The Unexpurgated Beaton

The Unexpurgated Beaton

THE CECIL BEATON DIARIES
as they were written

Introduced by Hugo Vickers

Weidenfeld & Nicolson

LONDON

First published in Great Britain in 2002
By Weidenfeld & Nicolson

Second impression 2002

A CIP catalogue record for this book
is available from the British Library.

ISBN 0 297 64599 4

Typeset by Selwood Systems, Midsomer Norton

Printed in Great Britain by
Butler & Tanner Ltd, Frome and London

Weidenfeld & Nicolson

The Orion Publishing Group Ltd
Orion House
5 Upper Saint Martin's Lane
London, WC2H 9EA

For Arthur
with love
from his father

Contents

Illustrations

The choice of photographs has been made to illustrate incidents in the diaries and some people not normally portrayed. The emphasis has purposefully been to avoid the very well-known Beaton images.

Between pages 116 and 117:

Cecil with his Rolleiflex.

THREE MONSTRES SACRÉES, LOATHED BY CECIL:
Katharine Hepburn, sketched by Cecil in *Coco*.
Marlene Dietrich – an early photo of the *diseuse*.
Elizabeth Taylor at the Proust Ball, 1971.

TRAVELLING COMPANIONS:
Cecil by Sam Green.
Sam Green by Cecil.
Mickey Renshaw in his villa in Cyprus, 1972.
Mona Bismarck in her villa in Capri.
Kitty Miller.

Between pages 180 and 181:

THE SPECIAL FRIENDS:
Lady Diana Cooper in her 'Happy Birthday hat', summer 1972.
Sir Michael Duff.
The Duchess of Windsor at the Proust Ball, December 1971.
Cathleen Nesbitt.

CECIL'S HOUSES:
8 Pelham Place, with Cathleen Nesbitt, John Betjeman, Eileen Hose
    (Cecil's secretary), and Lady Elizabeth Cavendish.
Reddish House, the beloved retreat.

Cecil as Nadar, at the Proust Ball.

TALENT FATALLY FLAWED:
James Pope-Hennessy, the writer, murdered in 1974.
Sir Francis Rose, artist, under the steps, with Cecil above.
Stephen Tennant, poet and novelist *gâté*, languishing in his bed.

Between pages 244 and 245:

THE STAUNCH ACHIEVERS:
Enid Bagnold, author of *The Chalk Garden* and *National Velvet*.
Kenneth Clark, art historian, and the suburban-looking glass window at
    the Garden House, Saltwood.
George ('Dadie') Rylands, Fellow of King's, in a room of his own, at
    Cambridge.
Sir Nicholas Henderson, British Ambassador, and his wife Mary on the
    Rhine.

WILTSHIRE LIFE:
The Earl and Countess of Avon at Reddish House.
The Earl of Pembroke at Wilton.
Irene Worth, actress and friend.

RETURN TO ACTION:
Bianca Jagger in the garden at Reddish.[1]
Cecil supervising Bianca's make-up in the guest room at Reddish.[1]
Diana Vreeland in her 'garden from hell' room on Park Avenue.[1]

*All photographs, except where otherwise indicated, are from the Cecil Beaton
collection, by kind permission of Sotheby's.*

[1] Author's collection (by gift of the late Eileen Hose)

Acknowledgments

The creation of these diaries proved very different from writing a biography. It was primarily a task of transcription, a task made difficult by Cecil Beaton's handwriting, which is almost impossible to decipher, but at least helped by my having twenty-two years of experience in reading it. The transcription was also made easier by my having read all the diaries before, when I was writing his authorised biography. Even so, there were some words that had to be taken at a run. A word like 'simmer' could be 'summer' or 'manner' , words were joined up, spelling was erratic (which in his writing might have been 'erotic'). It was not easy. But I was at least familiar with the cast of characters who appeared, many of whom I knew personally and all too many of whom are now dead, and I had a reasonably good over-view of the general content.

To create these diaries, I worked from photo-copies that I made between 1980 and 1985. When I had done all I could, I went up to St John's College, Cambridge to inspect the original diaries, to fill in gaps and to make sure that everything was in the right order. I am grateful to Dr Mark Nicholls and Jonathan Harrison at St John's.

The advent of a lecture cruise from Civitavecchia in Italy to Fort Lauderdale on board the *Seabourn Sun* enabled me to transcribe 65,000 words, and I am grateful to Philip Gosling and Elizabeth Sharland for putting me on board.

But I could not have done this on my own. I was helped immeasurably by Brenda de Lange, on the occasions when I could hi-jack her from looking after our three small children. As a former legal secretary, she not only typed at great speed, but was also able to unravel many of the mysteries of Cecil's hand-writing when my eyes were unequal to the task. This book would not have been finished in time without her help. She typed 79,000 words in twelve days in January in the course of otherwise very full days. It was a great pleasure working with her, but I fear I also owe her an apology.

I should have read through some of the pages in advance. There were occasions when the content of the diaries was other than what I would normally have chosen to read aloud. So much was this the case that there came a day when I dictated: 'Isaiah Berlin was in bed with lumbago', and Brenda instinctively gave lumbago a capital 'L'.

My editor, Ion Trewin, was encouraging and supportive throughout, even chasing elusive footnotes. Since he was undergoing the process of transcribing Alan Clark's equally illegible handwriting at the same time as editing my book, I felt a strong bond of sympathy.

I am very grateful to Lydia Cresswell-Jones and Grace Worthington at Sotheby's for allowing me to reproduce some unusual photographs from the Cecil Beaton archive. I am also most grateful to my friend, Richard Jay Hutto, in Macon, Georgia. To him I turned in despair about the more elusive American figures, and he never failed to produce obituaries from the *New York Times*, and newspapers as far afield as San Francisco. He unravelled Phipps family trees, perused the *Social Register* for me, and solved numerous problems that were keeping me awake at night. I was also helped in the quest for 'missing persons' by the Countess of Avon, Viscount Norwich (Cecil Beaton's other literary executor), Artemis Cooper, Mr Andrew Alpern, Kristina Stewart, Mr Samuel Adams Green, Mr Christopher Gibbs, Mr Nicholas Haslam, Countess Bunny Esterhazy, Mrs Ilsa Yardley for her perceptive and helpful copy-editing (solving mysteries from afar), Diane Solway (biographer of Nureyev), Mr Gerald C. Clarke (biographer of Truman Capote), Mr Claus von Bülow, Viscountess Stuart of Findhorn, Sir John Smiley, Bt, Lord Weidenfeld, Miss Melissa Wyndham, Mr Charles Biasiny-Rivera, Baron de Redé, Marquis de Ravenel, Mr Anthony Hobson, and Mr Charles Kidd (Editor of *Debrett*).

I would also like to thank my agent Gillon Aitken for his guidance, and also Lesley Shaw, and Mrs Doreen Montgomery, agent to the Cecil Beaton literary estate. Victoria Webb had the uneviable task of co-ordinating all the last minute changes.

Finally I would like to thank Mouse, my wife, for putting up with the frantic last days of editing, and for letting me have the help of Brenda at times when she needed her.

Hugo Vickers
July 2002

Cecil Beaton
1904–80

Cecil Beaton was a man of many parts – photographer, artist, writer, designer for screen and theatre, and arbiter of style. Jean Cocteau described him as 'Malice in Wonderland' and Cyril Connolly called him 'Rip-van-With-it'. Kenneth Tynan noted that if he arrived at your party, he would give the impression that he had just come from a very much better one upstairs. He was an elegant man, a man as much photographed himself as photographing other people. Above all, he was that very rare creature, a 'total self-creation'.

Diana Vreeland, the editor of *Vogue*, told David Bailey that Cecil 'realised that there's only one very good life and that's the life you know you want and you make it yourself'. Truman Capote agreed: 'There are very few people that are total self creations and he certainly is one, because nothing in his background... would in any way lead one to suppose that this person would emerge out of this cocoon of middle-class life.'

The Beatons came from Somerset and Cecil's grandfather, Walter Hardy Beaton, founded Beaton Brothers, a firm that imported railway sleepers from abroad. Grandfather Beaton ended his days as a portly figure, living in some style in a large house in Abbots Langley, Hertfordshire, and on his death in 1904, he left nearly £155,000, no mean sum.

Cecil's father, Ernest Beaton, was a timber merchant who made a good enough living to send Cecil to Harrow, but whose business collapsed in the 1920s, when roads ceased to be made from timber blocks. He married Esther ('Ettie') Sisson, a good-looking girl, who had come down from Cumberland to stay with her sister, Jessie, who was married to a minor Bolivian diplomat, Colonel Don Pedro Suarez. There is a suggestion that Ernest Beaton never met his wife's parents.

Cecil was born in 1904, and was followed in 1905 by a brother, Reggie, who, sadly, committed suicide when quite young, and two sisters, Nancy (1909–99) and Baba (1912–73). Cecil certainly did not know that his maternal grandfather was a blacksmith in Temple Sowerby. When, in later life, he found out, he was not pleased. As a child, he thought his mother was a society lady. He thought the same of his Aunt Jessie Suarez, who, in an enjoyably theatrical way, dressed herself up for diplomatic functions. As he grew up, it dawned on him that his family were not the cream of society, but he set about changing that. There was nothing much he could do about his father, but details of his mother's minor entertainments were sent by Cecil to the social pages. He dressed his sisters up, photographed them frequently as a pair and again made sure that their photographs were on the editors' desks awaiting publication.

The love of photography emerged from Cecil spotting a photograph of Lily Elsie ('The Merry Widow') lying on his mother's bed. Many of his life-long loves were engendered at a stroke. He saw a beautiful actress, and he saw a photograph of a beautiful woman. All through his life, the theatre was his first love, and his talent as a photographer the making of his career. A strong theatrical strain was evident in all his work.

As a youngster, he cajoled his sisters into becoming his first photographic models, designing their costumes, and entering them into fancy dress competitions.

Cecil went to Heath Mount School in Hampstead, where a fellow pupil, Evelyn Waugh, stuck pins into him. Not surprisingly, there remained a lingering antipathy between the two in later life. Next came St Cyprian's, a grim establishment on the south coast, where he developed chilblains; Eric Blair (George Orwell) and Cyril Connolly were there at the same time.

He went on to Harrow, where he prospered in the art school, and then to St. John's College, Cambridge, ostensibly to read history and architecture. His main contribution was to the theatrical life of the university, acting in and designing sets for the ADC and Marlowe Society. In 1925, he came down without a degree.

He spent some unhappy months working in the Holborn office of a friend of his father's for one pound a week, the friend being reimbursed by his father. In August 1926, he made an excursion to Venice, a first attempt to break out of his world into a brighter one.

This he achieved by his industry and imagination and the judicious use of publicity. He was an ace re-toucher of his work, drawing waists in, slenderising necks, removing unwanted lines, and presenting his subject as a vision of glamour. He made his name by taking glamorous photographic portraits of the 'Bright Young Things' of the day, who soon thirsted for his talents.

He needed a patron and found one in the aesthete, Stephen Tennant. They met on a dramatic day in December 1926, and Tennant instantly welcomed Cecil into his world. Tennant was everything Cecil wanted to be, rich, talented, good-looking, well-connected, a man with a host of ideas but lacking the drive or stamina to put them into effect. Stephen would say: 'Wouldn't it be wonderful to take a photograph of someone through the splinters of a broken mirror.' Cecil had no shortage of energy and put these ideas into reality. He went out with his hammer and created the image.

Advised to make friends with the Sitwells, he did so, and his ingenious portraits of Osbert, Edith and Sacheverell helped him gain employment with *Vogue*. He worked for the magazine as photographer, caricaturist, and illustrator, both in London and later in New York. In 1927 and 1930 he held one-man exhibitions at the Cooling Gallery, Bond Street, and presently produced his first book, *The Book of Beauty* (1930), which contained stylised photographic portraits of the great beauties of the 1920s.

In the 1930s his work matured as he fell under the influence of Jean Cocteau and Christian Bérard and his work became accordingly more complicated and baroque. He began to work for the ballet and opera, and designed revues for C.B. Cochran, notably *Streamline* (1934) and *Follow the Sun* (1936). Though he continued to photograph in London, New York and Hollywood, he was determined that photography would never be his life's work.

As he prospered, so, in 1930, he found Ashcombe, a derelict house in a glorious, Arcadian setting near Win Green in Wiltshire. He converted the house to his own style, and entertained his friends there, Rex Whistler, Augustus John, Edith Olivier, and many more. He staged a memorable *fête champêtre* and made films with the help of John Sutro. He loved Ashcombe more than any of his homes and never overcame his sorrow at being forced to leave when his lease ran out in 1945. He would be pleased to know that Madonna bought it in 2001, especially since she is a Cecil Beaton fan.

In the 1930s Cecil had photographed the Duke and Duchess of Kent, and in 1937 Wallis Simpson invited him to take the formal wedding photographs, on the day before she married the Duke of Windsor in France. Cecil's career was doing well, but in February 1938, he brought disaster on himself, by introducing some offensive anti-semitic doodles into an illustration for American *Vogue*. He was dismissed by Condé Nast, and did no work in the United States for a year and a half. The incident haunted him periodically in later life, though he rose above it with as much arrogance as he could muster.

His career was saved by two things. First, Queen Elizabeth invited him to photograph her at Buckingham Palace in July 1939. Cecil created glorious portrait photographs of her in Norman Hartnell outfits, the combination of which played an important part in establishing Queen Elizabeth's very particular style and image as queen. War was declared soon afterwards, but some of these pictures were released, serving as a reminder of a more peaceful life, and in stark contrast to the sinister images that were emerging, at this time, from Nazi Germany.

Secondly, the war itself was important. By 1939, Cecil was tired of photographing beautiful girls gazing languidly through bowers of flowers. He found an outlet in working as a war photographer. One of his most celebrated pictures was of a bombed-out child in hospital. This was chosen as the front cover of *Life* magazine in September 1940 and played a vital role in influencing American feeling during the war.

Cecil was taken on by the Ministry of Information, and photographed different aspects of the war effort in Britain, the Middle East and the Far East. Six books emerged from these years.

After the war, he veered to his first love, the stage, working on a number of theatrical productions, most notably John Gielgud's *Lady Windermere's Fan* in 1945, on which he lavished colour and style to serve as a tonic for post-war Britain. (The following year he even took the part of Cecil Graham in the American production). He worked on various Korda films, including *An Ideal Husband* and *Anna Karenina*.

Productions such as *The School for Scandal* (1949) and Noël Coward's *Quadrille* (1952) paved the way for the triumph of *My Fair Lady* in 1956, with its memorable black and white Ascot scene, a frieze of stationary ladies which caused an enjoyable gasp as the lights rose on them. Alan Jay Lerner, who wrote the play, pointed out that Cecil had that rare ability to create costumes that were both elegant and funny at the same time. Cecil repeated his success with the film of *My Fair Lady* in Hollywood in 1963, at the cost to himself of having to spend most of a year out there. The film of *Gigi* (1958) worked better, partly because some of it was filmed in Paris. *Gigi* won Cecil his first Oscar, and *My Fair Lady* two more – for costume design and art direction.

Cecil also made a marked contribution to the world of fashion. His best book (despite being more or less wholly ghost-written) was his look at fifty years of changing fashion, *The Glass of Fashion* (1954). Cecil remained a royal photographer too, and photographed all the Queen's babies from Prince Charles to Prince Edward, as well as being the official photographer at the Coronation in 1953.

In 1968 his career was crowned with an important exhibition of his photographs at the National Portrait Gallery. He continued to work hard photographing, painting, publishing volumes of diaries, and attempting to make a success of his play, *The Gainsborough Girls*. He travelled the world, recording his impressions by camera and pen. By the time we meet him as a diarist in 1969, he is struggling against health problems. One of the terrifying themes of the diary are the blinding headaches that assail him. They led to a serious stroke in May 1974, from which he made a valiant but only partial recovery. He died at Broadchalke on 18 January 1980, four days after his 76th birthday.

This book concentrates on Cecil, the diarist. They reveal an insecure man lurking behind the polished exterior.

Cecil was a man of great elegance. Through vanity, he always ordered his clothes a size smaller than he required because it looked better. While

Nancy Lancaster succeeded in creating homes that were elegant and comfortable, Cecil achieved the former, but ignored the latter. The winter garden at Broadchalke, for example, was impossible to sit in in comfort.

Cecil created illusions. People thought he spent a fortune on clothes, while often he picked things up cheaply on his travels. His day began early and he worked in bed. He might be checking page proofs, selecting photographs, writing his diary, or talking on the telephone, and he would not rise until shortly before his first appointment. If, for example, he were going out to lunch, he would shave and dress just before going out, thus arriving looking fresher and more clean shaven than the other guests who had been out and about all morning. He liked the image of Renaissance man or man of leisure. It was deceptive. He had been working very hard indeed.

He lived in two homes, 8 Pelham Place, in Kensington, a small house, which he shared with his mother until her death in 1962. He was there during the week, and the house was run by his secretary, Eileen Hose, who had joined him in 1953, and without whom chaos would have reigned. There was Ray Gurton, the chef, who later worked for Peter Sellers, and there were various other helpers who came and went. As soon as he could escape, he and Ray took the train down to Reddish House, Broadchalke, near Salisbury, the house he had found with Edith Olivier, and bought in 1948. He was never happier than when at home in the country as his diaries more than testify. Here there was his redoubtable gardener, Mr Smallpeice, whose wife worked in the house, as did Mrs Eide and Mrs Stokes. Sometimes Eileen joined them, and later Cecil bought her a cottage nearby, where her mother lived and where she settled after Cecil's stroke, when Reddish was his only home.

There is no question that Cecil was several different men, and he reveals several of these facets in his diaries. He had been an outsider when young, and he thus developed the facility to observe, first with nose pressed up against the glass, and then from within. For he succeeded in breaking into the world of society, and to numerous other worlds, those of the theatre, films, the arts, fashion, not to mention being a respected guest of royalty and a recognised figure in international society.

As he matured in years, Cecil achieved the rare distinction of making people vie to entertain him as an icon of style and all that was chic. He loved glittering society, though he could be critical, and more than anything else he admired genuine talent. He possessed an extraordinary visual sense and powers of observation. His lynx-like eyes took in every detail. One friend said: 'If there was a safety pin there, he'd find it,' while Truman Capote declared: 'The camera will never be invented that could capture or encompass all that he actually sees.'

Cecil also loved to explore what the wayward artist, Michael Wishart, called 'The Peacock Revolution'. Thus he became associated with 1960s stars such as the Rolling Stones, and not long before he died, he photographed a punk rock group.

An interesting question is to wonder whether Cecil really liked the people he now mixed with. His publisher, George Weidenfeld, suggested that part of him despised them: 'He would happily have witnessed their execution as long as he was given a good enough seat.' This is true in certain cases, but not all. He had friends to whom he was devoted and fiercely loyal. He loved Cathleen Nesbitt and Diana Cooper, and to a large degree, the Queen Mother. He loved Audrey Hepburn, and he was a huge supporter of young and emerging talent. Curiously, he was an ardent fan of Edward Heath, and would not hear a word against him. Some of his close friends appear in this diary – his travelling companion, Sam Green, Hal Burton, on whom he relied for advice, Alan Tagg and Charles Colville, and a host of Wiltshire neighbours

If once he had been dazzled by Hollywood stars, the scales had long fallen from his eyes. He leaves more than sharp portraits of Katharine Hepburn, Mae West, Elizabeth Taylor, and Marlene Dietrich. He was envious of tycoons, and yet drawn to their company. Best of all, he loved original, understated or possibly eccentric taste.

Cecil left a host of admirers behind him. The sale at his house in June 1980 and the two studio sales of his work at Christie's in 1984 and 1988 attracted intensely feverish interest. But Cecil also had his detractors. He was not an easy rival, and there were many squabbles in the world of theatre, film, opera and ballet. (When I told Diana Vreeland that I was going to interview Horst, she said: 'Hmm, that'll be interesting. One photographer talking about another photographer!') The lowest of his detractors were those who rose on his coat tails and then denigrated him for their own further advancement.

What is undeniable is that his was a life lived to the full, that he made an enormous contribution to many aspects of life. He gave pleasure to the world, and he did no harm. This is confirmed by his posthumous reputation which has never taken the dip that normally occurs when a famous man dies. Possibly he lived through the dip of the struggling years between 1974 and his death in 1980, by which time he was back at work again. Since his death, there have been numerous exhibitions, notably at the Imperial War Museum, the Barbican and the Victoria and Albert Museum. Sotheby's has an exhibition travelling more or less permanently around the world.

More exhibitions are planned, and even as recently as March 2002, in New York, Cecil was awarded the Theatre Development Fund 2002 Irene Sharaff posthumous award 'to recognize, celebrate and remember those artists who have pioneered the art of costume design, setting the standards for years to come'.

This book, which is published in advance of his centenary in 2004, affords the opportunity to read his private thoughts, to learn what the man behind the mask was thinking.

Introduction to the Diaries

My diaries in order to be lucid enough to be read necessitate an enormous amount of polishing and regrouping – even elucidating

CECIL BEATON – January 1972

Cecil Beaton edited and published six volumes of diaries during his lifetime, covering the years 1922 to 1974, doing so in what James Pope-Hennessy called a 'thirst for self-revelation'.

There remain 145 volumes of Cecil's manuscript diaries, written in large exercise books or beautiful marbled books from Venice also dating from 1922 to 1974 (when he suffered his stroke). He began keeping a diary at Harrow, but he destroyed it when he was about twenty because he was frightened that it might be found. Today only a minute fragment of this school record survives.

His day-to-day diary started when Cecil went up to Cambridge in October 1922 and filled fifty-six volumes with closely scrawled material, most of which was written on or soon after the day. This he continued until February 1927, by which time life was being led so fully that he could hardly keep up: 'I felt somewhat guilty at the sight of my journal lying apart like a discarded lover,' wrote Cecil, 'but life had become too busy for regrets.' Entries were written in a snatched moment, sometimes several months later. Therefore they lose the appeal of immediacy.

Cecil resumed a day-to-day diary on his first trip to America from 1928 to 1929, writing a great deal during times when he was lonely and bored, for example, during the war (twenty-two diaries) and his year in Hollywood working on *My Fair Lady* (nine diaries). At all other times, he wrote retrospectively, summing up a particular summer or weekend. After an occasion such as the Duke of Windsor's wedding, he would turn to the diary at once to record every minute detail, so that the most important events were covered in his attempt at all times 'to preserve the fleeting moment like a fly in amber'. Interestingly, Cecil wrote his diary in the morning rather than before going to bed.

Cecil told me that only one-tenth of his diary was published. This proved an accurate estimate. When he suffered his stroke in 1974, the diary was necessarily laid aside, but such was his recovery that unbeknown to anyone (though suspected by his secretary Eileen Hose), he resumed it in 1978. He filled three-quarters of a volume, writing with his left hand. The last entry is dated exactly one week before his death.

The first published volume, *The Wandering Years* (1961) took him from 1922 to 1939 and, of all of the books, is the one in which he rewrote passages, altered dates and names, and moved events sometimes five years out of sequence. An historian should always mistrust a diary edited by the diarist himself. In *The Wandering Years*, entries were rewritten with hindsight, some extracts were added that do not exist in the original manuscript diaries and events were kaleidoscoped.

In the early years the private diary was not written with publication in mind. On 9 October 1923 Cecil wrote, 'If I knew anyone had read this I'd almost go mad and yet I feel I have to write it. It's so much myself – the real self that not a single person alive knows.' On the same day he added, 'I don't want people to know me as I really am but as I'm trying and pretending to be.'

The Years Between (1965) covered the war years 1939 to 1944. Much of this had appeared in other Beaton books, notably *Winged Squadrons*, *Near East* and *Far East*. In this volume there is a fictional account of a day spent with his Delhi secretary, Jean MacFarlane, in 1944. This was in fact spent with his Cairo secretary, Pamela Burns, in 1942.

There was then a long gap until 1972, when he finally decided to risk all and publish *The Happy Years*, taking him from 1944 to 1948 and exposing his strange love affair with Greta Garbo. After that, three volumes appeared in relatively quick succession, *The Strenuous Years* (1973) taking him from 1948 to 1955, *The Restless Years* (1976) taking him from 1955 to 1963, and finally *The Parting Years* (1978), which took him from 1963 to just before his stroke in 1974.

In 1979 Richard Buckle, his friend and neighbour, made a composite selection, which was published as *Self-Portrait with Friends*.

Cecil treated the published diaries in much the same way as he treated his published portrait photographs. He retouched them shamelessly until he achieved the effect he sought. Thus, in the published diary, opinions are softened, celebrated figures are hailed as wonders and triumphs, whereas in the originals, Cecil can be as venomous as anyone I have ever read or heard in the most shocking of conversations.

A good example of this is his 1973 description of Marlene Dietrich. In *The Parting Years* (page 153), Cecil wrote,

I watched on television Marlene Dietrich's successful performance staged at Drury Lane. The quality of the photography was extraordinarily exact, and I felt I saw more and heard more than if I had been a part of the wildly enthusiastic audience. As for Marlene, aged seventy (actresses are always said to be older than they are), she was a quite remarkable piece of artifice. Somehow she has evolved an agelessness. Even for a hardened expert like myself, it was impossible to find the chink in her armour. All the danger spots were disguised. Her dress, her figure, her limbs, all gave the illusion of youth. The high cheek-bones remain intact, the forehead good, the deep-set eyelids useful attributes, and she does the rest.

Not much of a never-musical voice is left, but her showmanship persists. Marlene has become a sort of mechanical doll. The doll can show surprise, it can walk, it can swish into place the train of its white fur coat. The audience applauds each movement, each gesture. The doll smiles incredulously. Can it really be for me that you applaud? Again a very simple gesture, maybe the hands flap, and again the applause, not just from old people who remembered her tawdry films, but the young, too, who find her sexy. She is louche and not averse to giving a slight wink.

Marlene has created another career for herself and is certainly a great star, not without talent, and with a genius for believing in her self-fabricated beauty.

Her success is out of all proportion and yet it is entirely due to her perseverance that she is not just an old discarded film star. She magnetises her audience and mesmerises them (and herself) into believing in her.

I sat enraptured and not a bit critical as I had imagined I might be. The old trooper never changes her tricks because she knows they work, and because she invented them.

Compare this with the unexpurgated version on page 314.

The purpose of Cecil's diary almost certainly changed over the years. Yet in its unpublished form it remains a candid and thorough portrait of its writer, a valuable mirror to the many worlds in which he moved, and at times gives a devastating and wicked portrait of his friends and foes. Nor does he spare himself. Some of the images he presents of himself in later years verge on the vicious.

This new volume covers the most recent years – 1970 to 1980. It was a very full decade, and one which for a number of reasons Beaton skimmed over in 1978. He devoted a mere sixty-two pages to this period, for several reasons. The most obvious is that he was covering a long span in a short book, but the truth is that there were many stories that were too fresh for telling.

Since those days times have changed and, in presenting this new volume, I have transcribed only from the unpublished diaries. I discovered that between 1970 and 1980, Cecil wrote nearly a quarter of a

million words. It is presented here in as raw a form as possible. Like any
diary, there were some repetitive passages, while some of it was devoted
to travel, especially in South America, which tended to make tedious
reading. Just a tiny portion remains 'too hot to handle' even in 2002.

I therefore take issue with his quote that his diaries need 'polishing and
regrouping', but, as editor, I have done my best to 'elucidate' where
possible.

When I published the authorised biography of Cecil Beaton in 1985, I
made the prediction: 'As a diarist he will become increasingly important.'
This has proved something of an understatement, since a host of would-
be biographers have asked for snippets about their subjects and invariably
received these with delight. I was struck by how sharp and well attuned
Cecil Beaton was, when writing my life of Vivien Leigh (1988). In due
course I reached an evening in 1942, when he sat up late with her in an
hotel in Glasgow. He wrote two pages summing up her life, her stage
ambitions, dislike of films, her love for Olivier, her relationship with her
first husband, as she revealed it to him, while the dawn gradually rose and
cleaners swept around them in the lobby. I thought at the time that he
was spot on in two pages, when it had taken me 52,000 words to bring her
to the same point.

James Pope-Hennessy wrote that he thought Cecil's diary would be
'the chronicle of our age'. Talking to James Lees-Milne of the diaries of
Cecil and Eddy Sackville-West, he declared, 'We could not be hoisted to
posterity on two spikier spikes.' More recently John Richardson, a man
not wholly immune from the waspish comment, wrote that Cecil was
'historically important because he was an eye-opening recorder of the
passing show, a witness to his time. Like Horace Walpole two hundred
years earlier and Andy Warhol a generation later, Cecil had a homosexual's flair for seizing on the zeitgeist.' And I relish the comment of
Waldemar Hansen, an amanuensis, who helped Cecil polish his work:
'Cecil had his stethoscope on the heart of society, and when there was a
change in the beat, he wanted to know why.'

Here, then, is the man, his eye turned on those who comprised his
world, his family, friends and neighbours, the Royal Family, the world of
stage and screen, the world of society spread in countries far and wide,
and those who saw him at his happiest, a spate of work achieved, relishing
a summer's day in his house and garden at Broadchalke, to which he
returns with unfailing joy and love from the fray of life.

1970

Cecil Beaton entered the new decade at Reddish House, the country home at Broadchalke, not far from Salisbury, to which he had retreated regularly since he bought it in 1948. Here he was able to lay aside the studied image he wore in London and the United States, and relish all aspects of country life. His friend, Michael Pitt-Rivers, once asked him, 'Cecil, why is it that you are so loathsome in London and yet so delightful in the country?' Cecil mused a moment and confessed, 'It's true!' A sterner note was added by another Wiltshire neighbour, Mary, Countess of Pembroke, who stated simply, 'We wouldn't let him get away with it.'

Cecil was fortunate to live in a beautiful and historical part of the country, not far from Stonehenge and Old Sarum, near the great stately home of Wilton, seat of the Earl and Countess of Pembroke, and with sympathetic neighbours in and around the area of the Chalke Valley, the Earl and Countess of Avon at Alvediston, Michael and Anne Tree in Donhead, Lord and Lady David Cecil, Viscount and Viscountess Head, Richard Buckle at Semley, Billy Henderson and Frank Tait in Tisbury

This country life afforded him welcome respite from the more synthetic worlds in which he made his living, the magazine world of London, Paris and New York, and none more remunerative, yet more irksome to him, than the world of show business on Broadway and in Hollywood.

When in London, he lived at 8 Pelham Place, a late-Georgian house in South Kensington, which he had bought in 1940. He was there during the week, though at every opportunity he escaped to the country.

Cecil had indeed lately returned to Britain from a disagreeable stint in New York, designing Coco, a musical based on the life of the celebrated monstre sacrée icon of twentieth-century fashion, 'Coco' Chanel. She was a peasant-born seamstress, who became a legendary figure in the world of haute couture, creating nimble and stylish suits and freeing women of the encumbrances of formal clothing. Her empire has thrived since her death.

The musical starred the legendary American film star Katharine Hepburn as Chanel. She was one of the few great stars of stage and early screen to survive into the twenty-first century. Her 'apple-a-day' smile and her long, discreet affair with Spencer Tracy assured her a place in many hearts, if not Cecil's. She had mistrusted Cecil since he had written of her 'rocking-horse nostrils' and her 'tousled beetroot-coloured hair' in Cecil Beaton's Scrapbook in 1937, not to mention concluding that she was 'in close proximity very like any exceedingly animated and delightful hockey mistress at a Physical Training College'. Hepburn insured that, in his Coco contract, he was forbidden to publish a single word about her.

The musical was written by Alan Jay Lerner, the brilliant, nervous, highly *strung playwright, with music by André Previn. Lerner was normally partnered by Fritz Loewe, who wrote the music. Lerner and Loewe were the team which had created* Gigi *and* My Fair Lady. *Lerner once vexed himself over the line: 'Those little eyes so helpless and appealing, one day will flash and send you crashing through the ceiling.' Loewe reassured him: 'It's your lyric and if you want to crash through the ceiling, crash through the ceiling!' Lerner wrote the words for* Coco, *but unfortunately he and Cecil fell out badly during this show, because Cecil always needed a hate figure and this time it was Alan. Cecil blamed him for causing Rosalind Russell (the American leading lady in films who favoured roles as a career woman and starred in* Gypsy) *to be dropped in favour of Katharine Hepburn.*

This was the more strange, since the show was produced by Frederick Brisson, businessman producer, who had been trying to get the musical into production since 1954. He was a man of limited charm, who was married to Rosalind Russell. Elaine Stritch called him 'The Wizard of Ros'. He was the son of Carl Brisson, the Danish director, an international favourite of stage and screen, who made many films in Britain.

Katharine Hepburn and Cecil were not soulmates.

Coco and Katharine Hepburn in retrospect   [December 1969]

No cause for regrets. I knew the show would be no good with such a rotten book. I never fooled myself into thinking the book could be sufficiently improved. It's no good wondering if Alan Lerner[1] had not made a great mistake by throwing out Rosalind Russell[2] (done in such a dishonest, beastly way) in favour of Katharine Hepburn.[3] In fact RR would have given a better performance, would have projected the songs better, but the show would not have succeeded in becoming a smash hit, though it might have lasted longer than it will if KH is still determined to leave at the end of April.

It may, however, suit her to stay on to receive the applause of the multitudes. She is the egomaniac of all time and her whole life is devised to receive the standing ovation that she has had at the end of her great personality performance. As the play nears its end and she is sure of her success, she becomes raged, the years roll off her, and she becomes a young schoolmistress. Up till then she has, to my way of thinking, been as unlike Chanel[4] as anyone could be. With the manners of an old sea salt,

---

[1] Alan Jay Lerner (1918–86).
[2] Rosalind Russell (1908–76).
[3] Katharine Hepburn (b. 1909).
[4] Gabrielle 'Coco' Chanel (1883–1971).

spreading her ugly piano-calved legs in the most indecent positions, even kicking her protégée with her foot in the London scene, standing with her huge legs wide apart and being in every gesture as unfeminine and unlike the fascinating Chanel as anyone could be. Her performance is just one long series of personal mannerisms.

I would not have thought audiences could react so admiringly, yet the first time I saw a run-through rehearsal, I was impressed and even touched. But ever since I've found her performance mechanical, inept (her timing is erratic), she stops and laughs, she falters over words, she is maladroit, and she is ugly. That beautiful bone structure of cheekbone, nose and chin goes for nothing in its surrounding flesh of the New England shopkeeper. Her skin is revolting and since she does not apply enough make-up even from the front she appears pockmarked. In life her appearance is appalling, a raddled, rash-ridden, freckled, burnt, mottled, bleached and wizened piece of decaying matter. It is unbelievable, incredible that she can still be exhibited in public.

Fred Brisson[1] tells me that one day he will repeat the vile things she has said about me. As it is I have heard that she has complained about my being difficult, stubborn. She obviously does not trust me or have confidence in my talent. She pretends to be fairly friendly and direct, but she has never given me any friendship, never spoken to me of anything that has not direct bearing on the part that she is playing.

I have determined not to have a row with her, have put up with a great deal of double-crossing, chicanery and even deceit. She has behaved unethically in altering her clothes without telling me, asserting her 'own' taste instead of mine. (On the first night she appeared in her own hat instead of the one that went with the blue on her costume. Instead of the Chanel jewellery she wears a little paste brooch chosen by her friend[2] ... in quiet good taste.) She is suspicious and untrustworthy.

Never has anyone been so one-tracked in their determination to succeed. She knows fundamentally that she has no great talent as an actress. This gives her great insecurity so she must expend enormous effort in overcoming this by asserting herself in as strident a manner as only she knows how. She must always be proved right, only she knows, no matter what the subject. It is extraordinary that she has not been paid out for her lack of taking advice. But even if this is her last job, and it won't be, she will have had an incredible run for incredible money. She owns $20 million. She is getting $13,000 a week. But in spite of her success, her aura of freshness and natural directness, she is a rotten,

---

[1] Frederick Brisson (1915–84).
[2] Phyllis Willbourn, companion to the actress Constance Collier and then to Katharine Hepburn, remaining with her on perpetual duty until her death.

ingrained viper. She has no generosity, no heart, no grace. She is a dried-up boot. Completely lacking in feminine grace, in manners, she cannot smile except to bare her teeth to give an effect of utter youthfulness and charm. (This, one of her most valuable stage assets, is completely without feeling.) She is ungenerous, never gives a present, and miserly. She lives like a miser, bullies Phyllis [Willbourn] and thinks only of herself day and night. Garbo[1] has magic. Garbo is a miracle with many of the same faults, but Hepburn is synthetic, lacking in the qualities that would make such an unbearable human being into a real artist.

I hope I never have to see her again.

Cecil was fond of his Wiltshire neighbours. He was devoted to Michael and Anne Tree, and relished having them as nearish neighbours at Donhead. Michael was the son of Ronald Tree and his wife, Nancy Lancaster. Lady Anne was a daughter of the tenth Duke of Devonshire. They were rich and deployed their riches with style, commissioning Sir Geoffrey Jellicoe to create their garden at Shute House.

Cecil was reading Enid Bagnold's autobiography. Enid was best known for National Velvet *and* The Chalk Garden. *She lived at Rottingdean, an addict of vast doses of morphine. Cecil had fallen out with her over his sets for* The Chalk Garden, *which he designed in New York. To his rage, the sets were not used in the London production. Over twenty years of non-speaks ensued. Enid's autobiography (Heinemann, 1969) was a remarkable book. She had been scared to write it for fear of upsetting her children with an account of her affair, as a young girl, with the literary lothario, Frank Harris. This she covered with eloquence: "Sex", said Frank Harris, "is the gateway to life." So I went through the gateway in an upper room in the Café Royal.'*

Cecil was expecting the arrival of Eileen Hose, his secretary. She joined him in 1953 and stayed with him until the end, becoming housekeeper, nurse, amanuensis, accountant and best friend. After his death she served as Literary Executor and settled his affairs, donating his papers to St John's College, Cambridge, organising a sale of his drawings and paintings, and giving his Royal photographs to the Victoria and Albert Museum.

---

[1] Greta Garbo (1905–90), the first of many appearances of this gloomy Swede, who obsessed Cecil since the 1920s, and with whom he savoured an uncomfortable love affair. Film actrress, legend and nightmare.

Boxing Day, 26 December 1969

Such a wonderful illuminating view from the top of the Downs, looking over the distances of Fonthill as I drove out to my Christmas Day lunch with the Trees.[1] It was a sunny day and the winter scene was strangely soft and welcoming in a haze of sweet-pea colours, pale buff, pale mauves, pale blues and rose, the sight was eternal. It was of simple basic shapes, the distant woods were bare and just like patches of colour, no trimming, a living sculpture. Something breathing and alive, but unmoving. It was the best I'd seen since I left and I only now realised what solace to the spirit I have been missing. I was pleased with Anne's highly civilised conversation, so basic and honest and funny. She is one of the best that England produces, and I came away deeply satisfied with my happy outing to read Enid Bagnold's remarkably excellent autobiography.[2] This is a great lesson in depth and all her qualities are apparent (also her dislikeable-ness – she is *not* a nice person). But her honesty and strength of character are amazing and I feel sorry that she should have spent so much time writing plays at which she is no good.

Her description of past events reminded me of the Japanese film *Rashomon*[3] where so many people tell their varying versions of the truth. I knew so much that Enid believed in was not the same as I feel to be the truth. But the book kept me riveted for 2 days and it is a remarkable legacy for her to leave, an important and profound reportage in-depth of a strange, remarkable, original and warped life.

By degrees, the cotton wool gives place to sinew and muscle, and I am able to keep awake for a few hours. There are no pressing engagements and this gives me a wonderful feeling of luxury. The house is warm and scented with Smallpeice's,[4] pot plants and the neighbours I visit seem lively and bright, and when Eileen[5] arrives with Alan[6] and Charles[7], there is much laughter and the memories of 51st Street are fading quietly as my brain is filled with other music played on the record player.

---

[1] Michael Tree (1921–99) and his wife, Lady Anne Cavendish (b. 1927).
[2] Enid Bagnold (1889–1981), author and playwright.
[3] *Rashomon* (1950), Japanese cult film, directed by Akira Kurosawa.
[4] Jack Smallpeice (d. 1995) and his wife, Betty. He was Cecil's gardener at Reddish House for many years and his wife helped in the house.
[5] Eileen Hose (1919–87), Cecil's redoubtable secretary and the mainstay of his later years.
[6] Alan Tagg (b. 1928), theatrical designer.
[7] Charles Colville, companion to the above. Both were close friends of Cecil's and also of Eileen's.

5 January 1970

I kept this bloody diary every day while I was busy with idiotic events in New York. Now that I am quietly ensconced in the country, in my own adorable surroundings, I find I have not one moment of energy to even find where I have left this book. Ten happy days have passed. The first 5 were spent almost exclusively in sleep. I could not keep awake after I had had my late breakfast. I slept all afternoon and 12 hours at night. Then I started to read – Enid Bagnold – her autobiography – her plays. Then I started to write (the Sam Green[1] piece) and every day was filled. Social life at a maximum, dinners or visits of succour to recent widows – Essex, Pembroke, Radnor,[2] David,[3] Dot and Anthony[4] come to dine (spent from a pro-Communist on-thrust from Dot, which angers Anthony). The evening was a marvel of intelligence and delight and I was so pleased, when, as a result of the flowers Smallpeice has produced all over the house, Dot examining the dining table said 'You have banished winter'.

A recurring feature of Cecil's life was to be entertained by the super-rich. On the one hand, he loved the luxury and the chance to observe them. On the other hand, he was jealous of their riches and disapproving of their way of life. His hosts in Palm Beach in January 1970 were the Guinnesses.

Group Captain Loel Guinness and his third wife Gloria were supremely rich members of the Guinness clan. Loel was the father of Lindy, Marchioness of Dufferin and Ava. Gloria's past was less clear. She was the daughter of Raphael Rubio, of Mexico, and had been married to Count Egon von Fürstenberg and Prince Ahmed Fakri. She was popular with young aristocratic men, whom she

---

[1] Samuel Adams Green (b. 1940), see biographical note, pp.41–2.
[2] Alys, Countess of Essex (d. 1977), divorced wife of eighth Earl of Essex (1884–1966); Mary, Countess of Pembroke (1903–95), widow of sixteenth Earl of Pembroke and Montgomery (1906–69), daughter of the first Marquess of Linlithgow, Lady-in-Waiting to Princess Marina, Duchess of Kent, and chatelaine of Wilton House in the 1960s; and Isobel, Countess of Radnor (1908–98), widow of seventh Earl of Radnor KG (1895–1968). She lived at Alderbury, near Salisbury.
[3] Hon. David Herbert (1908–95), son of fifteenth Earl of Pembroke. Left the conventionality of Wilton for the louche joys of Tangiers, re-creating in exile much of the life from which he had fled, reading the lesson in church, Christmas pantomimes etc. A man of feline gossip, wholly immersed in all aspects of Tangerine life.
[4] Viscount Head (1906–83), former High Commissioner in Nigeria and Malaysia, and his wife, Lady Dorothea Ashley-Cooper (1907–87). They lived at Throope Manor, Bishopstone, close to Broadchalke. In his early days Head had been one of the young bloods who had propelled Cecil into the Nadder during the coming-out ball for Lord Herbert in August 1927.

initiated into the ways of the world. In later life, when people like Cecil complained that their private parts were getting smaller, she would mutter, 'I wish mine were.'

Palm Beach – Florida – Chez Guinness[1]   *18 January 1970*

I had been home for 3 weeks, all of 3 days having been spent in the country. I had recuperated from the efforts of the Broadway 'Flop' (which is now a sell-out) and had done some writing and was now tidying out, sorting papers, bringing forgotten scraps to light, losing page 70 of a mss and finding all sorts of helpful things instead...I was putting my house in order: I felt, as ever, the pathos of departure. I always wonder if I am leaving, never to return. This time I even expressed this feeling to Mrs Smallpeice as she did my bedroom.

While I was home I had several times telephoned to my remaining Aunt Cada.[2] I realised, as I told my sisters, that she was 'on the way out'. Tecia,[3] my cousin, confided that she didn't think the heart could stand up much longer and that, although Cada, the youngest sister and the one who had been so delicate in youth, who in fact had had most of her insides cut out, was the last survivor and had reached the 90 mark. In spite of her blindness (total), she had kept her spirits and her will to live. She was a fighter, and was now fighting to live to go to the marriage of her grandson. Tecia said, 'But I'm afraid the old girl won't make it.'

I telephoned to Aunt Cada once more for what I knew would be the last time. Tecia had said her mother was very breathless and weak but could talk and she was in fact full of vigour, her voice strong and quite cheerful, but nevertheless I would say resigned. Maybe she hoped she would survive until we all met at the family wedding, but maybe she knew this was the end of her life. She told me that she considered me, since my mother's death, as her son, that she thought the world of me, that I had been so good to her.

I fed her with silly pep talk about not trying to overdo it, keeping mum, not making any effort, and she seemed cheerfully resigned. 'Oh no, I'm taking time. There's life in the old girl yet.' It seemed so easy to talk to her for the last time. She robbed the talk of any pathos. I am sure she knew it was the last talk, and she had accepted the fact just as I had. 'Well,

---

[1] Group Captain Loel Guinness (1906–88), and his third wife Gloria (1913–80).
[2] Cada Chattock (1879–1970). Cecil's youngest maternal aunt, a daughter of Joseph Sisson, of Temple Sowerby, Cumberland. She married, as his second wife, Richard Chattock (1865–1936), of Solihull, and had two daughters.
[3] Winifred Leticia ('Tecia') Fearnley-Whittingstall (1907–92), Cada's elder daughter. She married Francis Fearnley-Whittingstall CIE (1894–1945).

goodbye dear, God bless you.' I hung up and felt very sad. I would miss her, for she was the last link with my mother's family. I had enjoyed the obligation of having to call her from time to time. Now there would no longer be that obligation. I was more sorry for myself than for Cada. She had had, by her own making, a wonderful life. And yet it had been a tragic one, ending in 15 years of blindness, and great things always about to happen – they never happened – but she was always cheerful and hopeful, and made her life sound so full and glorious. She had reached the extraordinary age of 90. One could not regret now the death of a blind old lady who was a burden in so many ways to her most dear and beloved.

Palm Beach   *January 1970*

Less than a week has passed since we talked and the telegram has arrived, telling me of Cada's death. In a way I am glad that she lingered no longer, that she has not had more to suffer. But remote as I am from her world here, in fabricated Palm Beach, the reality seeps through and I am sad.

For Cada was a bright, bird-like treat of my youth. The most wonderful glimpse of the countryside was spent staying in her cottage at Anley, in Gloucestershire. It was an idyll, with the apple blossom in bloom over the grey stone wall, and everything was a pleasure, including the first outdoor loo that I had ever experienced – it smelt clean and fulsome, of the carbolic we sprinkled when we had 'done'. Staying in the family house in Birmingham also had its treats for we were taken to the theatre to see *The Farmer's Wife*[1] in a try out for the Astaires[2] after their hardest run and were given outings that were not often part of our more staid home life.

She had foster-mothered Claud, who had been 'artistic', and was killed in the war, and Claud had inspired me, and I wept at the thought of his going into the Army and dying in the mud.[3]

Cada had always been the 'artistic' sister, friend of Barry Jackson[4] and the Malvern Festival people. She had known a lot of musicians and felt that every one of them was in love with her. She had a certain flair and, if

---

[1] *The Farmer's Wife*, a comedy by Eden Philpotts, first performed at the Court Theatre, March 1924.
[2] Fred Astaire (1899–1987), wizard dancer of the screen, famed for films such as *Top Hat*, and his sister, Adèle (1896–1981), also a dancer, who, in 1929 assisted Cecil to dispose of his virginity. She later married Lord Charles Cavendish (1905–44), younger son of ninth Duke of Devonshire. Fred and his sister were then a dancing pair.
[3] Claud Chattock (d. 1915), killed in World War One.
[4] Sir Barry Jackson (1879–1961), founder of the Birmingham Repertory Company. His father had made a fortune in the Maypole Dairies.

it had been necessary, could doubtless have expressed herself in more creative ways than being sympathetic and understanding to all artists. Now I
will miss going to the telephone in the library at Reddish and 'keeping in
touch'. But perhaps, although my 'faith' is very shaky, she is now in a
happier world, reunited with the others she loved, and being rewarded
for all the strength, goodness and courage she showed as the 'delicate'
youngest one of the family.

An older lady used a forgotten expression. She said (of Lily Elsie[1]) that
'She put her clothes on so well'.

This house is full of jokes. They are Loel's responsibility, and although
Gloria [his wife] does not enjoy them, she suffers them. Cushions have
comic mottos on them: 'You don't have to be crazy to stay in this house,
but it helps.' In the main room a plate is inscribed for weekend guests:
'When the hosts are drinking and they invite you to stay on till Tuesday,
remember they do not mean it.' Gloria asks, 'Do you know what the egg
said to the hen?' 'Now you've laid me, do you still love me?' Loel goes
back to George Robey[2] who said, 'Rather than block a young lady's
passage I would rather go to the edge of a cliff, and toss myself off.'

When the Wrightsmans[3] first took Mona Williams[4] home, they asked
the Guinnesses if it was right to swim in one's pool in the afternoon or
only in the morning.

It is quite amusing to find myself embarked upon a new job career. Each
morning I am called for by Jimmy Barker – a bright, black, curly-haired
Kentuckian, who gives me all the local colour (scandals) on his way to
escorting me to my sitter. I am now a painter and not a photographer. I
set up my very roughly improvised painting materials and, holding my
breath with tenseness, embark on a huge representation of the unknown
lady in front of me. The first was a somewhat tired and pathetic over-
middle-aged woman with a rich widow as mother. The house was all that
is lifeless and uncongenial in a Palm Beach pretentious style of decoration. While I drew, the widow prepared a lunch in the modern kitch-
enette for her pet poodle. The second sitter was on a grander scale,

---

[1] Lily Elsie (1886–1962), musical comedy actress and star of *The Merry Widow* (1907). A
huge favourite of Cecil's early life.
[2] Sir George Robey (1869–1954), British comedian of the musical halls, known as 'the
Prime Minister of Mirth'.
[3] Charles B. Wrightsman (1895–1986), and his wife Jayne. See biographical note,
p.77–9.
[4] Mona Harrison Williams (1897–1983), eventually Countess Bismarck. See
biographical note, p.81.

pretentious too, was her air of grace, but she's alright, in comparison to her revolting, brash, ugly, pushing sister, but that's another story.

My next sitter was almost my Waterloo. A Mrs Carola Mandel,[1] a Cuban who never stopped talking for an instant, the greatest woman 'shot' in the world – she has won 500 trophies and wished to be portrayed in evening dress, with long kid gloves (to hide her gun-spoilt hands), a dozen of her silver trophies and a gun. What could be more difficult? To add to my troubles, rain fell as only in India in the rainy season, so that indoors my cardboard became damp and the pencil strokes became incisors, rather than lines. The sitter never stopped talking. After 6 hours I had perpetrated a monstrous picture, which I hoped no one would ever see again. When Mrs Mandel showed me her collection of Bakst drawings, I felt like destroying my own effort but yet I did not for obvious purposes.

Virginia Beveridge[2] was next on my list. It was only after the sitting as we walked around and lunched at the Everglades that I realised what a strange and unusually delightful person she is. I was faced with an anaemic wreck, with sad bashed face, togged up in the glad-rags of a twenties kewpie doll, peppermint pink chiffon miniskirted evening dress, bobbed hair, a scarlet mouth. I later saw that she had the remains of what once must have been extraordinarily refined beauty. The drawing 'cost' me nothing. There are still 2 more to go. But to my chagrin I find that with all this effort I have not made more money than I did at the last show when more paintings were bought off the wall. When, on the telephone, I complained to Margaret Case[3], she said, 'You know we do an 8-hour work day here in New York.'

The last sitter was a funny little pixie man of 75, very rich, rather feeble but with a twinkle. His wife had commissioned this and had her husband in a tizzy of nerves. His hands twitched, but 2 vodka martinis seemed to help him a lot. I don't imagine they liked the drawing very much, but as Jimmy [Barker] said, 'Some people haven't ever learnt how to look at pictures.' All this activity was an excellent way (again Jimmy) of killing a day. But it has been quite fatiguing, and I wish I could have pocketed more. As it is, it amuses me to think I have this ability, but of

---

[1] Carola Mandel, born Carola Panekai-Bertini, of Havana, Cuba, m. 1938, Colonel Leon Mandel (1902–?), General Manager Mandel Bros department store, Chicago, who owned many large yachts. In 1958 her team came fourth in Moscow shooting competition (open skeet 200 targets).
[2] Virginia Beveridge (d. before 1998), wife of Albert J. Beveridge, daughter of John Barry Ryan, of New York. She was originally married to Major Edward Baring (1903–80), of East Sussex.
[3] Margaret Case (1891–1971), worked most of her life at *Vogue*, having been the mistress of Condé Nast in her youth.

course I should really do the thing more seriously, and bring my box of oil paints.

However it has been a good way of combining business and 'pleasure'.

Gloria's Mexican blood comes to the fore in so many instances. Whenever sex is in the air, she comes alive, and she is full of jokes and fun. Thirty years fall off her shoulders. My last evening with them in the house, she made an attack on Loel for the shaming, embarrassing way in which he sits on his back with his legs wide apart, showing to all the world 'this enormous bug' (bag). 'I don't know where to look – it's positively indecent. Why don't you wear something to keep that thing in?' Loel explodes, 'I want to be comfortable!' 'But you were so terrible leaning over in the aeroplane to look at the panel board and all those pilots and I could see between the cushions of your bottom, this enormous bug [*sic*]!!' Loel, trying not to laugh enjoys the situation. Gloria admits, 'I know I should be proud of you, but really it's too embarrassing in front of all those people!'

Driving me to and from the various sittings, Jimmy Barker gives me the scandal of the town – who shot who, who got drunk with who. It seems [one lady] had a Polish butler who one night appeared in her bedroom. 'I can't stand it a moment longer. I've been madly in love with you all these years. Unless you let me come to bed with you, I'll shoot myself.' 'Don't be so foolish,' she growled in her deep lesbianic voice, 'and go ahead and shoot yourself.' Whereupon her butler did just that. He fell dead at her feet.

Palm Beach   *January 1970*

It is a world apart, still a hangover of the days when privilege was everything. Mrs Phipps[1] drives her car against all police regulations, even on the pavement. When a young, uninformed cop remonstrates with her, she shouts 'Don't you dare get in my way! Move out at once' and she puts her foot down on the accelerator.

Mrs Phipps invites large numbers of people to meals, but she cannot be bored eating and hurries up the proceedings. She has brought the technique to such a pitch that she can now dispatch the luncheon guests from her dining table in 6 minutes flat.

---

[1] Gladys Phipps (1884–1970), of Heamaw, Palm Beach, widow of Henry Carnegie Phipps (1879–1953). Daughter of Ogden Mills.

A novice cop also arrested a lot of rich young people dressed like hippies. 'Get back to West Palm Beach', he told them, 'before I arrest you on disorderly behaviour charges.' They were horrified, told their parents and the novice was sacked. 'Everyone' knows the cops, whose wife is in hospital, whose relation died and the place is free of violence, burglaries are scarce. But the charm of the place has gone, the club rules are slackened and the place is now what Miami used to be, while Miami has become one of the most revolting places that exists anywhere on earth.

I leave few places that I stay in with regret. The Guinness visit has been very congenial, comfortable, effortless. I lay back and enjoyed the lack of responsibility. But when Loel and Gloria left and I was on my own for a day, all the faults in the setting seemed to have a life of their own. The pictures appeared worse, the décor mere trumpery. Outside the swimming pool was being emptied as the rain fell. I hung around saying goodbyes at the gallery, having no sitter on my last morning. I was quite ready to leave... and with the usual 'train' fever, caught a plane for New York with incredible speed (I remember it took days to come here when first Anita [Loos][1] brought me to Florida).

Cecil had become interested in a saga which involved a former film-star, Barbara Daly, now Baekeland, who was in pursuit of his friend, Sam Green (see biographical note, pp.41–2), as was her son Antony. Cecil had begun a novella or sit-com/musical, inspired by the stories that Sam told him, and in particular that Barbara went so far as to instruct an older girl to seduce her son. Cecil worked on this 'project' with Sam, and even seemed to predict the hideous outcome. The true story was told by Natalie Robins and Steven M.L. Aronson as Savage Grace *(Victor Gollancz, 1985). In that book Sam is quoted on the subject of Cecil's work: 'Thank God it was never published! Cecil was a photographer basically, but when he wrote he always settled for the most superficial frame around the picture. He revealed incredible tawdriness in his prose. But I hasten to his defense: he never displayed it elsewhere!' (Savage Grace, p.57). In 2002 Sam's opinion remains unchanged. It was 'profoundly shallow'.*

New York   *January 1970*

I returned to the St Regis. My rooms were occupied by a Mr Berger[2] of the 'Damned', so I was thrust into a terrible igloo of grey-green 'drapes',

[1] Anita Loos (1888–1981), tiny but brilliant author of *Gentlemen Prefer Blondes*.
[2] Helmut Berger (b. 1942), Austrian actor, known for his good looks and sinister roles. Star of *The Damned* (1969).

festooned to look like Marie Antoinette's boudoir. The bed, a vast arena, only made me feel lonely. However, a bright, smiling Sam Green soon arrived and we were launched on our 'communal' venture. He had strange stories to tell of his 'lovers', but none of the developments are useful to the story. The next 3 days were spent in the hotel. I moved from the igloo at half time, deeply engrossed in the latest draft.

Sam said he liked what I had written while in England, but as we came to go through it with a fine comb, the job of rewriting was an appalling lengthy one. However, we suddenly found ourselves a good collaboration team, and only on one extremely late session, when both totally exhausted and still trying to beat the clock, did we show the slightest exasperation with one another. Sam is brilliant, quick, persevering. I watched with enjoyment how, each day, he tackled the job of rubbing out, rewriting, sticking pages together, smoking and being altogether extremely vital. It is interesting that we should have met up with one another and so naturally found ourselves involved in this effort.

The telephone was at a minimum, since I had not told anyone I was here, and the New York weekend was one of more unreality even than usual. The streets seemed deserted. The outer world only appeared in the form of room service (and the price of the meals appalled us both). By Sunday night, with the help of double daiquiris, we got through the work and on Monday we reread our efforts of the night before to find that they were muddled and careless.

Another hard session of 3 hours and the typescript was put in an envelope to be picked up in the morning by Mrs Armstrong, the typist. My curious atypical New York visit was over. I was not at all sorry to leave New York in a cold, dreary sludge of dirty snow and drizzle. Not that I was particularly looking forward to spending 3 days in much-disliked Beverly Hills, but this was on my way to seeing Kin[1] in San Francisco, and since we have not met for well over a year, this would be an event in my life. This is to be my holiday taken in winter, instead of last summer, and I must try to make it into something that I will remember the year by with a 'first' in it, a first visit to South America or perhaps even a new experience of a different kind.

Beverly Hills Hotel   *January 1970*

By the time I arrived in LA (10.30 p.m.) it was the end of a long New York day and I was utterly depleted on arrival at the hotel I have hated so much at various times. The man on the night desk was dilatory and so

---

[1] Kin (b. 1934), Californian teacher. See biographical note, p.30.

boringly inefficient that the porter lost his temper with him and complained that I was not treated right. I was shown to a dog kennel. No sooner had I gone to sleep than the other man at the desk telephoned to say that he had a better room, but I was too tired to care.

With the aid of a pill I slept a long time, and woke with a headache to find myself in a no man's land, with grey skies, drizzle, wet pavements and no air, sinister, ugly. Danny Kaye[1] telephoned, before I had woken enough to make sense, to say the *Vogue* people had made as much fuss about his being photographed doing his Chinese cooking that it might have been as important an event as if the rocket had been let off. He loved that!

A free morning…We passed by Danny Kaye's for a preliminary glimpse of his kitchen.

In my solitude, I enjoyed the fact that there was enough time to do the usual routine without hurrying. I would get out the nail scissors, the pincers, put on hair lotion, lie in the bath, and this diary was a bulwark against the ugliness outside. This was one of those rare 'pauses' when I browsed in the drugstore – discovered Garson K [Kanin] had written a eulogy of KH [Katharine Hepburn] in *McCall's*[2] and ate a hamburger at a counter.

Cecil was commissioned to photograph the legendary screen star, Mae West, whose film, Myra Breckenridge, *based on the book by Gore Vidal, was about to be released. Mae West was a buxom and voluminous sex symbol of the screen, famed for remarks such as: 'Is that a pistol in your pocket or are you just pleased to see me?' She also delivered herself of the philosophical epithet 'You keep a diary and one day it will keep you'.*

On arrival at the huge twenties cement apartment block, which Mae West[3] used to own, I was surprised to find how small her own personal quarters are. Neither living nor bedroom are of any size and the dining room is minute with rough cased plaster ceiling very low. Everything was off-white, cream and pale yellow. Such a riot of bad taste as you could not imagine to be taken seriously and one wonders, does Mae West think it funny herself? I don't really think so. To begin with, I was fascinated. White carpets, pale yellow walls, white furniture with gold plate applied to

---

[1] Danny Kaye (1913–87), mule-faced entertainer and comedian, of stage, screen and television.
[2] Garson Kanin (1912–99), film-maker, one-time boyfriend of Katharine Hepburn, then enslaved in marriage to the tyrannical actress, Ruth Gordon (1896–1985), some 16 years his senior. He wrote a book, *Tracy and Hepburn* (1971), a sensation in its time. This was its forerunner. There was then some froideur between Kanin and Hepburn.
[3] Mae West (1892–1980).

the bosses of the Louis-style arabesque – a bower of white flowers, and not one was real, huge set pieces of dogwood, begonias, roses, stocks, all false.

Miss West's entourage consisted of about 8 people from the studio and her own Chinese servant, a tatty fag, and her bodyguard – Novak – an 'ex-muscleman'. Miss West was in the bedroom. She had 'finished her eating' and was feeling 'most uncomfortable'. She had put on weight over the holidays and her dresses would not fit. Meanwhile a lot of opportunity to examine the décor. The piano was painted white with painted 18th century scenes adorning the sides, a naked lady being admired by a monkey as she lay back on drapery and cushions, was the centrepiece of one wall.

On the piano was a white ostrich feather fan, heart-shaped pink, rose-adorned boxes of chocolate, nothing inside but the discarded brown paper. A box of Kleenex was enclosed in a silver head box. The lamps were converted from huge Victorian china figures of lovers and had rolling volutes of rushing for their shades. There was a great display of Mae West as photographed to her liking by still studio photographers, retouched beyond human likeness, all in tinny silver frames. One huge yellow china vase had a wedding posy sticking out at an angle. I discovered that this was to hide the break in the china. This led to other discoveries of unheeded wear and tear. Dust was covering everything not on view. In a nearby toilet a discarded massage table was caked with grey, and when I put my finger on it, I discovered the dark red artificial leather beneath. Everything was grimy. The rushing on the lamps quite black with grime. Perhaps Miss West likes to preserve every dollar she has earned.

She seems quite contented, or so it seemed from my short glimpse of her during the afternoon session. She at last bid me come to her bedroom. She was rigged up in the highest possible fantasy of taste. She could hardly be considered human. The costume of black with white fur was designed to camouflage every silhouette except the armour that constricted her waist and contained her bust. The neck, cheeks and shoulders, were hidden beneath a peroxide wig. The muzzle, which was about all one could see of the face, with the pretty capped teeth, was like that of a nice little ape. The eyes so deeply embedded and blacked were hardly visible.

She smiled like an automaton. She gurgled at the compliments. She seemed shy and nice and sympathetic. When I told her that Lady Cunard[1] had said she was dressed at a Sitwell party all in white like a vestal virgin, she pretended to be shocked. She moved very slowly into

---

[1] 'Emerald' Cunard (1872–1948), wife of Sir Bache Cunard. One of the great twentieth-century hostesses.

the living room and this extraordinary effigy stood, it could not sit, on its full stilt-fitted feet being reflected in the mirror. It was yellow, white and black and like some incredible, rather beautiful monster, in the ape house. She stroked her yellow fronds with fat, pointed fingers on which a dozen false diamond rings sparkled, her fingernails grown to several inches in length. She preened, and if she moved very slowly from one side to another, her audience gasped with admiration. 'Oh, Miss West, you have never looked so beautiful. The lighting is so soft.' The exhibit chortled in her too well-known voice. She did not need to speak. When she did have to ask a question, it was with the voice of a little girl.

As a prop, a young Adonis, a former athlete from the local University, USC, Tom Selleck,[1] had been corralled from the film, a more outrageous combination could not be imagined. This beautiful, young, spare, clean, honest specimen of US manhood and the 'pourriture' of this old 'madam' created an extraordinary paradox. Nothing will seduce Tom, not even this old transvestite, but to see her at work on him was interesting. I should have taken pictures of them in closer proximity, but I dare not.

One dared very little. Sam had asked if I would ask Mae West for a snip of her pubic hair – but oh no! That would have been considered outrageous. This great sex queen is a goddess, and empress, and there are only certain ways she must be spoken to, no bad language or coarseness.

She has a sense of humour and is able to laugh at herself. I liked her twinkle and her tentative quivery smiles. I liked her vulnerability. She started to walk across the room. Her feet were difficult to move. She teetered, but I caught her. When the whole thing was over, she said she would like to start again. I felt, by now, the apartment had become too cloying and airless. I longed to escape, and I thought of how lonely she must be when the moment came for her to be alone…

But, when we were packing up, and on the street was a mass of lights, cameras and the Adonis's evening clothes, and the Adonis told me how fascinating MW was as a raconteuse, I was sorry I had not had more opportunity to communicate with her. But for sheer artificiality and bad taste, the afternoon had been a top mark, and I'm glad that photography has given me this opportunity to glimpse such a remarkable phenomenon.

The most important thing about Mae West is her genuine belief in herself. She is not putting on an act. She believes everything she fabricates about herself. She asked an attractive young girl to lie on her bed

---

[1] Tom Selleck (b. 1945), until this time a model in print, billboard and TV ads, he made his film debut in *Myra Breckenridge*, playing a young man, interviewed for an acting contract and ogled by Letitia (Mae West). Later famous for a long run in *Magnum PI*, and films such as *Three Men and a Baby* (1988).

and look up at herself in the ceiling mirror. She said, 'You see that you are a Queen' and she believes that she is a queen.

She is still extremely sexy and always has a lover. At the moment she is being fucked by an ex-boxer guardian. She has for 20 years done little but look after herself, preserve herself with almonds and health foods, and become interested in the occult.

She believes she has extraordinary perception. She has few friends, but those who are around her are intimates who depend on her. Many of them are helping either to furbish her exterior (making hats and furbelows for her) or teach her about the occult. Recently the younger generation has discovered her films. She has had a tremendous 'come-back', and has appeared at many of their meetings and gave a talk on the cinema. She spoke in a perfectly normal voice until she talked of her mother. Then she transformed herself into the character that is her public one, who asks people to come up and see her. At the talk, she described how she always writes her own script, and how with W. C. Fields[1] she was revolted that he stank of cigars and beer. She even had it in her contract that he must not come near her when smoking. They had got along badly together...

I wanted to hear, after the sitting, if she had anything further to say about the procedure. She was worried when a telephone call came through from her producer, Bobbie Fryer,[2] that she had not finished the conversation about the photographs being 'passed' by her. It was in her contract... She became rattled. 'What was I saying?' She smiled into the telephone. But she is childishly excited about seeing the photographs. 'When will they be here? Not before 2 weeks! Oh!' So I telephoned next day. She was very gracious and quiet. 'Oh, I'm fine, dear. Only yesterday I was so tightened up and one shoe hurt. Have you seen the *Times* (LA) – it says this morning Mae West poses for Cecil Beaton. It's here, larger, here.'

I told her Prince Charles[3] had thought her *Chickadee*[4] was the funniest thing he'd ever seen. 'What a pity he saw me with W. C. Fields. I wish he'd seen me in something else... Well, goodbye, dear, and I hope we meet again.'

I pointed the camera at the self-appointed Goddess of Love, Diana of the

---

[1] W. C. Fields (1879–1946), silent film star and larger than life personality, famed for making rogues lovable.
[2] Robert Fryer (b. 1920), American film producer, also active on Broadway. Other films included *The Prime of Miss Jean Brodie* (1969) and *Voyage of the Damned* (1976).
[3] Charles, Prince of Wales (b. 1948). Cecil admired the prince as a young man, and thought him sensitive and responsive to the arts.
[4] *My Little Chickadee* (1939).

Ephesians, nineteen hundred style, standing in her funeral parlour décor. The mirrors reflected the figure standing as she wished to be presented, a trunk of artifice, a tall, svelte woman, who had with ostrich feathers, stoles, fur, high hair, created her own silhouette. But one would like to see more than the pretty, smiling, smiling little muzzle which was all that she allowed one to see. Even the beauty of the leonine eyes [is] hidden under the awnings of eyelids.

She pays great respect to her fan mail, always trying to send little souvenirs when requested, including clippings off her far too long fingernails, when the time for a manicure comes.

This lucrative photographic assignment over, Cecil was able to go to San Francisco to visit Kin, the friend he had met in March 1963, during his unhappy stint working for George Cukor on the film of My Fair Lady. *Kin was a graduate of Princeton University. He had fenced in the Olympic Games in Australia in 1956. He was a teacher in San Francisco, having undertaken graduate work at the University of California at Berkeley.*

The meeting between Cecil and Kin occurred in a louche bar called the Toolbox in San Francisco. They met regularly thereafter, and Kin came to live with Cecil in London for a year between 1964 and 1965. But he found the atmosphere stifling and went home. In many ways they were ill-matched, Cecil longing to be intellectual, but remaining always more visual, Kin perhaps a little too serious a character for the more amusing side of Cecil. Stephen Tennant described Kin as 'a great buffalo of a man', and Christopher Isherwood wrote to Cecil that he had 'somehow expected someone more slender and angular'.

Cecil kept three photos in his bedroom at Reddish House until the day he died. They were Peter Watson (see page 77), Greta Garbo and Kin.

Beverly Hills   29 January 1970

An empty half-day, not unagreeable, writing a bit and preparing for the journey by air to San Francisco to see, after a year-long interval, my dear friend Kin. (I remembered so well at the beginning of my *Fair Lady* sentence how, owing to the poor advice of my awful money-grubbing secretary, I nearly missed my plane for what was to be the most important event of my entire Californian experience.)

This time I allowed good time and was full of anticipation at the idea of seeing Kin with a beard. As I got off the plane and saw this unaccustomed sight, a terrible defacement, but his personality came through the ginger fuzz, I said, 'I am feeling a bit embarrassed!' 'What do you think I am?' he laughed.

We fought our way out of the airport (at the sight of others doing the same, one wonders if there is such a thing as the dignity of the human race) and once inside his Volkswagen station we resumed our former intimacy and friendliness. We were both very delighted to see each other, beard or no beard. When I later lay on the bed and Kin appeared head-first but backwards up the galley-like staircase, I would expect to see him as he used to be, and it was a shock when he turned around. But by degrees, I became accustomed to this perhaps not permanent addition, grown no doubt under the hippie movement influence (he has changed night bars to one that wears beads and beards instead of motorcycle clothes).

On arrival at 714 Kansas [Street], the garden struck me as being very successful in its Japanesey way, and inside there were marked improvements, and some tidying had been done, if not dusting. The house is full of Kin's taste and personality, with all the ancient farm implements displayed on the walls or used for utilitarian purposes today. The main colours are kitchen blue, glass of this colour everywhere, and scarlet red. The dining room is a Vermeer oasis of pewter and glass, and surprisingly neat. The Cinderella attic bedroom, with the sparkling, ever-moving lights of San Francisco outside the windows at three sides, is still dark, so that one does not notice the dust and dirt; the walls and ceilings are partly painted, partly of cracked painted wood. Over the bedhead is an art deco semicircular mirror. By the bedside blue dusty felt, some red roses (from last night's end of term party), all very impromptu and transitory for eventually Kin is going to do (himself) the re-plumbing of the house, the electric wiring, and the painting, as well as knocking down other walls.

We were tremendously happy to see one another. We went out to dinner, I as Kin's guest, to Emilio's. Here, in the back room, the strange bearded man beside me talked in a much freer way than he has ever done before.

I noticed the great change that has taken place. He is much more at peace with the world, more friendly, less inhibited, and more outspoken and demonstrative. He said that he loved me very much and that he was always afraid that one day the scales would fall from my eyes and I would wonder why I ever thought him intelligent, reliable, lovable or beautiful. This was something I had waited many years to hear and, although I accepted it easily, I forced myself to the realisation of how wonderful a thing it was to hear.

Friday, 30 January 1970

The day started slowly with Bach, Mozart and rock songs. It is rare that I lie back listening to music. It is rare that there is no hurry to get dressed and go out into the world. We pottered in the garden, we ate eggs, we thought nothing of the outside world – of movies, restaurants, or inevitable friends.

Sunday, 1 February 1970

Kin wanted to take me to the Glide Methodist Chapel for their Sunday morning service. This not the usual manner of worship. It was in fact a mixture of the Negro revivalist and a hippie service, the congregation mainly very clean, laundered hippies, Negroes, and the young who come for a pleasant 'workout', a 'get together' in a Christian frame of mind, aided by every modern device, including a psychedelic screen show above the altar on which every sort of picture was shown from a close-up of a girl's tongue, on which an acid pill was poised, to media shots and the information that Eichmann[1] was still alive. The place was gradually jam-packed with hundreds standing at the back of the hall, and the aisles filled with squatters.

A rock group started to play, Negro voices joined in, the gaiety was contagious, and the entire congregation started clapping in rhythm. The parable of the Good Samaritan was transposed to the New York subway in which the victim was bludgeoned then given supper by a Black Panther. Jesus Christ was referred to as Our Director, lyrics by Dylan[2] were sung, and a song from *Hair*[3] recited. The volume of music became unbelievable.

For one and a half hours a condition of euphoria was sustained. Kin, surprisingly outgoing, with his head waggling from side to side, was as well met as any of his neighbours, and when the time came he kissed the girl on his right, we all linked arms and swayed from side to side, and when after this catharsis of jazzed-up emotion we left the building, the Rev. Cecil Williams kissed each member of the congregation. The Rev. Cecil has a smash hit on his hands. This is the way religion is going. It gives the churchgoer a real reason to feel good.

By comparison what poor food the Rev. Neame supplies the congregation at Broadchalke. We motored to Sacramento and lunched at the Spirimaton and luckily avoided the great crowds coming out of town – hippies, zombies everywhere. The rest of the day was spent in Kin's house, cleaning and tidying and cooking for a party of eight (Ed, Gene etc.). The dining room made formal and pretty with good silver and 18th-century glass.

---

[1] Adolf Eichmann (1906–62), Chief of the Jewish Office of the Gestapo, a villain of the Second World War. He disappeared, but was found in Buenos Aires in 1960, tried in 1961 and executed the following year.

[2] Bob Dylan (b. 1941), folk icon of the sixties.

[3] *Hair*, popular rock musical, with nudity on stage.

The party was a success because so little was demanded. The food was excellent and dished out in vast medieval portions of which the company always helped themselves to 'seconds'. Kin stood in the doorway, with a wonderful laissez faire attitude, but knowingly incapable of steering or inspiring the talk...

Monday, 2 February 1970

We washed dishes, as the expression has it. It took a long while and I managed to sneak in a bit of surreptitious cleaning. It is strange how someone as orderly, neat and immaculate as Kin is, in some ways (he is always ready with the shoe brush), should not mind the house caked in grime. By contrast to the simple way of life, we lunched with Whitney Warren[1] at Trader Vic's. Kin laughing that he had been thinking just how much he would eat of what at W's expense (Whitney infuriated Kin for ever by pretending he had brought K into my life). W had the worldly manner of someone of Elsie Mendl's[2] last period and was as dated. But we were amused by and at him.

Went on to the Legion of Honour, where I am to have my photographs exhibited in June, and to Michael Taylor's[3] new house, a staggering accumulation of riches, gold, gesso, ormolu and lacquer, Greek fragments, put into a large villa that commands a grandiose view of the sea, with distant hills beyond. Quite beautiful, in a savage kind of way. When we had recovered from sleep (K takes one over forever to wake during the day), we motored to see *Curious Yellow*[4] and arrived so late as to see only half of it. It was interesting and amazing to think how much times have changed recently and how such frank sex can be seen by all.

---

[1] Whitney Warren Jr (1898–1986), philanthropist and agriculturalist. Overly rich bachelor operating in San Francisco. Son of the famous architect, Whitney Warren, who built Grand Central Station, New York, and many splendid hotels. A dreary old gossip and socialite, of whom Cecil wrote, 'He knows his mind even if it is a small one.'
[2] Elsie Mendl (1865–1950), interior designer, lesbian, famed for standing on her head, whose exquisite taste influenced the Duchess of Windsor. Married the British diplomat, Sir Charles Mendl (1871–1958).
[3] Michael Taylor (1927–86), interior decorator, who burst to fame that year, creator of the California Look. He used his house in foggy Sea Cliff, overlooking Baker Beach as a design laboratory to study forms, effects and combinations. Founded Michael Taylor Designs 1985.
[4] *I am Curious – Yellow* (1967), Swedish film, directed by Vilgot Sjöman.

Tuesday, 3 February 1970

We preferred a picnic on a wonderful mountain trip to the invitation to lunch in a seaside restaurant with W and his grand friends. Kin found a remarkable vantage point commanding Japanesey lairs of lower hills seen silhouetted in mist, colours grey blue, white, soft plush green and pale lion's mane. Trees dark dotted in isolated clumps and not to be noticed at first, isolated figures, like personages in a landscape painting. These, it transpired, were hippies, come to tune in and commune with nature – to try to learn the mysteries of growth, of a leaf, a tree, a lemon or a frond of the feathery mimosa.

I was engrossed in reading 'The Project'[1] by Sam Green and me (and I was bewildered). Kin went off to talk about acid and turning on with a group nearby. A girl in a state of bemusement walked by several times. I said how beautiful the valley was. She replied, 'It's weird!' Kin reported that the hippies on the mountaintop are more friendly than those in town, and are not to be feared or kept in caution, for they became different people once away from town. It surprised me how so many of these romantic wanderers get lifts back into town, and how others are able to drive when under the influence. Dinner again at Trader Vic's and always a feeling of closer harmony and intimacy, with barriers broken down, so that we feel there has been a progression in our relationship.

Wednesday, 4 February 1970

The plane taking us to stay with Nicky [Haslam][2] and Jimmy [Davison] at their ranch in Arizona was leaving mid-afternoon…

An hour's change of time, night at Phoenix, and Nicky in pale blue cowboy outfit to greet us and bring us painlessly to our night's haven and immediate friendship for Kin from Jimmy, Nicholas Lawford,[3] Horst[4] and another German, Hans, all cheery with liquor to such an

---

[1] The story about Barbara Baekeland, her son Antony, and their involvement with Sam. The family were very rich from the Bakelite fortune. See p.24.

[2] Nicky Haslam (b. 1939), interior decorator, friend of the stars and indestructible socialite, still plying his way through London life in the twenty-first century.

[3] Nicholas (or Valentine) Lawford (1911–91), former Foreign Office man, private secretary to Lord Halifax, who gave up his diplomatic career to live with Horst on Long Island 'I simply don't understand the *chemistry* of it,' complained Cecil. He contributed to magazines such as *Vogue*. Author of *Bound for Diplomacy* (1963) and a life of *Horst* (1984).

[4] Horst (1906–99), German-born protégé of Baron George Hueningen-Huené, he rose to be an international photographer, much favoured by *Vogue*.

extent that the travellers at first felt out of the fire and wine-warmed celebration. Nicholas showed himself drunk by over-repetition.

But whether drunk or sober, he is one of the most delightful, refreshing, un-selfconscious companions one could ever meet. He has an incredibly well-trained brain, never forgets a fact, date or name, is quite as flash, witty and kind. He knows that by now he would have been an ambassador if he had stayed in the Foreign Office, but he is in full deference to his breadwinner, Horst, who must put his name first in the visitors' book. It is good to see the world so well lost.

Thursday, 5 February 1970

The discovery, a bright sun, clear mountains, horses swaying or coughing, dogs bounding, Kin's eyes on sticks. We go for a walk to investigate the dried riverbed. All is dry and hot and about to burst into spring. When we return the others are all at the pool. I watch Kin's aquatics. He is in his element – a Triton. The water is so hot that it makes the atmosphere cold by comparison. We ride in the afternoon and, without Jimmy to conduct us, the expedition is much more adventurous than I have been accustomed to, and the horses galloped so strenuously for so long, although I was out of breath, that it was they, the horses and not their riders, who had to be considered, and so made to walk back to cool off in gentle stages. A very happy day, and I was proud of my brilliant friend, and sad the others were leaving by dawn the following day.

Friday, 6 February 1970

Kin and I went up the mountain walking in ravines, over rocks and arriving at a high mesa, two hours passed imperceptibly before our return in the ice-bright sun to the aquatic display from the bearded Triton (the 'acid' figure really coming to light with spouts of water from the filled cheeks and mouth). Again we rode, rather gently, up the mountain to command a marvellous panorama of mountains, sage, cacti. After a bath Kin urged me to look at the dying sunset. I went out without trousers and probably this was my undoing for a week. Dinner was nice, with music after and Kin to liven up the evening and give it extra point. I had started to sound hoarse and I wondered if I was going to have a cold.

Sunday, 8 February 1970

Got up for the usual cooked breakfast with Kin, but it took so much effort that sitting on the beach at the refectory table, I had to admit defeat and come back to bed for the day. I really felt awful. Kin talked sympathetically and intelligently but I was too ill to participate. Too sad as tonight he has to go back to San Francisco for his class tomorrow. When we said 'how sad' he said, 'No, it isn't – I love teaching.' But we said we were not thinking of him, of ourselves.

The day of a friend's departure is always painful and this was particularly painful for me, as I was feeling so inadequate to cope. I wanted to thank him for being so helpful about the 'project' and he even read my Gainsborough play.[1] (Halfway through he said it was 'handsome' and beautifully contrived. Later he said the last scene was a switch in mood.) He came to the room where I lay to do the packing and jolted me out of my inertia by the liveliness of his talk.

Suddenly we were confiding our thoughts to one another. He wanted reassuring of why I could not one day wake up to the fact that he was not what I thought him to be, and again I told him that our minds, so different, complemented each other, that I was flat in full admiration of his intelligence, his activity of interest and curiosity, his ever learning anew, his goodness of character which made me very inert in his presence.

In my weak physical state and in the darkness of evening, I started to blub and he was gently amused. We both agreed that the latest 'get together' had been perhaps the most successful of all. From many points of view (reality?) I think this is a miracle, and how lucky I am (and yet how lucky! He says he is!), wondrously beautiful, with his head, golden glistening, I watched him go out of the door and leave past the window...

Monday, 9 February 1970

In a haze I read half of *Wide Sargasso Sea*,[2] then suddenly could make neither head nor tail of it. My meals were brought to me, but I put on an overcoat and went over to dinner. Kin telephoned. The daffodils and blossom had come out. He was cheerful about his new class. Limp, I returned to bed.

---

[1] Cecil had battled on with his play, *The Gainsborough Girls*, for many a decade. It was produced on stage twice, in 1951 and again in 1959 as *Landscape with Figures*. It flopped both times.
[2] *Wide Sargasso Sea* (1966), evocative novel by Jean Rhys (1894–1979) about the first Mrs Rochester in Charlotte Brontë's *Jane Eyre*.

Tuesday, 10 February 1970

No improvement. Limp as a rag. But Sam on the telephone to give me a shock. Instead of a vision ahead of staying around swimming pools until my health had recovered, we were to fly to South America on Friday evening. Could I possibly be well enough in time? Only 4 days to go and I felt utterly incapable of making any effort. I coughed to stir up the deepest agonies in my chest. My head was swollen with sneezing, my eyes aching, my mind a daze. I crept back to my bedroom, suddenly become so bleak, so solitary, not that I even wanted to be seen by Kin. The boys were kind and cheerful and always so considerate with their *petits soins*. But I began to despair. I began to feel even older than I am.

I pile high the logs of wood in the hearth. The blaze is dramatic and heart-warming. The room glows. I sweat. I sleep. But on waking I am no better.

Syrus, the nephew of Indian Star, waddles in with breakfast tray. Before I have opened my eyes, he has asked, 'Will that be all?' and he is gone for the day. Perhaps the visit of Nicholas, Horst and Hans has strained the household, but suddenly it all seems very rundown, untidy and messy. Jimmy prepares lunch, and is very nervous at being caught doing so. His hand trembles above a bunch of lettuce decorating a plate of spiced sausages. I am an invalid, capable of taking in very little. Kin relished the various smells of fresh grass, the fragrant bushes, the tremendous scent of the oranges off the trees. I am a sack of old cotton wool, good for nobody. I sleep a drugged sleep, am happy to enjoy Jean Rhys. Will I be better by the end of the week?

Phoenix   *Wednesday evening, 11 February 1970*

The state of my health is deplorable. It has affected not only my body, but my spirits. I am quite abstractly depressed, which is something that occurs only seldom. I have had one of the worst colds I have ever caught…

The 'simple' (expensive) comforts of the ranch, the bathrooms, the best linen, the biblical food and the music and laughter and non-stop talk. Now either one or the other is away in Phoenix, the Indians are taking off 2 days a week, the hosts have a little squabble (and in the mirror I see Jimmy turn at the door and stick his little finger in the air. Nicky replies 'And yours too'). I sleep too much in the afternoon, and wake covered with sweat so that when it is the habitual bedtime I toss and turn, and my eyes ache too much for the calm of Jean Rhys.

I think about my early life and how magical all the childhood period now seems to be, and I try to think of the things that I have forgotten. Then I wonder what are the things that I am to look forward to next? And Eileen writes that I should 'not aim high, and to forget cameras'. Then she has to inform me that the lead pipes in the drawing room roof at Reddish have become perished, and the tiles are 'shaking, and letting the water in'. And that has to be paid for.

Meanwhile, I avoid my mirror as much as possible but occasionally one gets an unpleasant glimpse. I have become rather pleasantly sunburnt but even with this flattering veneer, my appearance is that of a very old woman, who becomes much more like my poor mother in her last gasp…

The drink of Bacardi goes straight to my head and by the time the TV programme is due I have the accustomed headache. However, the TV programme is no great help to me in my present mood. For it is Dick Cavett's tribute to the newly knighted Noël Coward.[1] With him to celebrate are his buddies Lynn [Fontanne] and Alfred Lunt.[2]

Noël makes a strange effect. He never lets up acting for a moment. He is very smug and pleased with himself at having become an oracle. He is like an old Chinese Buddha. He is 70 years old, only 4 years more than me, and yet he can hardly walk. He totters sideways, he has no hair, no teeth of his own, his face a wrinkled grimace. When the Lunts appeared the entire audience rose to its feet, for they are applauding 2 very old marvellous people. But Lynn is 84 and suddenly she looks it. She has collapsed into her own body, her face hardly recognisable. Poor Alfred with his black patch over his non-existent eye is the most spruce of the lot. Noël makes a few clever 'effects' and one marvellous joke. When Cavett asks if Noël, instead of being an actor, had ever had a wish to be anything else, to go in for animal husbandry for instance… 'Animals?' 'Well, I was just throwing ideas out into the air,' Cavett replied. 'But you can't throw animals about the air,' said Noël tersely.

It was sad to see someone who has been such a figure in one's life now at the end. He is not sad, for success has been his at the end as well as at an early age. But however much I may get involved with the young, and hope to learn from them, there is no gainsaying the fact that my generation is the one that fills the obituary columns, and one never knows for how much longer one will be spared.

---

[1] Sir Noël Coward (1899–1973), playwright, composer, writer and performer, of whom Cecil was undeniably jealous. Noël had made a rare TV appearance.
[2] Lynn Fontanne (1887–1983), actress of great distinction. Cecil dressed her in Noël Coward's *Quadrille* (1952). Married to Alfred Lunt (1893–1977), part of the celebrated theatrical pair known as 'the Lunts'.

Café society

The Fosburghs[1] took pity on the widow Miller[2] and asked her for a weekend. On the Saturday they all went to a nearby cocktail party. On the Sunday a list of names was found by the telephone. Kitty exclaimed, 'Oh, it's my list I gave to Suzy.'[3]

Thursday, 12 February 1970

Dare I write it? But it seems that at last I am better? My eyes less bunged and 'in myself' there is an improvement. I will go into Phoenix for a B1 shot from the doctor and I will ask his advice about flying tomorrow night. I will be horrified if I can't go. Meanwhile the *dégringolade* here continues.

Both boys were tired out and strained to the limit of their resources. Jimmy in Phoenix doing tiresome bank business all day, has had no lunch, and returned to find no dinner. Nicky said food crisis was extreme. Indians off for day and he had been busy making fancy dress costumes for Bob to wear at the horse competition of the year, so the chicken was not ready till 9.30. At dinner, Nicky most dictatorial, and uptight about his attitude to films, and what were *not* good of today. I sadly had to try to keep the peace. But the evening had no life of its own, only a batch of mail with strange assortment of news gave it any colour. A German magazine with a rival's pictures of Hepburn as Coco brought back to me all the unpleasantness of that experience, and my hatred of that unyielding schoolmistress.

There was an extraordinary photograph of me and Princess Margaret[4] (making her a matron) sent from last summer's party, a letter (surprisingly nice) from Prince Philip[5] in answer to mine about the death of his

---

[1] James Whitney Fosburgh (1910–77) homosexual painter, and his wife, Minnie (1906–78), one of the Cushing sisters, first married to Vincent Astor. The other Cushing sisters were Betsey Whitney (1908–98), New York socialite and philanthropist, said to have been worth $700 million, and Babe Paley.
[2] Kitty Miller (1900–79), overly rich American widow of theatrical impresario, Gilbert Miller. Daughter of the banker, Jules Bache. She gave an annual party in London to which guests flocked and about which they were exceedingly rude afterwards.
[3] Suzy Knickerbocker, alias Aileen Mehle, inveterate social columnist.
[4] HRH the Princess Margaret, Countess of Snowdon (1930–2002). Cecil photographed her many times. When she became engaged to Antony Armstrong-Jones (b. 1930), Cecil said to her, 'Oh, Ma'am, thank you for ridding me of a rival.' He was disquieted to hear that Armstrong-Jones had no intention of retiring from the photographic scene. Theirs was an uneasy relationship, but, as was revealed at the time of her death, Cecil did a magnificent job recording the ravishing beauty she enjoyed in her youth.
[5] HRH Prince Philip, Duke of Edinburgh (b. 1921). Cecil was scared of him and frequently complained of his 'barrack-room' attitude to him.

mother,[1] an account of Tony Gandarillas's[2] death (oh my Royal past![3]) and also an obituary of the man who recently inspected my sinus.

Hopefully I drag myself towards oblivion, and with the help of 2 aspirins found the night soon enveloped me, and here at last, the beginnings are felt of an awakening to life. It has been a bad patch.

Scottsdale

The winter resort. The doctor did not like the idea of giving me, as requested, a B1 shot. Instead he gave me an anti-tetanus injection. He explained that my sore throat with 3 large splinters still embedded, having come from a horsey surrounding, was the ideal place to harbour tetanus. I hoped, unlike Goldman[4] to Laura Canfield,[5] that he would not inject me with lockjaw. I came away stiff, bruised, tired, sorry for myself. Illness has robbed this holiday of its former charm. I am only anxious that vigour will return and that I can continue to enjoy things. As it is, I came back from S'dale feeling depressed at the ugliness of myself and fellow human beings. I slept for 20 minutes, took 45 to wake up, and yet at dinner was in no form to keep the others up to the mark. They were tired too, and were to be called at 5.30 to go to the annual horse event of the year.

Friday, 13 February 1970

I awoke painlessly and it was several minutes before I remembered how to feel how I felt. A relief to know that the result was not bad, that I was better. But the Indian servants do not make me feel at ease, at home. Although the day was brilliant, the ranch was lifeless. The hosts away

---

[1] Cecil had written to Prince Philip on the death of his mother, Princess Andrew of Greece, in December 1969, and received a handwrltten reply.

[2] Tony Gandarillas (d. 1970), Chilean, drug-addict, nephew of the famous Madame Errazuriz.

[3] Gandarillas was one of the characters photographed in costume for Cecil's book of spoof Royal memoirs, *My Royal Past* (1939).

[4] Dr Carl Goldman (1904–92). Leipzig born general practitioner, with fashionable practice at 1 Upper Wimpole Street. His patients included aristocrats and entertainment personalities. He spoke English with a classical German accent, which inspired confidence in some quarters.

[5] Laura Canfield (1915–1990), formerly a Charteris, then Lady Long, Countess of Dudley, Mrs Michael Canfield, and finally Laura, Duchess of Marlborough. After the death of Michael Canfield, she suffered intermittent ill health and was none the better for the ministrations of her doctor.

from early dawn to dark, showing their Arab ponies at the most important event of the Scottsdale year. I remained with a day to kill, but very
little spirit for the unexpected calm. I telephoned Kin, now engrossed in
his new term, and off to another emotional marathon orgy, and I did not
tell him of the anticlimax since his departure. But I felt dunched, and
anxious. Perhaps the complete change of climate in Lima will be a
necessary boost. Meanwhile enough of these unattractive, indecisive
self-pityings.

*Cecil then flew to Peru, to Lima, a town 'lacking in any appeal', accompanied
by his friend, Sam Green, with whom he had been collaborating on a
sit-com/musical about the soon-to-be tragic Baekeland family.*

*Samuel Adams Green, an entrepreneurial genius, was born in Boston in
1940, the son of Old American Stock academic parents, described by Sam himself
as 'nouveau poor'. He was a cousin of the famous Philadelphia art collector,
Henry McIllhenny, and was Director of the Institute of Contemporary Art in
Philadelphia from 1964 to 1968. During that time, he gave Andy Warhol a
retrospective exhibition, an important step in both their careers. He met Cecil
through McIllhenny, who recommended him as 'a guide for Cecil's prowls
through the avant-garde'. One afternoon Sam found himself introducing Cecil,
Babe Paley, Diana Vreeland and Cecile de Rothschild to all the gallery owners
with whom he did business in New York.*

*In 1968 Sam Green had embarked on a scheme to help Venice in Peril. He
had rescued Easter Island from being made into a refuelling jet station in the
South Pacific. He transported an Easter Island Moai (head) to the Seagram
Plaza in New York, to attract attention to the plight of the island. The following
year, working through the World Monument Fund, Green devised a scheme
whereby artists would give or design ties and scarves to be sold in aid of Venice.
Picasso, Miró, Dalí and Cecil were amongst those who agreed to participate.
Hermes agreed to manufacture them and Saks to sell them, but the project was
abandoned following what Green described as 'some greedy intrigue that
misfired'.*

*While in Philadelphia, Sam turned the downtown area into a huge sculpture
site, and was invited by John Lindsay, Mayor of New York, to advise him on
culture. He created another sculpture site there, and staged* Hair! *as the first free
concert in Central Park. Sam made his living by brokering works of art and
assembling collections – Egyptian art for John Lennon, contemporary art for
Blue Cross/Blue Shield insurance. For twenty years he had a big old house in
Cartagena, where he was able to entertain those who had entertained him
throughout the world. Today he is the Founder and Director of the Landmarks
Foundation, which undertakes projects in Turkey, South America, Central
America and Cuba.*

In July 1986 Andy Warhol wrote: 'I'd been reading Cecil the biography of

Cecil Beaton. I'm in it a lot when I knew him. And Sam Green was in every-body's life, such a big part – he's had Yoko Ono and John Lennon and Cecil Beaton and Greta Garbo and me.'

Sam Green described his friendship with Cecil as follows: *'I adored his company and didn't care about the obvious conclusions. I revelled in his erudite-ness, doted on his considering of who I actually was and what I might become. It was a mythical bachelor uncle handsome euphemistic nephew-type situation but (as far as I perceived) neither romantic nor sexual. Not that that wouldn't have been OK, but it wasn't; so that's not the correct conclusion. Fact is, Cecil never made a move on me'.*

Cecil explored Bolivia in search of information about his Aunt Jessie, about whom he was writing a book, My Bolivian Aunt (1971). During the trip, he and Sam Green visited Chincheros, where they ran into Dennis Hopper, star of Easy Rider, of whom Cecil left the following description:

Friday, 20 February 1970

Here, Dennis Hopper,[1] of *Easy Rider* fame is making his interesting film in the old village square of Chincheros. The church unfortunately shut, but it was exciting to see the film set, a mixture of fake cowboys and real Peruvians. The modern women in dark red shirts and plait flat hats, 300 of them squatting, spindling, and the 'Hollywood' technique of picture making at a minimum with most of the crews hippie dressed and bearded, Dennis Hopper in a quiet, dragging voice intoning about the story, of what the Indians make of the equipment left behind by a Hollywood cowboy film unit.

It ends violently with the torture and death of Hopper whom we talked to about the difficulties with the locals (once the terms of the deal were signed), and how after they had refused to let them pull down a bell from the tower, it fell of its own accord, with the tower. He seemed very calm and un-egotistical and a completely new brand of film star. We watched him being made up with face covered with festering wounds and bruises. The make-up man doing a sort of Francis Bacon job on his victim who, when in pain with the cuticle applied, unexpectedly would shout 'Fuck you!'. DH, like others, was not feeling too well in the altitude and com-plained to the doctor who gave him a shot which knocked him out for half an hour, and prolonged the incredible waiting periods, of which even the Peruvian leading lady complained.

---

[1] Dennis Hopper (b. 1935), American film star, who rose from juvenile roles into acting and directing. In 1969 he starred in *Easy Rider*, a tedious but popular film about two bikers crossing America. He was now making *The Last Movie* (1971).

DH said how much he had learned from *Easy Rider* and I thought how nice to learn from something that is netting him a great fortune and is being one of the greatest successes of all time. The Indian village behind the village is surrounded by blue and green hills, while Hopper told us the rock formation below the 'film-built city' was all pastel coloured. He is thrilled by the beauty of the surroundings, and is going to use many aspects, the water pools where the animals bathe among the willow herbs, and the electrical plant placed so paradoxically in this remote mountainscape.

Sam remarked that he understood and agreed with the actors who were 'acquiring' a small hill in this region, for they felt that the US had become so debased and life there so unattractive.

How good to be in these beautiful surroundings of hills and green pastureland, and with pools reflecting the blue mountain silhouettes, and seemingly contented personages standing quite alone in vast areas of unspoilt landscape. We were delighted with our visit to this mountainous countryside and tried to see a baroque church before sunset, but by now the altitude was doing its damage to me, and taking a page out of Billy Baldwin's[1] book, abruptly said, 'I've had enough – must go home now!'

Presently, Cecil returned to Beverly Hills.

Beverly Hills   *Monday, 2 March 1970*

About 8 telephone calls to discover my plans: nothing to keep me here so I decided to fly to Kin after a lunch with F[red] Brisson at Warners (*Coco* is beginning to show the first signs of taking off – KH as difficult as ever. The chorus girls complained to Equity that she demanded the theatre to be kept at freezing point. 'I don't care a shit about the girls,' she is reported to have said, 'but since they've complained, let 'em burn – turn the heat on to 100!') The flight from Burbank reminded me so much of the marvellous weekends when I was working at Warners and Kin and I motored throughout northern California. This time it was just as exciting a prospect, if different. Kin very wind-swept and blond, and wild-eyed, looked different but his regard so friendly and nice and honest. He looked like a romantic early Victorian sailor with his beard and blue trousers. On arrival I tried to get a ticket for London for tomorrow, only to be told there was a fireman's strike and the aerodrome closed. I had

---

[1] Billy Baldwin (1903–83), described as the dean of interior decorators, who, among other things, created the 'garden from Hell' drawing room in Diana Vreeland's Park Avenue apartment. His autobiography was published in 1985.

come from Peru and Bolivia imagining that my travel difficulties were over. These took quite a lot of time to overcome, and maybe I will leave tomorrow before Kin's evening classes.

His house looked tidier, the garden quite full of spring, and we went upstairs to the warmth to enjoy each other as intimately as only we have learnt to be with each other. All seemed so natural and inevitable and we were idling and giving one another Baden-Baden massage treatments when the sunlight turned to early evening. At Emilio's Kin again took the opportunity to confide his most secret sex difficulties. He is very worried about his major problem and when I asked why this had happened so abruptly he said it had been going on for half his life, but that he hadn't talked to me about it.

Tuesday, 3 March 1970

I did not sleep very well. Hours muddled up worked on my unconscious and I was very worried about Kin. He woke slowly to more revelations. He said he had no ambition, no satisfaction; when as a swordsman he had become a national figure, he had no satisfaction, he quit. He did not like any sport that meant beating another person. He did not feel his existence was justified. He was full of defects, could not have any self-confidence with other people. But in spite of 'dumping' his troubles on me, he felt he was beginning to feel he might be on the last lap of a difficult period, that he would perhaps soon find out where he was creating his own inadequacies...

Cecil returned to Great Britain and, as ever, was happy to settle in the country.

Play-going

After the desert of Broadway, an added pleasure to my return home is to find that play-going can be such a treat. During the 3 nights I have spent in London, the theatre has offered me 3 great pleasures. The first consisted of the acting of all the cast and the direction of Albee's *Tiny Alice*.[1] The play I saw in San Francisco is as remote as ever on a second visit, but in particular David Warner's[2] performance is masterly. He has acquired

---

[1] *Tiny Alice* staged at the Aldwych (1966), by Edward Albee (b. 1928), who also wrote *Who's Afraid of Virginia Woolf?* (1962), and *A Delicate Balance* (1966). Irene Worth was also in the cast.
[2] David Warner (b. 1941), stage actor, best known for Hamlet at Stratford. He also appeared in films such as *Tom Jones* (1963).

maturity. He has gained depth and his performance is full of variety, and even in such a solemn part, a great deal of humour.

The next play was David [Donald] Howarth's[1] *Three Months Gone*. I have always known him to be a tender and sensitive man of rare talent and after having had several of the worst failures it is possible to imagine, he has now, strangely enough, for it is a curious play, a popular success. (Yes, busloads will be coming up from the country.) The play, again, is miraculously acted by a Gillian [Jill] Bennett,[2] no easy quick admirer of hers am I. But even more remarkable is the timing, the reticence and reality of the vulgar Diana Dors.[3]

But of all the theatre joys nothing can compare with this present production of *Uncle Vanya*[4] – it is the best version of any Russian play I have ever seen. I have never known such remarkable acting. People behaved and sounded off in ways I have never seen on the stage before, and yet the effect was realistic. The imagination shown in the performances of Paul Scofield, Colin Blakely and Anna Calder-Marshall[5] makes one feel that actors have never before shown us that real inspired acting is choreographic in its insights and musical in the way that human beings sound differently when under various emotions.

At one moment Scofield, embarrassed, harassed at making a half-hearted love declaration, wound his arms in the air as if a cat was fighting. It was a little gem of observation. Likewise in the scene of hysterical exasperation he did such marvellous things with his hands flat upon his bowed head. His voice has lost its mechanical strangeness but sounds as if he was thinking and sayings things the first time. I admire and respect him as an actor both on and off the stage. He has none of the coarseness and vulgarity of the inferior being, Laurence Olivier,[6] but the adulation of the critics, students and general public alike is, in this case, absolutely deserved, for here is a wonderful instance of integrity and quality coming to the top without any extraneous boosting or propaganda.

---

[1] Donald Howarth (b. 1931), playwright, wrote *A Lily in Little India*. It played at the Duchess Theatre from March to September.

[2] Jill Bennett (1931–90), tragic English actress, who married John Osborne in 1968.

[3] Diana Dors (1931–84), born Diana Fluck, busty blonde starlet, who matured into mountainous middle-aged matron. A good actress, who nevertheless performed in such films as *Confessions of a Driving Instructor* (1976).

[4] *Uncle Vanya* (Chekhov) opened at the Royal Court Theatre on 24 February.

[5] Paul Scofield (b. 1922), legendary actor. Played Sir Thomas More in the film *A Man for All Seasons* (1966) and Salieri in *Amadeus* at the National Theatre (1979); Colin Blakely (1930–87), Irish-born actor, who joined the National Theatre company in 1963; Anna Calder-Marshall (b.1949), British actress.

[6] Lord Olivier (1907–89), leading stage actor of the twentieth century, who dominated the theatre for many decades. His second wife was Vivien Leigh (1913–67). He and Cecil came to despise one another.

Colin Blakely, when showing his forestation diagrams, put on the childlike 'exploring' voice that we never use at other times. When he said, 'You're so beautiful' to Gaerena [Yeliena] it was as if, in his passion, he had invented the words. As...Sonya, there has never been a better, or could be. This is perfection. One howls with pity for this little gauche creature that herself knows no self-pity. It is a masterpiece of true observation and feeling. One can only pray for her that one day she will be happy. Meanwhile her plight sears through every fibre. We suffer every particle of the way with her. I don't know when the director has begun or ended his work. He has chosen the perfect characters for each part.

The nurse is astonishingly 'right' – the grandmother of Gwen Ffrangcon-Davies,[1] with hardly a word spoken, is a presence not only on the stage but throughout the household that adds weight to everyone's misery. To see her with spectacles and ringed fingers reading a book on a sofa is to be spellbound and when she alters her position on that sofa, the whole play seems to take on new life.

The scenery is just as it should be, almost non-existent but full of atmosphere. Such a theatre joy is rare. I feel I would like to see the play every evening for the remainder of its run. Perhaps one would learn a little of what true acting is about. But all tickets are sold, and quite right that the public appreciates the very highest in stage art when it is given it.

Betty Somerset[2]   *March 1970*

Betty Somerset, as old as this century, telephones to say she has put her back out, and for the most ridiculous macabre reason. 'You see, I've always adored a waltz, I think that music could call me back from the grave. Well, the other night they had a programme on TV, about the waltzes of Strauss, and can you imagine it, but this old crone got up and started to dance when whack! I can't think why it should have happened because living my life, I must have waltzed thousands of miles.'

---

[1] (Dame) Gwen Ffrangcon-Davies (1891–1992), English actress of Welsh extraction, who began as a singer, and made her name as Shakespeare's Juliet in 1924, and as Eliza in Shaw's *Pygmalion*. Still to be seen in master classes on television in her centennial year.

[2] Bettine Somerset (1900–73), mother of the eleventh Duke of Beaufort. Widow of Captain Robert Somerset, who was drowned in 1965. She lived at the Round House, Netton, near Salisbury.

Dot Gossip *March 1970*

Dot [Head] telephoned to know if I was alright. She was so worried about dinner last night. The salmon had just turned. Was I poisoned? Oh, dear, she tries so hard to have everything as it should be and the cook is generally so good, but the Easter catering had been too difficult, with people turning up unexpectedly or not coming to the meals they said they would and so the salmon had been forgotten, and not put in the deep freeze. And it had been in the Frigidaire since Saturday.

'You do have such bad luck with your meals here. Do you remember the yak fat? When everyone farted and got so ill for weeks. It's a gastronomical risk for you to come here. You'll have to take a prophylactic or something.' I said, 'I thought it excellent' but 'Oh, all those things around it! It should have just had cucumber and French dressing, thin slices of cucumber, not all that rubbish. Those bits of egg and tomato and carrot! Carrots with salmon! Why it's like the Bull and Bush! My cook came to me, calling herself a colourful cook, and she will do these awful things. She'll say, "What about a nice colourful trifle?" And I say, "But you don't need colours! It's like a good wine. It doesn't need anything but its bush or whatever it is." I take her pictures. It's a sort of illustrated cooking course I give her, and then she sends me in a wonderful rice cream. She cooks like a dream, but it's covered with crystallised cherries and those awful spikes of angelica. And she is so nice. She gave me a pot of flowers, and I *do* praise her *so much*, on the telephone each morning. But when things go wrong I have to tell her and she is so upset about the salmon. Oh dear, this only happens to me!'

Dot on a Punk Gypsy Servant

'She put the cork down tight on a coffee machine and the thing exploded. Boiling coffee went all over the ceiling, and all over me. I was terribly burnt. Now she's done this awful thing to our Arplan. Just when we were having a Macmillan weekend lunch she had the inspiration to soap the linoleum floor all along the corridor, outside the kitchen. Of course Arplan went for six and crashed on the edge of the radiator cap, his mouth and jaw in a terrible shape. That's why you noticed the egg lump on his chin. It seems the teeth bit deep inside the mouth and caused this.'

'But the teeth can't get as far as the chin. I am trying and it can't be done.' 'I am trying too. Well, if it doesn't get better soon I'll have to take him to a plastic surgeon. I am terribly worried. But I asked the gypsy why she chose that moment to do the floor, instead of waiting till everyone had gone, and she said she couldn't think what else to do. Well, I said it was a most unfortunate inspiration. But we are all worried because we know she is going to do the hat trick and who's she going to do it to?'

The Salisburys[1] are recommended by the Belgian Ambassador[2] to take their chef and assistant. They are engaged for the Easter holidays. They arrive at Hatfield, are told by the butler to motor themselves to Cranborne. The butler asks Betty if it is OK to fill up their tank with petrol for the journey. 'Yes.' That is done and the chefs are never seen or heard of again.

A favourite figure in Cecil's life was Lady Diana Cooper, whom he first spied in Bond Street in July 1923. He followed her into the Times Bookshop *in Bond Street to get a close look at her. The daughter of the eighth Duke of Rutland, Lady Diana Manners was a legendary and uniquely unusual society figure, a great beauty and an actress in* The Miracle. *Though possibly destined to be a bride to the Prince of Wales, she married Duff Cooper, and became Ambassadress in Paris and the writer of three exquisite volumes of autobiography. Cecil made friends with her and, just as he was partly responsible for shaping her image, she was an integral part of his life. He photographed her in many different disguises over a period of more than forty years.*

She was known for spontaneous originality. When, in 1981, she saw Lady Diana Spencer, in her deep-plunge black dress, on her first public date with Prince Charles, her comment was, 'Wasn't that a mighty dish to set before a king?'

Diana for weekend   *Spring 1970*

She arrived with Doggie hidden in her basket and though stiff-kneed was able to walk around the garden, and keep up a pretty good commentary for the lunch guests (Salisburys) with all at the drinks party (Cecils[3] and Heads) and at dinner to give a *va et vient* of brilliance with quotes of Shakespeare, Donne with Dicky Buckle.[4] After dinner she reminisced about the pre-1914 war. She loved Basil Hallam[5] to the extent that Gaby

---

[1] Fifth Marquess of Salisbury KG (1893–1972), influential figure in the Conservative party, and his wife, Elizabeth (Betty) (1897–1982), daughter of Lord Richard Cavendish.
[2] Baron J. van der Bosch, Belgian Ambassador in London 1965–73.
[3] Lord David Cecil (1902–96), author and scholar, a happily dishevelled and eccentrically vague figure, and his wife, Rachel (1908–82), daughter of Sir Desmond McCarthy. They lived at Cranborne.
[4] Richard Buckle (1916–2001), ballet critic, who veered from the brilliant to the ridiculous. Author of *Nijinsky* (1976) and *Diaghilev* (1979). He lived at Semley.
[5] Basil Hallam (1889–1916), actor and vocalist killed in World War One.

Deslys[1] put detectives on her. Gaby was enchanting, *pottelée*. She said 'My legs are not padded'. To be vivacious was a necessity. She talked of the Casati with great sympathy, how she received in a huge silver bowl and gave to each arrival, announced by the beating on a gong by a Nubian slave, a tuberose. The Italians and French ecstacised about the elegance, the grace, the beauty – the English took the flower and said, 'Oh, what a lovely smell!'

She described how, at £2 a piece, she made £100 designing chiffon tunics in the Greek style, how her mother and people at that period always concealed their age, had it taken out of the manuals.

The following day Cecil lured his old friend, Stephen Tennant, from his life of seclusion at Wilsford Manor, Amesbury to Broadchalke to see Diana. Stephen Tennant was a bejewelled and heavily made-up aesthete, who assumed toad-like proportions in old age. He was Cecil's 'role model' when young, a man of effortless talent, good looks, but lacking in stamina or direction. Son of Lord Glenconner and his wife Pamela Wyndham (Lady Grey of Fallodon), he inherited Wilsford Manor and converted it into a retreat for himself from the rigours of the world. He spent most of his time languishing in bed, reading, writing poetry and designing book jackets for his never-to-be-finished novel, Lascar. He loved shells and fabrics, and his sense of humour never deserted him.

Next day Stephen Tennant[2] made a spectacular entrance for lunch having 'rested' all winter. He had not been out of bed, and I saw this extraordinary figure being escorted across the hall. He had a long white beard, was incredibly fat and wore, under layers of coats, jerseys etc., a red cotton bobble-edged shirt. As George, his chauffeur, helped him upstairs, the shirt fell, much to Stephen's embarrassment. It was an old tea table cloth that I had given him from New York, which he now thought to use as a disguise of the fact that he could not get into his trousers. An enormous gap displayed a pregnant stomach.

But once I was accustomed to seeing Stephen as an elderly man instead of the usual transvestite, I found the beard gave him enormous nobility and distinction. He looked extremely handsome like St Peter, and it did not matter that he had no teeth.

Diana, who knew him but little, met him square on and would take no over-emphasis. 'Oh, Diana, you are as beautiful as ever!' 'Oh, come off it, Stephen,' – 'Don't over-egg the pudding' – 'What, you've got a big stomach and you're hiding. You can't do up your flies?'

---

[1] Gaby Deslys (1881–1920), feather-bedecked singer and dancer, described by Cecil as 'the whole school of glamour that was to be exemplified twenty years later by Marlene Dietrich'.
[2] Hon. Stephen Tennant (1906–87).

The two were a good foil, Stephen reminiscing about Margot,[1] his mother, Harry Cust ('Yes, he was my father,' Diana said), Pavlova, Karsavina, Lady de Grey.[2] Talk was so high-spirited that it was difficult to follow, but one could only hope to keep up with the tide.

At one point Stephen asked Diana to sing some of the earliest songs as he knew she never forgot a lyric. This set Diana off, and Stephen too, who let down the tone from Gilbert and Sullivan to 'If you knew Susie as I knew Susie – ooooooh, what a girl!'. Then Diana told, in defence of Cynthia Jebb,[3] what a marvellous memory she has for old songs and how she, the Duke of Wellington[4] and Diana motored to Marlborough. For 2 hours they sang. As they motored through any big song, Gerry said, 'We must stop. We can't be seen singing through the windows.' But nothing stopped D and C, as they remembered another old favourite.

Later we went to see the Trees' new house [Shute House, Donhead]. 'Awful!' said Diana, getting back into the car. 'What a comedown after Mereworth, and it shows they have no taste!'

Unfortunately, before hurrying on to Reine Pitman's[5] for dinner, Diana, having refused my offer of a drink, said to Eileen, 'I'll just have a nip' and she must have up-tilted the vodka bottle. The evening, as a result, was a disaster – Diana noisy, non-stop talking, gesticulating. As she said about Ali Forbes,[6] 'You can't be amusing all the time. If you hold forth too much, you become a bore.'

Diana, when drunk, lurches and swivels round on dangerously precarious legs. She is a dervish, but her brain is acute. She never becomes fuzzy and remembers names, dates, quotes. But a lot of it has been heard before. She was, however, very graphic in word and gesture about twice being bound up by burglars. However, as usual, the result of this evening was that, once again, I felt enough is as good as a feast. One couldn't want more of her. The one and a half days is enough. Yet she is marvellous, as

---

[1] Margot, Countess of Oxford and Asquith (1864–1945), wife of H. H. Asquith, Prime Minister.

[2] Harry Cust (1861–1917), great-grandson of first Lord Brownlow, editor of the *Pall Mall Gazette*; Anna Pavlova (1881–1931), ballerina; Tamara Karsavina (1885–1978), ballerina; and Lady de Grey (d. 1917), Countess of Lonsdale, and later Marchioness of Ripon. Grandmother of Sir Michael Duff.

[3] Cynthia Noble (1898–1990), married Gladwyn Jebb, first Lord Gladwyn (1900–96).

[4] Gerald, seventh Duke of Wellington KG (1885–1972), aesthetic duke, formerly Lord Gerald Wellesley.

[5] Reine Ormond (1897–1971), artist, niece of John Singer Sargent, wife of Hugo Pitman.

[6] Alastair Forbes (b. 1918), writer and critic, who at that time divided his time between Switzerland and a cottage on the Firle estate in Sussex. Fond of Proustian sentences in his *Spectator* reviews and the master of many a long, searching monologue, which frequently disconcerted and on occasions offended.

she went to bed (to take 3 sleeping pills), she told Eileen to let me know she loves me. 'Does he know I really love him?'

Next morning, *very* groggy on her feet, but with Doggie scratching around the hyacinths I'd given her in the basket, she fumbled for her ticket in front of the collector, while I grimaced and kept up a commentary about the inclement spring, to take his eye off the basket. Somehow she is always in good hands, and Elizabeth Cavendish[1] found her, gave her a seat, and she was met at the station by that nice Lennox Berkeley's son.[2]

An invitation to lunch with royalty was now a regular feature in Cecil's life. He who had first photographed a member of the Royal Family in 1927, Princess Louise, Duchess of Argyll, could now count himself a friend to some members of the Royal Family, especially Princess Marina, Duchess of Kent. He was occasionally entertained by Princess Margaret and Lord Snowdon, and Queen Elizabeth the Queen Mother[3] had twice lunched with him at Pelham Place.

Cecil was almost a life-long friend of the Herbert family and was especially fond of Patricia, Viscountess Hambleden, David Herbert's sister. She was one of the longest-serving ladies-in-waiting and closest friends of the Queen Mother.

Cecil first photographed Queen Elizabeth at Buckingham Palace in July 1939 and, thereafter, she frequently commissioned him. He was sure that she obtained for him the job of photographing the Queen after the Coronation in 1953. He played an important role in the presentation of the Queen Mother's image. Eventually Cecil offended the Queen Mother by a silly reference to her in his published diaries[4] and, significantly, she was not represented at his Memorial Service.

Lunch with the Queen Mother   *March 1970*

Patricia Hambleden[5] is lady-in-waiting, and as such was to accompany Queen Elizabeth to the opening of a new wing at some Women's Institute half an hour away from Patricia's house at Henley-on-Thames.

---

[1] Lady Elizabeth Cavendish (b. 1926), daughter of tenth Duke of Devonshire, elder sister of Lady Anne Tree and friend of the poet, Sir John Betjeman.
[2] Sir Lennox Berkeley (1903–89), composer, had 3 sons, of whom, Michael, also became a well-known composer and broadcaster.
[3] HM Queen Elizabeth the Queen Mother (1900–2002).
[4] See Cecil Beaton, *The Strenuous Years* (Weidenfeld & Nicolson, 1973), p.114.
[5] Patricia, Viscountess Hambleden (1904–80), daughter of the fifteenth Earl of Pembroke, and Lady of the Bedchamber to the Queen Mother 1937–95.

The QM was to lunch before the stunt and Patricia asked Jimmy Smith (brother-in-law)[1] and me to make up a very informal party

Patricia opened the door, the house was tidy, a few pot plants around, but no feeling of gala, a small log of wood burning in the grate of a cold, forlorn drawing room on a cold, forlorn day. 'Is it too soon to make the cocktails?' 'Yes.' We talked about last night's *The Beaux' Stratagem*, then by degrees went to the grog tray.

As Jimmy was about to mix the martini, the old-fashioned car was seen, with a pink cushiony cloud in it, and soon she waddled into the room so like Aunt Cada, or the Helen Hokinson[2] ladies that wear elaborate feathered hats.

The Queen's manner was completely relaxed. I have never known her like this before. Generally she is putting on an act, but this was extraordinarily relaxed and easy. Moreover she sat on the arm of a sofa instead of the inevitable royal standing about.

Lunch was as spartan as the house. Asparagus, but not enough on the dish. The QM took three little fronds. I took four. There were scarcely enough to go round. Next, a very good chicken pie, pastry cooked by the Italian wife of the man who served us, light and excellent, followed by a very bad melon, unripe, green, no cream. But it was typical of the Herberts not to put on the dog, not to try to live up to the Joneses, and I dare say that QE enjoyed this.

Certainly never has she been more frank. We talked about our dreams. She said hers were so very unpleasant. It was very tiresome that her difficulties should continue at night. She was always late in her dreams and her proper clothes were never put out in time. (I told my equivalent, about being on stage without having learnt my lines.) QE talked about my collection of clothes, said she would try to look but always gave to the Theatrical Ladies Guild. Suggested I asked for Winnie, Duchess of Portland's dresses from Wemyss Castle.[3] Talked of how she hated the Japs, made criticism of the US and collapsed when told that SET [Selective Employment Tax] was over when one reached 70, and Patricia informed her that the let-up applied only to one servant. QE said, 'And it would have made a great difference to me!'

The food and wine produced a flush on the very fine white skin and I was amazed at the mauve pink-rose madder that appeared on the chin. The cheeks have formed their little crows-feet, but the effects of age are

---

[1] Hon. James Smith (1906–80), brother-in-law of Patricia, Viscountess Hambleden. Governor of Sadler's Wells and director of W. H. Smith.
[2] Helen Hokinson, cartoonist of plump ladies, in the United States.
[3] Winifred, Duchess of Portland (1863–1954), Mistress of the Robes to Queen Alexandra (1913–25). Her daughter was Lady Victoria Wemyss (1890–1994).

not unpleasant and are accepted with frankness. Jokes about the WI buildings and the awful fight against the clock. When the two ladies returned from 'retirement upstairs' and the detective said there was still '2½ minutes to go', the QM said, 'That's not enough. I have to write my name in Patricia's Visitors Book and that takes a long time.' When she sat with pen in hand, she did an imitation of a Helen Hokinson museum lady and the adept appearance was hilarious. Later Mary [Pembroke] told me that sometimes while playing bridge, the Queen has taken a strip of the brown paper from a chocolate box and has done an imitation of an old general telling who should play when and what cards.

The two ladies went off in the big car (the pink costume would make its usual great effect) and in the car Patricia would be amused by a running commentary, 'That's a good one. Look at that fat pig! Oh, I say!' They discussed the lunch and the Q said that I had been very amusing (I didn't think that I'd ever got airborne) but that the important thing was that I exuded goodness. This the greatest feather in my cap for I proudly think that the QM is a very good judge of character.

From time to time, Cecil liked to record a small vignette that amused him. This particular one was seen by many viewers of the 1969 television film, Royal Family. *The incident was excised on subsequent airings of the film, but by then it was a legend.*

HE Annenberg[1] to the Queen[2]

'We're in the Embassy residence, subject, of course, to some of the discomforture as a result of a need for, uh, elements of refurbishing and rehabilitation.'

Presently, Cecil returned to New York. He paid a visit to Valentina Schlee, the famous Russian dress designer, in quest of a dress for the exhibition of haute couture he was staging at the Victoria and Albert Museum in London.

Valentina was a creature of many dramas and susperstitions. She was born Valentina Sanina, and married Georges Schlee, described in many of Cecil's published diaries as 'The Little Man'. She was Greta Garbo's best friend in the

---

[1] Walter Annenberg (b. 1908), United States Ambassador to Britain 1969–74. He inherited a publishing empire, which he turned round and from which he made a fortune. As publisher of the *Philadelphia Inquirer* he became a friend of Richard Nixon. He was a generous donor to the British Museum and St. Paul's Cathedral and put two billion dollars into the United States education system.
[2] HM Queen Elizabeth II (b. 1926). Cecil photographed her many times between 1942 and 1968.

1940s, but lost Garbo to her husband, and when Schlee died in 1964, she turned against the sulky Swede and had her exorcised from her apartment. But the two ladies continued to live in the same apartment block, 450 East 52 Street, New York, for a further quarter of a century, trying never to meet, with 'Nin' Ryan, Rex Harrison and others for neighbours.

Valentina designed clothes that, as Irene Selznick put it, 'a woman could run along the road in and throw her arms around a man's neck without her dress riding up her back'.

Valentina[1] *– New York*   *April 1970*

Went to Valentina's apartment in order to get from her one of her theatrical dresses for my museum collection. I have not been to the apartment for 10 years, partly because of the Schlee situation v Garbo, and only because Valentina is one of the most crashing egocentric maniacs. Nowadays, in retirement, few people put up with her, so she was ready to give me all.

At first I was staggered to see how like Garbo's apartment this is. Maybe it's the same shape (it's in the same building) but the flush of over-decoration is the same, the bad ormulu mixed with the Grand Rapier Louis XV, the eczema of flower paintings (bad on walls). It's really kitsch. However, the shock was Valentina herself. Her teeth have been replaced by others, her nose looks fatter, her eyes smaller.

She is colourless now, whereas she once created a great effect of beauty. 'Darrlink, do you like my hair?' (She can't speak English yet.) 'I wash it myself, I cut it, you feel it.' She talked balls with over-emphasis of the hands, about the Windsors[2] and all the least interesting subjects. She eulogised an English/French-style chair. She put the lights on for her Monticellis, then she showed me a huge hibiscus tree. It had been given to her when small by Maggie Teyte[3] in exchange for a dress for *Pelléas et Mélisande*. She had nurtured it with vitamins, new earth, washing, every sort of care, and she said that each time she returned from abroad it put out a flower to welcome her. It had put one out for me today.

It is remarkable how she manages to preserve her Russian way of life in this very difficult period. Somehow she still has a couple of maids to look after her, but otherwise she is very much alone, and she treats every small

[1] Valentina Schlee (1904–89), Russian dress designer.
[2] HRH the Duke of Windsor (1894–1972) and his duchess, the former Mrs Wallis Simpson (1896–1986).
[3] Dame Maggie Teyte (1889–1976), actress and operatic vocalist. Performed in *Pelléas et Mélisande* at Covent Garden (1910) and again (1930).

event as a great milestone. I liked very much the fuss that she made in supplying me with a drink of tonic water, the amount of ice to be carefully judged, and to the maid, 'Now please go and cut a nice big slice of lemon.' Nothing offhand, great *soins* taken over everything. In her own way there is no denying she is an artist.

Then she brought out a grey chiffon wisp of a dress she had made for Tammy Grimes in *High (Blithe) Spirits*.[1] It was a masterpiece of cut and manoeuvring of mathematics. 'It's Chinese,' she said, as she fingered the seams. I realised that she believes completely in her talent being God-given and that it must be kept sacrosanct and not abused. Some manager had recently rung her for five costumes to be made in four days. She gave him the most appalling rebuke. When, having denuded herself of all but a pair of black knickers and a bra, she displayed the beauty of the dress in its manifold excellences, she then proceeded to pack it up for me. She was at once a marvel. The old beringed but delicate hands treated the silk folds with such exquisite care and bold gestures.

It was a work of art to see her wrapping the wisp in some rather crumpled pieces of silk paper. 'They are not new but they are clean.' This folded that way, that folded this way, up and over, she was leaning forward for a considerable time in an agonisingly painful position. (She has lumbago.) But she noticed nothing except what she was doing, preparing a work of art for posterity. As she manoeuvred the final gesture with the baby-like sleeves folded into a little roll, she leant down and kissed it. 'Goodbye,' she said. It was really very touching, because absolutely genuine.

New York   *April 1970*

Arrival for Tonys which I've been nominated for[2] (though may not get). NY very hit by money mortgages in all the housing trades, the slump imminent, Fulco[3] has been sulking because no one buys his jewellery and he has quit. Plays not coming on because of lack of production funds. But outside the hotel there is traffic panic, everyone on edge. The hotel a riot of visitors, all milling and making a terrible ear-splitting assault on one's nerves. Rudeness in language and gesture. I am calm and collected, but longing to get away at the earliest possible moment.

---

[1] Tammy Grimes (b. 1934), starred in *High Spirits*, Noël Coward's musical version of his *Blithe Spirit* in New York in 1964.
[2] Cecil was nominated for *Coco*.
[3] Fulco di Verdura (1899–1978), Sicilian duke and famed designer of stylish semi-precious jewellery. Author of *The Happy Summer Days* (1976).

New York   *19 April 1970*

The Antoinette Perry awards [the Tonys] took place at last, last night. They had been hanging Damocles-like for three nights since my arrival for them. What would one say if nominated as the winner? Was it tempting fate to prepare a little speech, and yet if one had nothing to say, how terrifying an ordeal in front of all and sundry. I had the secret feeling that I would win for my costumes since my rivals were really so very poor. (Sam Green was viciously amused at the idea of Bob LaVine[1] winning with his terrible *Jenny* costumes, a sort of modern *All About Eve* in another milieu. Bob was my assistant on *Raffles*.)

I would have been mad if I hadn't won, a terribly unnecessary journey. Nervously I waited for D. D. Ryan[2] to arrive for dinner. The stupidity of New York doormen cannot be imagined, as a revolting hired car was three-quarters of an hour late in finding her, so a rush to get to the theatre on time.

False alarm on arrival. Late comers were *not* penalised. In fact an hour's filling in before being on the scene of 20 million TV audience. I was the first nomination and Julie Andrews[3] read the citation and announced my name. Hurried through much voracious and surprising applause, suddenly embarked on speech – mercifully known by heart, and suddenly felt very shy, and voice dry.

But success tingled in the veins. The rest of the evening long drawn-out. Interesting surprises. Hepburn lost to Bacall.[4] *Coco* lost to *Applause* on all counts. Hepburn keeping up her tactics of being difficult, contradicting herself and making life a hell on earth for the poor Victoria Phillips.

Hepburn insisted on acting the last scenes of the play. They are the *worst*, and the audience loathed seeing it on a monitor and not 'live'. They will have done a lot of damage to the bookings, as no one who saw the sample scene will want to book for house parties now. The advance booking is very small. There's a chance that the show may not last much

---

[1] Robert LaVine (d. 1981), costume designer and one-time special consultant to Diana Vreeland. Author of *In a Glamorous Fashion – The Fabulous Years of Hollywood Costume Design* (1981); and his boyfriend, Robert Prairie (d. 1989). LaVine walked off with a dozen Garbo letters from Reddish House, which were sold in New York after Prairie's death.

[2] D. D. Ryan, daughter-in-law of Mrs John Barry Ryan.

[3] Dame Julie Andrews (b.1935), played Eliza Doolittle in the stage version of *My Fair Lady*.

[4] Lauren Bacall (b. 1924), film star, married to Humphrey Bogart, then Jason Robards. She starred triumphantly in *Applause* on Broadway in 1970.

longer. Meanwhile plans for taking the play in its present rotten shape, to London. Back late for tea, I found the mannequin statue being fitted quite ridiculous. Aunt Cada very masculine, the food situation quite grave...

The foregoing was written in the Jumbo jet, on my way home from New York. I was longing to sleep and was drugged with antibiotics, against sinus troubles. Little wonder it makes no sense.

New York gets you down, the beastly elevator man complaining at the Waldorf Astoria post Tony party about the number of people in the elevator. 'Stop complaining!' I shouted. The waiters are rude, the food unbelievably filthy, lukewarm.

On my return to London, went to a theatrical supper (after C [Carol] Channing[1] evening) at Savoy. There waiters so polite, efficient, relaxed, not hating, not subservient, food absolutely delicious, cigars, liqueurs. It makes New York barbarous in comparison.

Great joy to be back. The cold weather continues, and rain too, but the buds and bulbs have come out in spite of the cold. The countryside is at one of its best phases. The garden is full of daffodils and white narcissi and tulips, hyacinths, grape hyacinths, primroses, all at the same time, most peculiar. I long for sun.

I'm afraid I will miss the sun of spring by being ten days in hospital. Have to have my prostate out. I'm rather terrified and sad too – feel it is a loss of something that I have become accustomed to, and the implications are that it is the beginning of the end.

From the airport I telephoned to Kin, having tried all weekend, and miraculously he answered. He had not got my letter saying I would be in New York and had been away in Seattle. In the hubbub of the airport, in an open booth, I described to him the difference that the operation would make to my sexual activities, and that I was sorry and self-conscious, in case it would be off-putting to him. He was reassuring and made a comforting joke.

But I'm sorry the inevitable has to happen, that this has to be, but better not to have ambulance bells in the night or be in a state of emergency in Pueblo or Kotor.

---

[1] Carol Channing (b. 1921), best known for singing 'Diamonds are a girl's best friend' in Anita Loos's *Gentlemen Prefer Blondes*.

Shall I tell you about my operation?   *April 1970*

For the last two years I have had to get up to pee during the night three or four times. As one gets older the trickle is smaller, no longer that wonderful carthorse hose spurt, and when I reported this to 'Gotters',[1] he put his magic ray on my prostate and said he thought he could keep the situation in abeyance. Nonetheless it wouldn't be a bad idea to make an appointment with the specialist and have a proper examination. This I did. [Dr Howard] Hanley shoved a finger up my backside and after two minutes was more or less booking me into hospital. 'There's no immediate hurry,' he said, 'but it's better not to have ambulance bells in the night.' This phrase frightened me.

I decided to have the operation soon after my return from NY. I would have a few days' holiday in Somerset, to strengthen up, then a last look around at Reddish now that spring had arrived and the orchard was such a marvellous sight with narcissi and scarlet tulips, and the 'last Sunday' when the garden was open to the public was the first hot sunny day of a dreadfully protracted spring. Everyone's spirits soared. I stayed over until the Monday in a state of euphoria as the buds burst around me and the trees put on a hint of green. I also felt very sad. I did not, in fact, think that I would die as a result of the operation. Although my mother's family lived to great ages, my father and his brothers died quite comparatively early. But although I didn't feel I would expire under the anaesthetic, I did find myself in a strange state of elation. It is difficult to describe.

When I waved goodbye to Clarissa [Avon], after lunching with her and Anthony,[2] I felt that she wondered if she was in fact seeing me for the last time. When I drove home I found myself, instinctively, without volition, returning to the place that I loved most, for perhaps a final look at Ashcombe. I felt as if impelled by some force outside me. My body was exceedingly soft and limp, I moved with great ease. It was almost as if I was under the influence of a drug. The influence took me round the garden on accord that was not my own. It all looked so wonderfully beautiful, with the dappled sunlight through the earliest, greenest leaves. When I suddenly came upon the sight of the white-flowered orchard, it was as if it was the Elysian fields, I was deeply moved. I seemed to be

---

[1] Dr Antonius Rudolf Gottfried, Viennese-born doctor, with many fashionable patients. Cecil based Professor Higgins's rooms in the film of *My Fair Lady* on his premises at 75 Wimpole Street. He practised until 1979.
[2] Anthony Eden, first Earl of Avon (1897–1977), and his wife Clarissa Churchill (b. 1920). Clarissa Avon had been a friend of Cecil's since the 1940s, and bought a cottage at Bowerchalke. By this time they were living at Alvediston, a few miles down the Chalke Valley.

making a tour of all my favourite corners, and when back in the house came across so many unexpected 'souvenirs' of the past. The mood stayed with me all evening.

The next morning was different. This was an effort. Smallpeice, taking me to the station, said, 'This is a journey I expect you'd rather not be taking.' He was right. To make matters worse, the train was late on arrival from Exeter and I sat making conversation with Anthony Head, who has been particularly sympathetic about my being spliced open since he spent so much of his early life in hospitals, in fact nearly died at a tender age.

The journey eventually over, there was little time at Pelham Place for farewells, too many chores to attend to, then with the few things I'd need in hospital packed, a hire car arrived. (This so much more sympathetic than a mini with their rough drivers.) The arrival at the hospital was horrid. It happened there was no one to greet me, the doorman off on a chore. I waited patiently with a smug smile on my face. The porter arrived. 'Yes, room number 18.' The elevator wasn't working, he'd take me up by the service lift. We had to wait while a man kicked out a lot of huge boxes of discarded tins, cartons and unwanted left-over food.

The worst moment was that of arrival in my room. I was pleased and touched that my sisters had both sent me welcome flowers. They took the edge off the bleakness of the room. But suddenly I felt very sad. I found myself weeping. Soon a cheerful little nurse appeared and asked me to sign my own death warrant, and the signing of these various papers took my mind off my self-pity. From now on I was so busy that there was never a quiet moment. Pulse and temperature and blood pressure taken. Visits from many nurses of different denominations, all cheerful and nice, a visit of TV man, Dr Gottfried. He reiterated that he didn't want me to be operated on but in the circumstances of my being abroad such a lot, it was as well to guard against being ill in Kotor, or Pueblo, or even in NY. (I couldn't *afford* to be ill in NY!)

Visit of Hanley[1], who would cut me open in the morning and of the anaesthetist, with the mannerisms of the Queen Mother. Suddenly a strange old lady-like lady from the Red Cross who had come to do the 'flaars'. Very late, and he apologised for having only just got out of the operating theatre, was the good-looking doctor in green mackintosh hat, who set about shaving me with a Gillette razor from the stomach to the thigh.

This was a most horrible sensation, and a most horrible indignity. I hated the naked feel of myself. But mercifully a nice nurse came in and

---

[1] Howard Hanley (1909–2001), consulting urologist at Edward VII's Hospital for Officers.

gave me a painkiller and a strong sleeping draught. I must be up betimes in the morning in order to have my bath and be ready at 8.30. Everything very punctual and efficient, and yet done with gaiety, even charm. One of the nurses was so pretty, so delightful in manner and so sympathetic, that I could not understand why she had not been taken off in marriage by some Grand Duke. It was nice that she was the one to tend me early in the morning. I had slept well, no nightmares or horrid forebodings. A shot in the arm to give me courage.

I smiled and talked, even gabbled, as this pretty, nice nurse wheeled me along the corridors and up into the elevator to the operating room. I was reminded of Dr Kildare, and very cheerful was completely unmindful of the fact that these might be my last moments. (Yesterday, at Broadchalke, I had even thought that perhaps this was a good moment to go. Would it ever be so good again? I wanted to finish my 'Aunt Jessie' book, but if I went now it would be on a high note.) The welcoming team were lined up. From the stretcher I smiled at my executioner who shaved my private parts last night. He didn't seem too friendly, but the Queen Mother anaesthetist was there with a needle and that was that.

Quite a crowd in room number 18 when I came to. Gottfried, and God knows who else, but my dry mouth and teeth needed attention. Water pleased. I started immediately to describe my discomfiture. My bladder felt as though it were full to bursting, my privates so tender, I was gradually conscious of being attached to a saline drip, which poured drop by drop into a hole they'd made into my right hand. And the worst had happened. A huge rubber tube had been shoved up my cock, and was bleeding and peeing into a horrid plastic bag. I don't think I could live through two days that were quite as repellent and awful as the first. It isn't that I was in excruciating pain, but I just felt so desperately uncomfortable.

Why can't I be put out of my misery? Can't I have another anaesthetic, or more painkillers? My blood pressure had gone cold and I might be inclined to vomit if I drank some Codeine. Oh how *awful* this long, eventful, half-drugged day, and the long unpleasant night.

Marvellous attention from sympathetic nurses, but I wondered why no one had told me it was going to be as awful as this. I doubted if I would *ever* get right again. It was so terrible being marooned with these tubes. Gotters and Hanley said I was getting on alright, but I couldn't believe that other people had to put up with such misery. I couldn't imagine how I had got through such torment. The cheerful nursing no doubt helped me a lot. Full marks to Sister Agnes and all around her. The flowers that kept arriving were a great joy and I was thrilled that they took the edge off the clinical aspect of the room. Such a variety of people sent them, from Charlotte Gaffran[1] to Princess Alexandra.[2] Eileen was my first visitor, but I wasn't well enough to see anyone, but she seemed reassured that I would survive. Baba visited me and was kind and sympathetic, and Nancy[3] even warmer, and full-hearted.

June[4] was a marvellous visitor, the best, so understanding and sympathetic, and such fun, a wonderful, rare person, and John Sutro[5] is a most faithful old friend. I looked out at the remote world of Devonshire Street through a Lallie Charles[6] background window. There was Odin's Restaurant and it staggered me that all those people had such vitality to go out to dinner so late and so raucously.

David Hockney[7] and Patrick Procktor[8] came in and admitted they had been among the number at Odin's last night, and they'd gone on to some party given by the colossus Tony Richardson[9] until 4 in the a.m. I felt I'd never be able to do that again. By degrees my days took on a rhythm, early morning call with horrid cup of tea. At first I'd go back to sleep but as I got stronger, I'd read, *Madame La Tour du Pin*, Harold Acton's latest 'memoirs', Jim Lees-Milne,[10] but my eyes would ache with too much reading. The waking each morning was a bore, and yet it *did* freshen me up. But a continual anxiety lest one of the tubes should be wrenched from one played havoc with one's nerves. One did not want to take any risk so that getting in and out of bed was a great event. Would one ever be able to 'move one's bowels' again? Such a relief when it did happen.

More flowers, white freesias, lilies of the valley. Such pretty summer flowers, arrangements, and the best was cut by Bindie[11] from her

---

[1] Charlotte Gaffran, masseuse in Wiltshire, to whom Cecil was devoted.
[2] HRH Princess Alexandra, Hon. Lady Ogilvy (b. 1936), daughter of HRH the Duke of Kent, a favourite of Cecil's. He photographed her many times, occasions enjoyed by both photographer and sitter.
[3] Nancy Beaton (1909–99), Cecil's sister. Married Sir Hugh Smiley Bt (1905–90).
[4] June Hutchinson (b. 1920), wife of Lord Hutchinson of Lullington, formerly June Osborn. Cecil had wished to marry her in the 1960s, a match much encouraged by Lady Diana Cooper.
[5] John Sutro (1904–85), film producer and literary figure, a splendid mimic and raconteur.
[6] Lallie Charles (1869–1919), late Edwardian portrait photographer. Sister of Rita Martin (1875–1958).
[7] David Hockney (b. 1937), world-famous artist, who made a corner in swimming pools.
[8] Patrick Procktor (b. 1936), immensely tall artist, much liked by Cecil.
[9] Tony Richardson (1928–91), director and producer of plays and films, formerly married to Vanessa Redgrave.
[10] *Memoirs of Madame de La Tour du Pin* (translated 1969); *More Memoirs of an Aesthete* (1970), by Sir Harold Acton (1904–94), aesthete and writer, based in Florence; *Another Self* (1970), an enjoyable, though fanciful, volume of memoirs, by James Lees-Milne (1908–97), architectural historian and biographer, famed for his diaries.
[11] Viscountess Lambton, wife of Lord Lambton, soon to be a Conservative minister. A niece of Freda Dudley-Ward (erstwhile girlfriend of the Duke of Windsor in the 1920s).

Hampstead garden. Parrot tulips, pansies and morning glory. Bindie was enchanting, funny, courageous, and demonstrated by pulling up her skirt how she had now regained her figure after years of hospitalisation. The nurses all nice, except an Italian night nurse, and one or two South Africans without charm. The Spanish women who brought in the food were kind and cheerful.

Next door was Nico Henderson[1] looking deadly ill with tuberculosis of the liver, but he amazed me by being so mobile, and even went out to lunch and to see Regent's Park and drank champagne next door with Jo Grimond.[2] I felt I'd never be able to do anything again. Back to routine, visits from doctors, all reporting well. Early lunch then sleep, then perhaps a visitor. The wonderful Red Cross dowagers doing the 'flaars'. More flowers arriving. I feared with the first rush they'd give out, but they went on.

The evenings the most difficult because my eyes ached. The TV programmes were appalling and I didn't know quite what to do before being put down. And the nurses weren't ready to put me down before much too late. However, the nights went by in oblivion to the sound of traffic outside or the old man bellowing three doors away. I'm lucky not to be relying on sleeping pills as here I have been knocked for a loop by the two nightly Seconals.

The marvellous day came when the saline drip was taken away. I felt more mobile with only the hose attached to my cock and a bloody bag. The bag became lighter in colour and I was longing for but dreading the day when the catheter would be taken out. At last the morning arrived. The sensation as the quick tube was pulled down in 3 three-inch goes was one of the worst I have ever undergone. It was not actual torture. It was just as if an electric current was running through one 'til one could not bear it any more.

I felt like a Grünewald martyr in the extremest anguish. But when this was once out, oh, the relief of being mobile again. But without this tube would one ever be able to pee again? I was alarmed lest the same thing should happen as after my appendicitis. Then it seemed for ever before I could again pass water. This time, oh the relief, a little trickle, and the bottle had a small amount of pinkish yellow liquid in it. And now I could have a bath, and get rid of the musty, sickly smell of my hairless groin. The manoeuvring in and out of the bath was one of the things that have made me more on edge than I realise. I was by now longing to leave the

---

[1] Sir Nicholas Henderson (b. 1919), British Ambassador in Paris and Washington. Author of *The Private Office*, *Mandarin* (his diaries), and *Old Friends and Modern Instances*.
[2] Jo Grimond (1913–93), Leader of the Liberal Parry (1956–67).

boredom of the Lallie Charles window, but still the stitches must be taken out, and it was early days yet.

I read as much as my eyes would stand, and there were gardening programmes on TV, but by now I longed to get back to the garden and the burgeoning of spring. The day chosen for my release was the perfect one. If I had left a day earlier the effort would have been too much. As it was I could see the early morning sun was hot, and when Eileen arrived with the car I had only just had my bath. I left with gratitude, with no feeling of hatred or squalor at the painful things that had had to be done. If any nursing home is a cheerful one, this is it. The matron waving such a cheerful, jolly, funny farewell. Oh the relief, and oh the beauty to drive past Odin's and Devonshire Street and to see the flowering trees in the squares.

As for the park on this vivid summer's day, it was an unbelievably welcome sight, with may trees, chestnuts, lilac, and in the beds all the tulips were out. As we drove luxuriously in the hired car all the way to Broadchalke, England appeared a garden. Apple blossom, rock plant, bulbs, everything out at the same time. Unbelievably beautiful it all was. I was in a state of euphoria.

I know I looked white and pale on arrival at Reddish, but everyone was cosseting and kind and said I looked fine, and the garden looked fine. I walked around to see the marvels that happened since I left two long weeks ago. Everything was out now, or so it seemed, after the bleak long winter. I enjoyed Ray's delicious raffiné food after the hospital fare. I enjoyed going to bed for the afternoon, and feeling that for the next weeks I could stay in my own house and enjoy the best of all seasons.

As great good fortune had it, England was basking now in hot sun for one whole month. One could not believe it possible, yet day after day the sun shone through the ever-thickening green. The flowers came out and were superseded by others. The evenings grew longer and warmer, the signs of summer were more apparent as spring was left behind and the orchard was no longer at its best, while the terrace and the cottage borders came to life.

To begin with, I was not able to do anything but read, and look at TV, and sleep. Then one glorious day I felt I could pick up where I had left it, my 'Aunt Jessie' book. From then on this was my convalescent task. Some days I wrote worse than others because I felt more tired, but I made progress, and the work that I had done before paid off well in giving me something to polish and elaborate upon. I got more and more enthusiastic about the job, and only eye strain could prevent me from staying at it all day.

Eileen came for weekends, and I realised my resistance was low when she told me of some business irritation or frustration. By degrees I was able to move more freely in bed and at last was able to sleep on my left side, then even on my stomach, and soon I gave up taking pills.

Cecil hated being described as a 'royal photographer', but he certainly did not wish anyone else to be. He was summoned to Royal Lodge, in Windsor Great Park, to photograph Queen Elizabeth the Queen Mother for her forthcoming seventieth birthday on 4 August 1970.

May 1970

Yet I was far from strong and the idea of having to pull up stumps and motor to [Royal Lodge] Windsor to photograph the Queen Mother was a terrible milestone. I dreaded it. I did not feel I was ready for it, but one can't chuck a queen, especially at the last moment and the day was unforgettable as it turned out, like a visit to India with rhododendrons and azaleas like mountains growing in great alleyways among the well-tended Windsor Park lawns. The QM was her usual kind, good self, and funny; while posing among the azaleas she said, 'Gardening at Royal Lodge'. While we were having lunch *à deux* on the terrace, Eileen and Mrs Butler of the Broadchalke garage were being shown 'behind the scenes'.

Suckling,[1] the Queen's dresser, said she'd never seen the Queen slump.

The expedition (apart from a broken fan belt! which caused me to be forty minutes late) was so successful that I realised it had done me good, and made me realise I could get back to normal. Meanwhile another week of miraculous sunshine, more blossom, more blooming, nice neighbours, blue vistas through the green buds.

One expedition to London to see Gottfried who reported well. I went to a lunch at the French Embassy (crab, chicken *à l'estragon*, ice) and to Diana Phipps's[2] housewarming of 30 for her handmade home. She had cooked the meal, but this expedition was exhausting. With what relief I took the train the following morning for two weeks of uninterrupted country life. Still the sun went on shining. Still I worked on my book as much as I could (and it seemed to make little progress. But how lucky I am to have this heaven-sent task!).

By degrees the lilac is over, but now the laburnum is at full trumpet and the roses are coming out everywhere. The terrace is a marvel with

---

[1] Miss Gwendoline May Suckling, dresser to the Queen Mother, given the Royal Victorian Medal (Silver) (1971).
[2] Diana Phipps (b. 1937), daughter of Countess Sternberg, author of *The Journey*. She was a popular interior decorator and hostess in London in the 1970s. See also later biographical note, p.88.

valerian, white clematis, wild iris and, by degrees, I am able to do a lot of gardening without hurting the muscles of my stomach. It is very good to feel suddenly that that overpowering lassitude, which is so depressing, has given place to a return to vitality. Suddenly I feel I am able to move quickly again and not just sit blinking in front of me like an old pensioner. (And it's not a bad pastime, what with the birds and bees and butterflies, there is so much to watch.) But at last I am able to start writing this diary. I had meant to write the final excerpt on the day of going into hospital. But there was no time, and afterwards no energy, until today, a month later.

Whether or not the operation is going to be entirely successful, I do not know. I am sad that it had to be. I hate being tampered with and even though I might not have had a child it saddens me to know now I can't have one, and I don't know if it will make much difference to my sex life or to my attitude to sex. At the moment I feel as if I can never have any further interest in the subject. Meanwhile Kin has not written to me. It is unbelievable, yet not surprising. He is intent on torturing himself. I am intent on not letting him torture me. Sam G. has been solicitous and will come over soon and stay, and by degrees maybe I will feel able to cope with people. At the moment I am intent on my loneliness as it is the only way to recuperate and get on with my book.

Have done no painting. When in the writing mood it is impossible to switch, and to feel the lightness of the 'Aunt Jessie' book has come as a godsend. But what a mercy it is to have some craft to follow. I don't know how people who have no outlet can put up with things like recuperation from illness.

8 June 1970

E. M. Forster[1] died yesterday, 91. His death expected since many years. What a sweet man, gentle, self-effacing, kind, but with great moral courage, and a determination to fight for what he believed in.

His last novel written in the early twenties, it is a lesson that quality pays better than any quantity. He is one of the greats with an output of about five books.

A delightful friend, the last time I saw him was two or three years ago when the Italian Ambassador[2] and Madame Guidotti gave a gala for his

---

[1] E. M. Forster (1879–1970), author of *Howards End*, *A Room with a View* and *Passage to India*.
[2] Gastone Guidotti, Italian Ambassador in London, 1964–8.

having encouraged our understanding of Italy at a difficult time. He was invited to stay at the Embassy and to receive a gold medal. When he left Cambridge by train, he realised he had got into the wrong train and the limousine to meet him would wait in vain. He arrived, bedraggled and out of breath, at a lunch given in his honour.

I have always liked to know that he was still living in his room at King's.[1]

The news is desperately depressing. The imminent election looks as if it will be won by Labour by a huge majority.[2] I thought it bad enough when the Edens[3] said that it would be best if Labour did get in with a very small majority, as the difficulties are going to be so appalling in the autumn when all prices go up and wages are frozen. But now that the country seems to want them in, well, one wonders if one should not join the gang of expatriates. But where would one go? When the weather is as it has been here for the last month, there is nowhere more beautiful, and I know I'd be miserable outlawed. But in spite of personal conditions, we are going through a bad patch and the newspapers and TV news bulletins with Peruvian earthquakes and the incompetence of the government to cope, and the dancing in the streets at Peruvians having won a football match, is one of the many distressing things one reads. Others – Czechoslovakia, Dubcek,[4] the Middle East, Vietnam, Cambodia, and always our fear of those swinish Russians.

Diana Cooper visiting Iris Tree,[5] dying in the Sister Agnes hospital, says to the nurse, 'Of course I don't want to see her. I want her to see me.'

It was such a wonderful relief, at last, to feel my vitality was returning. I could walk up the stairs with as sprightly a gait as before. Then Mrs Smallpeice interrupted my writing by coming to do my room and, as I got out of bed, I complained, 'I don't know why, but I've got a stomach-ache.' It's just too damned bad. It seldom happens that one has an old-fashioned stomach-ache, but that's what I had, and it made me feel bad-tempered. My sister, Baba,[6] came to lunch on her way through from Somerset and the pain became so bad on the left side of the stomach that,

---

[1] Cecil photographed Forster in Cambridge in the 1950s. Forster's bedpan was visible under his bed.
[2] Edward Heath led the Conservatives to a surprise victory on 18 June 1970.
[3] The Earl and Countess of Avon.
[4] Alexander Dubcek (1921–92), elected President of the Central Committee, the Communist Party, Czechoslovakia, September 1968.
[5] Iris Tree (1897–1968), actress and poetess, married to the photographer Curtis Moffat, among others.
[6] Baba, Barbara Beaton (1912–73), married to Alec Hambro (1910–43). She was Cecil's favourite sister.

after our quick meal, I had to excuse myself and come to bed with 2 Disprins. She was worried so, when I woke up one and a half hours later and the pain had gone, I sent her a message to say all was well. But it wasn't.

An hour later I felt so ill that I had to call on Dr Brown.[1] He would come at 9.30 tonight, Ray[2] said. 'No, you must come immediately.' While we waited, I rolled about in agony, with a deep pain in my stomach. Brown gave me a painkiller and said that if I were not better, to call him later in the evening. By 9.30 I was, to use his expression, climbing up the wall. An appalling thud-like pain gripped me in the left loin. I was in extremis and terrified of the night ahead of me. Brown gave me an injection, another painkiller and a sleeping pill. They worked. We could not imagine why the pain travelled from kidney to stomach.

Yet another day of pain and, on finding my temperature was cold, I telephoned in desperation to Dr Gottfried. He said I must come back to the nursing home. I blew my top. I was quite rude. It is one thing to buoy yourself up to go to hospital for an operation, but to return there 2 weeks after one has been dismissed is more than one can bear. I felt terribly sorry for myself, but buoyed up and grateful for the sympathy of Mrs Smallpeice and Ray, who motored me to London. I saw Eileen for half an hour's hectic talk before her holiday and my return to Beauchamp Street.

Oh God, the horror of going through the ritual of signing papers again. This time I would *not* give them permission to cut me open and make a hamburger of my stomach. I was almost in tears but kept busy with nursing interruptions. For 2 days I did the usual boring things, was X-rayed, went into a Nazi torture chamber for a Barium test, and don't know how I withstood so many humiliations. Nothing definite was said. Meanwhile I was in a small cubbyhole (no flowers this time) with awful traffic outside and a beautiful summer being frittered away. Why, oh why, had this happened to me? So many people say the prostate operation was child's play. Now people were saying that lots of people had fevers or infections and it was a result of the ordeal.

It seemed for ever that I stayed, incapable of work, in my bed. My temperature would not return to normal.

My solace: Ray collected me to go for a run in the car and we visited Queen Mary's rose garden [in Regent's Park]. How she would have loathed all those vivid Day-Glo colours. Strangely enough the doctors and matron all agreed to allow me out to go to the Ball at Windsor Castle, but of this anon. I remained over the weekend, neglected, doctors

---

[1] Dr Christopher Brown (d. 1985), doctor to Cecil, Lord Avon and others in the Chalke Valley.
[2] Ray Gurton, Cecil's chef, who also worked for Peter Sellers at one time.

and nurses away, most of the patients too. I felt more depressed than for a long time. I felt no one knew what was the matter.

Meanwhile life was passing by so quickly. I could hardly believe that the young people I saw on television or the papers could lead the violent, athletic, sexy lives they did. I felt bereft. On Monday, more neglect, so I let off at Gottfried. He ran his head off to try and track down Hanley, the surgeon. At 3 o'clock Hanley telephoned to say the tests showed nothing serious, but that I had a kidney infection; that the left kidney, perfectly alright before, was now not functioning. But nothing serious, no antibiotics, just barley water. Since my temperature had come down, there was no reason why I should not go home. But when? Tomorrow? No, today, I said, leaping out of bed, and we contrived to get to Waterloo for the 6 o'clock train.

Never have I felt such relief. For the first time in 6 weeks it was raining when I came to Reddish under an umbrella. I made a tour of the garden in its summer's luxury and, thrilled to be home, sunk to bed and sleep without aid.

Next day, slight pain again in stomach, 2 Aspros cured it, but could things be right? In the evening my temperature went up, and my spirits really low. A quiet day followed, drinking barley water by the gallon, 2 Aspros, sleep, a bit of writing, the joy of the trees, the glades, the now-opened-up 'paddock', the roses, the garlands of palest pink. All this helped. But what if one has not one's health? I was not in top gear. My temperature had come down, but I must call Gottfried.

Things remain the same. Dot [Head] came to see me and we laughed as she is the best company. Then early bed and able to sleep without a pill, which brings on a headache, but I feel that the fever has gone to my balls. I call Gottfried early. He said Hanley had diagnosed kidney trouble. Maybe the pain was caused by gravel. Meanwhile, not to worry, not to give further treatment except barley water.

I am feeling better, but even so, the thought of starting another day makes me feel very sad. I can't stop weeping. I know it is through weakness, but I wonder if I am ever going to recover. At the moment I am in as bleak a mood as I have been for many years.

Have I told you about my operation? (continued)

I have some 'date' looming in the distance. The 21st July in Venice, to join the Wrightsmans' yacht. Will I make it? Closer is the dinner arranged three months ago for the Harewoods, Alan Rosses, Julian Huxleys, and the St John Hutchinsons.[1] June bullies me, 'You must

---

[1] George, seventh Earl of Harewood (b. 1923), son of the Princess Royal, and his second

cancel! You're not well, you mustn't make the effort.' I want to return to a bit of London life. Perhaps it will enliven my spirits.

On Monday evening I am dining with Anne Tree in her new house. When, by degrees after dinner, I realise I am leaving all the talk to Sam Green and to Anne, I am utterly limp. Fever tingles through my body. Obviously I have a temperature. Why do I feel so livery, jaundiced? We leave early. Next day, Sam tried to liven me up, but that's not what I want. Let me be crouched in misery. My balls ache. The whole of the lower regions are as if bruised and battered. I am glad I will be going to London on Wednesday to try to find out what is wrong. Gottfried has been a marvel of energy and intelligence. He was worried when I arrived, abject, on the Wednesday, straight from the train. He looked at my furred tongue, took my 100 temperature, found my blood pressure was high. He couldn't understand why I felt this was the lowest moment as I sat bowed on his patient's bed, my shoulders hunched, my long hair straggly, and my appearance uncouth. He had made an immediate date for me to see the surgeon.

Hanley kept me waiting three-quarters of an hour to give me a hurried poke up the arse and say: Yes, he imagined that since I had had an infected prostate this was all a matter of the infection spreading to the urinary tract. But why the aching in the balls? Why the aching of the kidney? He said he was worried that I had taken so long to recover. He had written Gottfried, recommending some female hormones. He felt sure this would do the trick. The after[many] months' notice dinner party was called off at 5 o'clock. I went to bed, feeling abject. How could I sleep tonight when I had slept fitfully all day?

Next day another wash-out. Gottfried visited me at Pelham. He seemed to put all his faith in the hormone tablets. 'Don't be surprised if you feel a tingling in the breasts and if they begin to enlarge!' What a joke! Nothing made me laugh. I lay in despond, sweating a lot, visited by Nancy, and upstairs was the rattle of Miss Leeney's typewriter. She could not understand where chapters 2, 3 and 4 had gone.[1] 'But you have them,' I moaned. 'No, Mr Beaton, that's just it!' My temperature must have jumped to 199. 'But you have copies!' 'No, Mr Beaton, that's just it. You see, there was such a panic when you suddenly said you wanted the last chapter to show Mr Green that there wasn't time!' 'But it takes no time to put in a carbon copy! That's a rule. I always *trust* you to take a copy. The marks are much too erratic. You must take a copy of everything!' 'I

wife, Patricia Tuckwell (b. 1926), an Australian; Alan Ross (1922–2001), editor of the *London Magazine*; Sir Julian Huxley (1887–1975), zoologist and philosopher, and his wife, Juliette Baillot (1896–1994), author of *Leaves of the Tulip Tree* (1986); and Jeremy, Lord Hutchinson of Lullington (b. 1915) and his wife, June.
[1] *My Bolivian Aunt* (1971).

am terribly sorry.' 'I know you are, but that's not the point. What am I going to do? Rewrite 3 chapters?'

I turned my face to the wall. For several days this added horror became a part of my illness. I had unpleasant nights of sad and horrible dreams. I was as weak as a rag. The sand very soon emptied in the hourglass. The days weren't even pleasant. Here was the garden at its best, and I lay in bed and saw the Picasso and Hockney engravings framed on my side wall, and the pictures were alliterated with the reflections from outside the window of roses blowing in the breeze, and the green marvel of the garden beyond. It was too pretty for words, and yet I took it all for granted. I was just not able to euphorise my garden. Such a waste of a summer. I suppose that if I recover and feel better in future, that all this suffering and disappointment will have been worth it. But, at the moment, I am very *éloigné* and incapable of enjoying what should have been one of the loveliest summers for years.

I am now back at Reddish. Sam has gone off on his adventures. Alan [Tagg] and Charles [Colville] are keeping me company There are visits from neighbours and Dicky Buckle is always interesting to discuss, his energy fantastic, his love affairs emotional and non-stop, but what does it all amount to? Meanwhile, I am so dunched with the thought of having to rewrite chapters 2, 3 and 4 that I am altogether turned off the Bolivian aunt work and am trying to gain energy to do fabric designs or work in other directions, one of which is to reread the volume about Garbo[1] with the possibility of severely cutting, and wondering if, after all, I will take the plunge and give the go-ahead to the publisher.

Cecil was invited to attend a Reception to celebrate 'the 70th anniversary of Queen Elizabeth the Queen Mother, The Duke and Duchess of Gloucester, The Earl Mountbatten of Burma and The Duke of Beaufort'. By December 2001 two had survived to become centenarians. The party was also memorable for the presence of Edward Heath, the Prime Minister, who had swept to unexpected victory in the General Election the day before and thus attended as Prime Minister in lieu of Harold Wilson, who had departed from Downing Street earlier in the day.

Cecil was glad to be able to go since he had missed a ball at Windsor Castle in April 1963, held a few nights before the wedding of Princess Alexandra to the Hon. Angus Ogilvy. He had been working on the film of My Fair Lady *and was forced to remain in Hollywood for many months, much to his undisguised fury.*

---

[1] Later published as *The Happy Years* (1972).

The Windsor Ball   *19 June 1970*

When I was stricken with my first post-operational 'setback' and was in actual physical torture, I kept wondering if, once more, I would be prevented from going to the ball at Windsor. The only other time I was bidden (to a ball in honour of Princess Alexandra's engagement), I was gratuitously prevented from flying over from Hollywood by the squeeze of the last-drop selfishness of Cukor.[1]

It has been a source of irritation ever since. Each time I asked a doctor in the country or back in the nursing home, if they thought I could 'make it' this time, they were all surprisingly sporting and wanted me to take the chance. Of course the nurses were tickled at the idea of hearing a first-hand account and even the matron joined the conspiracy.

At 6.30 I had the usual awful dinner, a pewter pot of gruel, followed by some tastelessness. Somehow I contrived to spread out the time of waiting till Ray arrived with my dinner jacket and a flask of brandy. Soon the hire car appeared. Ray later said, 'Mr B looked marvellous and out on the pavement in his big black hat, drinking from a goblet, brandy and ginger ale.' It was one of the most beautiful moonlit nights of a wonderful summer. The light was weakening and the lights went up in the delightful late 18th-century houses at Datchet. Windsor looked lively at this hour with crowds oblivious of the ball nearby, coming out of the theatre having thoroughly enjoyed *Dandy Dick*, or out of pubs and hotel bars. The castle in the distance was floodlit. Little possees of people watched the first guests, as with everything connected with the monarch, the organisation was perfect.

Polite policemen and Chelsea pensioners[2] at every standpoint. By now a steady stream of traffic in the direction in which we must go. On arrival in a very ugly, gothic hall, I was a bit baffled. I felt strange and out from another world as indeed I might, as my temperature was over 100. One had to battle with the battleaxe wives of officials.

The first woman I saw was the loathsome Lady [Adeane], the wife of the Queen's private secretary.[3] She is coarse beyond belief. She was wearing a brocade tube of gold and white stripes, which bulged in the bosoms, stomach and buttocks. Her hair was ironed. Her arms bulged above her white kid gloves. Her feet, in large silver leather slippers, plopped the ground heavily. I am told that this snobbish, horrible woman

[1] George Cukor (1899–1983), film director, who directed *My Fair Lady*.
[2] Cecil meant Yeomen of the Guard.
[3] Sir Michael Adeane (later Lord Adeane) (1910–84), and his wife Helen (1916–94).

simply splits her sides at all lavatory jokes. I thought better of asking her if she had pulled the plug.

One or two other people had to be overridden, but why shouldn't I do just that? A lot of cutting went on to begin with in the gothic hall which I now thought rather delightful, with the banners, coats of arms, and rows of fuchsias in pots. Then in a time that was my own, but somehow seemed a long way off, I found myself greeted by friends, Alice Winn,[1] Jimmie Smith, and then suddenly by a rush of devoted intimates who wondered how I was.

Certainly there was Anne Messel, the Countess of Rosse![2] Good God! She had really worked a miracle. Her appearance must have taken the full 3 weeks of planning since the invites arrived. She must have got up at dawn to start her witches' brew, to dabble with the pots and pans of liquid paint with which she disguised the ravages of age. Her face was now a masterpiece of shading, from a deep mushroom colour around the eyes, to a pale ivory, to give height to the cheekbones and a bone to her snout. The eyes had been painted with the blackest of mascara and not a bit overdone with false eyelashes. The little lips were rosebudded in the darkest black red and on top of all was the triumph of her wig, a limp coconut matting in front was the fringe, but even so it gave a warmth to the eyes that was not there before, and the back half of the head was one glorious mass of the silkiest, prettiest strands of curving red hair. The dress of spangled yellow cleverly covered all the danger points. The neck was muffled in sparklets, artificial and real, opal-colour sequins and the Rosse emeralds. The neck was then opened to reveal two highly perched bosoms. She is weighed by embroidery full to her fingers and to the floor. Her manner was the 'prettiest' you have ever seen, a sorbet wouldn't melt in that cat-smiling mouth, no evil thoughts would ever come through those girlish starry pupils, yet she was dividing her interests, regarding the silver and the porcelain services in the glass cupboards through which we passed, observing who was here, and at the same time keeping a close watch on herself.

It so happens that when I called my car to go back to the nursing home, she and her long-suffering spouse were also leaving. It was a Hogarth to the life that smiled with head to one side and raised its podgy

---

[1] Alice Winn (1902–2001), wife of Hon. Reginald Winn. She was the younger sister of Nancy Lancaster.
[2] Anne, Countess of Rosse (1902–92), mother of Lord Snowdon and sister of Oliver Messel. Cecil greatly amused himself by loathing her and created some vicious caricatures of her, which belonged at one time to Michael Tree and have now passed privately into other hands. Curiously, Cecil might have admired the style of Nymans and her garden there.

beringed fingers. All she needed were the black pox marks on her face and bosom.

Now we are back in the crocodile on our way to be received by the Queen. It is all very informal but efficient, no possibility of anyone getting past without their ticket. Surprisingly informal, in a rather cavernous light, the Queen is to be seen receiving at the top of this small flight of stairs. I have a good opportunity to watch her receiving those in front of me.

I watch her in cold blood. I have always wondered if, when one is presented, she makes any effort at conversation. Now I could see that she did not, but her smile was utterly dazzling. Perhaps it was that that knocks one for a hoof. When it was the turn of the person in front of me to be presented, I could see the marvellous sheen on the Queen's skin, her teeth, her lips, her hair. Yes, she was boringly dressed in white with some sparklets around the neck and her hair a bit stiff, she had made no attempt to look glamorous, but when it came to be my turn to be presented, I stared with great intensity at her, and I have never in my life seen such a marvellous regard as came from those incredibly bright eyes. In this light one could not tell their colour, only that they shone like no one else's eyes, and had a look of interest and compassion. I was utterly thrilled. Never have I been so impressed by her.

Suddenly the silence after 'Good evening' was broken by 'Are you better?' Then Prince Philip took up the badinage. 'What's all this about?' Explanation. 'I left the hospital to come here.' A laugh as much as to say, 'You must be mad' or 'What else is new?' He would have liked to bully me, but he must stay put and I must move on to be told by the waiting Patrick Plunket[1] to go, not in there, to the Waterloo Chamber, but to the long gothic gallery where a buffet stretched the length of one wall and the guests were occupying the rest of the space. The guests were old and young of all sorts. The party was to celebrate the 70th birthday of the Queen Mother, Duke of Gloucester[2] (he is too ill to appear), Duke of Beaufort and Lord Mountbatten. They've all been asked to invite their friends. Thus, from the latter list we saw a mass of Laycocks,[3] and that darling terrified Paula Gellibrand,[4] with a toy boy in tow. He had been forbidden to leave her side all evening and seemed happy to be with her only.

---

[1] Patrick, seventh Lord Plunket (1923–75), bachelor courtier, brought up almost as a brother to the Queen, due to the tragic early death of his parents.
[2] HRH the Duke of Gloucester (1900–74), uncle of the Queen. When Cecil went to photograph him in 1961, he sent a message to say that he did not want to be posed gazing through a bower of flowers. The resulting image was somewhat stern.
[3] Angela, Lady Laycock (1916–99), daughter of Freda Dudley-Ward. Widow of Sir Robert Laycock (1907–68), one of those who threw Cecil into the Nadder in 1927.
[4] Paula Gellibrand (1898–1986), Modigliani-style beauty, photographed by Cecil in his

We saw Prince and Princess Paul[1] and a lot of German Royalties and all sorts of young, including several long-haired young men. Xandra Haig[2] made a bloomer by putting on a tiara. Ava Waverley,[3] after a hundred telephone calls and visit to hairdresser and dressmaker, looked like an old dead woman by Dürer, her mouth fallen open and her eyes popping. But her white (in mourning for her brother she loathed!) was clean and pretty and her hair like a five-day-old chick, Diana Cooper a *tour de force* of aristocratic beauty in pristine yellow chiffon print, Caroline Somerset a beauty in white, David,[4] very tipsy, no Americans except the Whitneys,[5] she looking like the wicked witch she really is.

I sat with neighbour Mary (Pembroke) and the Hopes,[6] was visited by Sybil C[Cholmondeley],[7] Chiquita A[Astor],[8] and others who pretended that I looked well. I ate a bit of supper and drank two glasses of champagne.

The Queen Mother alluded to our cold picnic on the terrace and the hateful Griffin.[9] She was in a sort of redingote of pale moth-coloured chiffon with pelisses covered with solid sequins, a big pearl and diamond necklace and tiara. She only needed a wand to fly to the top of the Christmas tree. Princess Alexandra ravishing, long-tendril curls, a dark red satin dress and sheen on her skin, adorable of human beings she

---

Book of Beauty. Variously married to the Marques de Casa Maury, Bill Allen, and 'Boy' Long. A lifelong friend of Edwina Mountbatten. Her strange life was told in fiction by Enid Bagnold in her novel *Serena Blandish*. Later part of the 'White Mischief' set in Kenya. She ended her days in the Priory, at Barnes, her portrait by Cecil hanging above her bed.

[1] Prince Paul of Yugoslavia (1893–1976), ill-fated Regent of his country during the Second World War, and his wife, Princess Olga of Greece (1903–97), sister of Princess Marina, Duchess of Kent.

[2] Lady Alexandra Trevor-Roper (1907–97), daughter of Field Marshal Earl Haig. She was married to the historian, Lord Dacre of Glenton (b. 1914).

[3] Ava, Viscountess Waverley (1896–1974), widow of Viscount Waverley, formerly Sir John Anderson.

[4] Lady Caroline Somerset (1928–95), later Duchess of Beaufort, daughter of sixth Marquess of Bath; and her husband, David Somerset (b, 1928), later eleventh Duke of Beaufort, art dealer.

[5] John Hay Whitney (1904–82), US Ambassador to Britain 1956–60, and his wife, Betsey Cushing (1908–98). He owned the *New York Herald Tribune*. She was a New York socialite and philanthropist, said to have been worth $700 million.

[6] Lord John Hope (1912–96), by then Lord Glendevon, and his wife, Liza (1915–98), daughter of W. Somerset Maugham.

[7] Sybil, Dowager Marchioness of Cholmondeley (1894–1989), sister of Philip Sassoon. She descended from a prince of the moiety in the City of Baghdad.

[8] Ana Inez (Chiquita) Astor (d. 1992), first wife of Hon. John (Jakie) Astor and daughter of Miguel Carcano, former Brazilian Ambassador to Britain.

[9] Major John Griffin (b. 1924), Press Secretary to the Queen Mother. Knighted 1990.

exuded beauty. Princess Anne[1] with wild hair, fascinated by all she saw
and heard, Prince Charles with crab apple red cheeks and chin and nose,
so healthy and so full of charm, so intelligent. He asked me if I was still
photographing, which gave me a great opportunity to talk about the
recent visit to Royal Lodge.[2]

Patrick Plunket then took me under his guidance to see the Charles II
rooms recently redecorated with pictures rehung and redistributed from
Buckingham Palace. Some of the wall coverings are a mistake but in
general the refinement convinces and Patrick is responsible for redoing
all the flowers. Instead of the carnation and sweet pea arrangements he
has got the gardeners to grow vast quantities of green zinnias, tobacco
plants and alchemilla with which to fill the golden candelabra on the
buffet, and the four cones at the corners of the building and the vast
edifice in the centre, all spot-lit, were of white eremurus, white delphiniums, peonies. They were really a very great advance on the whole,
though I am not sure if the cones were as strange as they should have
been. They smacked a bit of Pulbrook and Gould[3] and wanted a bit of
something wild among the greenhouse productions. However, Patrick's
cutting down a whole syringa tree in flower and having it put in a vast
malachite pot in the supper room was a gesture on the right scale.

The evening was obviously being a success, everyone enjoying themselves and in a good mood, and the reason was that quite dramatically the
election results had returned a good Tory victory. We had been expecting to put up with Wilson[4] and his loathsome mob for another five years
and quite dramatically all was changed in the face of the polls. And here
was the new leader in person. I didn't see Heath[5] but he was here and
when he appeared a cheer went up and I was told that he blushed to his
collar.

I had so far had great luck and felt that I'd better be leaving before my
strength gave out. Perhaps a little pudding. Martin Charteris[6] got me
some caramel soufflé and just as I was enjoying this Princess Margaret
appeared, alone and lonely, very matronly. I didn't ask her where her
husband[7] was and quite imagined he'd have gone off to a hippie

---

[1] HRH the Princess Anne (b. 1950), now the Princess Royal.
[2] See p.64.
[3] Pulbrook and Gould, florists in Berkeley Square.
[4] Harold Wilson (1916–94), later Lord Wilson of Rievaulx KG, Prime Minister
1964–70 and 1974–6.
[5] Rt Hon. Sir Edward Heath KG (b. 1916), Prime Minister 1970–4.
[6] Sir Martin Charteris (1913–99), later Lord Charteris of Amisfield, inspired Private
Secretary to the Queen 1972–7.
[7] Antony Armstrong-Jones (b. 1930), by then Earl of Snowdon, a rival photographer to
Cecil, who never quite forgave him for marrying Princess Margaret. Nephew of Oliver
Messel, another rival. The Snowdons separated in 1976 and divorced in 1978.

happening but I was told he was already cornering Heath and telling him he must give more to the Arts Design Centre so that he could build more aviaries for them.[1] Certainly he was nowhere near his wife. I envisaged having to spend half an hour on my feet, making conversation. This I was too weak to do, so quite firmly, I shook her by the hand and left her.

There were many interesting sights to see, lots of people I hadn't spied out, but I'd got the message very clearly and the evening for me was more than replete. The return journey seemed to take no time and at the hospital two giggling Irish nurses were waiting by the front door for me. I felt like a prisoner, happy to return after his parole outing. I slept better than I have for nights and woke up next day with temperature normal.

Cecil flew to Venice to embark on a luxurious cruise as guest of Mr and Mrs Charles Wrightsman. He first went to Venice in August 1926 in the company of Alison Settle, of Eve, *and Mrs Whish, of the* Daily Express. *He was very excited to be going at the time and had to borrow the money from his father, who loaned it in the hope of 'something coming out of it'. Though he remained on the outside, it gave him an intoxicating glimpse of the high life, with sightings of Lady Diana Cooper, and afforded him the chance to show his portfolio of drawings and photographs to Diaghilev.*

Venice was to play an important part in his summer holiday life over many decades. Finding himself back there, he was in contemplative mood.

Interruption – Venice   *July 1970*

Venice is so full of ghosts for me that I found on this short visit that it is really no longer enjoyable. I did not love any more the place that, for so long, I loved so. The times that I have spent there seem to have gone by as in a dream. They have left no residue and are quickly forgotten. It is only on returning that I remember my first visit, with those appalling women journalists [Alison Settle and Mrs Whish], then with Oliver [Messel],[2] and Peter [Watson],[3] for it was here that I learnt to love Peter. There were the Odom[4] summers, and so many intrigues and activities,

[1] Lord Snowdon had designed the Aviary for the London Zoo in Regent's Park.
[2] Oliver Messel (1904–78), interior decorator and designer for the ballet. He had an affair with Peter Watson, while Cecil was in love with him.
[3] Peter Watson (1908–56), rich bachelor, turned patron of the arts, and founder of *Horizon*. Cecil was helplessly in love with him in the thirties and suffered accordingly. Watson kept him in close proximity but at arm's length.
[4] William Odom (1886–1942), Kentucky-born proprietor of Parson's School of Design in Paris and New York, and an important influence on decorative taste. For several summers in the thirties he rented the Palazzo Barbaro in Venice and Cecil travelled through Europe with him by car.

designing and sketching. Now, as the motorboat went along I passed the burial ground of Diaghilev,[1] which Simon Fleet[2] and Diana and some others of us had visited on the anniversary of his death.

And here was the little house that Catherine d'Erlanger[3] had made so magical with bits of tissue and silvers from the markets. Here were the hidden churches where we'd been to see little-known treasures. But there was not time for all the memories, only sadness that the Brandolinis[4] should be the last to have quitted their palace on the canal and have deserted Brando's family home.

There was no time to see the hordes of tourists who now are the sole support of the city. Raymond Mortimer,[5] very ill, was here recently and as he left he said quietly, 'I hope to see Venice again.' I do not feel this any more. It can never be for me what it once was. Even if its beauty remains intact, my eyes no longer see it with the passionate zest of youth. It is somewhere that no longer is part of the person that I have changed into. I would rather discover totally new places that have none of these associations with the past.

In his host, Charles Wrightsman, Cecil found an interesting study. Wrightsman was President of Standard Oil of Kansas from 1932 to 1953, and developed oil properties in Oklahoma, Kansas, Texas, Louisiana and California. He was a tournament polo player, and a munificent art donor to, and Trustee of the Metropolitan Museum in New York from 1958. He gave many works of art quietly and liked to quote his father's precept: 'I never saw a deaf and dumb man in jail.'

In 1961 he bought the famous Goya of the Duke of Wellington for £140,000, but the National Gallery matched the price and acquired it. Three weeks after it was unveiled, it was stolen. A nice cinematic touch was when James Bond spotted it in Dr No's house in the film Dr No. *The Goya was found in May 1965, in the left luggage office of New Street Station, Birmingham.*

There are eight Wrightsman rooms and three galleries in the Metropolitan Museum. Wrightsman lived at 820 Fifth Avenue, in an apartment where everything was of museum quailty: Aubusson carpets, Vermeers, El Grecos and

[1] Serge Diaghilev (1872–1929), great autocrat and impresario of the Russian ballet. When he died the Russian ballet died with him.
[2] Simon Fleet (1913–66), formerly Simon Carnes, companion to Lady Juliet Duff at Bulbridge House, Wilton. He also operated from a tiny house in Chelsea, known as the Gothic Box.
[3] Baroness d'Erlanger (d. 1959). Grand society hostess. She was giving a ball in Venice in August 1926, for which Cecil craved an invitation.
[4] Count Brando Brandolini d'Adda and his wife, Christiana Agnelli (b. 1928).
[5] Raymond Mortimer (1895–1980), literary critic.

Pissarros. The library contained Meissen and Sèvres, with Kaendler birds. Thomas Hoving, Director of the Metropolitan Museum and one of his many courtiers, described him as 'the most immaculate man I ever met. His silver hair was perfectly coiffed, his voice was gentle and cultured, his smile was gracious, studied, and he moved with a languorous grace as if participating in a minuet. His only true characteristic was an infectious, short bark of a laugh.'[1]

Hoving maintained that Wrightsman made his fortune of over $50 million by defrauding the shareholders of Humble Oil in the 1930s. He then dropped his first wife and married Jayne Larkin, who was a friend of the collector, Baron Eric Goldschmidt-Rothschild. They bought the Harrison Williams house in Palm Beach. They were avid golfers, but not proficient players. The story goes (Hoving again) that when Charlie hit his ball into the water he shouted at Jayne, 'Never play golf again! Do something else. Take up ... art.'

Jayne bought an art history book and they then began to form their legendary collection. Cecil particularly admired her, as she was completely self-taught. Hoving was less impressed. He hovered in anticipation of the Wrightsman bequest to the Metropolitan, but was disparaging of his benefactors: 'Both had a fierce grasp of the facts surrounding a picture or a piece of furniture or an object, but they had little comprehension of the spiritual sense of art.'

Jayne Wrightsman was said to have been an early mentor to Jackie Kennedy, when she first arrived at the White House. Jayne and her friend, 'Bunny' Mellon, were closely involved in Jackie's transformation of the White House. Apparently, she had her own scent specially designed for her and one evening, some years later, Brooke Astor greeted her and said, 'Jayne, I guess that dress cost at least forty thousand dollars?' Jayne replied, 'Thirty-seven thousand.'

Charlie eventually suffered a stroke and lingered near death for many years. Jayne, recognised as a highly cultivated art collector in New York, has been known to hire a private plane and dart about the countryside looking at Monets, and is the donor of giant trees to thank people for lunch, which then require the hiring of a van to take them to the country. She is an energetic figure in the New York social scene, a friend, for example, of the dress designer Oscar de la Renta.

She became a benefactor in Britain too, guided by Lord Rothschild. The National Gallery extension was the result of her generosity.

21 July 1970

I presented Jayne [Wrightsman] with my usual cruise present of a large box of Bendicks Bitter Mint chocolates. They are what Jayne adores more than anything and she could eat them by the hour. But this time Charles

---

[1] Quotes from Thomas Hoving, *Making the Mummies Dance* (Simon and Schuster, New York, 1993), pp.90–2.

took the box from her after only one round and hid it somewhere in his cabin. This was no joke. On the second night the box was produced for a few minutes after many requests. Margaret Walker and I took one each and when Charles was not looking slipped it [them] to her while Charles retired with the box.

Capri   *Sunday, 26 July 1970*

I wondered if as in so many instances, due to feeling so wretched, I would have to chuck at the last minute another invitation. But Dr G. said he thought I'd be strong enough to come for a fortnight's cruise on the Wrightsmans' yacht and indeed he was right. Just by a whisker I made it. How fortunate to have this nice invitation. It is just what the doctors would have ordered. Calm, change of air, no responsibility and, most important of all, an excuse to break the habit of my usual life.

Due to feeling so weak, yet determined not to waste the days entirely, I had made more of an effort than I should. I tried to get on with my aunt's book in spite of limited eye strength and headaches around the corner. Even if I am quietly alone at Reddish for 2 days, there was always more to do than I could undertake. In spite of the lure of the garden, still ravishing in the sun though the roses are over, there was only the minimum time to enjoy the new cutting garden, the linnet feeding its young in a nest under my bedroom window, or to watch the giant growth of the new greenhouse.

All this would have been usual, but my state of health prevented me from coping as usual. Even the train journey to London exhausted me and, having slept for an hour and a half in the afternoon, I would wake with a headache. I wondered how I could cope with the evening's activity, if for an exceptional treat I was going to see Gielgud[1] in *Home* or have the Sutros[2] for dinner.

The worst aspect of this phase of the illness is that I have not been able to enjoy. I was in a rut and everything was uphill. Better get out.

The trip to Venice was full of the usual delays. I had to comfort Dida Blair, who had mislaid her husband.[3] I waste a great deal of effort, and with the help of a short sleep on arrival at Anna Maria's[4] was able to go out and enjoy the Biennale exhibition.

Each year one wonders how is it possible that they can cap their last

---

[1] Sir John Gielgud (1904–2000), legendary actor, who contrived to outlive Olivier and Richardson.
[2] John Sutro (1904–85) and his wife Gillian.
[3] Ambassador William McCormick Blair and his wife, Deeda.
[4] Countess Anna Maria Cigogna, born a Volpi, with whom Nancy Mitford stayed each summer. A leading figure in Venetian life.

year's effort at shocking, or surprising. They succeed and this year's exhibit made the way-out painters and sculptors of before seem thoroughly old-fashioned. Paintings are now never done with a brush or paint. They are sensations, done by electronics, you go back through a laser ray and there is a terrible knocking around you. You move a large red globe and it lets off a scream like a siren. You go through a labyrinth made of bits of white string (rather romantic, this!). But neon and fluorescent light is the thing to create a work apart. There were exhibits of what looked like specimens of insect life in a natural history museum, and indeed the most elaborate and prize-winning exhibit of all was a series of huge glass cases in which bees were fed with synthetic honey from mother-of-pearl discs (instead of flowers) and were then lured through a tunnel to continue the ordinary life of a bee in its comb, or else to take to the open air full of artificial life.

It was difficult enough to walk round some of the exhibits with their raking floors (the French exhibit a sort of rooftop landscape on which two children were enjoying the crazy opportunities of swinging on ropes) but since we were accompanied by the delightful Johnny Walker,[1] Anna Maria was, with his laughing wife, a companion on the *Radiant* visit and since he suffered a serious polio illness as a child, the going was not possible. However, it was an amusing 'show' and we came away, baffled but stimulated.

Now three days later we have come through a slight storm and arrival at Capri. At dinner Charles said he was very on edge because he had just heard that he had made the biggest oil strike in his career. On this project he has spent $30 million, has been working for 18 years, and was about to retire on his gains from two 'salt' limes, but the third seems to be his biggest ever in 50 years of engineering, and he is only sorry that it has come so late in his life. He may have to leave the ship to go to Louisiana in the heat of August, to be plagued by flies, to suffer from all the discomforts that he knew in his youth and, although it is tough, at his age, the prospect is so tremendous that he may well be realistic and leave 'for a few days' while he watches the prospect of untold millions being added to his already vast fortune...

Charles tells us the lengths to which he goes to save a few hundred dollars. It is his sense of money that has made him what he is and, if things go for him as they have in the past, I cannot say that, in spite of setbacks and his selfishness, he is at 75 an unhappy man.

---

[1] John Walker (1906–94), patrician art connoisseur and Director of the National Gallery of Art, Washington, and his wife, Lady Margaret Drummond (1905–87), daughter of sixteenth Earl of Perth. Author of *Self-Portrait with Donors: Confessions of an Art Collector* (1974).

Later. Charles spent Sunday waiting for a call he had put through to Houston, Texas. It was not surprising that his engineer was out at 1 o'clock on a Sunday. Charles waited on tenterhooks all evening for the call to come through. Many false alarms. Then, his face 20 years younger, he returned to say, yes, they had found a very big oil well. It was his best coup since he started 50 years ago.

In Capri, Cecil called on one of his oldest friends, Mona Bismarck, formerly the American beauty, Mrs Harrison Williams, often cited as the best-dressed woman in the world. She started life as Frances Strader, daughter of Robert Strader, the Kentucky agent for the Palo Alto Farm of Leland Stanford. In 1917 she married Henry J. Schlesinger, son of the richest man in Wisconsin, but they were divorced in 1920 and the following year she married the handsome and athletic James Irving Bush, by then vice-president of Equitable Trust, a heavy drinker. They were divorced in 1924. Two years after that she married Harrison Williams, said to be the richest man in the United States and known as 'the mystery man of Wall Street'.

In 1936 Mona bought Il Fortino, at Marina Grande on Capri. Harrison Williams died in 1953 and in 1955 she married Count Eddy von Bismarck, her closest friend and adviser since the 1930s.

She then married, in 1971, Professor Umberto de Martini, Eddy's doctor. He became a count, behaved less than honourably to his wife and, in June 1979, drove off a bridge near Naples in his Alfa Romeo. 'Martini on the rocks,' said their friends, inevitably.

Capri

Mona, when I called her at the villa from the hotel, told me that she thought Eddy would not live through the summer. The cancer, which had appeared 15 years ago, had caused a tumour on the brain. The doctors had taken out a lump the size of an orange. One side of his body was paralysed. He was crotchety, perhaps in pain, she was dead tired, didn't want to see anybody and the doctors kept her busy enough. It was hard on her, but what can you do? Her voice was very matter of fact, a note of asperity had crept in. A great change, I suppose this is only natural when you are in such a situation. I was dreading the visit.

It is a long time since I have seen Mona, once one of the most beautiful women ever. Her garden was full of blossom, gardeners were doing their evening watering. Mona was weeding and clipping, as she does all afternoon. She was very wrinkled. Her make-up had faded, she didn't mind and she talked ruefully about the last 4 months. 'But come, we must go and see Eddy or he'll think I'm keeping you away from him.'

We walked through garden after new garden, sweetly smelling, not a bit formless and similar, to the terrace, overlooking Naples and Vesuvius. Eddy wore a little biretta at a jaunty angle. His hair, shaven for the operation, had grown again quickly. He was pleased with my enthusiastic greeting and compliments. His eyes were very big and pale, starry blue. He is thinner, he looked appreciative, his speech a bit blurred, but his brain still active.

I told funny stories about friends and he laughed. He wanted more gossip. He talked about going to Paris in the autumn. But he won't make it. He has had a dividend of 15 years, living in luxury and friendship with Mona. He has had a happy though vacant life. He has been one of the lucky ones in many ways. But Mona will miss him dreadfully. They were sitting together on the terrace happily when I looked back at them as I hurried down the labyrinthine paths, a bit uneasily in case the local taxi was not there to get me to the top of the mountain in time to join the others for dinner.[1]

The cruise   *July 1970*

Such calm seas that one could never believe they would ever become rough. But Margaret Walker's barometer indicated rough weather ahead and it was correct. So no Lifari islands, a slightly disturbed night on account of the swell, and we arrived early morning at Capri. The rocks higher than I'd remembered, a crystal day, with thousands arriving from the mainland. The long days of reading are perhaps at an end (I have bitten into so many varied books, E. M. Forster, Thackeray, Henry Williamson and a *How to Learn Italian*) for we have personalities and places to cope with from now on.

The Capri day was pleasant for me, for I avoided the crowds and went ashore only in the evening. The avenues of oleander and the operetta scenery were very pleasant. I don't know why I am not fond of Capri. Charles awaited the telephone, we had an excellent dinner at the best restaurant, by the avenue of oleanders with the locals making a fascinating pageant. Much sex apparent everywhere, the girls so sensuous, all wore the new midi skirts. One had forgotten how beautiful the Italians are ... and replete with lobster we returned down the terrifying hill. The great advantage of holiday being that for me, although moments of exasperation, it is a holiday, and my health seems to be returning to normal.

---

[1] Eddy died, aged sixty-seven, later that year.

Porto Cervo, Sardinia   *July 1970*

The new settlement inspired by Jacques Quelle[1] is original and endemic. The melting nougat shapes and textures are all a part of the rolling scene, all is painted white or pink or yellow. A great innovation and very well done. We were surprised to find ourselves next door to the Guinnesses' yacht and so we are bang in the middle of the giddy world of the young, intrigues to satisfy the wildest of gossips. Poor Dolores[2] surrounded by her family and the Aga Khan[3] with his new wife, pregnant, hunch-backed and by no means a beauty

Elizhina Moreira Salles[4] can expatiate on this subject by the hour and does. Dolores is in the process of losing her looks and her serenity has already been impaired, Gloria [Guinness] rising above all difficulties and making the best of her soul-destroying life, married to one of the richest but most selfish of men. A tense atmosphere when we are shown the old film *Jezebel* and discover it is about a girl losing her lover through her own fault. When the new wife appeared on the scene, the Begum Aga Khan shouted, 'Too late!'

Princess Alexandra,[5] not looking her best, but nonetheless admired for the adorable simplicity and honesty of character that makes her the most popular member of the Royal Family in England.

Dinner at Amin A. K. [Aly Khan]'s[6] very original house. A swirl of odd shapes, winding corridors, tangent stairs, unexpected terraces, everything off symmetry. White on white, huge coffee-coloured tiles, and in main room a whoosh of the mountain rock, like a vast piece of modern sculpture, everything in the manner of Quelle and asking for Giacometti decorations.

That old monster Kitty Miller hunched and wagging her head low over the huge table like a turtle, bemoans her losses. 'I'm playing with sharks!' She asks Gloria to give her a list of the tips for the servants – 'not that I can afford to pay after what I've lost at bridge'. However, when she gets

---

[1] Jaques Quelle, architect working in South of France.
[2] Dolores Guinness, daughter of Count Egon von Fürstenberg and his then wife, Gloria (later married to Loel Guinness), married to 'Tara' Browne, son of Loel Guinness and later Princess Joan Aly Khan. He was killed in a car crash in 1965.
[3] Prince Karim Aga Khan (b. 1936), son of Princess Joan Aly Khan. He married Sally Croker-Poole, formerly Lady James Crichton-Stuart, in 1969.
[4] Elizhina, second wife of Walter Moreira Salles (1912–2001), Brazilian Ambassador in Washington.
[5] Princess Alexandra and her young family frequently holidayed in Sardinia.
[6] Prince Amyn Aly Khan (b. 1937), younger son of Princess Joan Aly Khan.

off the boat, hated by all, she conveniently forgets to pay her debts. She and Gilbert were known to steal the clothes hangers from every house they stayed in. They liked them velvet covered. When a demand was sent by the Guinnesses for their return, they sent 12 plastic ones.

Radiant II   *July 1970*

For ten days now I have had wonderful rest, air, sea, bathing and sun. Perhaps when I return to the reality of a working life, I may find myself tired again, but at the moment I'm remarkably recovered. One does not remember how ill one felt at a certain time. But when slowly surfacing from a deep sleep, can now feel that my body is not going through those appalling changes, and being conscious of vaguely painful readjustments in the system.

To begin with the days were very quiet with only the Walkers aboard. We all read a lot, even in one another's company. Then with the arrival of the Moreira Salleses and the Yann Weymouths[1] things were more hectic. The fact that we were moored alongside the Guinnesses' yacht in Porto Cervo made the nights longer with the result that the mornings became shorter and the breakfast (underdone toast, horrid jelly marmalade) came in later. Then a few bits of the Italian lesson, no progress.

Then reading, H. Williamson's *Donkey Boy* filled me with adoration and unexpected tears. Kott's Shakespeare was contemporary, something I've always wanted to read, and I like being helped through the plays. A lot of E. M. Forster, very gentle, and the charm of his personality comes through strong. With him at her elbow, I even like V. Woolf, though she was a swine to me,[2] and in spite of her genius was in many ways a swine.

Surrounded by so many bright Americans I feel how very uninformed I am on general subjects, particularly on US subjects. Haven't thought about the emancipation of women, or how not to pollute the air, in fact never read the leading articles in the magazines. I have a good excuse, with my convalescence, to remain silent and make no effort, but oh, the abysses!

I feel very much more relaxed than I did last time I was on board, though it upsets me to see Jayne suffer. Her face twitches with anxiety when Charles is in a bait, and if he has not received telegrams about his oil wells, the weather is thundery. It is tragic to see how aged she has become, shrunk and wrinkled, and one wonders whether it is worthwhile

---

[1] Yann Weymouth and his wife, Lally, daughter of Kay Graham.
[2] Virginia Woolf refused to pose for her photograph to Cecil. When he published two sketches of her in *The Book of Beauty* (1930), she complained in print of 'a method of book-making which seems to me as questionable as it is highly disagreeable to one at least of its victims'.

suffering for so much of her life. Yet if she left him she would be penniless, and there is every possibility that although he is older, he will outlive her. No doubt it is a situation that Truman [Capote][1] is writing about in his next novel, *Answered Prayers*.

Meanwhile the boat has not kept to any schedule. We have moved off at a whim of Charlie's, or delayed, as in Porto Cervo, for an impromptu dinner engagement. It does not worry me in my relaxed mood as I am resigned that we shall not be seeing anything of interest on this cruise. After an eight-hour run, we arrive at Monte Carlo, less glamorous, more disgracefully defaced in the jumble of bad architecture, even than last year. No overall plan. It is very squalid now. But I am relaxed, and now once again amazed by the extraordinary talent of Patrick White.[2] He really does know how to write. He really is a writer by instinct. I feel that when I return to Aunt Jessie every page must be rewritten.

Monte Carlo

We have returned here after a little jaunt to St Tropez (the intention of Charles being that Jayne should here buy dresses exactly like Gloria Guinness's). The fishermen's port remains the same as it was when Daisy Fellowes[3] brought me to it forty years ago – (the woman who made paper hats, later to be copied by Suzy in Paris is long since dead, and the quai has now become a shopper's paradise for trendy clothes of all sorts. This year tie-dye is the craze). St Tropez is a place without charm for me and I do not understand Pam Berry[4] sinking so much money into a huge house here.

We then sailed for Portofino, in order to entertain 'some intellectuals', the Berlins[5] and Maurice Bowra.[6] As it happened, Isaiah was in bed with lumbago and Maurice in a bloated condition, over-egging every sentence and really giving so much that I feel he will burst. Mrs Hart, a friend, said he was terrified of death and did not think he would live long.[7] 'Why,

---

[1] *Answered Prayers* by Truman Capote (1924–84) was serialised in *Esquire* in 1975, and Capote became a social pariah, eking out his days with the aid of drink and drugs.
[2] Patrick White (1912–90), Australian novelist, whom Cecil met in Sydney in 1968.
[3] Daisy Fellowes (1887–1962), wife of Hon. Reginald Fellowes. A rich socialite and hostess, of a nervous disposition. She once telephoned a lover and said, 'I have news for you.' He listened and heard her hands go 'clap, clap, clap'.
[4] Lady Pamela Berry (1914–82), Lady Hartwell, daughter of the first Earl of Birkenhead. An important political hostess, who hosted extravagant General Election parties.
[5] Sir Isaiah Berlin (1909–97), philosopher, Fellow of All Souls, and his wife, Aline de Gunzbourg.
[6] Sir Maurice Bowra (1898–1971), celebrated Oxford don.
[7] Bowra died 4 July 1971.

isn't he the same age as me?' 'No, he's 72.' He certainly looked very highly keyed by the time he went down the steps to the waiting motorboat.

But as has happened on this boat most of the time, there was no opportunity for me to have a tête-à-tête with him. And I find myself as usual, unable to hear most of what Elizhina Salles was telling me in her very long roundabout way.

Portofino seems to have stood still. After Truman [Capote] and I had spent an agreeable holiday here, the place became enlarged and vulgarised. Now it has become a backwater again, the south of France is fashionable and loathsome, Portofino now has the charm of a water-colour of picturesque Italy painted on a Victorian fan. The port was delightful with orange lights, bobbing fishing boats, the mountains covered with dark greens; cypresses, pine umbrellas and the rocks going sheer down into deep green waters. This was beauty, after the ugly places we've seen, even after Sardinia.

Now we are back at Monte Carlo, which we left on a night of gala when the display of fireworks in the port was extremely impressive, with all the traditional beauties of multicoloured sequin showers, splintering squibs and roaring rockets, as well as the latest inventions of whirling fish designs and undulating tassel fringes. When the grand finale came with the crown of Monaco in lights and all the ships in the harbour let off their hooters or fog sirens, the nerves were obediently affected. It was a call back to the Onassis[1] period, when the neighbourhood was innocent of these unplanned sites of hideous skyscrapers.

Now my fellow guests have departed and I am on the boat for 2 more days, having to prepare for reality again. It has been an escape to luxury, which has made one very soft. Having every arrangement made for one soon has a pernicious effect, and for days I have been unable to go into a town to send a telegram or to see that my air ticket is confirmed. Of course the conflict was particularly unpleasant as nothing worked. My ticket not valid, no telephone answers. As Yann Weymouth said, 'In 1900 when one came to the Hotel de Paris everything would be in order, and the tickets, in the care of a human being rather than taken into the charge of a computer, would have worked.'

Lally Weymouth in her week on board delivered a rare gift for ragging Charles, for coming back at him without offensive, of ragging him every time he became difficult or crotchety. An incredibly bright girl, her hair

---

[1] Aristotle Onassis (1906–75), the Greek shipowner, who controlled the Sociéte des Bains de Mer in Monte Carlo in the late 1950s and early 1960s. He married Jacqueline Kennedy (1968).

is the thickest I know. She reads everything and is on to every manifestation of the young today. Her husband has a quieter mind, is deeply intelligent (though boyishly naïf) in a way that enables him to explain, with extraordinary clarity and simplicity, the ways of the weather or the workings of a submarine's atomic missile. Lally is one moment quite ugly with her lower lip protruding and her tongue hanging out like a village wight [idiot], then quite suddenly she is as beautiful as she was for her last departure from the ship.

My brain functions hardly at all. I dream all night, or so it seems, and I encourage these dreams to last until quite late in the morning. It is strange how I dream about things that have happened forty or more years ago, the profound impression that Peter [Watson] had over me still lives though he is long dead. The other night I dreamt that under a large flannel cloak of mystery he and Oliver Messel retreated for a whole night, while I waited for them. I wanted to have the courage to interrupt them, or to leave for ever, but I could not do this. I just hung around in misery while Peter hid his head from me.

We dined, the Ws and I, again at the Chateau de Madrid. I don't know why I resent so much the expense of this restaurant and the fact that there are still a few people rich enough to enjoy it. But these people are against the grain. I am not impressed, in fact resentful of being part of such a tawdry sort of people. Yet there is no denying the food is the best. I long for the grit and the guts of an artist's kitchen with baked bread and the things that Churchill painted.

This feeling intensified the following evening when again the three of us dined together, this time on the terrace of the Hotel de Paris in Monte Carlo. There was excitement around us for the Annual Charity Fête was being held, and crowds assembled to see Princess Grace[1] and the appalling clothes of the rich folk from the neighbourhood.

We had an excellent dinner, but I was choked with the atmosphere of over-indulgence, and the really terrible people who were present. Jayne did her best to keep the evening going and, in spite of the awful interruptions she has to suffer, has become an excellent raconteur, funny, sensitive, lively and extremely well documented. But she looked so poor and peaky tonight...

Tonight he [Charles] would interrupt the talk with a complete switch of topic. He would tell stories that he knew we had heard before. But he makes no concessions and is not likely to change...

---

[1] Princess Grace of Monaco (1929–82), formerly the beautiful blonde film star, Grace Kelly, from Philadelphia.

On the Yacht *8 August 1970*

Am about to leave. The first part of the holiday is over. It has been a wonderful rest cure for me and a miracle has happened in that I have felt so very well again. Now I am about to go to a simpler life and it should be quite delightful around Padua. But I am an apprehensive traveller, and I hate leaving one place for another and the *angoisse* becomes more acute, and since for 2 weeks now I have had no responsibility whatsoever, having to be on one's own again becomes a bit of a burden!

The anxieties proved unnecessary. The aeroplane, though late and having to fly through a storm (I tried to convince myself that it was only a bit of summer lightning), *did* bring me to Venice. The Hotel Gritti did in fact have a room for me (wonderful service, the best in Venice) and they arranged a motor for me to come to Esté, where in spite of all doubts, Diana Phipps was waiting for me, and I even managed to arrive in good time for lunch.

Cecil went to stay with Diana Phipps, the interior decorator, then popular in London society. She was born in Vienna, the daughter of Countess Cecilia Sternberg, who later enjoyed considerable success with a book about her life in European society called The Journey. *After a peripatetic childhood, Diana underwent her schooling in America. One day she announced to her mother that she had received a proposal of marriage from a boy in Calcutta, an American whom she had met in Paris. Her anxious mother consulted Eddy and Mona Bismarck, who assured her, 'She's a lucky girl. Not only is Harry nice, good-looking, intelligent and gifted, but he comes from one of the wealthiest families in America.' So, in 1957, Diana married Henry Ogden Phipps (1931–62), with her parents' blessing.*

Phipps proved an unhappy man and committed suicide when he was thirty. Of him, Cecilia Sternberg wrote, 'He simply would not accept human limitation and was to be throughout his short life as if haunted by some vision of perfection beyond mortal capacity to achieve.'

The first thing that struck me as balm to the spirit, after the arrivistic super luxury of the Wrightsmans' entourage, was Diana greeting me with a friend (Mrs Bendor Drummond[1]) carrying a large vase of yellow dahlias. All the guests were helping to make the holiday in this large shabby rented villa a pleasure to all concerned.

---

[1] Robert (Bendor) Drummond (b. 1933), keen yachtsman, married Phyllis Samper, daughter of Marshall Field of New York, divorced 1967.

Second delight, the lunch was floated down on a low table in the arcade by the front door. A wonderful basket of bread, some fruit to be painted by Bonnard, a rice dish and sweet corn on the cobs (and cheeses) and we must all help ourselves. This life has a patina to it. This is the sort of grit that is necessary. The contrast was so welcome from everything that had reduced existence to a degree where, for fear of offending Charlie, no one dare sneeze. Here was an untidy, overgrown garden, carpets that were worn, family portraits that had become darkened by the years. Here was a life of reading, sightseeing, enjoying the garden and the countryside.

Esté   *9 & 10 August 1970*

The Albrizzi who have owned this house since it was built have long since fallen on bitter days. In fact the present generation (the old Baron is over 80) have had to abandon it except for using part of the farm buildings for the administration of their wine produce. In summer, if lucky, they rent the house itself to eccentric English people who enjoy its shabbiness during the holiday months. In fact I believe Teddy Millington-Drake[1] took the house for five years and improved the amenities – but everything remains very down at heel, and utterly delightful.

After the hermetically sealed unreality of my two weeks on the millionaire yacht, 4 or 6 of us tended by a crew of 24, the contrast is just what I needed to balance the scales. And Diana Phipps, our hostess, with her offhand efficiency and athletic appreciation of the joys of living simply, is the perfect foil to the martinet crosspatch, Charles Wrightsman. He forbade one to walk on deck with wet feet, to put on oil for sunbathing, to take the newspapers to one's cabin. Here there are no rules, yet Diana must know how to organise the household, for in its vague casual way everything works. There are seven of us and two children. Diana has brought her Spanish butler from London, his wife helps and Diana does the cooking. The days pass without her seeming to make any effort, and yet some effort has to be made to provide the quails that we eat for dinner in the big rococo ballroom...

She organises that some of the guests motor to Venice to meet the Indian arriving from London on the same plane as her daughter Alexandra's[2] tutor from Gabbitas and Thring. Diana is extremely amusing about how she had only a day in which to arrange that someone

[1] Teddy Millington-Drake (1932–94), artist, son of Sir Eugen and Lady Effie Millington-Drake. Later he had homes in Tuscany and on the Greek island, Patmos.
[2] Alexandra Phipps (b. 1959), later twice married.

should come out at the last minute to give lessons to her daughter and her nephew. When a young man arrived at her London house from Hereford, she was undressed. There was no one else in the house so she threw on a long cloak and received the prospective tutor in the kitchen. He seemed amazed. He appeared not very sympathetic with his bush of black fuzzy hair and Negroid features.

But there was no time to see an alternative. 'What shall I teach?' he asked. What was he learning at Oxford? Political Philosophy and Economy. 'Then teach them Maths.' The young undergraduate has arrived, seems already to have taken in the situation with equanimity and has made a definite addition to the 'Month in the Country' atmosphere of the whole place.

No sooner had the young man arrived than, by the most extraordinary coincidence, I came across a quote from 'Letters from Ireland' in the book I am reading on the decline of the Man of Letters:

> To many an unknown genius postmen bring
> Typed notices from rabbit arse and string

Diana is convulsed.

Diana now finds the tutor more sympathetic than at first sight, though I doubt she will fall in love with him as Turgenev would have her do. Diana has had a tough time with her marriage, her husband having taken to dope and then committing suicide. She seems very independent and self-sufficient.

Yet she maintains a marvellous sweetness and is unbelievably resourceful, making her own décor, gluing and pinning up the wall hangings, making the curtain pelmets and sewing the upholstered banquettes. Here she is completely at ease, enjoying the shabbiness of the villa and its beautiful overgrown garden. The carpets are mostly threadbare, there is little matching china but the proportions of the halls and rooms are noble, and the house built when comfort on a large scale was understood. The loggias are peeling but beautiful with their tall honey-coloured walls decorated with the amphoras on brackets that have been found in the district.

The garden has broken statuary, a Neptune presiding over a green lily pond, there are dark green alleys of chestnut and limes, romantic and untidy, there are also rather well kept Hubert Robert vistas, of geometrical poplar avenues. There is a strange Japanese umbrella with ivy growing over its seat and up to the spikey 'toll' roof. There are abandoned winter gardens and greenhouses, an orchard, vegetable plots, fruit including *fraises des bois*, hens in their own sylvan preserve, a wonderful family of deer. There is nothing more exquisite and touching to me than these too timid animals. I long to make friends, but they are on the alert, and at a movement of my head are apt to scamper further away. The child, Alexandra, has shown how she overcomes some of their shyness by feeding them apple windfalls.

From this delightful place we drive in a curious mixture of motor vehicles, the cook's car, a rented limousine or local taxi, over the gravel paths between the beds of drooping, sun-tired roses, through the tall wrought-iron gates, to visit neighbouring sights. Sometimes these are too far for comfort and we return exhausted as, for instance, yesterday, when the traffic motoring into Venice was so hot, noisy and claustrophobic that we arrived an hour late for our motorboat trip to the Brenta. The joy of this was confined to the visit to Malcontenta.[1] Diana wondered at the most beautiful house, the most beautifully furnished that she has ever seen...

It was perhaps the only joy of the expedition planned by Bendor Drummond. He could not foretell the traffic jam, which started our expedition off so badly, but he must have known that with so many locks to be encountered on the canal journey the three hours he reckoned for the trip would be unrealistic. For me, still in a 'delicate condition' and told to 'go slow' after my operation, the day was a long drawn-out ordeal of noise. One could not hear oneself, or anyone else, shout. Peter Eyre[2] yelled, 'It looks like Antonioni's *Red Desert*'...

Cecil then described more sightseeing, decrying the noise that was such a feature of Italian contemporary life, the lorries 'letting off farts of stinking black smoke' and the 'reckless motor bicycles'. But he loved a Tiepolo of St Tecla and enjoyed a visit to Padua, the walled city of Montagnana and the gardens at Val San Tribio. He concluded,

There is no reason for me to hurry back home, it is a delightful life here, and, if I make up my mind not to go on exhausting expeditions, I have the excuse of my convalescence. Diana Cooper arrives tomorrow to jazz up the scene and she will be offended if I leave forthwith, so there is no reason not to lie back with my books to enjoy this very rare opportunity of being at such a delightful party in such a rarely achieved 'Wesen'.

Today, it being very hot and sultry, we all compared the varying states of lassitude in which we found ourselves recuperating from the too strenu-

---

[1] Villa Malcontenta, famous Palladian villa on the Brenta, restored by Bertie Landsberg, the lover of Baroness (Catherine) d'Erlanger.
[2] Peter Eyre (b. 1942), actor.

ous yesterday abortive sightseeing. Diana was busy about the house and looked tired. She looked middle-aged even. She looked quite plain. She is without feminine guile. She does not mind being seen at her worst. It means only that she is unafraid of reality in any of its forms. She never apologises for being seen around the villa in her negligee or bathing suit.

Then, after a quick visit to the kitchen to see that the pigeons and mushrooms and beans were properly prepared for dinner, she put on a long sheath dress of purple and emerald, tied a tight purple dog collar with a turquoise butterfly as brooch round her throat and pulled up her hair. She became a great beauty, her eyes dark velvety and so sympathetic, her smile so frank and healthy and honest.

Diana's blonde little daughter, Alexandra, has pale eyelashes and rather discoloured teeth, but she may become beautiful for she possesses many great attributes. Certainly she will become like her mother – a character. She took me to see the deer and fed them windfall apples. She has a way with all animals and she managed to get the company of timid creatures close around her, while one was bold enough to eat out of her hands. She has the quickest eye for an unusual beetle or snail. 'Good God! What have we here?' she asks.

Tonight her eleven-year-old daughter showed herself to be a tremendous character. She snapped at her cousin, 'We've long since stopped talking about the colours of people's eyes, we're talking about birds!' and she told me about her grandmother's aviary and how she had a mynah bird that had been with a tough innkeeper and how every time anyone knocked the bird shouted 'Come in, damn you!' 'And it sweared! It called someone a bugger!' She talked about her mother's married friends who are not getting along together. The Boxers were one example, and then on this dangerous ground she spilt the beans and talked about George and Sandra Weidenfeld,[1] and just stopped in time from mentioning her Uncle Bendor.

She asked how long her mother had been married and the date of her father's death, and when told just before her birth, she said, 'Then I was born to keep you company.'

Diana C. arrived having had the plaster cast taken off her broken leg only yesterday. Everyone said she must cancel her plans. But with extraordinary determination and characteristic courage she manages everything. She has little *gêne* about travelling in a foreign country without sufficient money or preparation. As is only natural she begins to show signs of old age.

I have not before noticed her deafness prevents her listening to others.

---

[1] George Weidenfeld (b.1919), now Lord Weidenfeld, Cecil's publisher, and his then wife, Sandra Payson.

She repeats herself, she is competitive and determined to be the centre of conversation for much of the time. But she is remarkable. After a night's sleep she admitted to me that her leg pained her a great deal, but she appeared at the bathing pool with a crook and her face painted dead white, pink and cerise in a way that one never sees today, and as she sat against the old brick gazebo in her shady hat, she still to me emanated the beauty that was so sensational fifty years ago.

Today was thwart day! Four of us motored through the appalling ugliness of Montcelice's factories to take the mud bath at Abano. But no, only in the mornings, and then after we had been seen by a doctor. Then on to see the gardens of Salgibeo. We saw only the magnificent proscenium-like gates and the statues mounting to the house, when we discovered we were locked out. Determined to avoid the noise and ugliness of the industrial world, we drove through the mountains. The road became alarmingly rough and unready for us. I had visions of our being stuck for the night while cowering from the oncoming storm.

We got through the green tunnel at last and called at the Duomo for another look at the Tiepolo. Each time the lights are turned on one sees more and more extraordinary planning in the picture. It is a masterpiece that grows the more one sees the many wonderful things contained in every aspect.

The menacing storm still held off. Meanwhile the heat was extraordinarily oppressive. We sat out in the loggia, quite a large circle, for the group has been added to by the arrival of Arabella Boxer[1] and of George Weidenfeld. I did not know that George had the gift of impersonation, and his performance as Annenberg, who has been sent as ambassador to London by Nixon,[2] was devastating and funny beyond belief. I don't know when I've laughed with such abandon as when hearing George imitate this rich voice with the phoney elocution lesson accent, as he tells his victims that if they will 'hear him out' that General de Gaulle[3] is going to fire ambuscades at Pompidou from the sidelines.

His encounter with George Brown[4] etc. equally funny and the description of the dinner given for the jazz trumpeter, Duke Ellington,[5] a gut buster. Mrs A., also reading a letter congratulating them for entertaining this great ambassador and signing himself R. N., which Annenberg 'explains to his British friends' does not mean 'Registered Nurse'.

---

[1] Lady Arabella Boxer (b. 1934), daughter of eighteenth Earl of Moray. Cookery writer, married to Mark Boxer, caricaturist and editor.
[2] Richard M. Nixon (1913–94), President of the United States 1969–74.
[3] Charles de Gaulle (1890–1970), President of France.
[4] George Brown (1914–85), Foreign Secretary under Harold Wilson in the 1964 Labour government, renowned for his fondness for alcohol.
[5] Duke Ellington (1899–1974), famed jazz musician.

George W. was extremely interesting about the great pact between Russia and Germany being the most important event of the epoch, and that it means the complete unimportance of the US in the future and a reshuffle of a balance of power with Germany, once more the most powerful country in the world, with France and England also-rans, and sadly all the occupied Middle Eastern countries still under the influence of the loathed Soviets.

At last I have done a drawing, the first since long before my operation. I wondered if I would ever get back to that medium again. Peter Eyre, with his long Dürer pallor, carroty-fringed hair and distorted proportions struck me as being an ideal sitter, and for long, almost empty days now, the opportunity to find the correct time has not presented itself. At last at lunch on the loggia yesterday, when it was decided we should not go on some discussed sightseeing trip, I asked Peter if he would sit. When Diana C. heard of my plan she said, after looking round the table, in a low sotto voce, 'Yes, he's the peak!'

We worked in complete silence in a good light in the hall. I was very concentrated. Peter was very still. I stared at his face intently, enjoying every shape. I was pleased with the drawing, a more careful effort than I have done for years. Then the subject, quite stiff in neck and arm, must sit for one hand, then the other hand. By now two hours had passed. I looked at my drawing as a whole, then at my sitter's hands and face.

The afternoon light was softer. I noticed more shadows on the surface of his physiognomy and he was sagging a bit. In his very deep rasping voice: 'Have I aged very much?'

Esté – Fin de Vacances   *August 1970*

I am leaving this evening for home. The eight days here have been a great contrast to the life on the yacht. It is true there were two Americans staying here for the first three days (Gordon Douglases) but they were quiet and civilised. For most of the time conversation has been quite high-class. George Weidenfeld has an extraordinary fount of knowledge of the widest variety. His historical sense is remarkable and there is no opera from any country that he does not know. Peter Eyre shares the same strange encyclopaedic knowledge, Diana Coo, perhaps less good on yesterday's events, is marvellous at evoking her past and she has a very adroit wit.

Diana, our hostess, is a cosmopolitan in the best sense, and she has escaped from Czechoslovakia, a penniless refugee, has had a turmoil of a marriage, but fends for herself well as a widow. She is imaginative and, by doing most of the cooking herself, is able to have a party of nearly a dozen staying in this very elastic house. The children, Alexandra and Maldwyn (Drummond), give the place great vitality with their stunts, owl hoots and gleanings from the swimming pool...

There are a number of young and impressionable people present, but so far there have been no dramatic developments in their juxtaposition. George W. says the scene in the drawing room is like a first act. I doubt if there will be an act II or III. No one has yet shown any signs of falling for the tutor.

How different from my early summer holidays. It was, from the earliest, always a time of romance, the love affair was probably unrequited, but oh the emotion of photographing one's beloved by the hollyhocks or coming out of a rough grey sea. How agonising the latest intrigues, the real dramas in the South of France and Venice.

This has been a very 'elderly' holiday for me. It has worked wonders in that I have returned to a state of health that I feel is almost normal and even seem bolstered. But I feel that I am treated as '*Il Vecchio*' (the waiter automatically brings me the bill) and I allow myself to be treated in a way that I have never before found agreeable. Yet now I am pleased if one of the children goes up to my bedroom to find a coat or a towel. But there have been no ecstasies, no real thrills, everything on an even keel. I have laughed and enjoyed myself, but it is sad to realise that perhaps for ever now summer holidays abroad are not what they used to be.

Diana Cooper

Diana C. is lying on her bed. Her broken leg has hurt her so much that she has had to leave the group. She keeps her bedroom door open so that she can waylay anyone coming up the staircase. I go in for a chat on my way to bed. She is depressed, she may go back to England to see her doctor. She does not want to be a burden. What bravery she shows, always pulling her weight, never complaining. Suddenly I felt a brute that I had secretly judged her for 'showing off', for not listening, for criticising the food, for being deaf.

Then I realise how unique she is, for she is nearing the 80 mark and she goes back to Victoria's day, talking about the fat quail from Turkey that they ate at balls and how her mother restrained her from knowing people like Oggie Lynn.[1]

She operates on one level, but her reactions are on a deeper one and after a long talk about the present party, and Greta, and Kin, I yawned 'I

---

[1] Olga Lynn (1882–1961), fat, musical lesbian who sang and taught singing. Her girlfriend, Maud Nelson, was Cecil's secretary for many difficult years.

must leave you, darling.' 'Good night, Kek, you're a kind and faithful friend.'

Reddish   *31 August 1970*

Back without too many travel difficulties. Had to stay in London to see specialist Hanley, good report, eye-genius Pat Trevor-Roper,[1] nothing serious wrong, and dentist, a broken root may give me future trouble.

Then at last the country. Here to wade into Aunt Jessie, forgetful of the bad weather outside my window. The headache–eye-ache that pole-axed me were proof that I can't do as much as I did before my operation, and I had to go more gently. After a concentrated spurt the end of the new rewrite suddenly seemed in sight. I was pleased and then started neighbour life...

But of all the visitors to the house, Cathleen [Nesbitt] has turned out to be the most easy and delightful companion. I have always admired her on the stage and considered her such a romantic personality, loved by the beautiful Rupert Brooke[2] and always of a high quality. I have never, as Emerald C [Cunard] used to say, 'asked her to the house'.

How lucky I am that she has been able to come for this long Bank Holiday weekend. She is so beautiful, so decorative, so easy about the house. She embellishes the garden and every room she sits in, and her talk is of the best literate quality. She shows a rugged sense of reality that no doubt she has learnt in the theatre. She alludes to Willie [Somerset] Maugham as a bastard, she talks freely of the functions of the body, she is clean living and clean thinking but realises the importance of the sensual passions. She is completely unbitter in regard to her present-day life and career. Other rivals have surpassed her in the theatre. She has no regrets. She knows they are not happy. She has an inner contentment. She does not think of herself, and she is generous, kind, unselfish and her sense of proportion is never 'out'.

Very impressive she is about knowing quotations from poetry, litera-ture and stage lore. She remembers the essentials, can relate the plot of any fatuous bygone play and can quote the essential line, is near to poetry of all ages. Moreover her brain is as quick and alert as ever, never at a loss for a name. It is incredible to think that she is 82 years old. Of course, the feast of reminiscences has been a rare one and she has told such enter-taining stories of Barrie[3] giving her advice while she wept as a result of

---

[1] Patrick Trevor-Roper (b. 1916), ophthalmic surgeon.
[2] Rupert Brooke (1887–1915), celebrated poet of World War One.
[3] J. M. Barrie (1860–1937), playwright, notably *Peter Pan*.

Basil Dean's[1] sadism before the production of *Quality Street*. 'We have to pay for all happinesses with sorrow. Better tears before than after.'

She related how, during the run of Flecker's[2] *Hassan*, she had become pregnant and how in one scene Henry Ainley[3] had to fling her to the floor, calling her 'whore' and how Cathleen *sotto voce* would tell him, 'For Christ's sake, mind the baby!' Ainley later said, 'You'd better leave the cast quickly or you'll be calling the baby Allah.'

She remembers the story of Mary Curzon[4] who was beloved of the King of Spain. A friend discovered some tooth marks on Mary's arm. 'Spain?' the friend asked. Mary replied, 'No, Portugal.' Looking at the pictures of the first Russian ballet classes in London she reminisced, 'Oh, Rupert took me to see *L'Après Midi …*' and she described how she took him to 10 Downing Street (in Asquith's day) for a party and R. B. sun-bronzed from Fiji, with dazzling turquoise eyes made more dazzling by his bright blue shirt, asked if he could go in his grey flannel suit and funny little straw hat. He did not realise that when people stared he was being admired for his corn-coloured hair and dramatic colouring, became put out and decided he would leave and go to Waterloo Station to wait for Cathleen to join him there. When she did so he had finished eating a strawberry tea. Cathleen said she'd like some strawberries too. 'No,' he said. 'You should have had them where you came from.'

Of her theatrical career, she talked of her Cleopatra in the OUDS (she married her Antony[5]), her Jessica with Moskovitch[6] as Shylock, her amusement at being in the same dressing room with Lady Tree for *Shall We Join the Ladies*, and her *fous-rires* behind a fan.

We paid a visit to Anthony and Clarissa [Avon]. It was a treat for Anthony to reminisce about his early stages. He had intended to act in *Cleopatra* and had read for a part, but realised that it would take too much time from his preparations for his exams. But he had this week talked to David Cecil who agreed that Cathleen had been the best Cleopatra he had ever seen (Dadie Rylands[7] also of this opinion), his admiration for Hawtrey.[8] Cathleen had acted with Hawtrey and could give very amusing

---

[1] Basil Dean (1888–1978), a stage producer who also directed films.

[2] James Elroy Flecker (1884–1915). *Hassan* was first produced in 1923.

[3] Henry Ainley (1879–1945). Hassan was one of his finest parts.

[4] Mary Curzon (1870–1906), Mary Leiter, from Washington, first wife of Marquess Curzon of Kedleston.

[5] Captain Cecil Ramage MC (1895–1988), President of the Oxford Union, played opposite Cathleen, but burned himself out, the marriage deteriorated and they parted. He spent his last years in Bournemouth, where he died, aged ninety-three in 1988.

[6] Maurice Moskovitch (1871–1940), Jewish actor.

[7] George Rylands (1902–99), Fellow of King's College, Cambridge. Virginia Woolf used his rooms as the basis for her novel, *A Room of One's Own* (1929).

[8] Sir Charles Hawtrey (1858–1923), actor-manager.

accounts of how professional he was while seeming not to act. Determined to play for once a serious dramatic part, he grew a beard and appeared as a tragic violinist. Out of nervousness he delivered an end of act speech at the beginning, and the curtain had to come down and the company to start the act again. The play closed on the Saturday. Anthony told Mrs Pat [Campbell][1] stories and rather disarmingly got them just wrong. He also quoted jokes that had made him laugh sixty years ago.

By the hour she could answer my avid questions with wonderful clarity of memory, able to evoke the whole atmosphere of the exciting day before I was able to cross the threshold of adult life ...

Of all the guests of recent years, I think Cathleen has been the most utterly delightful. She came early on Friday and left on Tuesday to avoid the Bank Holiday crowds. She was a 'new' friend, though an acquaintance of very many years (we had worked happily in the theatre) and she had been one of the stars of my boyhood ...

She is a great addition to the house and without much money at her disposal she manages to be so delightfully dressed. She is an adornment to the room or to the garden. As I said about old Mr Smallpeice, I would like to pay to have this decorative sweet-looking person just to sit in various corners of the garden.

And Cathleen is still wonderfully unartificial, her face as bright and clean in the moment of waking as others are after hours of preparations, as Dot Head said, 'She is the perfect example of how to grow old and proves how wrong it is to make too much effort in the ways of artifice.'

Each person that she met during a long and varied weekend was in full admiration. Raymond M [Mortimer] said she was a ravishing creature after he had a long talk with her on the terrace. I was not able to listen to their conversation and Eileen could only overhear a few snatches. But Raymond asked her if in later life she had come to rely on religion. 'No,' she said. 'I have no religion and no superstitions of any sort. Perhaps that has prevented me from ever doing anything great.'

She is very conscious of the fact that she has never succeeded in hitting the highest spots, and perhaps such unusual modesty in an actress has not helped her.

It was only when I was driving her to the station for her return to London (and a diet of cream cheese) that I popped the question of whether she would have married Rupert Brooke. 'Yes, I suppose we would have married if it had not been for the war. You see I only knew him for 3 years, and during 2 of those he was in America, and that's why there are so many letters ... I keep them in a cardboard box and should preserve them more carefully. But you see we were both recovering from

---

[1] Mrs Patrick Campbell (1865–1940), charismatic actress.

unrequited love affairs. I had that girlish crush on Harry Ainley with whom I was appearing on the stage and he was having an affair with a woman who became pregnant by him. He thought he should have married her, and she lost her baby and he felt guilt. Anyhow Rupert was studying for some Naval Reserve Course at Yarmouth and I went down to see him, or perhaps he came to see me when I was touring.

'Anyhow we were reading poetry to one another, I reading Donne to him and he reading his poems to me, and he said he thought he ought to be thinking about making a will, and he supposed we'd later get married, and which would I prefer, to be left his rather small possessions, or the rights to his poems. Then he went on to say he thought perhaps as he had just started with Lascelles Abercrombie, de la Mare and Gibson, a poetry magazine, and he would like it to continue, it would be perhaps best to leave the copyrights to the three of them.' If only it had been to Cathleen!

Not that she has regrets, but she has had to pay for her children's education and look after a drunken husband incapable of keeping a job. And after Rupert's death, Mrs Brooke, his mother, said it was quite *frightening* what a lot of money came in from the poems, that all England was mad about 'If I should die think only this of me…' whereas the other sonnets were far better.

Cathleen described his stocky body but graceful quick movements, the marvellous colouring, the jutting unclassical nose, almost a pug, and how that he had by dying so young achieved lasting fame. 'A young poet dying in a war is always the stuff of legend, and what if he had lived? Would he have developed as a poet? Rupert had wanted more than anything to be a playwright, and he had written two plays, but they weren't any good. Would he have become embittered? What would he have looked like if alive today as a man of 84?'

Perhaps all the sad things that have happened to Cathleen have made her face all the sweeter. Certainly I never came across a woman who has lived so intelligently in such a varied set of circumstances, and overcome all the disadvantages, putting them all down as part of life's experiences.

Often one has seen quite enough of one's friends by the end of a short weekend. One is conscious of their selfishness, over-indulgences or surplus of vitality. Cathleen one could not fault…

Not the same can be said for Margaret Case, and her weekend (obligation) was a short one. If she had left by 9.30 train on Monday as was expected of her, all would have been bearable. As it was, she blotted her copybook so much during the short time I saw her that morning that I could hardly be civil to her in the car on the way to the station. She had

spent a great deal of time telephoning on the landing and gave me a 10/–
piece towards the long-distance expensive gossips that she had indulged
in. She was rude (not intentionally, but by our standards nonetheless
offensive), off hand, patronising.

All this can be put down to 'compensation' for being unloved, an ugly
spinster etc., but it is tiresome nonetheless. She talks as if we were following the US steps all the time, even saying, 'Oh, I threw my papers away
on the train. Do you have them here?' 'Do you have previews here? The
Arlen son's book[1] will be coming to England,' etc. She embarrasses Ray
by saying, 'I'm lucky to have his genius', and 'I'd better have dinner at the
Miller house where there is a chef, a butler, a footman, two housemaids'
etc., etc. 'You don't have a household maintained in London, do you?' –
'I don't have a Bank[2] at the back of me, but I live comfortably...'

Anyhow she has gone and, apart from taking her to the theatre to see
London Assurance,[3] I am lucky not to see her again for a very long while.
She is a character. She 'never misses a trick', by which I mean she is on to
any little superficial effect but 'understands' nothing. She makes me
aware of the abyss between English and American more than any other
human being I know.

*In the late summer Cecil went to stay with Baron Philippe de Rothschild and his
wife, Pauline, at Mouton in France.*

*Owner of Mouton and king of the champagne empire Mouton-Rothschild,
Baron Philippe was a highly cultured man, as was his wife, the former Pauline
Potter, an American. Each year the Baron invited a famous artist to design the
label for his Mouton-Rothschild wines. One year the Queen Mother gave her
cipher, while artists have included David Hockney.*

Mouton   [August 1970]

Pauline[4] reminds me of how I made her laugh by telling her how little
interest I had in my sister's collecting of people. Nancy knows who
'everyone is', or, if she doesn't, she looks up their pedigree in the Peerage
or *Who's Who*. When trying to compete with her one day, I interjected,
'You're talking about that girl who was a Titchbore?'

'Oh no,' said Nancy gravely. 'She was a Snagge.'

---

[1] *Exiles* by Michael J. Arlen (1971), the fascinating story of his parents. Cecil would have
enjoyed it. Arlen's father, the novelist Michael Arlen, was best known for *The Green Hat*.
[2] Kitty Miller's father was a banker, Jules Bache.
[3] Boucicault's comedy was enjoying a successful revival with Donald Sinden at the
Aldwych Theatre.
[4] Baroness (Pauline) de Rothschild (1908–76).

Mouton

Pauline and Philippe[1] have spent all the years of their life together beautifying Mouton and its surroundings. They have not only made the wine
business into a great going concern with a name that has now become
famous throughout the world, but they have also made it into a unique
place of beauty, with the old Victorian house full of the most amusing
and audacious bric-a-brac of the period, but they have converted the farm
buildings into magnificent rooms furnished with Renaissance sculptures,
Venetian chairs, baroque statues, and a marvellous collection of books
and modern works of art.

Apart from this they have created an extraordinary legacy for future
generations, of precious objects, all connected with the grape and the
enjoyment of wine, goblets, Roman figures, and bottles, Italian glass, still
life paintings, engraved glass goblets, silver, early tapestries representing
the processing of wine, all placed and lit with originality and daring by
Pauline and placed in a marvellous museum full of things that Philippe
has bought to add to the great collection he inherited.

Pauline, like the rare American women the Duchess of Windsor and
Kitty Rothschild,[2] has this fantastic eye for works of art, but also the
determination to make the way of life *chez elle* into something quite above
the level of others. There is a woman and assistant whose sole job is to
arrange the exquisite still lifes of flowers, ferns, grasses and branches,
which she collects from the neighbouring woods and arranges on the
table, for lunch and dinner. We saw her miles away with a haul of mushrooms and berries to put into little Japanese pots on the elaborate
tablecloths.

There is an old man in a beret, who walks to and fro raking the white
gravel of the courtyard every day of the week including Sunday. There
are God knows how many servants. One sees pretty young girls in pink
emerging from an ironing room, and Philippe has a maid to look after his
toes and clothes. The linen is of the finest handkerchief lawn and is
ironed each time one lies on the bed. The breakfast trays are little masterpieces with every kind of toast and croissant, a pat of butter like the
moon and a minute basket of pansies.

---

[1] Baron Philippe de Rothschild (1902–88).
[2] Kitty Wolff (1885–1946), wife of Baron Eugen de Rothschild. A beautiful and
adventurous girl, she was the daughter of a dentist in Philadelphia, and married twice
before Rothschild. On the recommendation of Lady Mendl, she was the Duke of
Windsor's host at Schloss Enzesfeld in Austria for three uncomfortable months after the
Abdication 1936–37. A leader of international society, she eventually died at her Long
Island home.

By the bed are sharp pointed pencils, notebooks, various anglepoise lamps, a basket containing India rubber, a pair of scissors. These are placed also in opportune positions throughout the house. In one's bedroom the commode has a small bottle of whisky and Perrier in readiness. The plants are potted, a tuberose, stephanotis, orange, heather, lily. The bathroom is a haven with cotton wool, new Saponici Guerlain cakes of soap, big bottles of Floris bath scent, towels of every calibre and consistency.

As for the meals we sit down to in the various rooms (never in the same place twice) the menus, with the list of 4 or 5 different Rothschild wines, are one more remarkable than the other, crayfish, and partridge. Last night a row of ducks with the breast carved, everything a *raffinement* that does not exist elsewhere today. It is in no way vulgar, precious maybe, but it is the result of a wonderful combination between 2 people, one with the money to spend and the other with the character and taste to direct and promote the other.

Pauline, herself a work of art, with each appearance a subtle surprise (perhaps as during this visit she goes in for a 'boyish' look of white shirt and tight silk trousers), Pauline, lately recovering from a severe heart operation (the doctor last Sunday cruelly told her she might live another 4 or 5 years) emerges later and later from her beautiful room full of painted, stuffed or sculpted birds, and later and later does she go to bed. But during her hours awake, she is a masterly organiser of all this sophisticated beauty mixed with rural charm. The servants are dedicated in a manner that at first comes as a shock. The butler walks the length of the grand 'Salon' on his toes. An old woman about to bring a batch of bathing clothes, retreats on seeing a group of the household. Another apologises as if it were a tragedy that the grapefruit juice has not been properly iced and is therefore late in appearing on one's tray.

The fric, the wine, the coffee is attended with a perfection that no longer exists. The air is scented with lilac in late winter, now with tuberoses. There are plans for a new façade, a reservoir, a swimming pool, always additions that are imaginative and a great improvement to the general beauty. It has become a little principality on its own. 'Shell' people, through the good offices of some dishonest politicians willing to bring votes to themselves, receive permission to build a whole community of factories and oil refineries with their power stacks and the site chosen is in the centre of defenceless vineyards of France. On the horizon of this green-blue sea of vines, which dates back to the early Romans in the year 300, now there is to be seen, day and night, a vast flame volcanoing from a tall pipe that pierces the sky and bellows forth a long plume of black smoke. When the wind is in an easterly direction the stench is enough to make one wonder if there is not any minute to be an explosion of gas.

The tragedy of the cherry orchard has been brought up to date and multiplied a thousand thousand times, for these vineyards should be the pride of France and are part of the national heritage. Philippe sits in bed writing a manifesto which will be signed by all who own the neighbouring vineyards. But surely it is too late now to do any[thing]. Oil is here refined at the rate of thousands of gallons per week. It is sad that plans are afoot to enlarge this desecration, so that ten times as much petrol will be produced, and modern products of all hideous sorts with untold results to the wine. At the moment it is too early to tell how much the wine will be damaged.

One goes into the chais and imbibes the wonderful intoxicating scent of the fermented grape. One comes out into the museum to smell the foul stink of the worst of today. It is something so shocking, so vandalistic and ignoble that it would be quite understandable if Philippe should transplant his museum to England. As it is he is dying of the degradation of his home, of his life, while Pauline, with her wonderful abnormal control, will neither look at nor discuss the vile thing that has been sent from the devil.

Pauline has the Harewoods[1] to stay next weekend. She admires them but knows them little. She thought I would make things easier by being present. But to return to this luxurious ivory tower (on two floors) so soon would be trusting my luck too much and, in any case, am planning to make a motor trip to the Dordogne with Sam.

I woke early in the morning before my departure to receive a note from Pauline (who goes to sleep about 4 a.m. and sleeps till one o'clock). This was a subtle urging to accept her invitation, written in the most poetical style, but without any mention of the Harewoods or the worldly reason why she would enjoy my appearance. She is by far the most subtle person I know. One could learn a lot from her.

An unbelievable stroke of bad luck. Sam Adams Green wires me to get him a room in Paris and to meet him at airport. With difficulty a room is found at the small France et Choiseul, and he receives my message to say I will meet him for dinner at his hotel at 8 o'clock. I ask for Sam Green. The operator says no reply. I point to a card indicating his room and wonder why he wishes to be known as Adam Green. I wait forty-five minutes. In a fury I leave, my evening ruined. How casual can these people be? Is it worth going with him on a trip to the Dordogne if he is to be as unreliable as this? Back at Rothschilds' I receive a call from him. He

[1] The Earl and Countess of Harewood.

has been waiting in his room for over an hour. It seems there are two Greens, next to one another, Sam, and a Mr and Mrs Adam Green.

Pauline, while suffering Philippe's driving, 'Careful, or you'll make an accident!'

Waking at early morning to the gentle roar of doves, as one listens closely the sound is of many rollers, flattening the paths, at intervals stopping for a pause, like rollers on the seashore, or like oarsmen in an ancient Greek slave ship. Occasionally the cry of wings flapping.

Plebeian bathing scene devolving at side of Mercedes (!), potted not cut flowers in house. Huge lumps of sugar. Bomb-size butter pats.

The Windsors *September 1970*

Went to the house in the beautiful Bois de Boulogne to have tea with the Duchess. I did not realise what I was in for as I made the arrangement automatically to thank for the dress given for my collection. On arrival in this rather sprawling pretentious house full of good and bad (how quickly the second-rate becomes *démodé*), the Duchess appearing at the end of a garden vista on a crowd of yapping pug dogs, suddenly appeared to have aged, to have become a little old woman. Her figure and legs as trim as ever, as energetic as she always was, putting servants and things to rights, she had the sad, haunted eyes of the ill.

In hospital they had found she had something wrong with her liver, and that condition made her very depressed. 'People seem so much more amusing after you have had a couple of drinks!' When, at one time, she got up to fetch something she said, 'Don't look at me. I haven't even had the coiffeur come out to do my hair.' And it did appear rather straggly, and this again gave her a rather pathetic look.

She loves rich food. She is now on a strict diet and, accustomed to whisky and water, she now must not drink any alcohol. She tottered to a sofa against the light in a small, over-crowded drawing room. Masses of royal souvenirs, gold boxes, sealing wax stamps and seals, small pictures, a great array of flowers in obelisk shapes in baskets. These had been sent up from the Mill which, now the Duke is not able to bend down for his gardening, will be sold.

We talked as easily as old friends do. Nothing much except health, mutual friends, the young generation was discussed. Then an even greater shock. Amid the barking of the pugs the Duke of Windsor, in a cedar-rose-coloured velvet golf suit, appeared, bent on a stick. His walk makes him into an old man. He sat, legs spread, and talked and laughed with greater ease than I have ever known. He has never really liked me. We never got on well. At last, after all these years, he called me by my Christian name and treated me as an old '*copain*', of whom he has less and less. (In fact, it is difficult for him to find someone to play golf with him.)

There were moments when the Prince of Wales charm came back, and what a charm it was, but I noticed a sort of stutter, a hissing of the speech, when he hesitated in mid-sentence and was lost. Wallis did not seem unduly worried about this and said, 'Well, you see, we're old! It's awful how many years have gone by, and one cannot have them back!'

We talked of the current trends in clothes, hippiedom, nudity, pornography, 'feelthy' postcards etc. The thought struck me that had it not been for the sex urges of their youth, these two would not be here together today. They seemed to have forgotten the lure that sex still has. But they are a happy couple. They are both apt to talk at once, but their attitudes do not clash, and they don't seem to have any regrets that could have been avoided. He still talks of his Investiture and asked me to find out where the crown is that he wore at Caernarvon. He got to his feet (and stick) to look out some illustrations in a book, and talked of old characters – Fruity [Metcalfe], Ali Mackintosh, Freddie Cripps, Eric Dudley.[1] The usual question: 'Are there characters today?'

Talk of Queen Mary (and it seemed so odd to see little Fabergé frames with photographs of Queens Victoria and Mary in the house of this 'smart' American) brought me to James P-H [Pope-Hennessy] and I said how much I hoped he'd write their book. (If another has to be written, let James get the cash.) And when I said James was now busy on a life of Trollope, the Duke admitted his ignorance and asked, 'Who's Trollope?'

An hour passed quickly enough, but I felt we were perhaps running out of small talk when I looked at my watch and realised I must leave for an Ionesco play. The leave-taking was lengthy, due to many red herrings on the way.

The Duchess, leaning forward on tiny legs, looked rather blind and when an enormous bouquet of white flowers and plants arrived from Arene, she did not seem able to see it. She leant myopically towards it and asked, 'What's that? A tuberose, an arum lily.' The man corrected her: 'An auratum.' 'Ah yes. Will you please tell them how beautifully they have done them.' (This very nice of her.) I watched her try to open the card to see without her spectacles who this incredibly expensive 'tribute' must have come from. I'm sure it cost all of £75!

'Who's it from?' asked the Duke. 'Don't be so full of curiosity,' said his

---

[1] Fruity Metcalfe – Major Edward Metcalfe (d. 1957), long-suffering equerry to the Duke of Windsor; Captain Ali Mackintosh, author of *No Alibi*; Fred Cripps, second Lord Parmoor (1882–1977); and Eric, third Earl of Dudley (1894–1969).

wife, trying to read without glasses. 'It's from Jane Englehard!'[1] Who else could afford such an offering?

The two old people, very bent, but full of spirit and still both dandies, stood at the door as I went off in Liliane [de Rothschild]'s smart car. Through the passage of years, I had become one of their entourage, an old friend, and the Duke even said to me, 'Well, between these four walls ...'

Paris, 11 rue Monsieur

It has been a very good visit. My mood is good and my health does not trouble me. One day I got over-tired, but only naturally, for I visited three octogenarians, Marie-Louise Bousquet (miraculously still alive), Mrs Wooster, and Princess Bibesco.[2] They are all strong meat.

I bought flower seeds, soap, china cups, hair lotion. We had many delightful quiet meals in the house (food better than anywhere). It was a week of surprises. The last hours of the great Matisse exhibition with huge paintings loaned from the Hermitage, a Poliakoff and a Goya. A visit to the Windsors in old age, and to the latest Ionesco play about death. What a genius he is. How I laughed. I did not know I could laugh so much. (Lately I seem to have regained my facility for laughter. It left me for many years. Has come back since my prostate left me.) It has been a week of sunshine, the trees beginning to 'turn' and now I'm about to do a motor tour with Sam [Green] to the Dordogne, something I have dreamt about for many years, in fact since Cyril described the walnuts.

Cecil then went on a tour of the Dordogne with Sam Green, travelling via Tours and Chartres. They left Paris in a hired car in a bad rush hour. Their

---

[1] Jane Englehard, widow of Charles Englehard (1917–71), American industrialist and Chairman of Englehard Minerals and Chemical Corporation, whose fortune was partly based on circumventing South African restrictions on the export of gold ingots by setting up a jewellery business, which ostensibly exported manufactured jewels to Hong Kong. These were then melted down. His reputation was part inspiration for Ian Fleming's James Bond villain, Goldfinger. He owned the colt, *Nijinsky*, which won eleven classics, but was beaten by Mrs Arpad Plesch's *Sassafras* in the 1970 Arc de Triomphe, after which Englehard retired to the Ritz on a diet of Coca-Cola, and died soon afterwards. His widow, Jane, became a philanthropist and long-time board member of the Metropolitan Musuem of Art in New York.

[2] Marie-Louise Bousquet, indomitable party giver, where the fare was modest, but the guests top-rate; Mrs Frank Wooster, celebrated mother-in-law of Alan Pryce-Jones; and Princess Marthe Bibesco, author and friend of Proust.

spirits rose as they reached the cathedral town and went for a night-time stroll.
And so onwards they travelled to Chambord and Poitiers.

Driving with Sam was frequently an adventure in itself as Sam refused to
ask the way and they often got lost. On a warm morning in early autumn Cecil
relished seeing Chenonceaux 'through a nave of plane trees, more beautiful than
it proved to be on closer inspection'. They went to Villandry to see the gardens,
which Cecil judged 'well kept, the colours under control, mostly greens, and pale
yellow dahlia and dark red rose for colour'.

Cecil discovered he had taken photographs without putting a film in the
camera. They drove on, arriving in bad humour at a 'horrid' motel. Cecil 'woke
up in the middle of the night to pee, and pressed a button, so that a flow of muzak
filled the room (it is said that these rooms are supplied with music not so much to
be listened to, but so that lovers can enjoy one another's moans and groans
without being embarrassed that the neighbours hear what they're doing)'. Cecil
was 'not too unhappy at leaving the Loire and the big cities for what I hope will
be a sylvan end to the summer holiday'.

They headed towards Bergerac and further south, enthusiasm mounting for
'the rural delights for which we had been hoping'. Cecil loved the Dordogne,
'periwinkle blue and gently moving, seen from a mountain height or on the same
level, it was a child's idea of what a river should be, bordered with forests in
which fairy palaces with blue turrets were sheltered'.

Cecil and Sam arrived at a vieux logis, *and tucked into foie gras and truf-*
fles. They reached medieval Sarlat by night and continued exploring the next
day. A Madame Hamelin arranged visits to various chateaux, the first 'a really
marvellous yellow stone, blue stoned roofed chateau with moat, dovecotes, a huge
balustraded terrace overlooking the river'. Madame Hamelin took them to
the chateau of Hautesport, and on to Rastignac, a chateau burnt by the
Germans.

The owners of the chateau now live in a villa built nearly after the war
and of no interest. It was a wonderful Clérambard scene, the house is
owned by a lady in black aged 104, who sat drinking orange juice out of
doors, while her daughter,[1] married to an 84-year-old Englishman,
Fairweather,[2] lives with her brother,[3] once an enigma at French *Vogue*
and now a retired writer, and her son,[4] a gentleman farmer aged 60. She,
at tea, kept the ball rolling, incredibly vital and entertaining in her grey
chic wig, she had the grand manner, as she talked of Cléo de Mérode,[5]

---

[1] Ghislaine Lauwick.
[2] Harold Fairweather, Captain IAR.
[3] Jacques Lauwick.
[4] Cédric Fairweather.
[5] Cléo de Mérode (1881–1966), courtesan from the *belle époque*.

who left her everything in her will. Surprisingly, Cléo (christened Cléopatra-Diane) had got rid of nothing during her 60-odd years in the rue Tehran.

The concierge would bring up her breakfast, but I imagine she ate nothing, never spent anything, yet she left marvellous jewels, including a collar of seven huge diamonds. These are all in the bank while the present owner and her family are unbelievably frugal, having what meals they have at 12–3, tea at 6, and dinner at 10. When the couple were ill for six months, Mrs Fairweather and her entourage lived off pots of jam out of the cupboard, and the old ladies' cakes.

Mrs F. did not consider Cléo had been a *grande cocotte*, had lived with a French magician for ten years before the King of Belgium, who on meeting her after her performance on stage, asked, 'Are you one of my subjects?' to which she replied, 'No, one of your family.' He became her slave. She was never conscious of her beauty, though crowds followed her when she went out shopping, and when she danced with Rupert Doone who looked like nothing off stage, but had a great talent for stage make-up (which she had not), Cléo said, 'He is much prettier than me!'

Marcel Aymé[1] has written already so well of this group, but they fire one's imagination and, though one laughed, it was quite a ghoulish picture, with relics of the past, including Cléo de M.'s first music box displayed.

Cecil and Sam continued on their way, enjoying much delicious food, the beauty of the countryside, sometimes marred by mist, and the hazard of occasionally getting lost. But Cecil concluded, 'It has been an interesting week with beautiful things to see and the countryside has not disappointed. I am grateful that I have had this long wished-for dream to come true. But now it is over and I am impatient to get back to my own surroundings.'

Traffic jams, strikes, hijackings, Indians murdering ordinary English housewives and feeding their bodies to the pigs, outbreaks of cholera, famine, huge bridges collapsing, further clever coups by the Soviets and wars, these are our everyday diet. With more and more people behaving badly throughout the world, it is a relief to read that the real spirit of England survives in a number of instances.

A country woman saw a sand martin fall plonk out of a nest. She rushed to pick it up and see what damage was done. The bird was in a bad way. It could surely not survive. But she put a few drops of brandy down its throat and rushed it off to the local chemist, who she knew was an authority on birds. The chemist took the dying bird in his care, knew the

[1] Marcel Aymé (1902–67), prolific French author.

best things to give it and by degrees it showed signs of recovery. Its wings were pieced together and it responded to the diet. After many weeks the bird recovered.

But unfortunately it was now too late in the year for it to join the migration of its fellows to Africa. The chemist knew it could not survive an English winter alone, even if it were kept warm indoors. So what to do? Would it be allowed to remain here, most surely to die? No, it is next week being sent in its cage by BOAC to Lagos. Here it will be freed in order that it join the other birds who will, by that time, have arrived on those sunny shores.

Back in England, Cecil had agreed to take part in a documentary film about his life by the photographer David Bailey, called Beaton by Bailey, *eventually shown on television in 1971.*

Autumn 1970

David Bailey[1] dressed according to David Cecil like Edgar in *Lear* and Penelope Tree,[2] according to the same source, looking like the fairy Blackstick in *The Rose and the Ring*, have been here for several days as he is doing a documentary TV film about my various activities. It has been a disturbing influx with ten men with their wires and lights, their cigarette butts and dried sweat. It has also been extremely tiring, I do not know why, maybe the tension, however as a result of it I have had to tell Dr Gottfried that I feel chest pains, as if I had been running up a hill. He tells me that as a result of the various complications after my operation, my heart has been slightly pushed to one side and that the main artery that feeds it has a small dent in it. He does not seem to be worried but it is the first time that I have ever had anything said against my heart and I am rather appalled.

Altogether my state of health begins to worry me, for I have too many headaches, and it is a great effort to have to stop reading or writing (which I fear is the cause) and I am very loath to have to quieten down and become idle.

Perhaps if I allow myself a real convalescence during the next month I may regain my former strength. At the moment my mind is influenced by all sorts of horrid possibilities, and I am not in a mind to quieten down and slacken off before the grave engulfs me.

---

[1] David Bailey (b. 1938), cockney photographer, who rose in the sixties. Lover and husband of many a beautiful star. He married secondly Catherine Deneuve, thirdly Marie Helvin, and fourthly Catherine Dyer.
[2] Penelope Tree (b. 1949), hip model of the sixties with lynx eyes.

The TV technique might be something that one eventually took for granted as a means for expression. But I am too impatient a novice to endure the long delays, the hanging about. It is as tiresome as film-making and I am very little flattered. I have not seen the 'rushes' and may be horrified by my appearance. (The camera records states of health as well as every day of one's age.) If this sort of thing had happened early in life I no doubt would have been flattered. As it is it is merely upsetting. It has left me incapable of carrying on with my own life. I am too disrupted to switch back automatically to writing, and too tired.

However, the study of Penelope and David has been interesting. She is so subtle, sensitive and highly intelligent. He so cocky Cockney bright and completely uneducated. It seems that during the intervals of 'takes' she was standing between his legs as he sat on the kitchen table. Giving her a whack on her rump, he asked Ray, 'What do you think of this old bag? She's just a home-loving old trout, really.' Penelope seemed to love such treatment.

I find them both very strange but then I do not often realise when others are 'high' on 'pot'. Sam told me it was obvious they were 'feeling no pain' when they first came to lunch. I found them rather silent and, as a nervous host, tried to fill in the pauses between topics of conversation. It seems that the young consider these pauses natural and part of the intimacy of friendship. Seeing me clear up some cigarette ashes, P. asked, 'Are you a neat freak?' I admitted that I was. 'Oh, David and I are terrible. We make the most awful mess wherever we go.' I described the motel in [France] and how I hate the motel mentality. 'Oh, Bailey and I love it. We want to have our home just like a motel, with tuna fish sandwiches in cellophane wrappings for breakfast.'

David is extremely frank about his humble beginnings and tells how much he hates the working classes. 'They're a lot of good for nothing, idle bums.' I mentioned how good Ray is to his mother whom he visits every week. 'I'm good to my mother by keeping away from her as much as I can.'

God what a shock this ménage must be to the Tree parents.[1] I really feel acutely sorry for them.

The 'Aunt Jessie' book is quite a minor affair. It has been a very good way of keeping me going after the operation. Yet even this slim little volume has taken a terrific toll of me. An enormous effort has gone into it, but happily I begin to feel it is now in a condition where it can be shown to the publisher. It will be a terrible shock if it gets a bad reception.

---

[1] Ronald Tree (1897–1976) and his wife, Marietta (1917–91).

Margot Oxford[1]

D [David] Cecil tells how after Asquith's death Margot said, 'From now on I shall just see the King and a few friends. The opposing government have told enough white lies to ice a cake.'

[Robert] Carr[2] came down to visit Anthony Eden and said that when at last Heath's government got their hands on the papers left by the Wilson government, the situation in the country was so appalling that even if they had known the figures before the election, they would not have dared publish them as the effect on other countries would have been so damaging.

Since his defeat Wilson has been lashing out in all directions and has become completely and utterly discredited. George Brown, too, has behaved as a swine (still people go on saying, 'I happen to like George...') but altogether the recent Labour government has created an all-time low, not only in manners, but in ethics. As Clarissa pointed out, the French corral their government from the people, they are a pretty tough lot, but they (when in power) behave like statesmen.

Cecil invited John Gielgud to dinner at Pelham Place. As is inevitable in the theatre, there had been difficulties between them.

Cecil had designed Enid Bagnold's Chalk Garden, *when it was staged in Boston and New York under the direction of Irene Selznick. There had been a number of disagreements – the set was deemed too bright and sprayed down. When the production came to London, Gielgud had dropped Cecil's sets altogether and employed another designer. Cecil was enraged and for many years refused to speak to either Enid Bagnold or Gielgud. Enid wrote, 'All these years he has wiped me out of his life... Cecil bowed when he met me... A deep bow, very startling, out of Dickens. It made me laugh, though my heart ached.'*

Gielgud

We admire one another, but we are both rather shy by nature and the rift that was caused by the *Chalk Garden* has taken a lot of sealing up. We had an 'olive' branch supper at my house, but I found John very uptight. He didn't ask me back to him, but was solicitous at the time of my illness. I

---

[1] Margot Tennant (1864–1945), Countess of Oxford and Asquith, widow of H. H. Asquith.
[2] Robert Carr (b. 1916), Secretary of State for Employment 1970–72, later Home Secretary, later Baron Carr of Hadley.

decided to ask him again. He was delighted. I thought perhaps he'd thaw in the company of intimate friends. So I asked Cathleen Nesbitt and Irene Worth.[1] The evening was not entirely a success.

I have been suffering from bad neuralgic headaches and a rather slight one took the edge off my evening's enjoyment, but Irene was the real fly in the ointment. She has had a marvellous success as Hedda Gabler in Canada, but comes back to England raring to go and finds that no one is interested in offering her a part. Her behaviour is very understandable and it is disgraceful that Binkie [Beaumont][2] and gang say that she is not 'box office'. Yet this makes her very difficult company. She lashes out in all directions. Tonight she was strident. John arrived looking very much older, with white sideburns on his cheeks and his nose fuller than ever (it is not caused by drink as he is most abstemious). He is accustomed to competing with irrepressible actors, so he did not seem to mind Irene's overbearing performance, and argued with her without losing his temper.

Irene, generally so discreet, lashed out against Larry Olivier with such violence that John contorted his face and looked like an oyster squirted with lemon. He is so fair and good that he will not have his greatest rival denigrated. Irene was as if possessed. Cathleen, magnificent, heroic, dignified, modest and gentle, was all smiles and a sympathetic element as usual, while managing not to be a sycophant like Joyce Carey whom somebody said you could eat because she agrees with everybody.

Talk was entirely theatrical, *The Dream* of Peter Brook,[3] the bad notices for *Cyrano*, which John thought of doing until Olivier told him he was too old, of the disaster of the seventy-year-old Judith Anderson's *Hamlet* in the US, and of the way productions die unless, as with Godfrey [Granville] Barker, the director freshens up the performances all along the run.

Irene's contribution to the evening was her appreciation of Ray's supper, grouse and a pineapple sponge cake. She helped herself to a second helping of the latter with such relish that it was a joy to see. Ray said he would not like to work for someone like Sir John who obviously took no interest whatsoever in his food, bolted it in a jiffy and was contented with one small glass of wine. There is no sensuality about his personality and, much as I admire and like him, he is difficult to love. He wanted to be nice to me tonight and we had a brief talk after dinner when he amazed me at his memory, his total recall. He talked about the London that he first knew as a young aspiring actor. He met Robert

---

[1] Irene Worth (1916–2002), American-born actress much liked by Cecil.
[2] Hugh (Binkie) Beaumont (1908–73), theatrical impresario with H. M. Tennent. A monster in the theatre.
[3] Peter Brook (b. 1925), theatre director.

Farquarson[1] (a very witty sinister Aleister Crowleyish man) who was
'looking over' the young blood. He remembers Esmé Percy[2] and Dudley
Brown[3] at one party, dipping their fingers into a bowl of cream. Dudley
Brown! I had forgotten my first sophisticated friend at prep school who, a
year older than me, had taken to the 'low life' like a duck to a pond, and
had committed suicide in Paris before he was twenty.

John described how he tries to train his memory by conscious means,
how when he was filming in Turkey (Cardigan in *Light Brigade*[4]) he sat
alone in his dressing room, determined to recall the look of his first class-
rooms at school, and the names and appearances of masters and boys,
how when he sees some old bloated man in the street, he remembers that
they were contemporaries in the fifth form. He never forgets a name, a
face, an incident.

Suddenly he decides to leave. 'I don't wish to break up the evening, but
we had two performances today.' Formal thanks. When he leaves he
shakes hands and gives me a knowing smile. It is the most terrible
grimace. His eyes disappear into two little crescents on their sides. His
false teeth are seen, his nose stretches across his cheeks, he lumbers off.
He is self-sufficient, as resilient as be damned, with a wiry strength that
goes on, but he will not come out to one from his shell. One knows all
about him, one makes allowances, and one loves him.

Amazing how one does not see the obvious. I was looking out of my
bedroom at the paddock across the road, and suddenly noticed that the
gate to it was placed in a most inexplicable position and that it should
surely be central. This led me to realise that a path should be made across
the field towards the river and a clearing made so that one can enjoy the
amenities of the river. Perhaps plant a row of pollarded limes or Irish
yews each side of the path. Clarissa suggested pleached apple and this is a
delightful idea, as it would give an unpretentious *potagé* effect.

But how is it that I have to live in the house for 20 years before I realise
the obvious. If only I had had the 'brainwave' before, for it will open up
the property and give one not only a delightful walk to the river but also a
distant view of the façade. If only … the pleached apple trees would

---

[1] Robert Farquarson (1877–1966), effete actor, said to have sprung from rich Italian
nobility (real name – Robert de la Condamine), much in demand for highly coloured
figures. He effected a stammer that never afflicted him on stage.
[2] Esmé Percy (1887–1957), English actor, particularly known for playing Shakespeare
and Shaw.
[3] Dudley Brown (1903–25), at Heath Mount, where he attempted to enlighten Cecil
about the facts of life. He led a louche life and threw himself to his death from his
window in the rue Jacob in Paris.
[4] *The Charge of the Light Brigade*, directed by Tony Richardson (1968).

already be enormous and give one a great thrill of blossom each spring as well as the fruit in the summer.

Rushing down through the archway of Salisbury station to catch the train to London, I noticed an old monk in brown robes scurrying down the ramp towards me good-humouredly, carrying heavy luggage. We smiled at each other. As I went on he whirled round and shouted after me, 'Thank you for all you have done.' This gave me such a shock. My mind was so full of my own problems and the latest job (which I never think is up to scratch) having to be done in time that I did not realise that anyone was really conscious of my output. This is only the sort of thing that seems to happen to Godfrey Winn,[1] but it pleased me quite a lot for a few minutes.

Paris

Arrived without any preparations (rush too much, but have got *My Bolivian Aunt* off to the agent), and feeling utterly depleted. My heart valves have a dent in them and I get out of breath if I walk for any distance, particularly when carrying a suitcase. Having eaten lunch in the aeroplane, I had the lunch interval for sleep. I woke up to make an hour's telephone calls, then wondered where I should wander. I hate finding myself stranded far from a taxi, so walked down the street and found myself outside Chanel's. Well, I'd better go in and pay my respects.

This place doesn't have too many happy memories since the production of *Coco* but I felt I should visit the instigator of the whole project. I found that although everyone had said how feeble she had become, all was just as it always had been. The collection was being shown to quite a crowd of French women, and the clothes were as ever fresh, luxurious, under-stated, elegant, wearable, timeless. Again I was terribly impressed that the Chanel idiom seems to be indestructible. These were a confirmation, had nothing to do with what is going on in fashion elsewhere, but even so, they held their own so that one felt that anything outside would be ridiculous.

This isn't about the last of *haute couture* and again I went upstairs where Mademoiselle would receive me. I had been told that Madame Grumbach,[2] her social PR assistant had been sacked, but the poor woman was only looking older, having been several times fired, but then taken

---

[1] Godfrey Winn (1908–71), prolific, syrupy journalist.
[2] Madame Lilou Grumbach, press secretary to Chanel, and wife of Philippe Grümbach, an editor at *L'Express*.

back. I asked if Chanel would give me a contribution to my V & A Museum collection and she thought it best if I were to broach the subject. But it might be difficult.

Chanel was also looking older. Her hair the blackest of dyed wool, without shape or gloss, her eyes made up underneath to look like an aged dog, a dreadful white felt hat which [Katharine] Hepburn and gang would have discarded. It gave me a shock to see the room that I had re-created on the stage, the original so much more cluttered and personal, better in every way, but how could anyone achieve this effect of richness who did not have Chanel's sense of luxury? The old gypsy at once turned on her conversation machine and allowed me no opportunity to interject. She talked as usual of all the horrors of present-day life.

I found that I was able to understand much easier what she was saying, even so the torrent is extremely tiresome to follow and my mind wandered. I could not help thinking how utterly void of the mark Hepburn's impersonation had been. She had not got on to any of the obvious mannerisms, the sitting hunched with the hands pressing the short skirt against the knees, the frankness of the hands on thighs with elbows wide. Instead we got that banal impersonation of the typical Frenchman with the fingers clasped up high.

I had asked Grumbach to call for me after 10 minutes. The woman is a pig. She left me to make my own getaway 45 minutes later. In a way, though, it was marvellous that Chanel should *not* talk about the *Coco* show except to say disparagingly they were making a mistake to take it to London. It was over and forgotten now. Not a word about my work, no compliment, a lot of personality gossip, always a bit sly about other women who had started as cocottes and later 'made good' ... great abuse of those who spent their lives, like Maggie Van Zuylen,[1] at the bridge table.

'Poor Maggie, she got so ill and this made her thin and this pleased Maggie, who had all her life been too fat.' Then followed a diatribe against all fat people. 'They become so lazy and so stupid! They have all this bulk to carry around here and here (imitation) and they go on eating! The important thing is not to eat. It disgusts me to see the amount French people eat!'

In fact only she has the answer to life. She certainly has the answer to dismissing any attempt to leave. She fought like a dragon to keep the conversation going so that I could not say goodbye. Eventually I stood, walked to the door. On the landing she had a new lease of life and I was

[1] Baroness van Zuylen (d. 1969), born Marguerite Navvatella, an Egyptian, she married Baron Egmont van Zuylen, a Belgian diplomat. She was the mother of Marie-Hélène de Rothschild, and liked to sing saucy music hall numbers with Chanel.

trapped for another five minutes. Only when I was halfway down the stairs did she put on the farewell grin, which even today gives quite an effect of allure.

Downstairs Madame Grumbach asked how it went. Had to admit 'I didn't get a word in' and I would have to write her for a request for a dress for my collection. I'm sure it won't be given. I got away. I walked up the street and to Les Trois Quartiers and bought myself another silk handkerchief to wear as a kerchief round my neck in the country. I felt rather ashamed of my Trois Quartiers taste after Chanel's extravagance, but the fact remains that she is rich and grand and I can't afford to buy her silks.

Then my thoughts went back to Broadchalke and Major and Mrs Prest, who must live on a very few hundred pounds a year. For them it is a great extravagance to buy a packet of seeds and a dozen bulbs. They drink a port glass full of cider, and they give what they can to the village charities. They have one another and although they look sad, they are happy.

Yves St Laurent[1]

Apart from the Chanel scene, I have not been to any dress collections for so long that I thought it might be a good idea to become *au courant* by going to Yves St Laurent. He has such influence, is the one that all who know speak of in awed tones. Prejudiced against him and thinking he did nothing that Chelsea has not done. I was very soon under his spell. The clothes really are completely different from those that women of fashion would have worn two years ago. The point of view is completely opposite those of the early days that Yves knew when he worked at Dior. The spirit is against high fashion and good style. He has created a Callot-like[2] atmosphere with leather, suede, felt and tinker's bells trailing a pheasant's feather. It is not for the middle-aged or the aged, but it is in itself an extraordinary creation.

Apart from Callot, the inspiration I would guess is of the late teens: 1918, perhaps, with use of dowdiness to create a mood, pavane and squashed velvets remind me of my mother. Even at that time I thought the fashion dreary but now it is remarkable. It is an unsavoured, or at any rate forgotten, taste. The collection consists of long straight skirts over boyish (maxi) shorts with wool caps hiding all hair, of pleated fabrics that are woven in dull colours in geometrical designs, very dowdy bourgeois-

[1] Yves Saint Laurent (b. 1936), enduring couturier. Head designer of Christian Dior from 1957, opened his own house in 1962.
[2] Callot Soeurs, founded 1895 by three sisters. Finally closed 1948.

Cecil with his Rolleiflex.

Katharine Hepburn, sketched by Cecil in *Coco*.

Marlene Dietrich – an early photo of the *diseuse*.

Elizabeth Taylor at the Proust Ball, 1971.

Travelling Companions

Cecil by Sam Green.

Sam Green by Cecil.

Mickey Renshaw in his villa in Cyprus, 1972.

Mona Bismarck in her villa in Capri.

Kitty Miller.

looking tweeds made a rather wonderfully awful but original coat. Some boots are poor-looking, there is a prevalence of genteel poverty, governesses in distress who have had a windfall and have been able to go out and do a burst on one complete outfit.

His life in Marrakesh has influenced him in cloth and thread embroidery. There are dull soft brocades with old thread in them that have all the restraint of early Persian art, and there are Chinese influences worked in garish colours that are part of the pop scene and which remind me of the P. Brook *Midsummer Night's Dream*. The Chinese apple blossom worked in sequins over brilliant acid satins that might come from some fair. Except for some stars appliquéd on leather belt coats and hats and for some absolutely hideous travesties of the 1945 fashions with velvet turbans, square shoulders, short skirts and heavy clogged feet, his collection is all of a long restrained dowdy 'chic'. It is unobtrusively elegant, different, new, uncompromising. Y. has changed the values of former fashion.

This collection is entirely successful. The Ibsenesque suicidal heroines have come out of their black. It is all in a gravure of very subtle colour. Dark greys, greens, blues, browns, russets, and the fringed suede is often embroidered with little studs in a simple but beautiful design. There is much invention, but the interesting thing is that this man has gone his own way and created something without any mind to the public's reaction. He has done what he wants to do, and feels is fun to do. It gives him enjoyment and this germ spreads. It is this inspiration that keeps fashion from becoming static.

It is daring, refreshing, awful, mystic, wonderful. It has nothing really to do with Chelsea and Boutiques. It is of today, and today is more sombre and luxurious than yesterday. This strange creature has the gift to emanate the spirit of tomorrow.

The strength of his collection is masterly. He has the experience and authority not to mix too many elements in his choice. He takes a line and firmly develops variations around it, as a composer of music. The look is something that cannot easily be interpreted in drawing. I doubt if his designs create the atmosphere of the finished dress. Certainly the illustrations in the papers do not give a hint of this real germ of his invention.

Paris is full of dress talent. Grès[1] is still romantic and remarkable, Courrèges[2] goes in for his gym suits, but is now outshone by his disciple Ungaro,[3] and there are a number of clever young people who have

---

[1] Madame Grès (1903–93), opened her own house in 1942.
[2] André Courrèges (b. 1923), opened his own house in 1961.
[3] Emmanuel Ungaro (b. 1933), celebrated fashion designer, who founded his house in 1965. Now in Avenue Montaigne, Paris.

managed to throw over the old tenets and to forget the tenets of the older years. But here is something quite rare and utterly different, a young man who instinctively turns to a sort of beauty that has such strangeness in it, that it is difficult for most people to discard their old conceptions and accept the authority with which this innovator says to hell with sables, rich embroideries, glorious sables, and who finds poetry among the cowboys, and gypsy camp followers, the refined governesses.

Loel Guinness

He is rich. He knows how to look after his money. He knows how to spend it and he enjoys his life. He has known sadness, wives leaving him, his favourite son [Tara] killed, but he is as happy as a sand boy with his hobbies. His motor cars, jet aeroplanes, Rolls-Royce motor cars and his huge yacht. While staying the weekend at Piencourt, the ex-naval officer who looks after the estate said, 'Do you realise this costs you £400 a night!' Loel replied, 'Well, God knows what the yacht must cost then.' In addition Loel has a large apartment in Paris, a home in Lausanne, and in Palm Beach. I don't think it worries him that in order to save taxation he is only able to come for a few days to England.

A few little things impress me perhaps more than the big expenses (like the golf course which has taken a year to make etc., the new room built on and filled with newly acquired works of art). For instance, on a quiet Sunday morning I wake to look out of the window and find a man walking up and down the velvet of the croquet lawn pushing a machine to gather up every fallen autumn leaf. An old man was walking up and down the gravel drives rhythmically raking the stones into a geometrical pattern.

Cecil celebrated New Year's Eve at Monton with Philippe and Pauline de Rothschild.

1971

It was only three days ago that Smallpeice brought me to Salisbury station and now he was meeting me again for the weekend. How happy and relieved I was to be coming back to my Wiltshire home! The winter is being horrid. For days now a raw, cold fog has enveloped the countryside and although we notice the beginning of spring shoots, it is still deep dark winter. Nonetheless to come away from London is a benefice.

I was particularly relieved this time as I had awakened early to read the final chapter of my 'Aunt Jessie', so that it can now be retyped and sent to the publisher. The relief is gigantic. I have discovered that the headaches from which I have been suffering seem to vanish when I am not under pressure. If, as at Mouton, I spend the morning reading or writing diary, I am not afflicted later in the day with neuralgic pains over the left eye. But if I have to concentrate on my writing for more than two hours, I am likely to suffer. I put on a very good spurt of four hours before catching last Tuesday's train. I had to pay for this.

For most of my London visit I was working under the disadvantage of not feeling well. The photograph sitting with Julia Foster[1] of *Lulu* was such a strain that I felt the pictures would not be good, and when that night *The Duchess of Malfi* was being performed at the Court Theatre, the strain of sitting for three and a half hours was too great, and I caddishly made Felix Harbord[2] leave with me in the interval. The short London visit had its moments of pleasure, when Lee R [Radziwill][3] gave me her marvellous collection of dresses for the V & A, when the osteopath, Johnson, worked on my spine. There was an outrageous and amusing little dinner at David Somerset's, when talk was so outspoken that even I felt a bit shocked. No holds barred.

But we had arranged for many things to be done in such a short time and the strain was awful. It was not a very good birthday for me either. To read in the paper that I was 67 gave me a shock. One goes on floundering in a limbo of agelessness. If I was asked how old I felt I would admit to 37. I know that on seeing myself unexpectedly reflected in glass, the shock is awful. I know I am not able to do as much as I used to without total exhaustion, but I do not feel like an older man, do not think or behave like one. Sometimes there are sops to the birthday horror. Not

[1] Julia Foster (b. 1941), British leading lady, in *Half a Sixpence* (1967) with Tommy Steele.
[2] Felix Harbord (d. 1981), interior decorator, fond of theatrical effects, sometimes nicknamed 'Felix Cardboard'.
[3] Lee Radziwill (b. 1933), wife of Prince Stanislas Radziwill and sister of Jackie Onassis.

this time, merely avoidance, a lot of work, and no celebrations. Perhaps that is the best way.

Anyway, here I am in the country again, with an empty weekend in front of me, so that I can pick up threads, write this diary, and possibly do a lot of writing. But the pressure is off, and the house is filled with pink hyacinths in bowls, and I have lots to be thankful for.

Turandot   *January 1971*

Joan and Garrett [Drogheda][1] invited me to their box at the opera to hear Nilsson[2] in *Turandot*. I thought I would sit back and enjoy the production that I had designed ten years ago and for once have no feelings of responsibility towards it. I did enjoy the music. It swept over me like a tidal wave, and for several days afterwards was hearing it in my inner ear. Nilsson's voice seems as great as ever.

But the evening was disturbing for me since my work seemed so outdated. The impact had gone. There was no punch of surprise. I could understand the audience not reacting with fervour, Fulco [di Verdura], Brando[3] etc. in the audience, not even mentioning my work to me. The critics have never liked my work on this production and again talked of the 'restricting' first set being 'self-indulgent'. This I do not understand.

But I realise now that although it was hard work I did not do enough research. I did not dig deep enough. I relied upon a lot of facile gimmicks. These have been copied so many times since that the result no longer surprises. I remember when this production opened, Liz Hofmannsthal[4] sent me a cable to Hollywood saying, 'This is beauty.' I couldn't now see what she saw. But I am, as usual, being harsh on myself, for very few ballet décors remain valid after ten years. Picasso and Dérain are timeless. We lesser fry, working in this evanescent medium, have not got what it takes to produce something that is not only right for the moment, but is likely to last. It is as if one asked of a fashion designer to do something new that would remain fashionable for ever. I now see why ballet décors are redone every so often and I, unlike Oliver Messel, would not be hurt, for I know that most designers have a short run.

---

[1] Eleventh Earl of Drogheda (1910–89) and his wife the pianist Joan Carr (d. 1989). He was Chairman of the Royal Opera House, Covent Garden. They died within days of each other.
[2] Birgit Nilsson (b. 1922), Swedish operatic soprano.
[3] Brando Brandolini, Venetian count.
[4] Lady Elizabeth von Hofmannsthal (formerly Paget) (1916–80), daughter of sixth Marquess of Anglesey. One of the great beauties of the age. Maid of Honour to Queen Elizabeth at the Coronation (1937).

As I sat in the box I wondered how on earth I would set about doing the job today. It would be very different no doubt, but no inspiration springs to mind. Meanwhile I am going to try to make a few minor alterations.

Chanel died on 10 January 1971. Having reached the peak of fame in the 1920s, she became a living legend. She became the richest couturière in Paris. She retired in 1938, but made a spectacular comeback in 1954, introducing cardigan suits, pleated skirts, short chiffon dresses, neat blouses, and 'junk' jewellery. The Times stated that her success was 'the result of immense flair coupled with ruthless good taste'.

It was said that Chanel died in Paris and that her body was taken by car, propped up, as if alive, to die officially in Switzerland, in order to avoid the astringent death duties in France. Cecil had his own valedictory words.

Chanel

She will no longer make the effort to climb all those mirror-walled staircases to her atelier. She had gone on doing it, day after day for so long, that one thought perhaps she was, with the help of her doctors, able to continue for ever. Certainly, once she got to the top of those stairs, and started to work, the results were as vital and fresh as ever.

But suddenly Chanel is dead and one can no longer take for granted the fact that she is always with us to prove over and over again her great talent. For she was a genius to be able to prove herself right for such a long time. For fifty years she went on proving that her taste was impeccable, that she had a strong, daring, sure approach that made others fade into insignificance. Never anything extraneous and fussy, she believed in utter simplicity. She was a female Brummell. Just as the Beau got rid of frills and furbelows overnight, so too Chanel proved that nothing was more chic than fine linen, navy blue serge and lots of soap.

Not daring to speak French in front of her, I was not able, at the height of her allure, to get to know her, and she was very forbidding. But her appearance in the twenties and thirties was so unimaginably attractive. She was no beauty but by her allure she put all other women in the shade. She was unlike anything seen before. Even in old age, ravaged and creased as she was, she still kept her line. She was able to put on the allure. Most of the time she sat complaining in her rasping, dry voice.

Everyone except her was at fault. But you were doing her a service by remaining in her presence, for even her most loyal friends had been forced to leave her. You tried to leave too, for your next appointment. But she had perfected the technique of delaying you. Her flow of talk could not be interrupted. You rose from your seat and made backwards for the door. She followed, her face ever closer to yours. Then you were out on the landing and down a few stairs. The rough voice still went on. Then you blew a kiss. She knew now that loneliness again faced her. She smiled a goodbye, the mouth stretched in a grimace, but from a distance that grimace worked. It contained the old allure.

I found myself outside the shop a few weeks ago. I hadn't seen her since *Coco*. I thought I'd pay her a call. She was older-looking than ever. No gypsy has ever looked so old. The hair was like black wool, the eyes darkened on the lower lid, no make-up would remain on the dark skin. Her hands appeared enormous at the ends of such long, stringy arms. The chest was almost concave. She eats nothing and one feels it is only her spirit that keeps her going. Her servants and the others who work for her are cowed. But she knows that she will always continue to have the whip hand, and she wields the whip.

One can say horrid things about her. She was never a friend of mine, though I have known her for so long. But she never had any feelings of friendship for me, so I am not disloyal when I write of her venom, her lack of generosity and her disloyalty.

But these are apt to be failings that other women have. But Chanel had qualities and talents that are very rare. She knew she was exceptional, and she was. She was unfeminine in character but totally feminine in her attitudes to enticement. One felt she was not at all a physical type, yet she exuded sex appeal. She had an 'eye' to quality and proportion that was unbeatable. She had daring, freshness, authority, conviction. She had genius and all her faults must be forgiven for that one reason.

Broadchalke   *Monday, 18 January 1971*

So many humiliating things to suffer as a result of my operation. Due to the female hormones I have to take daily, my breasts have enlarged and the nipples are quite painfully delicate. I don't mind this much, as I have no desire left. I have had three unexpected wet dreams (one with a surprising emission, the others going in backwards!) but I have no lascivious thoughts and to add to my feeling of *éloignment* I am utterly mortified that my cock has shrivelled. There is hardly anything to take hold of when I pee (or as they said in *Steptoe and Son*, 'point Percy to the porcelain').

But this weekend (I am here alone tidying up lots of writing now that Jessie is through another phase) I have had to suffer another degradation. I woke up to find I had a low comedian's red nose. It was not sore, there were no signs of an oncoming boil. One side was worse than the other and slightly swollen. Ray and Mrs Smallpeice commiserated but couldn't help smiling at the same time. With age, all sorts of awful things appear. My forehead, chest and shoulders have broken out in huge freckled spots, and one toad-like mark appears under one eye with very bad results, but what if I have to go through the rest of my life with a drunkard's nose?

I still try to battle against all physical odds, and to try to wear clothes that are sufficiently attractive and unusual to take people's eyes off the horror they camouflage. And someone told me a day ago that I had been counted as one of the best-dressed in a 'list' compiled in the USA. But what's the point of my going over to Gillingham and ordering a new suit if it has to be worn with a cherry on the tip of my nose? Frank Tait very kindly motored over with a tube of unguent. He thought it was an infection below the skin and must be dispersed.

I have applied the grease all night long and have eagerly looked at myself each time I go to the bathroom. I don't know if it is too early days yet to report an improvement, but I have a suspicion that the schnozzle is slightly less red today.

My neuralgic headaches continue. If I read or write for more than two hours in the morning, at six o'clock in the evening I am burdened with this heavy pain over my left eye. I do not like taking aspirin and I'm afraid it may form a habit if I rely on it too much, but the result is that I have had to reserve my reading (and writing) entirely for 'Aunt Jessie'. There are a dozen books at the foot of my bed that I am longing to read, but I feel that my own work comes first.

However, in small doses, I have been picking up Lord Moran's diary about Churchill.[1] It is really a great document and very important historically. But the old man has got into very hot water for publishing it, has been cut at his club (and I believe he cares). It gives me another pause to wonder if I ought to go ahead and publish the Greta diaries. However, I think after this interval I have decided to do so, and must steel myself against adverse comment. Quite by accident (in order to look up something connected with 'Bolivian Aunt') I read my early Vol. I after an interval of five years. I was amazed to find how outspoken it was. No wonder my sisters got a bit windy at the prospect of Aunt Jessie! In one's youth one is apt to slash out left and right. I certainly did so, and anything I now write is mild in comparison.

I have also dipped into Harold Nicolson's Vol. III.[2] It does not come

---

[1] *Winston Churchill – the Struggle for Survival 1940–1965* (Constable, 1966). Lord Moran, Churchill's doctor, wrote, 'It is not possible to follow the last twenty-five years of Winston's life without a knowledge of his medical background.'
[2] *Harold Nicolson – Diaries and Letters 1945–62* (Collins, 1968), edited by Nigel Nicolson.

up to the others, but it is delightfully easy to read and golly he's not afraid of putting down the most trivial detail. It is perhaps going too far to say that he spent the evening looking at *Panorama* without saying what the subject was, but it inspires me to jot down a few of the things that happened to me during this very quiet and dull weekend.

Weather grey, misty, lifeless, rather too warm and damp.

Anne and Michael Tree brought their two children (adopted) to Sat. lunch. Ray was very pleased that on arrival in their shocking pink ponchos, they were told by Anne to say 'How do you do' and shake hands with Ray. I am tremendously impressed (as I am with Smallpeice's display of flowers – pink hyacinths, freesia, paper whites and Christmas roses in urns). It was such a wet, horrible morning that she had been prevented by downpour to go out into the garden but I thought it amusing that she gave me a very long description of the 'pathetic' little bunch of early flowers she intended bringing me as a belated birthday present. Ray produced stuffed pancakes with curry sauce, beef stew with carrots, artichokes, mashed potatoes and a marvellous pudding – half American cheesecake and half crème coeur. The children were disappointingly quiet, only 'got going' when told they couldn't talk or weren't being invited to have a certain food.

The beginning of a cold made me stay indoors and prevented me from sweeping up leaves. There are so many *still* to be made into valuable compost, and I decided the fog would be an excuse for my not going to Tania Stern's and my combined birthday party. The more valid reason being that I was 'imposing sanctions' against Jimmy Stern[1] for his unbearably selfish and rude behaviour when he came to lunch last Sunday, and kept us all guessing whose posthumous letters he was editing long after we had lost interest. In any case we did not know or care about John Davenport. He inflicted his sadistic attitude towards his wife by shooting her down by sarcasm or sheer contradiction each time she tried to express herself.

Since TV programmes are so bad on Saturdays, I took a chance on having a headache and read a piece on the delightful Victorian photographer, Paul Martin,[2] the result of clever research by a very nice young man, Mr Jay, who runs *Album* with Tristram Powell,[3] who has asked me to write an introduction. The photographs of Victorian children on the beach, watching Punch and Judy, picnicking in the rain, views of sea storms, a cottage, of lowlife of the city, are utterly delightful. When I had

---

[1] James Stern (1904–93), novelist and critic, and his wife Tania.
[2] Paul Martin (1864-1944), photographer. Photographed Queen Victoria's funeral (1901) and the Coronation of Edward VII (1902).
3 Tristram Powell (b. 1940), son of Anthony Powell, the novelist. Film director.

read this piece I turned on the TV and found, to my delight, that the late hours entertainment provide programmes of great interest. I have generally gone to bed by the time *Omnibus* or *Horizon* or whatever come on, but at 11 o'clock I found myself faced with Mick Jagger,[1] Schiele and the Norman Succession Show, my favourite William Rushton[2] and Jonathan Miller,[3] showing off his vast brain and knowledge of philosophy.

(While writing this, Mrs Stokes [Cecil's cleaner] came into my bedroom with an elevenses cup of coffee, and I wished to finish the paragraph without keeping her waiting too long – hence the worse than usual writing.)

Sunday

After I'd picked a bunch of white flowers for Frank Tait, I slept, until his car was outside. 'If red nose isn't better in three days, I'd go to your skin doctor,' he said. We gossiped about the Snowdons. He told me S. refused to have Pss. M. come but once to the nursing home, when he was being treated for piles. He wouldn't allow her to telephone (she is a born nurse and would have loved nursing him) and he was furious when the newspapers displayed the story of Lady Jackie R. Isaacs [Rufus-Isaacs],[4] who had visited him continually. Frank said he was appalled at S.'s bad behaviour to Pss.M. in public. She is miserable, but there is no possibility of a divorce.

Took Ray to the station in fog, returned to watch TV. The Anne Boleyn episode in the series on Henry's eight wives.[5] Old fashioned but gripping and [Dorothy] Tutin[6] always a good actress, very moving and convincing, a terrible glimpse of the brutality of the times. It was good to have one's history brought back to mind even in this popular form.

Cat on green velvet chair almost all day, went out for hunting or mice catching for a short sortie, then whines and scratches outside my door. I was pleased to find I had gone to sleep so quickly. The cat jumped on the bed, and we slept soundly till Mrs Stokes brought in the egg-laden tray at 8.30 with the newspapers filled with the usual terrible news and the prospect of there now being a postal strike. This is a disaster for the entire country.

[1] Mick Jagger (b. 1943), lead singer of the Rolling Stones. Knighted 2002.
[2] William Rushton (1937–96), actor, author, cartoonist and broadcaster.
[3] Jonathan Miller (b. 1934), stage director. Knighted 2002.
[4] Lady Jacqueline Rufus-Isaacs (b. 1946). Her name was publicly linked in the press with Lord Snowdon at this time.
[5] Popular TV series with Keith Michell as Henry VIII.
[6] Dame Dorothy Tutin (1931–2001), actress.

One joke

Mary P [Pembroke] and I laughed a lot on the telephone. She had been to pay a rare visit on the extremely forbidding mother-in-law [Beatrice, Countess of Pembroke]. For once Mary had 'really felt quite sorry for the old girl' for not only had her Italian couple left without a by your leave, or indeed a warning, but she had been pestered beyond endurance by a man who had spent a weekend at Wilton when a boy. He had been a school friend of Sidney's and asked home for the holidays. He had never recovered from this and all his life had sent letters to Lady P., accompanied by bottles of drink or other presents. Occasionally Lord P. would be the recipient of a whoopee-bed shout – 'A bottle of Dubonnet from Dickie Dormer!' 'Who's he?' 'The boy that came to stay during his school holidays thirty years ago.' 'And what are you going to do about it?' 'Drink it, of course, but I'm not going to thank him.'

Well, it seems that after Lord P. died, Lady P. would periodically receive telegrams, pages long, declaring his love for her. Recently the overtures had been revved up. More bottles of drink, more telegrams and more telephone messages. 'This is Dickie Dormer speaking from Buckingham Palace.' Sometimes he would appear on Lady P.'s doorstep. In fact he appeared yesterday. Lady P. had rung up to complain. 'There was this stranger on my doorstep,' she explained. 'Yes, we know that,' said the police. 'Mr Dormer came to us for your address.' 'Well, will you tell him not to bother me again.' The police explained to D. D. that Lady P. was now a very old lady, very easily upset. But D. D. had no intention of harming her. On the contrary he wants to marry her. 'Name the day,' he writes in a telegram. Long letters are sent about their honeymoon plans, accompanied by a bottle of the 'long' for her to toast their future happiness. I think perhaps she does wrong in ignoring him. She is very lonely and he might be a fourth at bridge or even give her an occasional game of Patience.

At last, after a four-month delay, the Harewood dinner took place. We had just the same food and company as we would have had that night, so long ago, when, at the last moment, I had to put them off, for I was feeling so ill. The Hs both quite relaxed, he very clear-skinned, bovine, acutely intelligent. She very bright, a bit common or is it merely Australian? The Julian Huxleys enjoyed themselves inordinately. It was their week for earlier on he had been given a gold medal for his work preserving wildlife. He can be a bore, talks without contradiction of his listener, but I had a quiet moment when he was fascinating about the habits and cleverness of birds. She is tremendously intelligent, intellectual, and as pretty as a periwinkle. June and Jeremy [Hutchinson] were as nice as only they can be, without airs, completely natural and without pretensions, so alert. Dicky B. [Buckle] a washout. The evening such a success that it lasted till midnight. I was still in a weak condition and tired out, and sad that I had to admit to myself that I was glad when the evening was over.

Jakie Astor[1] is the only one of the Astor sons who has inherited any of his mother's wit. He says really funny things very often. Dorothy Parker,[2] during her lifetime, made the wittiest remarks of all. (I particularly liked her opinions on a photograph of three elephants. One wore a top hat, another a bridal wreath and veil, a third a clerical collar. After looking at it for a few seconds, she said, 'I give it six weeks.') But for most of the time D. P. was sympathetic and sad, but never funny. Jakie keeps up a flow. Of his brother, Michael,[3] who has intellectual pretensions, Jakie said, 'To see him with the inties [intellectuals] is like seeing a dog reading *The Times*.' About the aquiline Mrs Wyndham, he said, 'Don't point your nose at me, it might go off.' Less good are his references to Michael's weddings. Re Barbara, who he had made enceinte, as Jakie as best man went up the aisle with his brother he asked, 'Is your journey really necessary?' And on his marriage to the third, Judy Innes, he said, 'Michael, you really must start to diet a bit. You don't want people to refer to you as Paunch and Judy.'

London   *Thursday, 28 January 1971*

We knew it would be a hectic day, as the time is short before starting on what might be a six-week holiday in South America. If I could get through all the appointments punctually, and generally they run over time, I would prefer to leave in the evening by the 6.10 from Waterloo and wake up to a new day in the country. The house has become a factory with Mrs Antrobus, the assistant to Eileen, Isabella the re-toucher, Karen, the Scandinavian daily, all running in circles. William J. to see me about the introduction to Paul Martin, and bringing a great pile of his snapshot albums, things of touching poetry.

Communications about plans, tickets, finishing touches for publication

[1] Hon. Sir John Astor (1918–2000), son of Nancy Astor, an MP in the 1950s.
[2] Dorothy Parker (1893–1967), American writer, poet and wit, at the centre of the Algonquin Round Table in New York.
[3] Hon. Michael Astor (1916–80). He married first Barbara McNeill (div. 1961), then Pandora Jones (div. 1968), then Judith Innes.

of *Bolivian Aunt* (Tony Godwin[1] has written a most amusing blurb). Lunch Proppers,[2] preliminary to photographing old Spanish husband, rather a beautiful Tintoretto face, but my body tired and aching.

Back to Pelham to find Eileen had brilliantly Sherlock Holmesed a young man to decorate the fashion exhibition for the V & A and that he was arriving immediately and at the same time as Anna Calder-Marshall, the very brilliant young actress who was so memorable as Sonya to Scofield's Uncle Vanya and it now to be Shaw's Cleopatra to Gielgud's Caesar. She is like a young calf and as such is beautiful, with dun-coloured hair and pale eyes. But today she was all masked eyes and dye for a hippie part, and not looking as she should. Also it was very disappointing to find that the very interesting and brilliant daughter of very intellectual parents should have acquired the breathless, over-enthusiastic projection act that is so ordinary and inevitable. But I had no time to get to know her. She listened to me with some interest and I hope to see her under less difficult conditions. Likewise Mr Haynes upstairs, for he seems to be a talented young (with it) artist.

Prints arrived for Isabella, very disappointing batch of Princess A [Alexandra], Then Bloggs, my old friend, now Lord Baldwin of Bewdley[3] arrived, his son, Lord Coverdale, and daughter-in-law, nice bright, clean young people, and the son has acquired many of his father's mannerisms and modes of speech. But whereas in the son it does not 'work' and appears pompous, in the father it appears refreshing and funny. 'A splendid man, a good fellow.' He gives to these phrases a new meaning. He would *pay* me for the photographs for, at the time of the marriage, they were *lavish*.

Bloggs is unique. I never see him, but each new meeting is like a tonic. When, after an appalling train journey, the engine ground to a halt at West Byfleet and we were more than an hour late, I arrived to find Bloggs had called, but would call again. Early morning and Bloggs to say he had seen me coming down the stairs, looking as tall and elegant and thin as ever. But when we sat and talked, he saw that the merriment had gone from my eyes, that I must have suffered a great deal as a result of my illness. He had not known, otherwise he would not have imposed on me to take these pictures. It was an effort that I was making and for that alone I would go straight to heaven.

He is a sincere and kind and wonderful man, and I am happy that he should consider me a friend.

---

[1] Tony Godwin, Cecil's editor at Weidenfeld & Nicolson.
[2] Eduardo Propper de Callejon, Spanish Ambassador in Washington, and his wife, Hélène ('Bubbles') Fould (1907–97), writer and artist, and grandmother of the actress Helena Bonham-Carter.
[3] Third Earl Baldwin of Bewdley (1904–76) and his son, later fourth Earl (b. 1938).

The relief at going to bed at last was one of the joys which become more acute as others fade.

I was saying how exasperating I found it that the Japanese, when embarrassed, took recourse to laugh. The more lost one's taxi driver becomes, the greater his inane laughter. Diana [Cooper] said, 'But I like the theory.'

What it costs to keep going! During the short midweek visits to London, I visit the doctor, the osteopath, Dr Johnson, and Charlotte [Gaffran] comes early morning to give me exercises and massage. This week I had also to visit McKenna, the skin specialist, who wanted to check up on the removal of a wart on my forehead. I showed him that a freckled blotch under one eye had not responded to his acid so he decided to freeze it off. Each time I go to see McKenna he congratulates me on my fortitude. He says so many of his patients carry on like stink while in the process of being put to minor disturbances.

But even I had qualms today, for while he was standing by my side preparing the electrical equipment with which to needle me, he was unable to fit in a large-sized bulb, so had to substitute it for another. As he unscrewed the bulb, it exploded with the most shattering report, a whiff of smoke and a storm of broken glass. I felt rather pleased with myself for not remarking, 'What a good thing that did not happen while the thing was on my face.' The incident was soon forgotten but it did lead me to realise how lucky I had been to avoid such a nasty accident.

Amazing how freshly one enjoys everything on the return to Reddish after only two days in London. During the interval all seems renewed. Sometimes the house seems less well-warmed, but there are always things to be done to give it life, and I enjoy these things, putting a few books about, bringing in the plants from the winter garden. Mrs Smallpeice has the delightful habit of finding what flowers there may be to put on the dining table and also at the bedside. These give me great joy. My London clothes are thrown on to the bathroom chairs in exchange for leather and corduroy, and the garden always presents some innovation.

After this week in London culminating in the awful train journey, the reveille in the country was particularly pleasant. The greatest joy was to see, from my bed, reflected in the glass of one of my framed Hockneys a moving procession of white and pink flowers. It was not someone going to Covent Garden market, but Mr and Mrs Smallpeice bringing in all the new bulbs for the weekend guests' enjoyment, and for mine. And they were happy too, for they were the produce of the new glass house, and bigger and better hyacinths and sweeter Roman hyacinths one has never smelt. As for the freesias!

Cecil had a particularly difficult friend in Sir Francis Rose, a painter and baronet,[1] who was a friend of Gertrude Stein and the inspiration for her saying 'Rose is a rose is a rose'. He was a mercurial character, blessed with an exotic background and an inherited fortune, but cursed by a fatal strain of self-destruction. A childhood friend of Sarah Bernhardt and later of Isadora Duncan, he smoked opium with Cocteau in his youth and burst to short-lived fame in a retrospective he shared with Salvador Dalí in Paris in 1938.

Rose soon lost most of his fortune to a swindler boyfriend and disposed of what was left on the green baize of the casino. There was a drunken stoker boyfriend who jumped from a window and perished in his arms; Rose himself was said to have been in the bed of Ernest Roehm in Munich in 1934, when Hitler rounded up the dissidents.

Many years later the actor Timothy West recalled him as a figure in Brighton, in scarlet-lined opera cloak. Rose was commissioned to design The Trigon, *and would appear and 'suddenly spin out of control and he would squeal exotic obscenities at all and sundry'. When they opened in Wimbledon, Rose arrived on the set with three canvases and had to be restrained from going on stage to hang them as the audience were already seated.*

When, inevitably, penury arrived, Rose would turn up on Cecil's doorstep at Pelham Place, demanding the wherewithal to survive. (When Cecil gave him an old suit, he would boast, 'I have the same tailor as Sir Cecil.') Of Rose, Cecil wrote, 'His life is a long succession of suicides, killings, fatal accidents. In his wake, he brings chaos'. He was apparently twice married, his second wife being the travel writer Dorothy Carrington (who specialised in the history of Corsica and died in 2002).

Francis Rose   *February 1971*

For long periods one does not hear anything of Francis Rose. After some awful crisis he has got married and there is silence until the marriage breaks disastrously. Then he is begging on one's doorstep. A few months ago he had sunk to the depths of the Portobello Road. He was without money. Then silence. A priest in Wales wrote to say that he was in his cottage, ill, penniless and in need of friends. I sent £20 to be doled out in small sums. Suddenly Francis reappeared in London. He had been robbed. The £20 and his return ticket to Wales had gone.

Again he was on the doorstep and violent this time. Acquaintances said he had been arrested for being drunk and disorderly. After two days the case was dismissed. I would give him the return ticket to Wales but nothing

---

[1] Sir Francis Rose (1909–79).

more. It was disastrous, it was cold. Francis had nowhere to go and Eileen, from upstairs, during a staff party, watched him lurch down the street.

A week later he was back in Wales and we read he had thrown bricks through church windows in order to be arrested and have a roof over his head. He was remanded, dismissed. He came to London again, banged furiously on the door, after an abusive scene with Ray (I was away). Later more banging and a note put through the door for me to tell me he had never thought that I would not open up to him and that he was going to commit suicide, leaving me his heir.

I was very worried when I returned and Eileen told me that the solicitor had rung up, that Francis was in his room (Eileen could hear him talking non-stop) and that although eccentric, Francis was not insane and would be calmed if I would say that I could speak to him on the telephone that evening. I worked myself up into a nervous state and each time the bell rang for Ray, I was convinced it would be a final call from Francis. Ray said he thought Francis would be drinking away the £5 given to him by me earlier in the day and would forget to telephone. But Ray's instinct was wrong for once.

After a quiet and agreeable evening talking about painting with Patrick Procktor, I came up to bed. The bell rang by my bedside. It was Francis's very quiet, serious voice that I listened to. He was going to kill himself tomorrow afternoon. He would go to the National Gallery to look at the portrait of his ancestor (who?) and would do it there. He was leaving notes to all the press saying that my name was not to be mentioned but that I was his heir. He could not, at his time of life, endure such an experience as spending a night out of doors in the cold. He had lain on a platform seat. He had no regrets of dying. He had been very much loved, but he was not afraid of death and quite happy to go. It was not 1880, or even 1930, and it was legal to kill oneself. I would find that he was leaving me much of value, his pictures, books, bits of jewellery, and that in 20 years' time a great fortune would come from Spain and he wished me to make a trust for promising young artists.

It was very disturbing to hear about the end of his life and as he talked on quite calmly, I could hear a male voice shouting at him to hurry up with the phone. 'Where are you talking from?' I asked. 'A hotel.' 'The one where you are staying in Bloomsbury?' 'No, one where they don't charge me for the call.' Francis said that I was the one person he had always loved, not sexually of course, and that there was Bob whom he loved now most of all. But I had been the one person in his life that he could rely on. There was no time for me even to wonder how I had got involved with F.

I never liked him. From the first meeting I found him revolting. He is not a nice character. He does have a certain genius and a flair for beauty in its most rare forms. But I don't know how it is that he has become for forty years my great cross.

At last I was able to ask if he didn't think it would be a good idea to wait a few days before doing something so definite? No, his friend Bob was in hospital with only four months to live and Francis wished to go first. 'But if you delay something so disastrous?' 'How can I live? I have no money and I'll be out on the streets if I don't pay the hotel £12 by tomorrow morning.' 'If it's a question of £12 I'll help you.' 'But what about my solicitor, and I have to have food, and if I go to a monastery, there would be £10 a week to pay.' 'Well, come and see me tomorrow morning, Francis, after I've seen my publishers.'

Francis, after all he has been through, looked quite a great character, in a strange hat, with long hair, a brilliant shirt, a paste brooch and my old grey suit. He talked quietly for an hour, giving his version of what had happened during the last two months. The Father Beddoes was his enemy and would not live long. He was a wicked man. Black magic was involved. I could not understand much of what Francis was telling me, but he did not allow me to interrupt. 'Francis, two women are arriving for a business talk in ten minutes. Will you please let me ask you what you need, though I can't afford to keep you.'

Eileen, poor girl, of course got involved. Arabella von Hofmannsthal[1] arrived and gave Francis an address where he could sell some trinkets. I gave him another fiver and a cheque for his hotel and for his will. He hurried off down the street in the pale winter sun, looking like Verlaine. I was worried so that I felt very fraught all day and knew I would have one of my bad headaches, as indeed I did. But Francis did not telephone to say he had decided to keep up the fight for life, though how on earth he is going to be able to live, for not only will he not help himself, but he is no longer able to earn his keep, so the inevitable faces him, and for me the awful shock that his threats *have* been carried out and that he has succeeded in some devious way of making one feel responsible.

Bertie Abdy[2]

I was at home at Pelham, as I have been each night this week, and was looking at the latest volumes of the Wrightsman collection,[3] when most suitably Bertie Abdy telephoned. This delightful man was suddenly

---

[1] Arabella von Hofmannsthal (b. 1942), daughter of Raimund von Hofmannsthal and his second wife, Lady Elizabeth Paget. Divorced wife of Piers von Westenholz.
[2] Sir Robert Abdy, fifth Baronet (1896–1976), very rich art dealer.
[3] *The Wrightsman Collection Catalogue, Vols III & IV: Furniture, Goldsmith's Work and Ceramics*, ed. by Sir Francis Watson (1970).

telling me about how incredible butterflies were, that some had antennae that could spot out love 25 miles away. He went on to talk about Maeterlinck, who told us so much about bees and other insects he had known, who had lived in great splendour near him at St Germain. 'But how did he afford such splendour?' I asked. 'Oh, you've no idea how his books sold and in those days, authors really made money. Do you realise that Kipling made one million pounds out of *Kim*?'

Early in 1971 Cecil returned to New York, on his way to Brazil

New York   *13 February 1971*

New York isn't what it used to be. Neither am I! The excitement of arrival has gone, now this afternoon almost relief that there were no unforeseen disasters. We waited one hour at the start of the journey at Heathrow for our turn in the air traffic, having been searched for bombs. We were not hijacked. The arrival was quite peaceful and quick. No complaints. But instead of the old thrill of being greeted with sparkling sun and electric atmosphere, it was a dull day, grey, abnormally cold, and there was comparatively little traffic about. Somehow I felt the recession may be just imagination, but maybe the sparkle had gone out of me.

My arrival was sadly automatic. I went up to my rooms. They looked quite pretty, having been freshly painted, and started 'getting in touch'. But the telephone system has gone to pot, and the reserves of energy were soon exhausted. I slept. I wondered if I would recover sufficiently to go to a play, but I was past that. Later someone asked me to go to a supper party for Nureyev,[1] Jackie Onassis[2] and gang at the de Cuevas house. It would have been an amusing thing to do, but I was past it. The last few weeks I have been an invalid, and the days spent in the air and in a new atmosphere might help. I turned off the telephone at an early hour and spent the night watching the hours go by. It was very relaxing and peaceful.

Baffling number of impressions have gone through my head since arrival yesterday afternoon. Little wonder that I am tired and the fact that snow was on its way gave me a baffling headache. The first morning's telephoning is always an event. I got bits of news from old friends, Anita

---

[1] Rudolf Nureyev (1938–93), brilliant, dissident Russian dancer, who defected to the West in 1961.
[2] Jacqueline Onassis (1929–94), widow of President John F. Kennedy and, later of the Greek shipping tycoon, Aristotle Onassis.

Loos, who told me that Tom Wolfe's *Radical Chic*[1] was a milestone. Ruth Gordon[2] here to be photographed for *Vogue* at the age of 75, gyrates as if listening to a way-out pop group and uses all the teenage phrases. She is flapped and flipped and everything is groovy. Her performance is so slick that now she listens to nobody. Everyone enjoys the hot ticket *Nanette* revival,[3] because it seems the audience gives such a great performance. Some don't like Brook's *Midsummer Night's Dream* (which got epoch-making raves) and the recession is not called a depression but people talk of tight money.

Travel and luxury restaurants have suffered whatever you call it and the future with smog, crime and greater taxation seems very bleak. I went to the [Gertrude and Leo] Stein family show, a miraculous collection when you think that no big money man paid for anything. Poor Francis Rose not included. Vultures for culture in expensive clothes there in their thousands. Beautiful exhibitions of Walker Evans[4] and at Doubleday great books on Lartigue,[5] and the Stein collection, and more pictures than I've ever seen before of Garbo in a $40 book on four beautiful cinema faces.

Cecil then saw Truman Capote, the wickedly provocative genius of a novelist, who sprang to fame with Other Voices, Other Rooms *in 1948 and went on to write* Breakfast at Tiffany's *and* In Cold Blood. *Cecil had encouraged him as a young man and introduced him to England, but later felt let down by him, for two reasons, his great success with* In Cold Blood *and the damage this did to Capote's character, and his betrayal of those who had befriended him, such as the William Paleys in* Answered Prayers. *By this time Capote was an outcast, depending heavily on alcohol and other stimulants.*

Unexpected dinner with Truman and an unknown anonymity [Danny][6] who (surprisingly) paid the Lafayette bill. T. a bit bothered, said he was

---

[1] *Radical Chic* (1970) by the brilliant American writer Tom Wolfe (b. 1931).
[2] Ruth Gordon (1896–1985), American actress, remembered for the films *Rosemary's Baby* and *Harold and Maud*. Quick to write memoirs of friends who died, to the point that Noël Coward said he dared not die 'for fear of the file marked C coming down from above the bed'.
[3] *No, No Nanette* was a huge success in New York in 1971, starring Ruby Keeler, Patsy Kelly, Jack Gilford, Bobby Van, Helen Gallagher, with Susan Watson as Nanette.
[4] Walker Evans (1903–75), photographer of Negroes and architecture, much encouraged by Lincoln Kirstein.
[5] Jacques-Henri Lartigue (1894–1986), French photographer, best known for romantic images of *belle époque* France
[6] This is one of the 'men without faces' – boyfriends of Capote, who passed through his life at that time. He was disguised as 'Danny' – see Gerald Clarke's *Capote: A Biography* (1988), pp. 419–28. The above description of him is Capote fiction.

not well, and had been in and out of hospital, and did not believe in psychoanalysis which he'd tried in vain. He was drinking less and seemed less socially orientated, which is a good sign, and made me curb my harsh criticism of his recent outpourings in the press about Mrs Jackie and other unworthy subjects.

Truman telephoned to ask what I thought of [Danny]. I said I'd never been more surprised than when he paid our bill. 'But he's a tycoon. At 32 he has 12? 30? factories making a sort of parachute stuff.' He's a big timer, being very kind and given T. a Mercedes. As a result of which T. thought he must go to bed with the boy. It was quite a success but T. thinks he will now call the whole thing off by degrees. I thought the boy just a nice young Jewish student.

5 February 1971

Captain Shepherd,[1] considered an old man at 27, walked or worked on the moon today. I felt, in the St Regis, before the impetus of my usual NY existence had started to build, like someone in outer space. The early morning was sinisterly quiet and fears of the worst weather were proved hideously correct. A combination of ice, snow, sleet and fog. Very few people abroad, and I remained quietly in my room when suddenly the bell broke out on the telephone and people invaded the suite with instructions of redecorating the rooms.

A new tourists' camera arrived, air tickets for Palm Beach, and theatre tickets. Lunch interval, my old friend Eleanor Lambert,[2] who is bright and appreciates wit but presents everything in such halting dullard terms that the result is boredom. How different from my evening with Lincoln K [Kirstein].[3] He asked me to dine at his downtown house, where I have not been for so many years. I imagined a vast joint of beef or a turkey served by a coloured Massine.[4] But Massine has got old and spasmodically ill, so instead Fidelma, the wife, who has also got *terribly* old and grey and small and thin, prepared 3 trays while Lincoln talked non-stop about his likes and violent dislikes (K. Clark among the latter) and his reaction to everything he has seen in every form of creative activity. No one has such energy.

[1] Captain William M. Shepherd (b. 1944), NASA astronaut, who had spent 159 days in space.
[2] Eleanor Lambert (b. 1903), widow of Seymour Bergson (d. 1959), born in Indiana, founded Coty Awards and Council of Fashion Designers of America. Established best-dressed women list 1941; still running her own PR business.
[3] Lincoln Kirstein (1907–96), founder of the New York City Ballet.
[4] Léonide Fedorovich Massine (1895–1979), dancer, choreographer, ballet master and teacher.

He sees all plays, films, ballets. Tonight he was excoriating Ken Russell's *Tchaikovsky* film as the worst ever, and from a master too. He took me to the ballet and said there were two promising dancers: Massine's son, also a choreographer, and John Clifford,[1] who indeed proved himself like a cricket. His movements quite unlike any other dancer. He is very young and easily upset, but when 'boos' were heard after he'd done a cowboy dance, he brushed them aside saying they came from people who'd refused to go to bed with him. The nicest dancer of the troupe, Anthony Blum,[2] who is intelligent, enthusiastic, but unfortunately looked a bit like A. Armstrong-Jones, has been through a trauma experience. His mother, a nymphomaniac, was found in her apartment by her son, lying on her bed, having been raped, then gashed with knives and her head cut off.

Lincoln steadfastly refuses all society life, spends little money on himself, but fortunes on philanthropic schemes, and for the arts. The New York City Ballet is of his creation and although he is a pessimist (and the two ballets we saw were very old hat and tepid) it must be marvellous for him to see what he has built, a company that fills that vast theatre for forty weeks in the year. It is under the direction of Balanchine[3] who seems to be in his prime. Tonight his lips and cheeks were so pink that he looked as if he were wearing make-up, but no, the everlasting youthfulness is natural and his vitality is unimpeded. He exuded electricity as he railed against this evening's assistant conductor, taking the *Tchaikovsky Suite No. 3* so fast, then with equal zest described the various wines of Bordeaux that he preferred. I was not impressed by his protégé Massine and thought him a fatuous bore when he asked, 'And do you like vin rosé?'

Truman   *February 1971*

Later. Sunday morning is a great telephone marathon, at last an opportunity to ask T. about his 'troubles', leading to nervous breakdowns. T. found himself more in love with [Danny] than anyone he had ever known, a mixture of physical attraction and nostalgia for the type he had liked as a boy. Sex plus nostalgia reduced him to a state of such misery that a psychiatric doctor had to come to him, as he lay jittering in a bed, and take him to a hospital for five weeks. The breakdown attacked his central nervous system so that his whole body shook and he could not

[1] John Clifford (b. 1947), dancer and choreographer.
[2] Anthony Blum (b. 1936), principal dancer with the New York City Ballet.
[3] George Balanchine (1904–83), American dancer and choreographer.

hold a glass of water. He gave up smoking as he couldn't keep a cigarette in his mouth. He recovered, he went back to Palm Springs, continued his 'affair' with [Danny], then suddenly left again. He had a psychiatric breakdown. Far worse. He is still battered, unable to work. He must see his doctors twice a week. But he says he could never have imagined it happening to him. It has been the greatest emotional impact and he thinks it will take him a year to recover.

Saturday, 6 February 1971

Charles Biasiny,[1] my clever assistant, roared with laughter when I told him I wanted to buy an 'instamatic' camera and simplify life. I thought he was as amused as Liberman[2] who had thought it a great sale, but no, it was a corroboration of his own feelings about photography at the moment that amused him. He too had felt there were too many gadgets, lenses, too much technicality. He too wanted to get rid of the 'bullshit' and just take tourists' equipment with him everywhere. I was delighted to find how simple the camera is in design and trust great things may come of it. I am sick of getting results that are not 'spot on'. Charles said he was thinking of giving up photography in NY and going to live in the country to have bees and animals, and possibly raise a family.

Almost everyone I know seems to want to get the hell out, including Bob LaVine, who got attacked by three thugs who broke the nose of his friend, B [Bob] Prairie. When the three were had up in court in front of witnesses, it came to light that they already had three convictions for brutality and violence. Yet the judge dismissed them with a warning. The prisons are full up. NY City is pretty unattractive.

I used to love going to Hamburger Heaven but when I went with Bob L. prior to a matinée it seemed squalid beyond enjoyment.

It was wonderful to see *Midsummer Night's Dream* here in NY. The Peter Brook production still held its magic, though of course the initial impact of this marvellously original production wears thinner. But Shakespeare is at the fore, and it is good to see something first rate when surrounded by such trash as one is here. My mood was a bit restless and the audience coughed insistently [*sic*] but I admired most of the performances more than ever, Theseus, Oberon, being particularly real and impressive and his asides about players and reality deftly pointed.

---

[1] Charles Biasiny-Rivera, apprentice to Cecil, went on to work in magazine and fashion photography, now director of En Foco Inc.
[2] Alexander Liberman (1912–99), Managing Director of Condé Nast and photographer in his own right He was later responsible for ousting Diana Vreeland from the editorial chair at *Vogue*.

What a contrast to see the hot ticket revival of *No, No, Nanette*. This has created such a furore that the audience, overexcited, makes the evening by applauding before the highlights begin. I never liked Ruby Keeler[1] in her heyday forty years ago, but it was an extraordinarily moving experience to see her doing the same thing today. Her hair is still shingled, though grey, her legs as pretty, though the body is a bit thick, but it is riveting to see her facial expressions, the way of opening her wistful eyes, pouting, or opening her mouth in wonder, throwing back a stray lock of hair with a large well-bred hand, with fingers that were such an innate part of the dance that she went into, with fingers bent back-wards and thumb sticking out like a curvy banana. It was such a surprise to find her being able to dance so diligently with such lightness and style. It was so absolutely of her epoch, so real, that one could not but admire and respect her. The fact that she was a suburban housewife today and was able to go into these routines without any humour, always serious, made the performance utterly endearing. I found myself weeping (though this may be due to my being overtired and nervously depleted). The show is *awful*, but there is dancing on a large and wonderful scale, and we have missed this. Busby Berkeley[2] gave the girls real 'period' style. Today's young choreographers know nothing of yesterday. The sets were art deco and with the exception of Act II, surely the ugliest thing one has ever seen, they afforded one great interest. But the costumes were hideous and completely lacked the allure that every period possesses. Still, an evening's entertainment with marvellous songs and Helen Gallagher[3] and a young string bean named Van,[4] who danced like an angel.

A mainstay of Cecil's New York life was the legendary editor of Vogue, *Diana Vreeland. Until her enforced retirement from the editorial chair, she bombarded Cecil with exciting commissions, sending him off in quest of elusive ballerinas, curious locations and other assignments, always original. She lived in an apart-ment on Park Avenue, with her dining room/drawing room decorated by Billy Baldwin to resemble 'a garden from Hell'. Here sat Vreeland, with her black lacquered hair, invariably adorned in 'pants' and pullover, with sharp jewellery, her vodka glass in one hand, her cigarette in a holder in the other, contemplating the world and expressing her opinions in her unique idiom. She was famed for*

---

[1] Ruby Keeler (1909–93), diminutive singer and dancer, who went a long way on a small talent. Appeared in films of *42nd Street* (1933) and *Dames* (1934), among many others.
[2] Busby Berkeley (1895–1976). Best known for magnificent precision dance routines in Warner Brothers films in the 1930s and also briefly an important figure on Broadway. Supervised the revival of *No, No, Nanette* in 1970.
[3] Helen Gallagher, dancer, who performed in *Pal Joey* (1952), *Anything Goes* (1953), and later *Tallulah* (1983).
[4] Bobby Van (b. 1930), song-and-dance man, who later made his name in television.

her epigrams, once declaring 'These girls... If they've got long arms, long legs and a long neck, everything else kind of falls into place.'

Sunday, 7 February 1971

Sunday lunch at Vreeland's. I'd hoped It would be *à trois* with Penelope Tree, but found Fred Brisson would also be there. I arrived to find a group. I told Diana of my disappointment that the Moreira Salleses[1] would not be in Brazil as they had come to New York hospital with their son [Peter] whose leg has become putrefied. Diana looked deeply grieved. 'I've had a terrible morning of bad news. Leland Hayward's[2] had a terrific operation on his brain and is trying to get out of bed and come here. Penelope has a temperature of 104.' We sat down to lunch, telephone, a maid put the message at the table. 'May I borrow your glasses?' D. read, 'Peter (Mrs G. Miller's butler) found dead at bottom of swimming pool this morning.' Each time the telephone rang, Fred B., not the most tactful or sensitive of people, would say, 'Another death.'

The stories he told of K. Hepburn on tour are unimaginable, and even her best friend, Michael Benthall,[3] before leaving, told Fred that the only place for her was Bellevue Hospital in a straitjacket. When Freddie announced the death of Chanel, K. H. responded by asking how the weekly takings were.

New York   *February 1971*

Decided to be extravagant, so hired a limousine from the hotel to take me to the airport via the Met Museum, here to report on the plastic cases in which the masterpieces of the world are shown. Very beautiful and impressive variety of objects, unimaginatively shown. Once more in my lifetime, took the plane to Palm Beach, luckily not realising a hurricane warning had gone out. We bumped, but avoided the bulk of the storm, and arrived in a

---

[1] Walter Moreira Salles (1912–2001), Finance Minister under João Goulart 1961–2, banker and twice Brazilian Ambassador to Washington in the 1950s. He founded Unibanco (the fourth largest bank in Brazil) in 1975, played a major role in the negation of Brazil's debt, sometimes described as 'the richest man in Brazil'; and his beautiful second wife Elizhina, later divorced. She claimed poverty despite a huge settlement and jumped to her death from a window. Their son, Walter, is a brilliant film director in Hollywood.
[2] Leland Hayward (1902–71), agent and film producer, married to Pamela Churchill (later Mrs Averill Harriman).
[3] Michael Benthall (1919–74), opera, theatre and ballet director. Artistic director of the Old Vic for nine years.

rain-sodden, untidy Palm Beach. It looked its worst, particularly since the 'recession' has also hit it. Shops empty, not nearly so many visitors. Aimée de Heeren,[1] an all-out hostess, no detail is spared by her, she is good, warm, beautiful, a character, and talks non-stop. I was allowed very little time in my room for on arrival at badly kept house (such a contrast to the Ws! [Wrightsmans]), Mrs Rose Kennedy[2] was on the telephone, to know if she should wear false eyelashes. Obviously she wanted a lot of reassurance. She giggled when I told her not to get flustered.

Never have I felt my age more or in a less good state of health than in comparison to Aimée, who was a tornado giving help to untalented but willing Portuguese-speaking servants. All the old Palm Beach names made me realise that it is a lifetime since I first came here, yet it still has the rich spending enough to make it a magnet for the likes of me. A lot of the old names came to dinner. With what joy I went to bed, knowing I could sleep late.

And I did. So that by the time I'd prepared my cameras and was about to get in the bath, the Kennedy car was at the door. Mrs K. with eyelashes (I'd told her not to add any) greeted me in silver. She showed off dozens of dresses for me to choose and was upset that she had no new ones for her pictures. She is publicity mad and thrilled to appear for the first time in *Vogue*. She is an old toughie, treated her secretary pretty severely and was a blockbuster to direct. But we got on well together, and she was grateful for suggestions and my patience. Two and a half hours all out. Every sort of picture. (Would they come out? I always have this agony.) Complete exhaustion as Aimée would not let me be, wanted advice about gardens and deposition of pictures, objets etc. indoors. Without a rest, had to go to 'Wrightsmans' Residence', Jayne, in a head scarf, had obviously just had her face lifted. She was without lines, smooth, shiny and appeared siliconed up to the eyes. However, I don't think it's a bad job, probably an improvement. Charles ill upstairs. The house has lost its point as the good things have gone and she's now gone in for cottons. It's neither one thing nor another. The faux Louis furniture is appalling. I too tired to enjoy, luckily slept before dinner, but the prospect of taking plane at Miami at 2.30 a.m.! The trip most exhaustingly arranged, could have flown direct to Rio, instead of jig-jagging to Panama, Peru etc.

To add to the exhaustion, bad weather in the mountains around Quito delayed us by two and a half hours. I feel I'll never get to Rio.

The journey made me wonder once again at Aunt Jessie's patience and endurance. We eventually flew over La Paz and Titicaca but the clouds

---

[1] Aimée de Heeren, Brazilian with homes in Biarritz, Paris, New York and Palm Beach.
[2] Rose Kennedy (1890–1995), widow of Joseph Kennedy and mother of President John F. Kennedy, and Senators Robert and Edward Kennedy. She died aged 104.

prevented any but a sudden glimpse of the vast craters. In fact bad weather made a bad trip horrid. We bumped and banged intermittently and when night-time and a storm came on at São Paolo I thought we'd crash. The others in the plane, mostly young and to do with airlines, kept up a continual noise and seemed cheerful. I read Tom Wolfe, Mainwaring and Segal's *Love Story*,[1] which by the last page succeeded, as with God knows how many million others, in jerking out the tears. Thank heavens that Walter M. Salles sent his nice secretary Maria to help with customs and Julio [Senna] was at the airport. I came through the night to the Copacabana apartment in a daze of fatigue.

Cecil had hoped that Walter Moreira Salles would oversee his stay. While he benefited from his hospitality, he was left in the care of the interior decorator, Julio Senna, a then fashionable figure in Rio, who had worked on at least one of Walter Moreira Salles's houses. Julio made many plans for Cecil, some of which worked and some of which did not. There was a lavish dinner at Julio's house, during which the decorator declared that he had been trying to get Cecil to Rio for twenty-five years.

Next day, at lunch, Julio enthused about his party. He 'made a great ploy of the difficulties of eating a mango. It is the messiest business and must be done elegantly. He has a childlike – is it Brazilian sense of humour? – and tears rolled out of his eyes at the idea of serving only mangoes to the women at last night's party, which he confided consisted of the crème de la crème.'

There were one or two surprises in store for Cecil, one of which occurred on 12 February, soon after his arrival, in his hotel room:

I started to read *Kim* for the first time and no sooner was I engrossed than my dinner arrived. As I sat drinking coffee, I picked up a 'coffee table' book on Casanova and dipped into some racy pieces from his memoirs. Unexpectedly the telephone rang. The rasping voice of a child trying to speak English asked if Mr Moreira Salles was there. (It had called two days ago and I said he was away in NY.) 'Ooh is spikking?' the voice asked. 'I'm a friend. My name is Beaton.' 'What nem?' When I repeated it, the voice asked, 'Not Cesshuhl Beaton?' 'Yes,' I confessed. 'Oh 'ow nice?' I was surprised that she had ever heard of me. Instead of hanging up, I explained I did not know when Mr M. S. would be back, that he was now in NY etc.

This morning I was very amused by Julio telling me how Brazilians love to fuck. To explain this he put the tips of his first fingers and thumbs together and pressed them tight to make an imitation cunt. It had given

---

[1] *Love Story* by Erich Segal, later a popular film starring Ryan O'Neal and Ali McGraw, which does not pass the test of time.

me quite a shock. Now I had been let into one of Walter's secrets, and I was amused to think of this quiet, gentle little man having these late night calls. The rasping childlike voice continued, 'I'm in Room 6 Ohrr 7 in this hotelle and I've got a friend here who would like you to come down and have some champagne.' I panicked. I talked very fast knowing that the poor creature could not understand me, but I could think of no excuse. I was going out, was here with friends, I was ill, I was in bed, I must go now. The call made me realise how completely homosexual I have become, how undaring and unversed I am in the ways of the world.

To begin with I would be appalled at the prospect of being 'gypped', of having to pay a great sum of money for something so alien to my nature. When I say that I have few extravagances in my life, to the list of negations I should add that of women, who cost most men a very great deal. Here was I, pushing 70, feeling like an abashed student on account of a telephone call from a no doubt well-meaning, wide-eyed little bit of fluff, who in astonishment realised I wanted none of her and in a friendly, baby voice, said, 'Well, bye-bye!' I can smile at myself now a little while later, but I realised how very unlike I was to the book I was reading. Casanova's adventures no longer amused me. I went to bed.

Cecil was partly in Brazil to relax and gain strength after his operation of the previous year. The next days were filled with expeditions and parties, and he was pleased when the Ambassador wanted to meet him.

'The British Ambassador has come specially to meet you.' With an armoured car in front of his Rolls, Sir David Hunt and his Greek wife[1] arrived very late, a very straightforward, uncut diamond, he talked about his sister in Croydon, and his only recent study of South America. We talked of the Avons and I left the lunch party at six o'clock. A whole day given over to it. But I did not complain to Julio for I am on vacation and have nothing to do but try to get my health back, and today had not been tiring and the waterfall made me very sleepy and full of well-being.

Another quiet evening in hotel room. A mouse scurried behind the radiator as I came into the sitting room for dinner and the telephone rang. But I was terrified that it was Walter's little tart downstairs, so left it unanswered.

Cecil attended mass, and went to Brasilia in a private plane. Presently Walter Moreira Salles arrived from New York. Because he was a rich man, Salles had to have a bodyguard. Cecil noted, 'It is perhaps typical that when we came out

---

[1] Sir David Hunt (1913–98), Ambassador in Brazil 1969–73, author and winner of *Mastermind* 1977, and *Mastermind of Masterminds* 1982; and his second wife, Iro Myrianthousis, married in 1968.

into the night to go home, bodyguard and chauffeur were nowhere to be found.'
The next days contained varied experiences:

19 February 1971

Luncheon at the British Embassy, and impressive too, as it should be.
The decorations are awful, pretentious without being amusing, and the
colours just wrong, but the replica of an Adam house done twenty years
ago is certainly well designed and convenient for living and entertainments. The Office of Works have supplied excellent 1800 silver and the
V & A lent a wonderful Dutch tapestry. The present Ambassadress is
perhaps responsible for the presence of artificial flowers in huge urns and
in fountains, and when she produced her own paintings one realised the
full impact of her lack of taste.

The Ambassador, David Hunt, held the very difficult party together
(eight very mixed types) and gave it any life he has (his wife certainly
helped very little). He was full of statistics, dates, figures, facts, and interesting information, and could relate funny stories. He was, it would
appear, at the height of his powers, enjoying his job and his health and
accumulated knowledge. He talked with great vividness of the recent kid-
nappings and the dangers of the experience of the American diplomat,
who, after 40 days in a cell, was released to come and take refuge here.

The cheek of Julio! Some woman comes up to him at the party and asks if
Mr Beaton would like to come to her gala tomorrow. 'Oh no, Mr B.
never accepts invitations for two days in succession.'

Brazilians are very fond of decrying themselves. Over and over I have
heard them say à propos of some poor person spending a thousand
dollars on a costume for the carnival night: 'Not bad for an undeveloped
country.' They refer to me as being 'civilised'. 'We're not civilised.
You're educated but we're just savages, and we know it.'

Rio   *20 February 1971*

The hotel swimming pool crowded with people arrived for the carnival,
including US journalists and Valentino,[1] the Rome dressmaker. I can't

---

[1] Valentino (b. 1932), Italian couturier, who opened his first atelier in Rome in 1960,
and went on to rival Saint Laurent, Givenchy and Karl Lagerfeld. His clientele included
Jackie Onassis, Gloria Guinness and Elizabeth Taylor.

work up an enthusiasm. The hotel upside down with the result telephonists say, 'Don't answer' automatically and I remain waiting for one hour upstairs while the chauffeur waits downstairs. A visit to see the mass of black bodies on a beach, and a locked church was the day's way of using up all energy. My fatigue showed itself in a drawing that I did of Julio's profile as he sat sipping a long glass of champagne and making a great effort not to talk.

Cecil looked forward to the Carnival, which was to be the highlight of his stay in Rio. Meanwhile, for the second time, he photographed prostitutes in the Quartia Reservé.

Julio was extremely good-natured to accompany me with good humour as we did the same routine. The atmosphere was a little impregnated with the spirit of carnival, but there were still a number of whores who did not wish to be photographed, and at one moment a terrible fight took place when one of the girls rushed at the man who had been fucking her as he tried to make off without paying her. He was pushed into a coffee stall, ricocheted into a crowd that was unsympathetic to him and followed his ebb and flow like waves.

Squawking as a chicken, faces at every brothel window, I fled in retreat with the 'bodyguard' and watched the fight from a distance. It appeared that all the girls formed a circle so that the man would not escape, and the outraged victim stripped the man first of his shirt, then of his pants, and left him naked. Whether she got her two dollars due, I don't know. Some of the photographs should be a bit more interesting, for certainly the coloured interiors, red, orange, turquoise, should help the general effect even if the girls themselves are neither attractive nor grotesque.

The long-awaited Carnival took place on Sunday, 21 February:

Grey skies, heavy heat, the chauffeur an hour late. My stomach upset not improved, a bad beginning to the day, but in early afternoon the carnival processions of sambas have started, and from a stand where workmen are still banging and sawing, we are unable to find our places, quite expensively booked, as information is not one of the best talents of the coloured people. Rhythm, energy, health, yes, and an innate dignity of movement. Thousands of dancers old and young sambaed their way down the main thoroughfare wearing red and white dresses of all descriptions.

There would be no knowing why they were dressed as Creoles, or Carmen Mirandas, or Louis XIV courtiers. The inconsequential is part of the charm. Suddenly in one group a particular dancer will be stricken with an attack of sheer madness and improvise a little marvel of energetic frenzy, eyes lost to the world as his feet become stars. A huge old lady wobbles in a dozen different layers of fat. These schools of samba have assembled from neighbourhoods of varying distances and after preparations that have absorbed them for most of the year, the various clowns walk in their costumes to the main arteries of the city, often a long journey in itself. Then the strenuous dancing lasts for many hours of most days.

Feelings of theatrical rivalry are very strong, everyone is a vedette in his or her own light, and sometimes the jealousies burst out in terrible anger. A year ago, a man in the leading part of a samba (red and white to be seen tonight) murdered a rival. Some friends of the deceased threatened their revenge. He would be shot at the next time of the Carnival. Sure enough, yesterday, while he was putting out all the shoes to be worn in his 'school', and mindless of the warning, he was shot dead. The body was buried this afternoon and tonight the show goes on. It seems that the local archbishop has chosen this very bad moment to die, but in accordance with His Holiness's wishes, Carnival must continue.

The social significance of the festivities is quite remarkable. Here are people who are usually poor, who work terribly hard all the year round with very little to spend. Yet they will afford money and time to make extremely elaborate costumes that are in themselves the symbols of riches. The elaborate prince and princess or king and queen costumes are worn by cooks, household servants, nurses, waiters, who are all willing to go 'banco' on the one big occasion. Walter M. S. was telling me that often when downtown he does not wish to go to his club for lunch where he will meet too many people anxious to talk to him. He prefers a small restaurant where the patron looks after him with solicitude.

The patron is Portuguese, over seventy, extremely tall and very heavily built. He is a man with children and grandchildren. Walter wished him 'good Carnival' and added, 'I'll see you next Wednesday.' 'Oh, no,' said the patron. 'For four days I dance in the Carnival and that is so tiring that I must have two days of rest.'

The music is very African and monotonous, but there is no monotony about watching the unforeseen and the unexpected. This afternoon the grey skies suddenly opened. It was very sad that there has been no rain for six weeks (and this is the 'rainy season'), yet suddenly it had to come now in torrents. All in a moment, the streets were flooded. Visibility was nil. You saw drenched couples trying to take shelter under a tree. But later in the day the sun came out again.

The huge red and white procession was just passing as we fought our way to our seats. Julio's promises were fulfilled and the elaboration of the costumes was all he suggested they would be. The murdered man was forgotten in the general abandon.

Everyone was happy, everyone had forgotten their cares, they were being applauded by a great anonymous public. They were indeed 'stars' for the occasion. They were kings and empresses, with a public as enthusiastic as for a football or movie idol. Thin and fat, hair-lipped, squinting, young and old, they were all giving everything they had to give. That extra reach of the voice, the little stretch more of the hips, the twinkling of toes. It was a very happy sight to see so many people having the time of their lives without any slight degree of regret. Euphoria here was in supremacy. Huge fat mamas whirling in silver crinolines, huger fat men were parading with trains many yards long, holding wands, sceptres, waving flags. Everything was spangled, glittery, shiny bright, everything in a style that has been evolved through the years and has a style of its own – not sophisticated, perhaps it would not even be valid on the stage, but for this purpose it was perfect, unassailable.

After the thousands and thousands (perhaps 30,000) of dancers had passed and the drummers brought the procession to a climax of frenzy, the crowds belched forward to take possession of the thoroughfare, while the next 'school' was being prepared. Julio and I walked behind the stands to the behind-the-scenes preparations for the next procession. These costumes were all pink and green, the green of a metallic butterfly, spangled green, pale lettuce. There was a group of fat ladies dressed in pink and green roses, another lot as can-can dancers, some pink and green 'twenties', some shiny diamond and gilt pink and green of the court of Louis XIV, white cotton-wool wig on top of black faces, some like Picasso harlequins, clowns, pink and viridian, every variation of pink and green.

Some flower girls were particularly charming for they carried baskets of violets. Everything unexpected, imaginative, some of the best costumes were made from utilitarian objects, 'petrol' containers cut in half, milk cloudy plastic bottles, ping-pong balls, but most things glittered whether it was the spangled breath of a harlot or a hangman, or death's head, a few sinister Ku Klux Klan children. Only the exhaustion that is beyond conquest drove me to ask Julio for leave of absence. No doubt we would have stayed all night. But I felt we had had just the right amount of Carnival and more would have lessened the enjoyment. I felt it had been the great sight that everyone had said it would be, and I was relieved in many ways, above all that I was not disappointed, when at last I got to my bed.

From Rio, Cecil flew to Buenos Aires, where he met two survivors from his childhood, the Alberdi sisters, Beatrix Gausbeck and Carmen Knight-Searles. They were the nieces of his beloved Aunt Jessie, who had married a Bolivian, Pedro Suarez, known to Cecil as 'Uncle Percy'. Aunt Jessie lived at 74 Compayne Gardens, Hampstead, and Uncle Percy's sister, Madame Anna Suarez Alberdi was so devoted to her that she built a French-style house opposite

Aunt Jessie's, in order to come over and sit and watch her. She spoke little English and had many daughters. But she died young, and Beatrix, in particular, became a companion to Aunt Jessie and, despite the difference in their years, almost a sister to her.

Recalling Beatrix as a young girl, Cecil wrote, 'Beatrix wore her marcelle-waved hair flat like the coiffures in Grecian sculpture, but she lacked the Greek column neck and, in the fashion that was about to start, sat rather hunched with head thrust forward. However, this gave her an opportunity to look up with her large prune eyes more full of commiseration than ever.'

To meet Beatrix and Carmen again after all these years was to prove an emotional experience.

Buenos Aires   *February* 1971

I am writing this now so that I can throw off my mood of sadness and try not to return to It. The experience has been too upsetting.

A clear childlike voice of utter femininity answered my telephone call with complete surprise. On arrival here from the aeroplane, I looked up in the local telephone book, and there, as if the improbable had happened, the name was there: Gausbeck, Beatrix. 'Where are you, Cecil?' the voice cooed. 'In Buenos Aires.' 'In Buenos Aires!' Never has such complete astonishment been registered. 'And how long are you staying?' – 'Is that all? Well, we are not prepared, Carmen and I, we haven't had our hair done or our clothes from the presses. But what does that matter. We must see you. We'll come to the hotel at five o'clock. Whereabouts is the hotel?' I was waiting in the reading room. I had changed into a white suit and a dog's tooth shirt.

A completely unrecognisable Carmen, light-haired, but with a sweet expression and a friendly smile, came up to me. She was a nice-looking, middle-aged, elderly woman. I steeled myself to meet Beatrix. It is *so* long since I've seen her, perhaps thirty years or more. Even then she was no longer the beauty who had played Titania and been such a figure at Compayne Gardens in my early boyhood. It had all become very vivid to me since writing this book, so the impact would be terrific. It was.

I came face to face with someone who had Beatrix's big, thick eyes, but nothing else. At once I was struck by the enlarged mouth, stretched with false teeth. It completely disguised her and I noticed that the bone of the nose had been taken out to get rid of the aquiline beak. The hair was slightly but well dyed, the complexion much as it used to be, but Beatrix the buxom had shrunk into a little old lady. She had been very ill and could not eat much, but it was difficult to find out exactly what was her illness, so much avoided – unspoken.

We sat at a table, Beatrix soon revealed the habit acquired of wiping her wide mouth with large hands as if to apologise for the shape of the new mouth. She still looked up with big eyes, but leant forward more than before. We talked of Argentine and Peru, the way the poor have been better looked after, but the expense of everything! We talked of Bolivia and what a pity I hadn't gone to Santa Cruz, and told her that I was writing a book. So many people could have helped. She wouldn't listen to the fact that I had not known, at the time I went to Bolivia, that I would be writing about my aunt. 'What a pity you didn't do this and that.'

I turned to Carmen. She was a shorthand typist working for a shipping firm. It was a good job and interesting, but she had to be at the office at 8.30 a.m. They neither of them had servants. Bea had cooked lamb for lunch but it was so bad for her liver. She had to be so careful since her illness. New York was so dangerous she daren't go out at night and Anita's boyfriend had been almost killed on the streets, four months in hospital and back again for another operation. Brothers dead, other names long since gone. Bea's husband had had large properties in New Jersey and given them to her, but the Americans took everything from her. Hard luck stories, missed opportunities. 'We went to the beach today but the wind blew the sand everywhere.'

These two sisters have little in common except blood. Carmen is at least twenty years younger than the eldest. But they love each other. Now that Carmen's daughter is married, and I felt that Carmen was by far the most capable of making her own life, but she must now look after Bea. In fact, after a disastrous war marriage, she had earned her own living and brought up a daughter. But she was incapable of making me believe she had been the beauty that she had once been. Bea so kind and silly. Bea could not even keep a conversation going. If one tried to explain the simplest fact, she was incapable of listening. Yet she was so nice, so sweet and so kind, and she had dressed herself very charmingly in a navy blue dress with a white bow, and a nice large bag, and her shoes were good.

After an hour's conversation, 'How's Nancy? Baba? Tecia? Tess?'[1] she suggested I would want to return to my friend and go sightseeing in Buenos Aires. After a bit I realised the strain of the threesome was beginning to tell, that I would never be able to get going with Carmen while Bea put up a smokescreen.

So Bea got to her feet. Her legs are slightly fat, still, though so much of her body has shrunk. I remember the sturdy legs so well from my early boyhood. They were so South American. These legs now staggered a bit, Bea always had an ungainly walk, her head was always thrust forward.

---

[1] Cecil's two sisters and his two cousins.

Now it was positively hen-like as she looked right and left. Could I recognise the profile? No, the nose had been too altered, only the eyes remained, and this 'made-over' lady went towards the door of the hotel, Carmen, dignified and quiet in the background. Bea was still the star, but it was all a bit difficult for her, and her teeth made it hard to smile without it becoming a grimace.

As she staggered through the revolving doors, I suddenly had the knowledge that I was seeing her for the last time. She appeared ready for her grave. I watched very carefully as she turned and as I blew her a kiss, she gave me the grimace smile. I staggered a few paces back into the shadow of the hallway, and suddenly I realised I was appalled by the sadness of life. I saw myself in the mirror and realised that I looked like a dressed-up clown that was suddenly weeping. I went to the elevator in floods of tears. By the time I got to my room, I was bellowing, sobbing, hiccuping with tears. I stood saying, 'Oh, God! Oh, God! How sad!'

I was weeping not so much for silly sweet Bea, as for my own lost youth. I was weeping for all the dead people I had loved. I was weeping for Aunt Jessie, and perhaps my mother, and my brother, and all who had been part of my childhood. I was weeping for the whole of a lost era, the 'Edwardian' era of large, cosy family parties, and holidays, and treats, and evenings by the fire. I was weeping for the demolition of 74 Compayne Gardens and the atmosphere that once that magical house created. Bea was just an excuse for me to weep for the mysterious sadness of life. What was it all about? What answers are there? Why were these people failures? Why had their lives gone so wrong? And what about my own? There was so much wrong with that too.

My sudden onslaught of old age, my appearance, my not feeling well, the pointlessness, struck me very strongly. Eventually I lay on my bed and wept aloud, and I feared that Julio, in the next room, would hear me.

Eventually the sobbing stopped. Perhaps out of sheer breathlessness and exhaustion. In my bedroom there is a cupboard with mirrors placed so that I can see dozens of reflections of myself. This mercifully happens to me seldom. The images of myself in my present state filled me with such depression that again I started to howl. I watched myself putting my hands up to my cheeks to smear away the torrent. My nose was swollen and red, my hair, what there is of it, on end, my stomach bulging out of a tight pair of trousers, my hormone's breasts enlarged with full nipples – God, what a creature!

A while later I felt strong enough to telephone next door about plans for our journey. 'How was your meeting?' he asked me. 'Very sad,' was all I was able to say, for suddenly I was again convulsed. Julio, typically, said, 'Well, don't let's talk about it because it will only make you sad.' Perhaps I wanted to be sad. Anyhow, the mood was on me for a long while but I was not learning anything from it and I felt that perhaps the best way to dispel it would be to write about it now, rather than let the sadness return again when once I have, I hope, regained enough strength to put on my armour against the inevitable and the unanswerable.

Time passed and it was soon to be the hour of rendezvous for an evening out under the auspices of Miguel Carcano.[1] No possibility of moping. I hurried into a bath and smarmed my hair down. I looked a bit sinister. That at any rate was an achievement and, with eyes still red, I went down into the hall and soon was in smiles and full admiration of the marvellous, vital human being who carries his eighty years without any seeming effort.

The above is no doubt an indication of my somewhat poor state of health. Had I not been overtired, perhaps by the recent journeys and terrific heat, I don't imagine I would have 'let go' so foolishly.

Next morning, before leaving BA for Cordoba, I went out and bought Bea and Carmencita thirty pounds' worth of gloves and handbags.

Even after a bath, I was still red-eyed for the arrival of Miguel Ange Carcano, my host at Cordoba, who unexpectedly was in BA for a few days. He called to take J. and myself out to dinner at the Jockey Club. Never before has Miguel appeared more elegant, more charming-looking in appearance, so witty and amused and amusing than this evening. He is over eighty years old but seems absolutely in his prime. He has the grand manner, charm that is seldom seen now, in all respects a gentleman who is shocked if others are not gentlemen too.

He took the evening in his stride, introduced us to the leading members of this most rich club which, having been burnt by Peron in an effort to destroy the flower of Argentine aristocracy, has now been rebuilt in the home of an old lady of great wealth, where the additions have cost so many millions that Miguel was shocked at the unnecessary extravagance (they pointlessly bought a Lawrence of the Duke of Wellington and a marble bath worth five hundred pounds!), so declined the Presidency.

On arrival the doormen refused admission to Julio for not wearing a tie, although he was in semi-sport outfit and looked much more elegant than most of the people in their badly-tailored lounge suits. In fact the members looked a pretty mangy, unremarkable lot, and the bad taste of the Victorian pastiche is really quite appalling. How can they have re-created the ugliest of the 80s here today? BA is cold after Rio, in fact, by any standards. We chose a table where the 'air conditioning' was the

---

[1] Miguel Carcano (1889–1978), Argentinian Ambassador to Britain, father of Chiquita Astor.

least violent, and kept warm by eating a large and rather so-so meal. But the evening was a delight on account of Miguel who talked about his country, my country and its visitors, and was altogether a remarkable and beautiful example of what a great gentleman can still be today.

Footnote

At one point, while eating fish, Miguel was telling a story with such relish and emphasis that he spat out a morsel of fish which landed on the upper part of an arm. Instead of drawing attention to this, he ignored it until a later moment when others were talking, and then he flicked the fish flake off with a napkin.

Cecil then went to stay at San Miguel, the Carcano ranch, which he found more than congenial. He was thrilled to meet Stella Carcano, Miguel's wife, which brought back many memories.

I was so touched and happy. We kissed fervently and I saw that although she had become old, she had all the charm, authority and character of before. She has had a wonderful life, so full of adventure and experience, born of an important and no doubt rich Argentine family, she has benefited by the success, so well-warranted, of her delightful and brilliant husband. They have, apart from all else, the gift of friendship and are much loved by groups of intimate friends throughout the world.

Their social success started in the days of the Prince of Wales, when he came to the Argentine and was so pleased when a fanatic ran up to him on the golf course shouting, 'Viva il Principe democratico!' Ever since, the Carcanos have had an easy way of discriminating the true from the false, and have never been beguiled by café society. It was when they came officially to represent their country during the war that I got to know them, and was so touched when, on the eve of my departure to the Middle East, they gave a lunch party for me (Georgia and Sachie [Sitwell] were there, I remember), and they wished me bon voyage in champagne (that most rare of drinks).

And here was Stella, seemingly a little smaller, her hair sand-coloured, her skin freckled and a bit wrinkled, but the dark eyes were as full of life and change of mood as ever. It is altogether a fascinating face for it is the embodiment of all her thoughts. When she is amused or surprised, hurt or astonished, one can see to what exact degree.

Leaning slightly forward in the way that older people do, she took me to see the Arcadian view from her garden. Nothing could be more lovely in the clear mountain sunlight. Among the stretches of green were riders on horseback and groups of children were picking the harvest of dark red apples. ('They pay for our trip to Europe,' Stella said.) We were shown her rock garden and heard how, for two years now, they'd had no gardener for the last had sold all her plants, mostly to the Martinez de Hozes[1] (which perhaps was the reason for a certain froideur between the former such good friends). We saw the wooded copses with two or three different streams, and loved the effect of the sun in patches lighting ragged clumps of tall, yellow daisies and of hydrangeas of all colours...

Cecil and his hosts had much to discuss, and while he found them generally positive and sympathetic, he noted that they could 'both be quite sarcastic, as they are about Dulce M. [Martinez] de Hoz, who has obviously irritated them very much, no doubt because of neighbourly rivalry'. One afternoon, a survivor from Cecil's 1930 Book of Beauty came over.

Soon a motor appeared, within it, Clara Uriburu[2] and various members of her family (sister Duggan and husband, son and daughter-in-law). I had not seen Clara for forty years when she was one of my first sitters and the Ambassador's sophisticated daughter in London. She is hardly recognisable, for not only have fashions changed, but her manner has changed from mouse to matriarchal authority. We talked of the past and again I realised what fun she had had among the most privileged in the land. She was friendly and kind. We had not much to discuss by mid-afternoon and the siesta was more than ever welcome.

Above all, Cecil awaited the arrival of Dulce Martinez de Hoz. This occurred on Saturday, 28 February.

Return to find the Martinez de Hoz party had already arrived for lunch. This long-awaited moment when I should set eyes on this great beauty again after five years was at hand. Would I be disappointed? She has had such a build-up. Still beautiful, everyone said, but quite different.

I was disappointed, for although she is a remarkable 71, and looks 50 at most, she has become like Bianca Mosca. Her dark grey hair too 'coiffed', her suit too tailored. But after the initial shock I soon realised that here

---

[1] Dulce, wife of Eduardo Martinez de Hoz, described by Cecil as 'such a great *star* in the fashionable world of Paris for so many years, and then she takes to meditating about the Bible and thinking that there is more to life than racehorses and Vionnet... and she has built herself a bastion in the Argentine Mountains'.

[2] Clarita Uriburu, daughter of Dr J. Evaristo Uriburu, Argentinian Ambassador in London in the 1920s. In his *Book of Beauty* Cecil described her as '... an exquisite puppet, five feet in height, delicately proportioned...'.

was one of the great beauties of our time, with allure and charm and natural gaiety undiminished.

It is an interesting story. The fabulously beautiful girl who married first a fabulously rich old man, a journalist, then an equally important breeder of horses, who had kept Chanel and Dorziat[1] among his many women, and Dulce became the best-dressed woman in Paris, with jewels so heavy and numerous that when the two escaped via the Carcanos out of Biarritz, the Germans thought they were carrying the contents of Van Clef and Arpels and arrested them. (The C.s got them out, made such a fuss about the jewels that the German Ambassador in BA arranged for them to be given back.

(The Carcanos, at the end of the war, even got the Germans to pay recompense for the marvellous racehorses which the Germans had eaten. In fact the Carcanos played a great part in their subsequent lives, for it was after staying with the C.s in Biarritz, that Dulce, Madame de H. having lived for years at the Ritz in Paris, acquired a taste for gardens, came to these mountains to stay at San Miguel, and from here decided to build and settle on a neighbouring mountain.)

Before the war, Madame de Hoz was acclaimed the most fêted beauty and crowds at the races cheered her as she made her way to the paddock. Once Bébé [Bérard],[2] on seeing her arrive at a ball, rushed up and kissed the hem of her ball gown.

As for me, I hardly ever saw her. When I first arrived in Paris to take photographs for French *Vogue* I [was] ill-equipped, I could not speak French, the cameras and lighting were very heavy and cumbersome. In front of the camera Madame de H. looked plain. I became desperate. She knew I was upset because she was not *photogénique* and said she would return in the afternoon. She did not. The few pictures I took were terrible. She has never been well-photographed or painted. But all that part of her life was over when she came to this department. She became ill, had to remain in bed for two years, was convinced the air of the mountains was the only cure, so remained.

Here she got the taste for solitude, for being close to the earth, for reading. Her trips to Paris became more and more intermittent. The Parisians said she was spending her time asleep in the mountains to keep young. Then Dulce discovered literature and the arts. She studied a Froissart version of the Bible, changed her character to greater kindness, and devoted her time only to flowers and planting trees and planning the landscape. And here she was in her new guise, with delicate hands of a peasant who does weaving or sculpting with clay.

The charm is the same, the neck thrust forward, the eyes wistful and

---

[1] Gabrielle Dorziat (1881–1979), French supporting actress.
[2] Christian Bérard (1902–49), Parisian artist and a strong influence on Cecil.

forehead questing. The voice deep, she laughs full of bubble and fun, the legs quite shapely but surprisingly solid.

We talked with ease although I was nervous and found it hard to find time to eat (a marvellous lunch with stuffed pancakes, a medieval joint of veal which Miguel Ange carved, and a soufflé cake-meringue combined), and later discussed the difficulties of her not being *photogénique* as she walked about the garden under a parasol. A delightful magnetic person. No wonder she has always been and remains a star. The party stayed on 'til late and tomorrow we go to her famed house, then I spend my last night there. So it is a 'Dulce' gala from now on.

Stella, earthy and maternal and wonderful, asked what I thought. A sweet, kind woman, without pretensions and completely unspoilt by the adulation her beauty, combined with her riches, has brought her. No wonder that her husband, now over eighty, still loves her to distraction and says that she gives way to his every whim, whereas it is she who manages to have her own way in everything. She is touched by his devotion, though at one time she fell in love with a brilliant Frenchman named Barachin. She wished to marry him and told her husband. When a large bouquet of flowers arrived from the lover, the husband fainted. Dulce was so moved that she decided to live with her husband for ever more.

Cecil's stay with the Carcanos was coming to an end:

Later we started reminiscing about old friends that we had all known and how the Prince of Wales ran from her advances and how badly T. Beecham[1] (a common fellow) had treated her, talked of Emerald [Cunard] and Augustus John[2] being so generous in bad ways as well as good, of the Duke of Sutherland[3] frightening a young lady at Dunrobin by telling her of the ghosts, and then when, with his white face and long night shirt, he appeared in the night in her door and she screamed, he put a finger to his lips and said, 'Ssh, it's the Duke!' A lot of the people were just a bit older than myself and very grand so that they always had great glamour for me. It was interesting to hear behind-the-scenes stories of what they were really like.

In Buenos Aires Cecil had a modest lunch with Bea and Carmen. He then endured an unpleasant experience:

[1] Sir Thomas Beecham (1879–1961), well-known conductor.
[2] Augustus John (1878–1961), artist.
[3] Geordie, fifth Duke of Sutherland (1888–1963).

Then back to the hotel to pay for a new fur coat, a puma of great beauty, and to pack. Gradually it dawned on me that two of my cameras were missing. Then, searching everywhere, I was convinced that they had been stolen from the room. No one had visited me here, I had last used the Rolleiflex on my arrival here to take the Rodin statue. The manager was called, servants looked everywhere. One maid looked very upset and may be guilty. Here I was, left without a camera. I was appalled. Such an awful feeling.

Julio said he would make a scandal and tell the press of the world. The manager, quiet and upset, said he would recompense me. But I left the nice hotel in a state of shock...

In Rio, Cecil had a further shock:

Elizhina [Moreira Salles] had said her maid would unpack for me, but I suddenly had a desire to find my pocket book with pounds and dollars and cheques in it. But as I searched, I realised that too had been stolen. I was too upset to sleep for a long while, and at seven o'clock, I shouted, 'Oh no!' as I suddenly realised that the envelope containing cruzeiros changed at Walter's bank was also missing. The thief had done a good job. I was sad that this had happened in the Argentine and in that hotel. It took the edge off my pleasure at being there. It brought on a headache, but I was able to go to sleep again, until the telephone woke me with a shrill ring two hours later.

Cecil was aware of the differences between the two countries he had visited:

Returning to Rio, one realises some of the differences between Argentine and Brazil. The latter honky-tonk, no elegant buildings, no culture, the future is everything. BA has not developed since the Perón era, nonetheless life is more agreeable still. There are no poor, no Negroes, excellent food, particularly Argentine beef. Here Elizhina says, with no regrets, 'There are no good restaurants.' In fact 'no regrets' is a typically Brazilian attitude.

Julio chooses his servants more for their looks than their abilities. They are like children. He is never exasperated with them. (I would blow my top all the time!) From BA he sent a telegram to tell of his return. Late at night he found no one at his house to greet him. One servant was asleep. When Julio woke him, the servant said, 'Oh, how nice!' and turned over and went to sleep again. Julio assumed that this was typically Brazilian. His telegram arrived the next day.

Cecil now longed to leave, but was glad when Elizhina Moreira Salles summoned her private plane from São Paolo to take him on a two-day jaunt to Ouro Petros and Congoulnas. Before he left, he had to endure an evening listening to some music composed by Julio.

All the optimistic attempts by Julio for me to make a lot of money by taking photographs has dwindled into thin air, like many of his schemes. But he remains optimistic and starts a sentence by 'I have good news for you'. But the revelation is seldom a *fait accompli*. He tries hard for me, he has been a good friend and I have more than repaid him.

This evening was my greatest test, for I have agreed to hear his music for an operetta on the Romance of Madame Santos and Emperor Paul I. He wrote this seven years ago, and it seemed as if it was conceived in the 30s at the latest. It was quite appallingly old-fashioned, and so monotonous that I was almost lulled to a doze.

Three sad women were involved and a nice Negro who is well known in the Rio theatre and TV world. Out of friendship to Julio he may direct it, but I had to say what I thought, and tried to be kind but constructive. It is obvious an enormous amount of work must be put into it, before it ever goes into rehearsal. I doubt if it will ever materialise, and knew the evening was an utter waste, even so better than dining with the Marguerite Veigas, whose invitation I turned down, for although they have swamped me with kindnesses, I found neither at all sympathetic.

Julio laughs easily. He laughed when I said that Carmen was à côté and, with her white and black-painted eyes, looked as if she had come out of the jungle and all she needed to complete her appearance was a ring on her nose. An early bed in preparation for an early call.

After Ouro Petros and Congoulnas, Cecil returned for a last evening in Rio.

Tonight should have been particularly charming as Donna Louisa is the most cultivated, delightful person I have met here. Her home outstandingly nice in an unpretentious white, modern, Portuguese, African style, with long balcony running the length of a façade. Here we drank champagne and ate foie gras sandwiches before sitting down to an excellent dinner of three courses, shrimps in pink peppery spiced sauce, chicken in heavy curry sauce, and a very rich ice cream with pistachio and melted syrupy sugar. Perhaps I was too tired to eat, but even so I did, with very bad results.

My hostess, so interesting as she talked about Herbert Read[1] being the best advised on modern painting, or how she felt that for someone like herself it was essential to study, to see what modern painting was about. But I found myself trying to suppress yawns.

---

[1] Sir Herbert Read (1893–1968), artist, poet and art historian.

The other guests were all equally intelligent and interesting, the set I would like to move in if I were unfortunate enough to live here, but I was glad when at midnight the party broke up. In bed I had a twinge of pain in my stomach but I was too tired to get out and take a Lomotel pill. Instead I had to get out of bed half a dozen times during the night as the contents of my bowels had turned to water. Such a deluge, such a cascade, and followed by pains. I felt I was poisoned. *Could* it have been Marie Louisa's shrimps? Not possibly, perhaps my own stupidity in eating too much in such heat.

Wednesday, 12 March 1971

God, I felt awful. Hardly able to move. More visits to the bathroom as I wondered whether to squit on the loo or be sick into the basin. Perhaps after some time I'd feel better. Elizhina was sending her maid and a packer and governess to translate about where I wanted which things. Before I knew what was happening, I spewed up over the bed and my pyjamas as they rang the doorbell. The governess was very reassuring. She would send for some medicine.

Meanwhile I lay watching the big dark mammy packing with such expertise that it was a work of art. Never have my clothes been so beautifully treated. By degrees my health recovered enough for me to dress to go out with Julio to return borrowed cameras and try in vain to do some last-minute shopping.

How I longed to leave! How I hated sitting around the pool for the last time. I went to say goodbye to Elizhina in her house. How different if I had stayed in that oasis, and was staggered at the *tenue* of her *vie*, servants, trained to be subservient and deprecated in a manner we see nowhere else today. Her maid dressed up in white gloves, hovered while the butler did a dance of 'bows', while emptying ashtrays, bringing the tea, offering the endless dishes that remained untouched while Elizhina talked of Rio's provincial life, the awful publicity, the lack of culture. She ordered special food for me, a huge plate of peas in boiled rice to be followed by boiled bananas with lots of sugar to calm the liver...

Cecil's plane was delayed, but eventually he took off after what he called 'the sauna bath penance'. He was determined he would never return to Rio and allowed himself some parting thoughts:

Certain South Americans exude a strangely smelling sweat. It is unlike any I've known before. Julio has it. It's leathery, tangy, pungent, and once or twice Stella Carcano, and even Miguel gave off whiffs of it. And often in crowds I'd come across it. It seems native to this continent.

Julio's promise of making money by taking commissions of his rich friends came to nothing, like many of his optimistic schemes.

Before returning to Britain, Cecil spent a few days in the more familiar territory of New York.

March 1971

Anita Loos. I asked her what she liked in the theatre, the revival of *No, No, Nanette*. 'But', she said, 'if you hated that, you'd kick a puppy.'

Broadchalke   21 *March 1971*

Typical that I was not able to continue drawing once I arrived in New York. The air journey quickly over, we landed in grey, drab New York, but I was never more pleased to be here. The climate of Rio had been more of a strain than I realised, and later discovered that others too feel bereft of energy there, even in the comparative cool of winter.

A Harpo Marx brother taxi driver bringing me to the St Regis told of the appalling abuse and expense of welfare in New York and how many big corporations were transplanting themselves in order to avoid city taxes.

Discovered Sam [Green] was in the city, in good form, and we went to exhibitions and plays (*Alice in Wonderland*, via *Gregory à la Gratowski*) and for three nights running he became host. First to a hippie group for dinner and the slides of his recent journey to see the Stone Balls (prehistoric) of Costa Rica, the figures on Easter Island, and surprisingly our trip to the Dordogne followed by wonderfully evocative shots of Reddish garden in full summer sunlight, or at any rate, late evening sunlight. He is a remarkable photographer, not knowing the limitations of the camera, takes pictures in almost darkness and they come out.

Next evening he took a party to Albee's *All Over*, a very excellent play, that stands little chance of commercial success, for it is glossy. But how well-written, how deeply felt, how articulated and movingly acted. Then a dinner for me of ten at a restaurant called the Grenadier, that has rare atmosphere and charm. In Sam's 'set' people do not resent being asked at the last minute. His thirteenth-hour guests included Renata Adler, a fashion expert aged 22 named Sable, and Rex Reed, a clever nice group.[1]

---

[1] Renata Adler, author and reviewer (*New York Review of Books* etc.). Rex Reed, Texan-born film critic (*New York Observer*), also an actor: the man who had sex-change operation and turned into Raquel Welch in the film of Gore Vidal's *Myra Breckenridge* (1970), and, as himself, in TV episodes of *The Critic*.

Margaret Case was also in town and so helped and appalled. We lunched with Vava [Aldeburg] and as I put their names in my book, I realised that this was for the nine thousandth time. They appear since 35 years! Vava was tied to his bed for seven hours while coloured people shot themselves full of heroin and robbed him of all his cherished old Russian tabernacles. When giving evidence in court he said, 'No, I was not frightened. I've been through two wars and one revolution.' Admitting there was such a thing as a depression, the perennial optimist said that the TV people had lost millions by the government ruling to prevent advertising. Margaret, always social, said, 'Have the Paleys[1] lost a lot?' 'Twenty million.' Margaret tut-tutted. I made the most unpopular remark of her year by saying, 'It's no skin off my nose if the Paleys have lost money so long as some people have been prevented from killing themselves.'

High spot of my week. Lunch with Diana Vreeland. She had been in bed for three days, so was rested, and I got the full effect of her freshness. Her brain ticking over with extraordinary quickness and clarity. She was in a rare confidential mood and regretted the break-up of her son, Frecky's, marriage, and the way her work at *Vogue* had become so menial. She even has ideas of coming to England to live, and asked me to find out how much it cost me to keep the London house.

She was euphoric about the South American photographs, particularly those of Congoulnas, which *are* very beautiful. I'm pleased with all except Dulce, who just is *not photogénique*. I was thrilled to have first news from home since the seven-week postal strike and to hear, in spite of my anxieties, that all was well. When, after the most pleasant week in New York that I have spent for years, it was time to leave, I was more than impatient to leave.

March 1971

On arrival in London John, the chauffeur of Regency Hire Car, says, 'Something wonderful has happened in London. The film of *Death in Venice*[2] is the most beautiful there has ever been. See it, then realise.' Everyone, but everyone I speak to, then tells me it is perfection – Dot, Eileen, Buckle, everyone says it is so fearless. Irene Worth was seen in tears as she came out. (The audience does not speak as they file out.) And Dicky [Buckle] kissed her saying, 'Yours is a wonderful profession.' Everyone talks of the silence, the unbearable beauty.

---

[1] William S. Paley (1901–90) and his wife 'Babe' (Barbara Cushing) (1915–78).
[2] *Death in Venice* (1970), directed by Visconti, and starring Dirk Bogarde.

It is sad when young people of promise become successful, then prove themselves to be shallow phoneys. For all his brilliance such is the case of Leonard Bernstein.[1] As a young man haunting the Everard Baths and spending the weekends in the company of Gian Carlo Menotti[2] etc. and other musicians, he was a live wire. He continued to be too lively. His ambitions were without end. He even married and had children. He became a popular composer, a conductor and great publicity figure. But he stank.

He is too much the charlatan 'show off'. He is now discredited by serious musicians, though his career soars, in spite of the devastating mistake he made in allowing Tom Wolfe to come to his cocktail party for the Black Panthers and thereby becoming such a laughing stock that he and his family are threatening to come to live in England.

He appeared on TV at the concert he gave with the Vienna Philharmonic. He shut his eyes, swooned and smiled ecstatically, danced up and down, tossed his old grey Jewish locks. He was disgusting and repellent. Following the programme of the Wandsworth Grammar School choir, with its remarkable and pure leader, whom B. Britten[3] has written special works for. What simplicity, seriousness and purity! TV delves deep beneath the surface. This was a really splendid person. You could tell the gold from the dross we'd just had exhibited to us.

There were a number of people in London who gave annual luncheons and dinners for Queen Elizabeth the Queen Mother. These continued into 2001. With the passing of time, the various hosts and hostesses died. Among those who gave such annual parties were Lady Diana Cooper (who also entertained Harold Macmillan once a year), Maureen, Marchioness of Dufferin and Ava, who gave an annual dinner for twenty, with guests coming in after dinner, and the Dowager Marchioness of Cholmondeley.

Cecil was a regular guest at such events and now he was summoned by Lady Cholmondeley to her London home in Kensington Palace Gardens (a private road, dubbed 'Millionaire's Row').

4 April 1971

'Cecil, will you sit next to the Queen?' Sybil said, with a vague point to the empty chair on the Queen Mother's left. Really I felt I'd come up in

---

[1] Leonard Bernstein (1918–90), conductor of New York Philharmonic Orchestra and composer of *West Side Story*.
[2] Gian Carlo Menotti (b. 1911), composer.
[3] Benjamin Britten (1913–76), British composer.

the world. It was a lunch for eight – the Salisburys, Heads, Jeremy Tree[1] and myself. It was very agreeable and casual. I felt completely at ease and almost critical of the Royal lady of whom I am fond and to whom I owe so much. I found her affectations a bit tiresome as she made such play with Anthony [Head] and rather overworked the facial gestures, as she showed surprise, wistful longing for Bobbety [Salisbury]. But she looked really rather plain too, in a colour that 'did' nothing for her, and her face is fatter than ever, but yet wrinkled.

We talked of everything except her family (although she said Prince Philip was as tough as old boots). She thought Heath had put on stature, and I was amused to see that, when served with our lobster, she looked round the table to see what implements the others were using. No fish knives for Sybil, we were, I suppose, meant to use two forks, but this is difficult with a hard fish like lobster, so having started off with two forks, Queen Elizabeth then, in imitation of Bobbety, took up a knife, and so did we all. Sybil seemed very much at ease, in fact so did all, and when QE left, Bobbety said that the greatest quality his friend has was her enjoyment of everything. She was never blasé and really loved these private outings more than anyone else.

Cecil then went to inspect the rushes of Beaton by Bailey.

TV

The week has been given over to the final week of shooting the Bailey film. Eileen and I came to London mid-Monday to watch the rushes for two hours. It was as if I were looking at my obituary. Quite an uncanny feeling to have these various people, Audrey Withers,[2] Hugh Francis[3] of the Ministry of Information, Twiggy,[4] David Cecil etc. saying nice things about me. As for myself, I was quite pleased to see that I had, in most cases, been photographed with kindliness. Nevertheless in some shots, as with Nancy and Baba [his sisters], I was a sniggering, giggling, comic old man. There is no getting away from the 66 fact.

However, I am pleased with the effect of the film in general, and if Bailey has patience and talent for the cutting, then I think all will go well.

---

[1] Fifth Marquess of Salisbury and his wife, Viscount and Viscountess Head, Jeremy Tree (1925–93), the rotund racehorse trainer.
[2] Audrey Withers (1905–2001), editor of British *Vogue*.
[3] Hugh Francis, who was in charge of publicity at the Ministry of Information during the war, and responsible for sending Cecil on various missions at home and abroad.
[4] Twiggy (b. 1946), wafer-thin model. Cecil was quoted saying of her: 'If I say she has the sex appeal of a child, I'll probably get run in.'

The week of filming was full of variety – Hampstead Heath, the Ritz (for tea with Cyril Connolly,)[1] the hatters in Bond Street,[2] the V & A and the National Portrait Gallery were some of the locations before coming down to Reddish again to do some early spring shots of using the flame-thrower in the paddock and walking through the village etc., etc.

Whereas I had found the first weeks of shooting deeply upsetting and disturbing to the routine, this time all seemed calmer and the crew had become friends and individuals. An Indian photographer had replaced an Australian and he gave a great sense of calm and security to the proceedings. One felt he knew what he was about. In fact, when the whole troupe left in their vans and cars, I felt quite bereft and sorry that something so much discussed was over. Notwithstanding it was with a wonderful feeling of relief that I came to my bedroom and knew that I could remain here for at least a week, until after the Easter holidays.

7 April 1971

There's always so much to do and think about while spending a quiet ten days in the country. The mail brings in a great wad of stuff from Francis Rose. Rather than give him more money to spend on drinks and boozer boys, I try to encourage him to go on writing. (He has the impertinence to say he is 'bored' in the monastery where he is so kindly being taken care of.) Most of the stuff he sends in is utter waste, but there are grains of gold to be found in the great mass (I am reminded of the goldmine near Belo Horizonte) and so I look to see if *The Magician's Tea Party* is worth working on.

I became involved. Two mornings (which in my present condition of bad headaches amounts to two *days'* work) is spent trying to find the glistening grains. Eventually I look at some of the other articles he has sent me and I become as incensed as if he were present. I scribble abusive notes – 'Rubbish' – 'Don't waste my time or money in getting this amateur rubbish typed or read!' It is no good. But then other people are a bit exasperating...

Stravinsky[3] is dead. He wanted to die for the past four years, I was told. He was 88 and one can have no regrets except that he is one of the greats of our day. *Still* too advanced in some instances for one. But his Diaghilev

---

[1] A memorable scene, in which the pair sing 'If you were the only girl in the world...', while the waiter hovers nervously with a plate of cakes, until despair sets in and he fades from view. Cyril Connolly (1903–74), school friend of Cecil, critic and author of *Enemies of Promise*.

[2] Herbert Johnson.

[3] Igor Stravinsky (1882–1971), influential modern composer. He died 6 April 1971.

contributions were high marks of one's 'heyday', *Petrushka*, *[The] Firebird* are classics by now but he never rested on his laurels. Like Picasso he was always renewing himself.

Most touching of all his music to me is *Apollon Musagète*.[1] This soaring, ecstatic romanticism haunts me every time I hear it, and I would like it to be played when I die.

How *extraordinary* is the Cavendish family. Nearby lives Rachel Stewart [Stuart].[2] Her husband died six weeks ago and his incinerated remains are in her potting shed until she goes to Scotland in a few weeks' time.[3] Her food and the cold of the house probably killed him, and certainly drove him to cosier beds and hearths during their long marriage.

Recently Lady Rachel called on her old friend, Betty Somerset, and asked if she could lend her a piece of wire? 'Why?' 'Well, I've swallowed a fish bone and it's stuck in my gullet and every time I turn my head to the right, it's very painful.' 'But you must go at once to Salisbury hospital,' says the aghast Betty. 'No dirty wire is going to do anything but danger.' Rachel got sick of waiting in line for the National Health doctor. She telephoned Betty again. 'Have you a pair of pliers? I'm sure I could get at the thing with those?' 'But what if you swallow them? Then you *really* are in trouble!' Later Rachel telephoned triumphantly. 'Well, I borrowed a pair of pliers from a neighbour, and I've got the bone out!' 'But did you sterilize the pliers?' 'Oh, no.' 'Well go at once to the medicine cupboard and tell me what's there to use as a disinfectant – TPC [TCP], Listerine?' Rachel came back: 'There's a bit of gargle left in an old bottle of James's. I'll wash my mouth out with that.'

Reddish   *Easter Sunday, 11 April 1971*

How the wretched English population do suffer! There are precious few holidays during the year, and it is at this time that unions do their damnedest, meanest to interrupt services. This year it is the trains that

---

[1] *Apollon Musagète* (1928), neo-classical ballet, choreographed by George Balanchine.
[2] Viscountess Stuart of Findhorn (1902–77), born Lady Rachel Cavendish, daughter of ninth Duke of Devonshire. Lord Stuart, Joint Chief Whip in the wartime coalition government, and Minister for Scotland, died 20 February 1971. He is remembered as an early suitor of the Queen Mother and the man who inadvertently introduced her to the Duke of York in 1920.
[3] The saga was complicated. Lady Stuart buried her husband's ashes in a deep hole at Findhorn in a 200 Purdey cartridge box. It fell to their son to convey his mother's ashes to the same resting place. They were in a purple plastic casket. The ashes attracted the attention of airport security men, who sniffed and tasted them, lest he was smuggling drugs to Inverness.

are 'going slow'. No holiday is more looked forward to than Easter for, hopefully, it portends the end of winter and the advent of that marvellous miracle of an English spring.

This 'Good' Friday was as cold, raw, windy, wintry and bleak as it is possible to be. Nothing to do but stay indoors. Fortunately for me Alan [Tagg] was staying and we took the opportunity to change the furniture and 'effects' in the dining room, winter garden and other rooms. Alan has a wonderful 'eye' and sees things that are no longer 'valid' and that I, through living with them daily, no longer see. But for most people on holiday the day was a loss. Easter Saturday brought out the sun, the bulbs, and peoples' spirits were raised. Alan went for a walk before break-fast and the day was spent out of doors discussing with Smallpeice, of all things, the construction of a lake across the road.

Then we planted the iceberg roses, then at Alan's suggestion, we went for a walk to see the village. This was a splendid suggestion, as from a car, one misses so much, the cottage garden built on such a high slope with the beehives and flowering red currants and the topiary cut in the shape of a circle. One does not see the 'improvements' that would-be Percy Throwers[1] have made to their gardens with rustic arches and curving paths. One does not see the spring that bubbles so clearly and coldly and the watercress beds, one has not had time to see how many new houses have sprung up in the very small available space or how ugly is the lack of 'taste' with which almost every home is furnished (through the windows we could see some pretty expensive record players and tape recorders). Faces at windows were as interested in us as we were in them.

We walked up to Clarissa [Avon]'s erstwhile cottage [at Bowerchalke] to find that her valley has been completely de-romanticised by rows of bungalows and a stone, derelict house converted into a ghastly desirable country residence. Clarissa's Rose Bower was full of life, a whisky and soda on a mahogany coffee table, splayed daffodils in a cut-glass vase and the garden looked puny. We reminisced about C. and Anthony, and Dicky Buckle's tenure.

We stood in awe at the end of the round cottage, now derelict, that was once lived in by Mr and Mrs Stacey, now both dead, the gardener who had helped us out and was such a character was now so long since forgotten. The cottage falling down, the garden a shambles. We thought how impressive a shot would be of the front gate, now padlocked but still with its sign to beware of the dog, the low yew arch, the old tree trunks of laburnum and pine.

The wintry sun was now at the end of a long span of light. We watched a beautiful barn owl, dove-biscuit coloured, with a large wingspan. It

---

[1] Percy Thrower (1913–1988), radio and television gardener.

winged its way around the valley, it fluttered, soared, prospected, then landed. It walked, it rested, then was on the wing again. We saw a rabbit hurry over a steep hill to its safety. Alan's quick as a flash eye discovered some blue flowers that were rare with dotted leaves. The heads at windows were now preparing dinner. How good it looked but we just wondered how good it would be in comparison to our kipper mousse and rich mutton, and celery and cheese.

The fresh air and sun had completely drugged us. We could not move while a real eccentric Englishwoman living with roosters, goats, sheep and dogs galore, gave an interview on the telly. She was one of England's great eccentrics, and in her upper-class voice she said, 'I know people think I'm mad, but I know these things do happen.' A very early peaceful bedtime.

Next day, another wonderful walk, this time over the hill and on to the dams opposite my house. It must have been ten years since I last took this very precipitous but wonderful trek into a country that seems so remote from my garden. It was as open and void of humanity, as if one was on a mountain in Switzerland, and there one could surely see a chalet. Here, no sign of a dwelling. It was a cold day, but the sun shone, the sun was a clear azure-winter-blue. There were a few enormous hares, a number of rabbit corpses (myxomatosis has returned?). Every sort of birdsong could be heard, at times though I could not identify the various sounds which made a continual twittering in the back of one's consciousness.

I felt I had had a real holiday by the time we got back for hamburger lunch. The water life in Broadchalke is a fascination of which I've not had enough. It is so soothing to the spirit to watch the flow of the Ebble and to see an animal splash to denote where a trout is swimming upstream. We are planning to use our meadow marshland as a water garden and I hope that in my *really* old age it may content me to sit and watch the ripples.

Sylvia Henley

Judy [Montagu]'s Aunt Sylvia[1] is a woman of quality. She is now nearing her nineties but she is totally in command of every situation. She walks as straight as a dye. She never forgets a name, or gets tired when sightseeing in Rome where she recently became friends with Ann Fleming, who she says has a remarkable quality of being very good at giving people a 'free rein', but she knows exactly the moment to 'jib'.

---

[1] Sylvia Henley (1882–1980), daughter of fourth Lord Stanley of Alderley (also fourth Lord Sheffield). Her niece, Judy Montagu (1923–72) married Milton Gendel.

I went to collect a 1918 dress from her. She told me its derivation. Her husband and Boy Capel[1] had at one time been in partnership together and B. C. had Chanel as his mistress. Chanel, wishing to make a gesture, specially designed this dress for Sylvia to wear at the peace conference celebrations in Paris.

'Aunt Sylvia' was pleased with a maxim that the mother-in-law of Mabell Airlie[2] had told her, 'A brick that is good enough for a wall will not remain on the street.'

Dame Edith Evans

Alan [Tagg], breathless from Chichester, where he is designing *Dear Antoine* in which Edith Evans appears, says that she has been very fussy and devious. When she can't remember a line, she interrupts with some red herring. Sitting on a sofa (she complains that in this production no one comes nearer to her than six yards) she picked up a cushion and said, 'This object is a designer's peccadillo.' She took against it. The director asked her, 'Do you like cats?' 'Yes.' 'Well that cushion is a cat.' From then on she stroked it. It seems that when making *Nicholas Nickleby*[3] she had to have a cat in her arm for one scene. The cat scratched her mercilessly, but in spite of it being agony, she continued to hold it until the 'take' was over. Then Dame Edith complained to the cat, 'You're very naughty. You tried to steal that scene, and you're not an important part in this film. After all, we're not doing Dick Whittington.'

Went to a Foyle's lunch for P. Daubeny[4] (and rather impressed by my treatment). And Wilfrid Hyde White,[5] the old rogue, told me that when offered Alastair Sim's[6] part in the current William Douglas Home play,[7] he said, 'Well, I've never replaced anyone before, but our play is closing

[1] Captain Arthur Capel (d. 1920). Father of June Hutchinson.
[2] Mabell, Countess of Airlie (d. 1956), daughter of fifth Earl of Arran. Lady of the Bedchamber to Queen Mary. Author of *Thatched with Gold*.
[3] Dame Edith Evans (1888–1976) had played Miss Betsy Trotwood in the film of *David Copperfield* in 1970. Bryan Forbes attributes this incident to that film. See *Ned's Girl* (Elm Tree Books, 1977), p. 265.
[4] Sir Peter Daubeny (1921–75), founder and artistic director of London's World Theatre Seasons. He was described as 'a theatrical Marco Polo exploring the international scene as no impresario ever had before'.
[5] Wilfrid Hyde White (1903–91), actor, played Colonel Pickering in the film of *My Fair Lady*.
[6] Alastair Sim (1900–76), inimitable actor of stage and screen.
[7] *The Jockey Club Stakes* by William Douglas-Home (1912–92), opened at the Vaudeville Theatre 30 September 1970.

on Saturday. I don't want to move out of my nice, comfortable dressing room, so if you'll bring the production to the Savoy, I'll accept.' They did.

Henry Herbert, [Earl of] Pembroke as he now is, was standing on the front doorsteps after an Easter party and looked at the line of fruit trees recently planted in the vegetable garden opposite. 'Does that belong to you?' he asked incredulously. I don't think that his question is the reason for my wanting to improve the prospect from the front of the house, but recently I've realised how wasteful it has been that no benefit was gained by this charming river scene at the end of the paddock. How could we arrange it that it becomes part of the domain? We have pondered for months as to how to cope with the bogginess of the land beyond the ash trees. Could we afford five hundred lorry loads of hard core? No, if we could, it would be more ground to look after. A Burmese bridge? A runway of rubble, could we bring the river in close? Smallpeice one morning suggested we should have an ornamental lake. But how? We have now seen many 'authorities' including two men from the River Board, the local contractor and others, and it seems a wonderful possibility could be within our reach. River plants, reeds, iris, white king cups and Muscovy ducks. It is a thrilling prospect. I am waiting to hear how much it will cost.

27 May 1971

Nancy's marriage to Hugh [Smiley] has worked extremely well and they are extraordinarily happy together. They seem to have complete understanding and Hugh in his happiness has become much nicer than in the days of pomposity and wealth. But it is sad that as a silly young army officer, he should have spent so much of his inheritance. He lavished jewellery on a lady who had three lovers and then married the Duke of Bedford before committing suicide.[1] Nancy came in for aquamarines, and each year the reality had to be faced with greater strictures that Hugh could no longer afford to live at Great Oaks, nor indeed in the smaller house they bought, but that in order to cut their cloth according to their means, he must live in a cottage that was not even *orné*. For seventeen years now they have been happy in a hideous little dwelling with low ceilings and the furnishings have become poorer each year.

[1] Mrs Clare ('Brownie') Hollway, first wife of thirteenth Duke of Bedford, who succeeded in 1953. Her health declined after the birth of her son Rudolf in 1944, and after a row with her husband, she died in 1945 from an overdose of sleeping pills, mixed with dry martinis. An open verdict was recorded.

They manage a certain amount of entertaining with Hugh, a superb chef, doing the cooking. He has been known to go down to the kitchen in the middle of a night's sleep to see if he put a lobster roe through the sieve for the fifth time. But their most favoured guests are invited to their annual treat of motoring through wonderful country lanes and forested highways through Petersfield to Chichester, to see the four plays of the season and to dine afterwards on the cold buffet in the theatre caravanserai.

I have enjoyed my previous outings very much indeed, for although I think I did not enjoy the productions (Clements,[1] the present chief, is a second rater) the beauty of the motor journey was one of the joys of an English summer. Never has anything appeared more green than the beech accidia, the chestnuts, candelabra, the Queen Anne's lace in the hedges. The theatre itself is a beast, always with a howling gale or air-conditioning draught, blowing down one's neck. It is not a good place in which to act – nonetheless for N. and H. it is always a big excitement and one has not the heart to drop a word of criticism.

This year Nancy asked me to see *The Rivals* but this is a play I have seen once too often. I really could not manage that, but begged to be allowed to see *Dear Antoine*, the Anouilh play which Alan Tagg has decorated and told me would be so good because the entire cast was excellent and Edith Evans in particular was in her best form. At rehearsals she was apt to forget her lines and in order to cover up would insert some excuse for an interruption. Then she would ask the prompter, 'Where was I?' and given the missing words would continue. I was full of expectancy when, after an idyllic sunlit drive, we arrived through the mazes of white may blossom at the theatre. The audience was either eating a pre-performance snack or else wandering their way to the foyer.

It is odd how one can tell from a distance if something is out of the ordinary and if there is some crisis. We noticed a huge olive green stationary Rolls full of women, over the one in the back R.-hand seat, the chauffeur was bending solicitously, as if pampering a child or an old invalid. The invalid seemed to have a familiar profile. Surely it was Edith Evans. Was she being told to hurry and get into her dressing room? Isn't she cutting it fine? Surely she would prepare for her performance long before this? Yet I could see that it was Edith in her well-known white chauffeur's jockey cap, of pale beige with the pale being stronger beneath it. She was obviously being very tense and on the alert for danger. A rather hippie-looking fan stood by the open door of the motor, waiting

[1] Sir John Clements (1910–88), actor, manager and producer. Director of Chichester Festival Theatre (1966–73).

perhaps to ask her if she would oblige with an autograph. But very slowly, as in a funeral procession, the Rolls moved off. I was very baffled.

Surely it was too late for her to drive off in the opposite direction of the theatre? We went into the dark, dreary theatre, saw Alan's funereal set and were given a programme, out of which fell a slip saying that, owing to the indisposition of Dame Edith Evans, the part of Charlotte would be taken by her understudy.

Disappointment was forgotten as the lights were lowered and Joyce Redman[1] started to give the performance of the evening. The play disappointed, there was much to criticise about the direction, but the whole evening was ruined by the absence of Dame Edith. Glamour had gone, star quality was missed and her understudy had none of Edith's charm or wit. One closed one's eyes, one heard the same intonations and one could imagine exactly how Edith would play the part, how she would get her laughs, and give it pith and wit. But the woman imitating her vowels, her musical cadences, was completely lacking in the essentials. Obviously Edith had given a run of the mill, Lady Bracknell portrayal which I don't think is what Anouilh meant, but she gave it grandeur and fun, and this the audience missed.

The evening went off at half-cock. Anna Calder-Marshall, in the interval, told me that Edith had had a nervous 'crise' at the thought of facing an audience. She had the weekend to think about it, and that had been too long away from the stage. She was only happy if acting continuously. Sundays were a trial. By Monday evening she had worked herself up to such a pitch of nerves that a doctor had been summoned and in her dressing room had told her that she should not go on.

She has been rather odd at rehearsals. She hates first nights, the telegrams, flowers, messages, excitement. The management decided not to tell her when the first night had come on them. On the morning of the opening, her chauffeur telephoned the theatre. Dame Edith had not ordered him for the evening. Was she not wanted at the theatre? Yes of course. How important that you enquired, but don't let her know it is a first night. Edith had, according to Eileen, who was seeing the first performance with Alan, appeared very tense, but the audience had applauded every word. It had been a personal triumph, probably her last.

For what we had witnessed quite by chance outside the theatre was poor Edith's final exit from the stage.[1] She is eighty-three. She has

---

[1] Joyce Redman (b. 1918), Irish actress, who first appeared at the Playhouse, London in 1935. She joined the Old Vic company at the New Theatre in 1944 and the Shakespeare Memorial Theatre Company at Stratford-on-Avon in 1955.
[2] Bryan Forbes, Dame Edith's biographer, confirms that Chichester was her last appearance in a play on stage, though in 1973 and 1974, she appeared in *Edith Evans ... and friends.*

difficulty in learning her lines, is wobbly on her feet and getting a bit deaf, so it is difficult for her to take a prompt. She is still able to play bits in films and television, but from what everyone says, this is the end of a long and wonderfully productive theatre career. It is sad that she should have to go, but she has had a good innings.

Gladys Cooper,[1] who is a year or so older than Edith, was quite unsympathetic when she heard my news. 'Her trouble is that she thinks too much about the theatre. She should go out and forget it, but she's so ingrained and self-centred, she has no other interests, except her performance. I have my grandchildren, and all sorts of interests to keep me going, but I don't think about my part when I'm out of the theatre, and I don't think about myself if I can help it. A young man rang me up for an interview on the psychology of acting. I said I didn't know anything about it. I was too busy housekeeping and looking after my friends and as far as the theatre is concerned, I feel jolly lucky that I've got a good job.' Gladys has always been a realist. She has never treated the theatre seriously and it has stood her in good stead. She is packing them in at the Haymarket for a revival of *The Chalk Garden*[2] and when I asked if she was tired, she said, 'Tired? Not a bit of it!'

30 May 1971

This diary has been neglected: I have had wretched headaches, and have had to restrict my writing (reading) as there has been proof correcting and quite a spate of diary extracts to polish for Vol. IV. I do not know where the springtime has gone. I have been most of the time in the country, squeezing as much as possible into the limited time in London, so that I can come back by a that much earlier train, and here there have been lots of excitements. As a result of Alan's visit, the Blick workmen came in and stripped the dining room bare. It is now a monastic cell and very beautiful in its austerity. I am pleased to get rid of the junk, the bad Delft, which has become such a blue and white cliché. It was time to make a clearance. Now too the winter garden has been freshened up with a layer of lily of the valley leaf green paint. The linoleum walls and bamboo panels had been there for twelve years and have become drab.

The biggest change however has been brought about by the arrival of a huge prehistoric mechanical giraffe, a digger which has bitten into the

---

[1] Dame Gladys Cooper (1888–1971), had played Mrs Higgins in the film of *My Fair Lady*.
[2] *The Chalk Garden*, Enid Bagnold's best-known and most successful play ran, in the revival, from April to August 1971.

soggy marshland at the bottom of the field, opposite the front door, and has created a little private trout stream and a lake with an island, all for my own benefit. It was extraordinarily exciting to see at night from my bedroom window, the remnants of the light in the sky reflected in the winding ribbon of water. It brings a whole new interest to life here, the element of water is one that we have not enjoyed. Even in the appalling muddy condition with which the landscape is at the moment disfigured, one can tell that here will be a lovely place to look at, a new form of nature, with fish and all sorts of birds that are different from those on our terrace. Already the bird life is amazing with doves and greedy thrushes and blackbirds, added to which can be heard the squeak of a moorhen and ducks have explored the new terrain, and swans have been seen...As for the trout, it seems I should spend my old age being a fisherman. Charles II said these were the best trout in England and it is said that sixty trout appear whenever the gardener next door puts his garbage down for them to eat off.

Of course it has been a time of great frustration too. I seem to have a jinx on all machinery, even when removed at a distance from it. Twice the digger broke down and the driver said for the first time in four years, then the rain came down and lorries got stuck in the mud. Smallpeice, who is becoming gloomier, said it was madness to continue in these bad conditions. But a digger costs a fortune a day. I became rather rattled watching the various snags happen, and I am too sensitive to overlook the displeasure of the neighbouring Bundys. Ever since the son drove his tractor through our chalk wall, they have disappeared at the sight of me. Today the son gave me the cut direct.

I came back to 'flake out' but my siesta was a very spasmodic affair with wondering what was happening to the Flanders Field opposite. Had the digger sunk in the lake? No sound could be heard. I looked out of the window once more. The driver in his seat appeared to be reading his newspaper. On the other side of the domain, a lorry was churning up mud, stuck in its attempt to dump a lot of earth in the top field. (It is Smallpeice's one wish to level our lawns so he need not get off his mowing machine once it starts. I see his point, but with the levelling a lot of charm will go too.) It is really rather a relief when the time comes for all the workers to dump their machines and depart for the Whitsun holiday.

3 June 1971

Panic stations to be ready for 10.45 appointment with a German woman who wants to see if a little blob of dried pus should be cut off the tip of my nose (the result of a streptococcic boil) or whether to leave it be for the rest of my days. Proofs of Cathleen Nesbitt article to be corrected, letters of thanks re the costume exhibition to Philip Hay[1] – Princess Alexandra and Duchess of Kent.[2]

No time for telephoning. A rush without handkerchief or rail ticket. The German woman pores over my face, says it needs cleaning. She pricks my cheek with electric needle. 'I am very brave,' I tell her. 'Most men aren't, but women are. They have to be, they know they'll get no sympathy.' The little bump should stay.

I rush out to Canadian TV interview and in my hurry, pull the curtain back on to a view of a woman lying with her legs apart, having an electric needle applied to her twat. The nurses laugh. A beautiful Japanese interviews me. All goes well until a loathsome imitation Barbra Streisand fails to materialise with the promised taxi and I am anxious and angry as I am late in the traffic for Kitty Miller's awful but somehow unavoidable lunch. I am the last to arrive and first to leave. No *gêne*.

Relief to go to the country and anxiety to see the new lake and island since the second visit of the digger. Smallpeice rather a wet blanket. He never informs me of anything. One has to drag information piecemeal from him, he is seldom enthusiastic. He is sorry to have missed the opportunity of having several dozen tons of earth dumped for future use near the lawn which he wants to level. He says the digger has departed. The result is 'alright'. I am however extremely pleased with the effect. The mud is heavy and wet and dark but when it is levelled a bit, the landscape is a delightful shape

I am pleased with a great new interest to life. A trout appeared, then another, the birds were merry. I went up the garden to pick flowers for the house, my much enjoyed therapy. By degrees tension slackened. TV Percy Thrower (alas without the Countess of Rosse, who appeared with him last week, never has any slut appeared more gracious!). Early bed and the prospect of an easy weekend – DV.

Francis Rose   *June 1971*

Agonising situation. He has really reached rock bottom. He has not one penny in the world and cannot make any money. He is incapable of looking after himself and the church has kicked him out, or rather the Father at the monastery which housed him for a month has sent him back

---

[1] Sir Philip Hay (1918–86), former private secretary to Princess Marina, Duchess of Kent.
[2] HRH the Duchess of Kent (b. 1933), formerly Katharine Worsley.

to London without any suggestions as to how he can keep himself. No place to lodge. He has found a doss-house where he joins the other down and outs and looks like any of them, hair to his shoulders, not shaven, my old suit unrecognisable as a tramp's garment. Why could I not allow him to lie on the floor of the dining room for a night? Because I'd never get rid of him, the room would somehow be ruined and all the servants would leave.

I have given him 'tips' which last a day or two. When in extremis he comes for more, but he is not grateful. 'Why do you only come to me when you're desperate?' 'Because you're my best friend,' he says. He arrived with a portfolio of about a hundred drawings. 'No, Francis, I can't keep them here.' I did not want more excuses for him to return. The portfolio was left in a telephone booth and stolen. It is the last act of a tragic farce. Ray says Francis will find it very hard to die. He threatens me with his suicide, says he can't bear the burden much longer, and in fact I cannot think how he has survived this long. But he has a monumental strength and anyone else who has drunk and drugged as he has would have long gone.

Meanwhile there is a short lull, and miraculously *New Horizons* have taken pity on him and once they are responsible for someone, they will not allow them to go without their guidance. It is quite extraordinary that there are these people who will devote their lives to those they know to be fundamentally crooked. Francis is no crook. He would not steal, but he is a liar of major proportions, a bully, a sycophant when need be, and it is only a tragedy that he has not left behind him a great monument of work that would justify his behaving like a Corvo.

Stephen Tennant, Reddish *June 1971*

With David Hockney and Peter Schlesinger[1] here, I decided to telephone to see if Stephen would receive us. Surprisingly the answer was 'yes'. Stephen, like a beached whale, was in bed, fatter than ever, his red-dyed hair down his back, his fingernails two inches long, his beard sprouting through make-up. He was in a 'new' bedroom, and it was certainly much cleaner than the one he has occupied for the last year. And when I say 'occupy' I mean it, for he seldom leaves his bed. Daylight was kept at bay. I peered through a slit in the curtains. 'How is your garden, Stephen?' 'I really don't know,' he replied. He was intent on showing us his enormous fan, a black Japanese prey-bird of a fan, and lots of others. 'Could I have

---

[1] Peter Schlesinger, a Californian art student, who was Hockney's lover and favourite model. They met in 1966 and in 1968 Hockney brought him to London.

this lace one renewed by Duvellroy?' 'I'm afraid, Stephen, they are no longer in business.'

He then showed, from a basket, his jewels, turquoises, Mexican bracelets and rings galore. Nothing good, or to my taste, but he was funny, witty. He soon talked of old songs. He and his servant, George, had been singing old songs such as 'One Night of Love, Two Hearts Entwined'. I laughed too loudly. 'What's funny about that?' he asked, rather waspishly. 'It should be called The Higher Mathematician's Waltz,' I explained.

He was a little uncertain of me today and spent his energy regaling David and he succeeded. He talked of Thomas Hardy, whom he knew, and told of his first poem. When he completed two lines, Hardy felt he really was a poet. Stephen said his first wife objected to Hardy playing the lute in the summerhouse as she considered it too unconventional and Hardy's pictures did not do him justice. 'He was much more interesting and impressive.' Stephen recited 'Lyonesse', surprisingly word perfect. S. knows much of Shakespeare by heart and quotes readily from many sources. When he reads, he remembers. It is his life. Imagine the loneliness, being by himself in bed all the time!

He regaled us with his recollection of America, staying in Palm Beach with Willa Cather,[1] appalled to find Los Angeles was a 'mass of shacks'. Stephen allowed himself to be photographed, therein making a mistake. He said he was regaining his youth. He gave me a photograph of himself, the skinniest person there has ever been, and yet there was no regret in his voice. We drank half a bottle and two quarter-bottles of champagne. We looked at the house hurriedly, and the two boys felt they had never seen anything to compare with it, and would never forget the experience. Incidentally, the new 'woman' has tidied up the house considerably and S. does not seem to mind.

June 1971

A busy week. Monday alone, a day in which to recover from the nervous irritation of the visit of Ossie Clark,[2] his wife and baby, who arrived one hour late for lunch and behaved just as badly as David Hockney and his friend, who were staying, behaved well. It is always a strain to have people for the day. They have nowhere to return to, and one feels that having made the effort to arrive, they can't be left alone. At last I got down to a

---

[1] Willa Cather (1876–1947), American novelist with whom Stephen Tennant was obsessed.
[2] Ossie Clark (1942–96) dress designer. Subsequently murdered.

bit of painting, though much activity to cope with. The entrance drive being paved, the water garden being bulldozed once again, and inevitably getting stuck in the mud. Arrangements to buy bamboo, which must be put in during the next ten days or we miss a year's growth. Headaches in evening so visit to neighbouring Pitt-Rivers[1] and peers to see their gardens and get tips. Tuesday a wonderful dividend of a morning as I found I did not have to go to London for any appointments before an emissary from the publisher coming to see me at five. Ann Fleming[2] gave an amusing dinner and supper, mostly political, Fred [Ashton][3] and I the exceptions. The Roy Jenkinses (he seems to be doing an impersonation of a boy pretending to be a man), she exceptionally good, the Longfords, he too complimentary, the Amerys and Maudlings[4] etc. afterwards.

Cecil had been working for two years on a fashion exhibition at the Victoria and Albert Museum. He collected dresses from the Queen, the Queen Mother, Princess Anne and other members of the Royal Family. In quest of some of Queen Mary's hats, he went to Leeds to visit the Earl and Countess of Harewood.

Next morning dawn called to go on a quest for a toque to Leeds. But as the toque was once Queen Mary's,[5] my journey was really necessary. Almost a week of rain seemed to culminate into days downpour (yet it continued till I left England) and the view from my comfortable train window was one of bleak squalor, slag heaps, miserable rows of houses, flatness, drabness everywhere, and the outskirts of Leeds an appalling sprawl.

In the dank coldness Patricia Harewood to meet me to take me to Harewood House. Princess Mary[6] had a great glamour for me as a boy. I was in the crowd, up for the day from Harrow for her wedding. It gave

---

[1] Michael Pitt-Rivers (1917–1999). He lived at Tollard Royal and was sent to prison in the Montagu of Beaulieu boy scout case.
[2] Ann Fleming (1913–81), formerly Viscountess Rothermere, and widow of Ian Fleming. Political hostess.
[3] Sir Frederick Ashton (1904–88), ballet choreographer.
[4] Roy Jenkins (Lord Jenkins of Hillhead) (b.1916) and his wife (Dame) Jennifer (b.1921); the seventh Earl of Longford (1905–2001) and his wife Elizabeth (b. 1906); Julian Amery (Lord Amery of Lustleigh) (1911–96) and his wife Catherine (d. 1991); and Reginald Maudling (1917–79) and his wife Beryl (1919–1988).
[5] HM Queen Mary (1867–1953), wife of George V.
[6] Princess Mary (1897–1965), later the Princess Royal, only daughter of George V. Married sixth Earl of Harewood.

me a feeling of 'small-town boy makes it' to be staying with her son forty years later. I had seen the house on the tour with Kin, so chose to see the collection of birds rather than the contents of the house after lunch. Perhaps this was a mistake as the cold 'up North' is far worse than in Wiltshire during 'flaming June'. The white owl was the star bird, but others with marvellous colours, and the setting quite magnificent. But the big moment was when we delved into the past and in a cupboard room smelling disgustingly of Olive, the mad maid's dog, we opened up boxes of Princess Mary's carefully preserved wedding garments, the shoes, stockings and headdress all together. The dress from Handley Seymour[1] just as it had been taken off.

The poor 'shy' bride, and she never lost her shyness whatever else she lost, had sweated the arm holes, and the silver embroidered net was a little discoloured and the dress was always rather ugly, but now it was a period piece, though the going-away dress of a particularly dowdy blue, embroidered with a particularly dowdy pink, was a fine example of the strength of Royal dowdiness at this time. We discovered that Princess Mary (later [Princess] Royal) had never thrown away a BOAC fan, or memento of some trip. Little handiwork bandeaux of leaves had been carefully preserved, also feathers, aigrettes, snippets of lace, decorations for shoes.

Likewise she had preserved a great number of Queen Mary's hats. At first they were disappointing. One expected to see a large loaf-like toque, instead the proportions were so very small. But I suppose the great white wig on top of which they were perched gave such an effect of height. Many of these toques, all in splendid condition and very well made, were also of this particular dowdiness that struck me so forcefully at a time when I craved for just the opposite of these determinedly dull effects.

I was terrified that George [Harewood] would not allow me to take away anything, having thought perhaps the Queen or someone would criticise him, but no, I was able to choose half a dozen of the 'smartest' and felt that my quest was completely successful, and dare not risk displeasure by asking too much, and wondering if perhaps also his mother's wedding dress...

I discovered that George is by no means an easy person to live with, but Patricia seems able to cope with the incessant flow of vitality, the over-life-size manners and on occasion the bullying. There is, in spite of all his remarkable aesthetic and musical sensibilities, a coarse grain of militarism in him, and he insists on everything being done in a most absurdly ritualistic manner. When his grandmother's 'effects' were being

---

[1] Mrs Handley Seymour, designed the Queen Mother's wedding dress and her dress for the 1937 Coronation. Later superseded by Norman Hartnell.

opened, he became quite wild that his wife was not putting them around in 'any order'. He is the one never to be interrupted, and this must be difficult as his flow of (good) talk is almost continuous.

That George has broken away completely from the Royal tradition (to have a bastard son was quite an event) shows his strength of character, and mercifully the change of wives has worked well for him and neighbours told that the change of atmosphere from tension to ease was quite remarkable. Marion[1] was a bad housewife and is the one to suffer now.

Patricia is what one of the neighbours (Lord Raleigh) would call a sycamore, not quite a hardwood, not soft. She talks with a certain gentility that covers up her Australian descent, but she has a good sense of humour and is remarkably efficient, and she has a tough job. She told me that the house carpenter had warned her that a four-poster bed should not be used by her and her husband as if it were given any 'undue activity' it would collapse.

Early next morning I left Leeds with Queen Mary's toques. Never would I have imagined that the hall at Pelham Place would one day be littered with these majestic creations.

Cecil then went to Lake Garda on behalf of Vogue *in order to photograph d'Annunzio's house, on the northern shore of the lake, Villa Il Vittoriale.*

The name of d'Annunzio had to me only vague connections, mostly with women, [Eleonore] Duse, the [Marchesa] Casati, some romantic queen etc. I had seen photographs of his extraordinary house, but I had never read anything by him. Did not know if his poems and plays were first-rate, or the reason for his now being completely outdated and in eclipse. That I will have to find out, meanwhile the house is of an extraordinary astonishment. The whole complex of buildings, with theatre, lecture auditorium, gardens, mausoleum, ship banked among the cypresses, colonnades, arches, terraces, stairways. But the small private house beggars all description. To begin with, it is so dark (except for one room, the study) that one can hardly grope oneself about. When one's eyes have their right adaptation, they see the most gruesome mixture of things of fantasy and the macabre.

It is all a triumph of originality but of bad taste. I admire his abandoning all tenets of purity, of classicism and form. He has run amok in a Stephen Tennant madness of egomania, everything to *épater*, nothing fresh, clean, pure, banal, all golds and black, Oriental mixed with Florentine renaissance and Victorian Danteism. Dolls, Chinese figures,

---

[1] Marion Stein (b. 1926), first wife of Lord Harewood. Divorced 1967. Married 1973, Jeremy Thorpe.

badly gilded plaster casts, plaster casts trimmed with jewels and draped with gold lamé, it might be the eyrie of a black magician, or the heart's desire of a raging faggot. It was fascinating to try to deduce the man from his legacy. Here were rows of encyclopaedias, thousands of books marked with his tags, chairs for reading and study at every point, so he was a man of real intellect. But the surface frivolity is appalling.

Obviously this syndrome amused him (though I doubt his sense of humour) but mostly it was done to impress, to make himself a talking point. He was a sort of Dalí of his time, but we know Dalí was a great draughtsman.

In this awful darkness one was, after two hours, quite exhausted and ill. I am not generally sensitive to vibrations and atmospheres, but this I felt was really rather macabre and evil. The airlessness, the slightly dusty veneer and the mothballs, produced a sort of pain in the chest. After two hours' photographing I felt utterly and totally exhausted.

The following morning it was not any better. The sun was out for the first time here in a month (a terrific Thomas Mann climate had been created) but inside d'Annunzio's house the same darkness prevailed. Again, after two hours, I felt not only 'bushed' but had a headache. Fortunately we stopped at midday to go to San Vigilio, loved by Duff and Diana, where Walsh, the proprietor, has just died, and *The Times* obituary which I have brought was written by John Julius. A lovely place, simple, free, airy, completely unlike Il Vittoriale. We visited Sirmione, then as rain was coming on, tried to ferry to d'Annunzio before another storm.

By the time we left I was again exhausted beyond repair and even a sleep before dinner in a *boîte* was not enough to revive me, and I sank into bed as if I was caught in one of d'Annunzio's aeroplane propellers. He has cast a great spell and I see his influence everywhere I now look.

More d'Annunzio

He was a small man. He made all doorways low and the rooms are small, with two exceptions. Everywhere bad taste. He enjoyed buying useless objects and would perhaps buy forty pieces of junk all at a go. The whole minute arrangement is carefully loved and tended by an old man who was with the Master for seventeen years. I am sure it will not be long before he is found dead on his Master's bed or sunk on a pile of fifty cushions.

The stink of camphor, the lack of air, made a two-hour working stretch terribly tiring. As it is I have worked so quickly that others would take a week to do what we have in three days. Let's only pray the results are as good as they should be. The house is certainly *photogénique* and I

Lady Diana Cooper in her 'Happy
Birthday hat', summer 1972.

The Duchess of Windsor
at the Proust Ball,
December 1971.

Cathleen Nesbitt.

Opposite:
Sir Michael Duff.

8 Pelham Place, with Cathleen Nesbitt, John Betjeman, Eileen Hose (Cecil's secretary), and Lady Elizabeth Cavendish.

Reddish House,
the beloved retreat.

Cecil as Nadar,
at the Proust Ball.

James Pope-Hennessy, the writer,
murdered in 1974.

Sir Francis Rose, artist, under the
steps, with Cecil above.

Stephen Tennant, poet and novelist *gâté*,
languishing in his bed.

can't think why already a film has not been done of the loves of d'Annunzio. The gardens are not inspiring and clearing up the odds and ends of the job was tedious and tiresome, but it should be well-paid and I have to make extra money now. We all discussed the dismissal of Diana Vreeland from *Vogue*, and it seems that the finances of the magazine are in a very bad way. Future blanker. I will have to go to Milan.

Nice outings to eat in good rustic restaurants around the lake. It is very much a *Death in Venice* life in this hotel, so good to get out. The Sunday crowds are appalling and we motored to Verona and felt the solidity of this ancient-walled town with great squares and magnificent palaces and churches on a grandiose scale...

A final look at the d'Annunzio garden, to photograph the beached ship, today overrun with holiday crowds. The success that d'Annunzio enjoyed in his life followed him afterwards. The effort of walking up steep hills made me feel very old. I became depressed at how stiff I was. My body has lost a lot of flexibility and I must ask Miss Gaffran to limber me up, but there's something about my attitude to myself and the attitude of others towards me which makes me feel very aged...

David Bailey is never in one country for more than a few days. When he is in London he is hot on our tracks in connection with the film he has done on me. But when we try to see 'rushes' he is nowhere to be found. I did not wish to discover that the film was a 'send-up' and that it was too late to insist on alterations. However, after many delays, Eileen and I were allowed to see it. It is entertaining. It is good value. But it is not a good film, badly edited, inconclusive, superficial.

I don't even think it has Bailey's imprint, let alone mine. I come out of it as a rather pleasant old buddy, distinguished-looking and with a sense of humour. It shows only a small part of my work as a photographer, very little of my life and none of my other interests.

A lot of valuable stuff has been frittered away – D. Cecil, C. Connolly, D. Vreeland, A. Withers go for nothing, a pity, for they said interesting things. The war years, confined to England, are rather moving, and I suddenly felt I was seeing my own obituary. It was quite upsetting. But later, when I had got over the shock, I realised what a lost opportunity this was, how interesting and varied an entertainment it could have been! A pity that so much time is wasted.

Truman C [Capote] in a very bad way. He says in the film that I don't know what I'm about, that I would really like to be Noël Coward. How very far off the mark he is. I would have liked to have been N. C. when I was 18 to 23, but then everyone would like to have been N. C. at that time. Truman also says 'I make enemies like most people gather roses'.

Diana [Vreeland] tells me he recently came to lunch, leapt on the sofa and said, 'Well, now I've had *everything*!' And went on to describe how his 'home' on Southampton Beach with all his papers and possessions had been pitch-forked into the lake, and all lost, and no insurance. A long description. Diana telephoned to her daughter-in-law who lived nearby, to ask if her house had suffered in the recent storm, earthquake. 'No.' 'Well, will you motor and see if what Truman says is true about his home.' Betty Vreeland returns, 'T.'s house is there alright.'

It seems T. is putting all the fantasy that went into his early books into his life and nothing into his writing. He really does seem to have gone round the bend in a very unattractive way.

Richard Buckle planned to stage 'the Greatest Show on Earth' at the London Coliseum on 22 June 1971. The purpose of this was to raise money to purchase Titian's Death of Actaeon *for the nation. The picture was due to be sold by Christie's on 25 June. Buckle promised 'a succession of crazy events'. One was a performance of* Garden Party *by Bach, to a previously un-staged arrangement by Diaghilev. Then there would be* BreakfastDickyBuckle, *hopefully starring Margot Fonteyn, Anton Dolin, Lydia Sokolova, Alicia Markova and the Indian dancer, Ram Gopal. This would be followed by a* Come Dancing *spectacular with Victor Silvester. An auction would take place on stage. The performance would end with what Buckle declared as 'all the most divine people who happen to be in London at the time dancing on in masks before being introduced individually.'*

That was the plan. Alas expectations proved too ambitious. When the tickets were reduced in price, it was re-described as a 'répétition générale'. Fonteyn and Desmond Kelly danced in an Ashton arrangement of a romantic duet by Liszt, Wayne Sleep went through some new steps devised for him by Peter Darrell, and then, in the words of the disenchanted Times *reviewer, John Percival, who sat in his seat from 7.30 pm until forced to meet his 11 pm deadline, 'amateurish lantern slides of some professional paintings' were displayed, not without hitches, to mime by Wayne Sleep.*

Danilova, Dolin and Ilzikova appeared in Diaghilev costumes in front of ill-lit Bakst settings. The performance was 'exhaustingly long' and Percival missed the promised pas de deux *by Fonteyn and Nureyev.*

Cecil was in the house:

The Greatest Show (Off) on Earth

Poor Dicky [Buckle]. A meeting with A. Warhol sent him off his rocker. He at once thought he could command the same publicity as Andy and started to show off in a most atypical manner. He has been a distinguished writer and critic for years. Now he wanted to be Dickybuckle, a character and his *folies de grandeur* were frightening! He seemed to believe he could sell his posters for ten thousand pounds each. That he could make two million on a gala to save the Titian or, he wasn't quite explicit, to make a museum of the performing arts. I was supposed to give one thousand pounds towards a harpsichord to be made of mother-of-pearl. He would not listen to any suggestions for economies. He lashed out at critics of his extravagances. It has been a difficult time for his friends.

The gala started on such a grandiose scale that by degrees he has had to accept reality. Tickets, instead of being £100, were reduced to £10, but not before he had spent thousands and thousands and we feared the worst when at last the gala which, in spite of all difficulties, *did* take place, Dicky's contributions were puerile. As Fred Ashton said, 'If he had had to write a critique of someone else's work, he would have been scathing.' There was a disastrous moment or two when Buckle talked about himself into a microphone that did not work. The audience pretty nearly booed, but when the worst was over we were given some great vaudeville turns by the best dancers, a Venezuelan, a Japanese (named Hideo!), a great *coup de théâtre* by Zizi Jeanmaire[1] in black, with chorus boys with pink ostrich feather fans (Zizi has surely the best legs of today in the world!)

Fred [Ashton] did an idyllic love dance to Thai music. Margot [Fonteyn][2] appeared as young as ever, Nureyev looked loathsome and was monstrously brilliant, so the appearance was stupendous. Our hearts were in our mouths when Dicky appeared lest he should gag this 'The happiest moment of my life'. But mercifully he merely paraded his stars like a showman with his Lippizaners. Mercifully he was dressed in sports white, no hippie nonsense. Mercifully the curtain came down without disaster.

But the critics panned the evening – 'The Greatest Show on Earth' was a whimper and Dicky will never have anything but docks and weeds surrounding his cottage, and he may well have to fill up the cottage itself, though I'm sure the bills go as far as the bankruptcy court. So sad, and Dicky has his great *Nijinsky* book up his sleeve. It will doubtless make his reputation, if not his fortune. (But the madness of the past three months has made him a 'laughing stock' and no one takes him seriously.)

Francis Rose, another madman, has eventually been sent off to Spain (thanks to a lot of poor young people clubbing together at *New Horizons*), to be put at the mercy of some priest who imagines Francis to be a grand aristocrat painter (he has been told Francis has eighty Spanish

---

[1] Renée (Zizi) Jeanmaire (b. 1924), dancer with her husband Roland Petit.
[2] Dame Margot Fonteyn (1919–91), ballerina.

titles). Now, after one week, the Foreign Office rings up to say Sir F. is destitute in Spain and says I am responsible for his visit and have guaranteed to send him home when necessary. I cannot dismiss from my mind the horror of the situation in Spain!

Weeding   *24 June 1971*

The unusually heavy rainfall during this past month has wrecked the roses but done untold good to the weeds. I try to keep the cracks between the stones on the terrace as my own private weeding job, pulling up tufts of grass, pruning thistles and plantains, and doing my best with unknown trespassers, but this afternoon I felt that Smallpeice must be helped and that I could relieve him of the 'easy' job of pulling up the thriving harvest of groundsel (we could feed a million canaries for a week!). On my way to the top garden, armed with trowel, knife, secateurs and trug, I noticed an iris had fallen.

I picked off the stalk, as the flower was dead, I dead-headed a few roses and some nut brown clusters, then by slow degrees, tidying a bit as I went, arrived in the cutting garden and set to among the beds. Two kinds of weeds were predominant, groundsel, or white flowered little spikes which were easily pulled out. Luckily the rainfall has made weeding easy, and if one is in a happy frame of mind, weeding is a very pleasant occupation. If one has anything unpleasant on one's mind, one is apt to dwell on it. If one is actively worried then it is not the sort of thing to do.

Mercifully, apart from the illness of Ray, and wondering whether he will be able to continue with us, and wondering whether the new water garden and paved forecourt are going to be the final straws on my way to bankruptcy, my frame of mind was halcyon. Yet I found, as I pulled up ten more sheafs of weed, I kept saying to myself, over and over again, "Tis like an unweeded garden, things rank and rotten grow wild...' or I found that my mind was asking the same silly question, 'E contana da qui?' or repeating something asinine like S.E.T. [Selective Employment Tax], Solzhenitsyn[1] or the Butler wedding.

Time is notated by the things that get stuck in my head, like a faulty record. At one time it was Bendit Cohn – Cohn Bendit – then Colombey les deux Eglises. Then for a spell Julia James, the old actress who I had lately discovered went mad and ended her days in an asylum, was on my mind as I bent over and tugged at a stinging nettle or a dock.

But the afternoon passes pleasantly in spite of these little irritations. There is a pretty lost minute frog in the border of Juliet [Duff]'s giant

---

[1] Alexander Solzhenitsyn (b. 1918), Soviet author.

bluebells. The seedlings that I planted from what used to be penny packets (and are now at least ten new pence) are becoming night-scented stocks, or big green plates of nasturtium leaves. The bird life is going on at the back of my ears, and children are the other side of the wall.

The hours pass, the trug is full, yet so much more to clean up in the flower border, not to mention the beans. Why do I do this? Why don't I stop? Is it because I want the villagers to be impressed when the garden is 'open' on Sunday? No, I don't care all that much. Is it a sign of old age that I find this a delightful occupation in spite of the back-breaking effort? (Sweat is now pouring down my forehead.) The trug will not be heaped any higher.

As it is I have to dig my hand through the fading green mass to find the handle, and at last take the lot to the rubbish dump by the compost heap. I heave the trug in the air, turn it upside down and give it a good shake, so that its contents will fall among Smallpeice's carnation stalks. As in drowning, the past falls before me, but these are the contents of one afternoon. There among the groundsel the bits of stinging nettle that I dared to clutch, the nasty large hairy leaves of a few thistles, a lot of dead roses, and brown lilac clusters.

Oh yes, there is that mildewed peony that I had topped as I stopped to admire the pink and white garden at its height now, and there the iris stalk. Lastly caught in the wooden slats of the trug a few little tufts of weed that spell two o'clock when I first came out on the terrace for the afternoon's activity. And Smallpeice, relaying the news from his wife, tells me that tea is ready.

7 July 1971

At last the unbelievable has happened and high summer is here, and I am in Broadchalke, the best of all places to enjoy it. I walk on the early dew in bare feet, and do the same at night when the dew falls fast and early. I can't paint, shut up in the studio, so have taken my easel out to do terrible governess calendar paintings of the herbaceous border. The garden is at its best, the roses recovered from the month of wet, the stalks of the sweet peas are over a foot long and smell of childhood, everywhere sweet scents, malmaison, huernia (which gave Smallpeice and me a rash which kept us awake at night), pink lilies, curry angel balm, verbena, new dawn ramblers, and even one or two candidum. And apart from the usual joys, there is 'work in progress'.

The house is now seen proudly standing on a paved forecourt. Instead of a gravel path of uneven design, we have a very formal slice of green lawn, with paving stones coming to the edge of the box, and the yews. It is a great improvement and is not only a delight to me, but to the passing visitors. All that is now needed is some herb growing beneath the cracks in the stones, and things like white foxgloves, sprawling in clumps at the edge of the drive and steps.

The water garden is taking shape and gives new joys. At dusk bats fly over the water in waltzing circles, eating the mosquitoes that have escaped the trout that leap from below at them. Eileen has her first fishing lesson from Offley. (I know I haven't the patience, and I hate worm and I can't bear to hit a fish on its head or see it with a pin in its throat) and we noticed the Dutch cheese circle of moon come up and be reflected with a star in the lake. There are squawks of moorhens, an owl plops in the water, and this house like a toy with lit indoors in the distance, seen to an advantage never before available. The water garden supplies a new world.

12 July 1971

David Somerset, who has recently taken up flying as his hobby, said about the incessant cold wet beastliness of June that he felt like crying. He summed up many an opinion. It seemed just too cruel that the month that we had looked forward to all our cold, grey winter long should prove such a total disappointment. For the farmers it was a tragedy, for the gardener a heavy burden too. Everything we had hoped for was dying by degrees, or not showing any signs of growth. The peonies never flowering and leaving a small brown football on a rotted stalk. Roses a mushed mess of Kashu colour. Too cold to do without a fire. Whitsun Bank Holiday a wash-out.

Then suddenly all is changed with a vengeance. Could one believe that it would ever be too hot? The drawing room, such a large room to heat in winter, is so hot even with all the blinds down that the freshest flowers die in their vases in two days. Even the hall and dining room and kitchen corridors with their stone floors are not cold to the feet.

The terrace, always a sun trap, is an oven. Timothy sleeps in the shade of the herbaceous border. Strawberries and cream go off in a jiffy, the cream 'turns', the ice runs out. Windows and doors are open yet never a draught blows. Coffee out of doors (one could dine out of doors) and as the evening comes on, the water garden gives me new pleasures. There are trout jumping and an otter perhaps, or a water rat or a vole. Moorhens, where before was nothing but a stinking bog land, the little spring has been discovered with its source at the side of the ash trees.

We light the bedroom and library lamps to make a pretty effect as the house, never as even before, is reflected in the water. It is all so overwhelming and soothing and compelling that one cannot go to bed until with sheer excess of pleasure that one wondered if it could still exist, or was it part of one's youth, one is worn out and without curiosity to open any books, or newspapers and turns out the bed lamp to sleep naked, knowing that tomorrow one will wake up to an equally lovely experience.

Holiday – Sandwich   *August 1971*

Dates not gelling, people I wanted to go to couldn't have me at the right time, so have filled in an odd week by doing two days' work in London, between visits to Sandwich and Houghton. Both Kent and Norfolk old childhood holiday haunts.

When we went to Sandwich it was to a cottage on the ramparts, not to smart bay with Prince of Wales and Astor houses and golf links. Now I went in splendour (Astor house taken by Prince Paul and Princess Olga and Elizabeth of Yugo[1]) and longed for the excitement I felt at inner stirrings at growing up. At the time we were in the cottage and a purchase of an engraved glass and a sprig of jasmine were incentives to art and snobbery. The little town is unchanged in its Dutch charm, but alas the ramparts have become a colony for mod-con villas and labour-saving and smart, and the cottage is nowhere to be found. No doubt the owners fell for the blandishments of the property developer.

The visit to the bay was, as usual, depressing. The wind blows incessantly, the sea is muddy and the sands, as a result of bombs at Deal, have become a pebbled beach. But fascinating to hear the Pauls talking of having recently met their old ladies' maid from their palace in Belgrade. The loyal old servant had arranged to meet her daughter in Munich and had written to her former mistress to ask if she could come to see them. The Pauls went to see her and had a meal in a private room in a hotel. The maid told of how the Germans were very 'korrect' in occupation but the Russian soldiers rushed wildly into the private apartments, stood on the bed of Princess Olga and slashed the hangings and covers, forced open Princess Olga's dresses, the ones in which I'd photographed her in B.P. [Buckingham Palace in 1939] and proceeded to put them on. Naturally they were too small so they were slashed open. They took away in hampers and sheets all the *bibelots*, and one object fell, and was found by the maid, a gold Easter egg, and this she kept until she was able to send it safely to her mistress.

---

[1] Prince Paul of Yugoslavia (1893–1976), ill-fated Regent of his country in the Second World War; his wife, Princess Olga of Greece (1903–97), sister of Princess Marina, Duchess of Kent; and their daughter, Princess Elizabeth (b. 1936).

Prince Paul told of how the soldiers cut the Savonnerie carpet in the hall into square rugs on which they lay sunbathing in the garden. They described the recent visit of the Snowdons to Tito,[1] who had behaved with greater grandeur than anyone in former days, with private yachts, aeroplanes and his own vineyards. When complimented on the grandeur of her palace, the peasant-wife said, 'Oh, it is not mine. It belongs to the people!'

It is sad to see Princess O [Olga] in exile and she has never got accustomed to being treated as an ordinary citizen (one evening she got up from dinner and wanting us to stop our conversation, said 'I'm standing', to which P. P. shot to his feet, bowed in an exaggerated, way and said, 'Oh, I beg your pardon, Madam'). But P. P. is an exceptional man with great flair for and knowledge of the arts. He is a most highly civilised human being and I am only sorry that he should feel, and he has every reason to do so, that life has 'deteriorated' ever since the 1914 war.

Phyllis Monckman[2]

The legend is that Prince Albert, later King George VI,[3] was a backward young man and the courtiers were beginning to worry. He showed no sign of the usual interest in the opposite sex, so perhaps some delightful, trustworthy young woman could be chosen to initiate the young Prince into the rites of sex. It was agreed by all who knew her that the well known dancer and actress Phyl Monckman would be a suitable person. She was attractive with dainty little legs & ankles, sprightly & gay & a very sound character. The young Prince responded as expected. He enjoyed the sex experience very much. Phyllis gave the young man a cigarette lighter & although the relationship could never be considered more than an affaire-ette, whenever they met in public the Prince who became King would produce the cigarette lighter to show he had not forgotten.

I have to keep in check a certain nostalgia for old actresses that I fear could get the better of me, if encouraged, but I have often thought I would like to ask P. M., whom I would occasionally see through a taxi window, hobbling on a stick like the Fee Carabosse, but still looking game and appetising. I heard she had had both hips operated on, was now

---

[1] Princess Margaret and Lord Snowdon visited Yugoslavia for a week as guests of President Tito (1892–1980), in June 1970.
[2] Phyllis Monckman (1892–1976), star of the theatre in the 1920s. She first appeared as a dancer aged 12, and was principal dancer at the Alhambra in World War I. She was later a leading lady at the Comedy Theatre.
[3] HM King George VI (1895–1952).

recovering from a bad knee, but since she had a weak heart could not take the anaesthetic for an operation. Rather than sit in her bedsitter and mope, she would go out into the world, show an interest in everything new and defy her seventy-odd years.

I wrote to ask her to the Arnold Weissberger[1] lunch (a dread) and she appeared in a tangerine-coloured coat, very neat, a legacy from the recently dead Mrs Emlyn Williams,[2] and her complexion was as fresh as a day rose. No nonsense about Phyl, she talked about having no money, no health, but enjoying life and knowing everything about the theatre today.

Of course it was only natural that she should know about the theatre of her day, but it was remarkable that her memory was faultless. If I asked her questions about certain old favourites, she gave a real answer. 'Yes, Gaby Deslys was attractive, not beautiful, carried on an affair with both Basil Hallam and Gordon Selfridge[3] simultaneously As Hallam left by the garden door, Selfridge arrived by the front.'

One day Phyl was asked to help Gaby out at a charity bazaar. At lunchtime Gaby said, 'You will excuse me if I take an hour off. I must lunch with Mr Selfridge.' She pointed to a black pearl in one ear. When she returned from her lunch it was with the white pearl pin in the other ear. In some ways she was extremely extravagant, in fact seldom appeared before the public in the same dress twice. She had a woman permanently employed copying her expensive original Reggie de Venille design in every colour. But she was also French in that she could be very stingy. She lost her pet dog, was in a frightful state. After three days she offered a £25 reward. The dog came back. Phyl said, 'How thrilled you must be,' and Gaby replied, 'Yes, but think of the £25!'

Her house in London was filled with artefacts and she had little talent, but knew how to put herself across. She told Phyllis she was foolish to show herself too much. 'You shouldn't go to the Embassy ([or] Ciro's?) every night. You should be like me and make it an occasion. When I go out to a nightclub they call the police to keep the crowds back.'

Phyllis talked of June,[4] the exquisite thistledown and apple blossom dancer, who married rich and is now in London staying at the Connaught Hotel where the equally rich contemporary, but less successful dancer,

---

[1] Arnold Weissberger (1906–81), American theatrical agent, who gave incessant parties for his actors and actresses.
[2] Mrs Emlyn Williams (d. 1970), Molly O'Shann.
[3] Gordon Selfridge (1858–1947), founder of Selfridge & Co. (1909).
[4] June (1901–84), actress and vocalist in musical comedy in the First World War, who married Lord Inverclyde and later Edward Hillman, Jr., from whom she was divorced. Author of *The Glass Ladder* (Heinemann 1960).

Anita Elson,[1] is also staying. Anita has to have a full-time companion with her as she has had a stroke, and June has to push a sort of perambulator contraption in front of her. Her legs have gone, her hair is white, her face fat, but she is still pretty when she smiles.

I thought perhaps I had given Phyl a rare treat, that this would be one of the few outings of the summer, but two nights later I saw her again, the centre of attraction among a group of rich old queers who were thrilled to take her out to dinner at the Connaught.

Stephen T [Tennant] with dyed-red hair down his back, waddled out of his car to pay a high summer visit for tea. Surprisingly he did not touch the cucumber sandwich which, but that's another story, had been such a damned difficulty to procure. He said he was getting fat, the euphemism of all time.

But he sat absorbed in talk of the past and his memory is extraordinary. He remembered being taken on *dear* George Curzon's knee and how thrilled he had been to hear him say, 'If only I could have a son like you,' of Grace Curzon's[2] difficulty in being received by London society. On her arrival as a rich widow from the Argentine, she said Mrs Greville[3] wrote 'I've invited that pretty Mrs Duggan to lunch'. It would have made all the difference if she had left out the word 'that'. Poor Stephen, if only he could deliver the goods and prove his talent. His life is made up of 'make believe'. He is still preparing a box of poems and he asked me if I liked the title *A Spice Box for Dew*.

'Elegance is a condition of the soul' – Anne Tree.

Anne's father [the Duke of Devonshire] used to cut up wood in the drawing room, hence her love of turning the drawing room into a work room where she paints, pins her butterflies, dissects frogs and dries her wildflower collection between blotting paper.[4]

---

[1] Anita Elson, popular soubrette, friend of June (see *The Glass Ladder*).
[2] Grace Curzon (d. 1958), formerly Duggan, widow of George, first Marquess Curzon of Kedleston (1859–1925).
[3] Hon. Mrs Ronald Greville (d. 1942) – Margaret (Maggie), daughter of Rt Hon. William McEwan, married Hon. Ronald Greville (1864–1908). DBE 1922.
[4] Tenth Duke of Devonshire died in 1950, chopping a piece of wood, before trust arrangements had been settled. As a result, there were harsh death duties and the Devonshires sacrificed Hardwick Hall to save Chatsworth House in Derbyshire.

Diana Cooper and Old Age

Took Diana to the *Lear* of P [Peter] Brook and Scofield, thinking we'd have a memorable evening. We didn't, v. disappointing film. But Diana didn't talk throughout as is her wont and was very 'piano' when we went on to the Savoy with John Julius and Anne [Norwich].[1]

Next evening we were both invited to the *Anastasia* ballet in the royal box with the Colin Andersons.[2] I arrived to find Diana, her eyes glazed, but upper lip lengthened by an inch and lower lip hanging out. She was completely drunk and continued to be throughout the evening. She could hardly get herself to the supper in between acts and her legs were completely out of control. Next night she came to stay at the Heads, went to drive with Anne and Michael [Tree], and while Anne was out of the room putting the children to bed, Diana secretly went to the grog tray and for the rest of the evening was completely blotto.

It is outrageous. One would like to smack her, but it is tragic. How terrible the *dégringolade* of a great character who is also a great beauty. How awful that she should be lonely and *have* to go out every night, and because she doesn't have enough repose, have to take a snorter. If you ask her if she'll have a drink, she'll say 'No'. If she is given a chance she'll become a greedy child and finish half the bottle of vodka. She is brave, she is good, she is wonderful, but as Dot Head sadly said, 'She should be living in the country with her books, and a garden, but she's done it the wrong way round!'

It is ghastly to see her, with her gammy legs, taking off down a flight of steps or driving in traffic in her Mini. It *must* end in disaster. She must kill herself. Perhaps this is what she wants. She has had enough of life. She has a great strength still but old age is a traumatic experience to all. To Diana it must be an even harder test of character. I fear there is little one can do to stop her. To warn her would be of no avail, and she would put on that fierce, proud expression and you would know that it was terrible impertinence to talk on such a subject.

Sybil Cholmondeley

A really intelligent woman, with tremendous personality. It is difficult not to copy her idiom. She speaks in a deep voice with 'e – verry – syll –

[1] Viscount Norwich (b. 1929) and his wife, Anne Clifford. They were divorced in 1985.
[2] Sir Colin Anderson (1904–80), Chairman of the Royal Fine Art Commission, and his wife, Morna MacCormick.

abble' most carefully enunciated. 'They surely don't work on a Sat – urr – daye!' As a young girl she was given a very severe education, worked tremendously hard learning four languages, music, being given special tuition in history of art, politics.

Now she is over seventy and a widow, she runs Houghton with avid interest. 'Let us go and see the new digger of corn.' It is a most colossal German machine which she understands and talks of with expertise to the Norfolker who is in charge of its running. She takes us to see other beautiful houses. She motors into Holt to buy the lobsters, soles and crabs which have to be just the right size.

She is extremely funny and quick. She uses old-fashioned phrases that come out with surprising freshness. 'I was bowling along at a grrreat batte' – 'Oh, the poor child was more than dead!' Someone is 'v. boresome'. If things get too serious then its 'goodnight' and her manner with servants is very daring but they never seem to take umbrage, in fact they adore her (though knowing they can't play any tricks on her – she can be severe). The old parlourmaid, Norton, in a wig, is about to leave the room. 'Don't go, Norton. I wish to speak to you. Draw nigh. Now tell the cook that she can have the day off tomorrow. We'll just have cold for lunch, and if that doesn't suit her, tell her to go to hell.'

Sybil and Rock[1] have seldom allowed anyone in to see Houghton and guests for the weekend are very privileged. I enjoyed my 'family' visit enormously, though whether it was the excess of rich food, the strong Norfolk air or merely a chill on the liver, I don't know, but the result was an appalling stomach upset which caused me to have a ghastly night of diarrhoea, so that on my return to London I had to take to my bed.

Cecil had his first chance to see On a Clear Day You Can See Forever, *since its release in Britain.*

In March 1969, Cecil had undergone a stint in Brighton, on location with the film, having designed the costumes and dressed the Regency sequences, some of which were filmed in Brighton. The film was written by Alan Jay Lerner, directed by Vincente Minnelli, and starred Barbra Streisand.

On a Clear Day concerned a girl who was hypnotised to stop smoking and then went into trances, recalling previous incarnations. Cecil had been pleased to get hold of an in-house questionnaire, in which Streisand observed that Cecil was 'a beautiful man and a beautiful talent'.

Pauline de R [Rothschild] and I went to see this film which has only just

---

[1] Fifth Marquess of Cholmondeley (1883–1968), Lord Great Chamberlain. Sybil Cholmondeley was once asked by a granddaughter if she could bring her boyfriend to Houghton, to receive the answer: 'The house is not open to the public on that day.'

come to London having opened to bad notices in the US almost a year ago. The notices were deserved. How Hollywood in its appalling financial condition can have put up money for something so inept, and then spent so much more on it than they ever bargained, is just another example of the stupidity which has, at last, brought about the downfall of the film capital.

My visit was the finale to a very long experience, for originally I was to have designed the stage version. But mercifully I got out of that, but not before I had to endure countless conferences in all parts of the world. When the film was made I was engaged to be responsible for the Regency sequences. This was quite a nice, neat little packet to be exposed only in Brighton. Of course, it necessitated going to Hollywood at least twice, and being at the beck and call of B. S. [Barbra Streisand].

But although the clothes were mostly made here in London, the time spent in going to Tangier to get cheap tissues, and supervising each individual ball dress, was quite considerable.

Now I see the film and see the appalling waste due to the fact that no one had prepared a proper script. One whole ballroom sequence with B. S. in dark red satin, and all the others in specious stoned velvets, has been cut. B. S.'s best dress cut, many scenes cut, and the laying down of cobbles in Lansdowne Crescent (Brighton) and the hedges especially built, all unnecessary, all cut. If Alan Lerner had delivered a carefully considered script, many hundreds of thousands of dollars would have been saved.

But this is nothing in comparison to his extravagance on *Paint Your Wagon*,[1] which almost succeeded in bankrupting Paramount. Why does Alan L. have the authority to do all this? Why is his name still valuable? (It is at least twenty years since *My Fair Lady*.)

It may be said that I was well paid for the job and that is all I should worry about. But that isn't the whole story. I really sweated to see that things were perfect, and that is the only way I can work. But if another job arrives along that I don't really believe in, will I remember the lesson of *On a Clear Day*? I rather doubt it.

Cecil then took a holiday with Michael and Anne Tree, and David and Caroline Somerset at the Trees' holiday home on Spetsai. He wrote that the Trees were his 'best friends and I love laughing with them and exchanging confessions'. But he regretted his physical deterioration, describing his stomach as looking 'like a horrible drained pig, pink and swollen', and observing, not for the first time, that

---

[1] *Paint Your Wagon* (1969), a musical Western, originally on Broadway, starred Lee Marvin, Clint Eastwood and the tragic Jean Seberg.

his penis had shrunk 'to the size of a crab apple'. While on Spetsai, bad news reached him from New York.

Cecil heard of the death of Margaret Case, society editor of Vogue, *and his first true friend in New York as far back as 1928. On 25 August 1971, Margaret Case put on her raincoat and scarf, and jumped fifteen storeys to her death on the concrete of the courtyard below. She had worked for Condé Nast for forty-three years and had been depressed by the recent acquisition of the maga-zine by the Newhouse family, and the firing of Diana Vreeland as editor. Significantly, Margaret Case had left* Vogue *on 1 August, 'because of her advanced years', as the file put it. She drew up a new will to take care of her housekeeper on 18 August but only began to act strangely on 23 August, when she appeared seriously depressed. Though friends thought she might have been worried about money, her estate was worth about $570,000.*

Cecil, of course, did not know the precise details as listed above.

Margaret Case

The most unexpected bad news. Telegram received here on Spetsai to say Margaret Case is dead. No details. I always thought she'd see us all out. She had the strength of a dozen youngsters, but I was wrong. No doubt the Condé Nast behaviour to Diana Vreeland has something, even if indirectly, to do with it. Margaret, generally so optimistic and sighing about national and personal crisis, had suddenly been got down by 'second raters' taking over, the general decline in standards. She wrote to me that she was shocked and frightened, a letter to which I replied saying it had brought out the best in her, her underlying loyalty and courage, in a world of artifice. But her friends did mean everything to her and she would do battle for them against the greatest odds.

Margaret was my first friend in NY. I arrived late for a large lunch at C. Nast's apartment and she was impressed that I had already seen the Grecos in the Hispanic museum. She showed a friendliness that few others did and by degrees she became a very important person in my American life. She maddened me. I hated much that she said, her reac-tions could show that she did not understand what one really meant. But my God she was a hard-working friend. If I asked her to buy a dozen pre-sents to take back to England, the telephone calls would continue until I was sorry I ever asked the favour.

When in trouble she would be terribly upset. I remember when my career was just about finished as a result of the Walter Winchell row,[1] I was hard

---

[1] Cecil was fired by Condé Nast for introducing anti-Semitic slogans into a caricature to accompany an article on society by Walter Winchell in February 1938.

and metallic and defiant in the face of losing everything, and she, the first to come round to my hotel room, sat weeping on a sofa. She realised, more than I did, what a blow had befallen me, and she was helpless to do anything for me. Margaret was the first person always to telephone as I arrived at the New York hotel. She it was who got the theatre tickets for me, reserved the table of the restaurant and was always 'at the ready' at the last minute.

Now she is dead. Perhaps in her melancholy she took an overdose, though being a staunch Roman Catholic this does not seem likely, but whatever the reason for her loss, New York will never be the same for me. I will miss her more than I realise, and it says well for her that maybe twenty other people feel the same way.

M. C. Postscript

The even worse news of her death is followed by the manner of it. It seems the unhappy soul jumped from the window of her bedroom on the fifteenth floor. One cannot imagine the misery of the mind that caused her to have such terrifying last seconds before crashing in smithereens. The unhappiness is a shock of a terrible kind, for Margaret seemed to have so much to keep her interested. She was indeed dreadfully upset at the sacking of Diana and the direction in which *Vogue* was going, headed by a lot of ghastly go-getting animals.

But she kept *au courant* with books and all the new plays, and as for people she never stopped making new friends and was the most loyal of all to her old lifelong cronies. However, they did not make up for the emptiness of her life and she no doubt realised that she was going round like a squirrel on a wheel, to no avail, when reality in the form of cruel businessmen delivered a *coup de grâce* that she could not survive.

Now that she is dead, people rally to her and are suddenly aware of all that she gave to them. She was such a strange and strong individual that no doubt she would have reacted in some unexpected way to their sudden display of affection. But all her friends have written just the things she would have liked to hear and darling Diana has even gone so far as to say the first time she ever saw her she looked so pretty. This is adorable of Diana for it is a charming lie. Margaret was never pretty, in fact her ugliness was no doubt one of the reasons, although she rose above it in an heroic way, that she was never courted and never married.

The picture of her taken recently and published in connection with her death is a most wonderful character study of her in a benign, amused, interested mood, as she arrived, as chic as be damned to spite her ugly face, at some exhibition where she was caught by a cameraman who no doubt never realised what an emotion his picture would create in so many hearts. The sight of it went through me like a stab, so vivid and vital and immediate does she appear, that for several nights here on Spetsai, I have been haunted by her, both sleeping and awake, as I have relived so many of the times, during the last forty years, that we have spent together.

Air Journey from Greece to Italy

More and more do I have *angoisse de départ*, and this time leaving Spetsai I felt quite sick at the thought of such a complicated journey, and not knowing one word of Greek. After ten very salubrious days relaxing in sea or on balcony in the wonderful pure air, I felt much better in my physical state and only hoped the journey to Capri would not undo all the good of the holiday. It almost did.

Anna, the adorable old Greek lady of high birth who is acting as housekeeper to the Trees, took me in a cab to the ferry boat which was lying in the harbour. Here my three pieces of luggage were placed. Then on to Olympic Airways to get my ticket which they said [was] all supposedly in order, or as much as could be. I then waved goodbye, went on the ferry boat and could find my luggage nowhere. It was not on the ship. No sailor knew a thing. It gradually dawned on me that it had been put on the 9 o'clock ferry boat instead of the 9.30. I *knew* I would never see my luggage again.

As we passed the ferry on its way back from Corinth, a sailor with a loudspeaker signalled to the boats to stop, and as our boat slowed down he shouted and a Greek lady translated that the luggage had been taken off the boat and I would find it on arrival at Corinth. No luggage. I asked at a restaurant, at a hotel, someone said my luggage had gone to the nearby airport.

I was in complete despair at the thought of all my work of the holiday going for nothing. I had been mean about not giving away my drawings, because I felt they were too good and had taken too much out of me and the watercolour sketches and my diaries, and my cameras! Surely not *again*! I was sweating in the sun with rigours of despair going through me, when someone said here was my luggage, coming over in a little sailing boat. Anna had sent Nicholas with it. Can I describe my delight and relief? Well, all day was spent in a misery of heat, delays, noise and muddle.

Rome airport is the hell of all time. I will never go there again unless impossible to avoid.

With some sort of unborn energy I managed with patience to go through the appalling difficulties of the journey, though it is no wonder I had a return of my neuralgic head. I had hoped that maybe I could arrive in Capri by dinner time, but no. Darkness closed in at Naples and I had to go to the Excelsior where, more dead than alive, the first hot bath in nearly two weeks revived me and I was lucky enough to find Georgia and Sachie [Sitwell][1] in the dining room.

The S. Sitwells and I came over in the hydrofoil together to Capri, where, according to Sachie, who is a purveyor of delightfully odd bits of information, the lizards are electric blue and not green. In their company the tourist element could be overlooked and I enjoyed my half-day with them, listening to Sachie's stories of Nijinsky and being taken after the ballet to the Carlton Grill for supper.

Here he saw Gaby Deslys having supper with her mother and a young man, Jimmy Forster, who had been challenged by his fellow officers in the regiment to sup with the notorious Gaby and do the necessary afterwards. The evening would no doubt be very expensive for him. But Gaby, although wicked, was nice, and all her co-workers in the theatre adored her. She knew how to *éblouir* people with her white car and jewels, and her home near the Albert Hall with the rich décor and crucifixes, and Sachie told me that Gaby Deslys had made two films, the last quite excellent of its sort with a touching goodbye scene made especially poignant by the fact that two weeks later Gaby was dead of cancer of the throat.

We walked through the streets of Capri doing shopping, and Sachie was made by Georgia to buy a straw hat. Sachie's eyes, which appear to see nothing, are as quick as an insect's. He seemed not to look at himself in the glass but said, 'In that hat, I look exactly like Edith!'

Sachie gave me palaces and churches to see around Turin and I wondered why it is that I see so little of one of the people I have always liked most.

Mona Bismarck   *Summer 1971*

The last year has not been a good time for Mona. For six months she watched Eddy die in the extremes of paralysis, and when all was over had a nervous breakdown. When I arrived at the Fortino today, I saw a group of elderly people sitting at lunch on the terrace and I had no idea which was Mona. On closer inspection I was horrified ... I did not expect to find that all traces of her beauty have vanished. She was one of the most beautiful women I've ever seen. She is now suddenly a wreck. Her hair, once white and crisp and a foil to her aquamarine eyes, is now a little dyed

[1] Sir Sacheverell Sitwell (1897–1988), the youngest Sitwell, poet and author, and his wife Georgia Doble (1905–80).

frizz, and she has painted a grotesque mask on the remains of what was once such a noble-hewn face, the lips enlarged like a clown, the eyebrows pencilled with thick black grease paint, the flesh down to the pale lashes coated with turquoise. When she later appeared in a bathing costume, it was terrible to see the shrunk, wizened, wrinkled, sagging skin. She was like a starving Pakistani.

But worse, she seemed in such a terribly high tension state, her hands trembling as she gestured or lit another cigarette. Oh my heart broke for her. Mercifully she seemed to rise above the lost beauty and was completely unselfconscious of the fact that she made such ugly faces as she listened intently to some guest telling her of New York today or Russia before the Revolution. She is still interested in what is happening in the world though regretting the present trends and for the past. She finds nothing of beauty is made today, and I suppose it is as well that she does not assume a false interest.

The result is that her house is a period piece. The amount of money spent on it is fantastically exaggerated. Workmen for two years have been making walls and terraces so that she can have an alternative way down to the sea. A huge room has been made for an annexe to the bathroom, changing rooms, and a new garden made just like the dozen others that already give her so much trouble, fighting incompetent gardeners and the hard, dry climate.

Yet this is the life she has chosen and she is in most ways quite happy. She has no longer a desire to travel and go in for excitements. She is preparing for her death, and unless she puts on some flesh it may come before she realises it. Poor Mona, she is a good sweet person, and it made me aghast to watch her careering around her garden paths, an old Cipriani eccentric.

Margaret Case

A week or two later and I still cannot believe that such an immediate spirit is lost to us. I cannot think of her in the past tense.

Paris   *10 September 1971*

After lovely laughing talk on telephone with Nancy Mitford,[1] who has been in the extremes of agony for the past months (in fact two years

---

[1] Nancy Mitford (1904–73), novelist, who moved to Paris to be near the man she loved, Gaston Palewski.

desperately ill) she has found five days ago a pill that relieves her pain (cancer of the spine is said to be the cause). She no longer screams when a lorry passes the house and the vibrations torture her. She is dying, free from pain, in a state of euphoria. After our talk she said, 'Yes, I'm *in* heaven. Goodbye,' and I wondered if this was the last time I'd talk to her.

Reddish   *14 September 1971*

The holiday which, as they ask on the forms, was a question of 'business combined with pleasure' was entirely successful. The change of air, the sleep, the swimming, has done me all the good necessary, and I have to boot a booty of the clothes I needed for my collection at the V & A.

The only disadvantage was that in order to get these clothes I have had to have a great deal of change of scene, and the air travel was exhausting and harassing. I was very pleased when, after three days in a stranger's flat in Paris, I was able to leave. I longed to get home and my anxieties about getting the clothes through customs were unnecessary. It was a smooth homecoming and soon I was on the train for Salisbury.

Never have I been more pleased than I was to see my house, and although autumn had approached, there were still signs of summer, and on awakening the first morning a marvellous sunny picture greeted me. My spirits rose. I was in a state of euphoria when the Sunday papers arrived and in the [*Sunday*] *Times* was Raymond [Mortimer]'s notice of my Aunt Jessie book. Never have I been more pleased, the review so brilliant and incisive, so protective, was not only a marvellous piece of work, but the ultimate in praise for me. It was a crowning triumph. I remember the days when I first started writing, and I felt that to be reviewed by Raymond Mortimer would be my life's ambition. Not only has this happened but the piece is in the nature of a rave.

Weidenfeld did not think the book stood much chance and my sisters thought of it in the nature of a private joke. No one really had much encouragement. Suddenly this has happened. I was near to tears as I finished the review and exclaimed to myself, 'Divine – Divine!'[1]

Cecil's exhibition, Fashion, an Anthology by Cecil Beaton, *was due to open at the Victoria and Albert Museum. It ran from October 1971 to January 1972.*

17 October 1971

Never have I known a longer week. When on those few lucky occasions I am able to stay at Reddish for a continued spell, the week goes by in such a flash that Sunday evening is upon me before I have realised that full days of activity and work have sped by unnoticed. Due to the 'Anthology of Fashion' opening I had to come to London on a Monday, remain there throughout the following weekend for the pre-opening on the following Monday, to be followed by the public opening on the Wednesday. Unfortunately to add to my burden, I was stricken by a bug and whenever I could get away from the million chores at the museum, had to stagger back to bed. Never before did I realise the efficacy of sleep.

By almost non-stop sleeping on Sunday, I was well enough to help with the finishing touches a few hours before the 'Friends of the V & A' arrived expectantly...

The exhibition went off marvellously well. It looked dazzling, sharp, and transcended the shop level window. Distinguished guests included Clemmie Churchill.[2] I was pleased, but after the opening, time lay heavily. The anticlimax was softened by a few 'dates' – TV and BBC, but the pressure was down. I had considerable time on my hands, I didn't enjoy it, for I could not settle down. I went to *Bloody Sunday*[3] one afternoon and could not believe that Thursday wasn't Friday and made a 'balls-up' with the dates. I couldn't go to Broadchalke as months ago I had said yes to Mary Rothermere's[4] nice invitation to stay in Warren Hastings's house in Gloucestershire. Would Saturday never come?

It is extraordinary how many things one can fit into a week without any feeling of satisfaction. God knows I had enough excitement during the Monday to Wednesday, then as well as seeing a film, I went to the Osborne play[5] and to a ghastly piece of rubbish about 'Kean',[6] but that feeling that I never have at Reddish, that the week had not been productive, and merely an interim wait, made me feel sad and empty.

I got into the train at Paddington, dozed, woke to find winter rain and fog had superseded the brilliant autumn days. Then arrived at a house

---

[1] Cecil was especially pleased since so little had been expected from this book, a eulogistic tribute and a labour of love.
[2] Baroness Spencer-Churchill (1885–1977), widow of Sir Winston Churchill.
[3] *Sunday, Bloody Sunday* (1971), film directed by John SchlesInger, starring Glenda Jackson, Peter Finch, Dame Peggy Ashcroft and others.
[4] Mary, Viscountess Rothermere (d. 1993), third wife of second Viscount Rothermere. They lived at Daylesford House, Moreton-in-Marsh, Gloucestershire.
[5] *West of Suez* by John Osborne, with Sir Ralph Richardson and Jill Bennett.
[6] *Kean* by Jean-Paul Sartre, with Alan Badel and Felicity Kendal.

party, something I have not done for so many a year. A beautiful Cotswold stone house built on an unusual blue point, with rooms circling the main room and a completely circular room. Relics of India everywhere, great perfection and luxury, and an assembly of unexpected guests, the Roy Strongs,[1] David Hemmingses,[2] etc. and for two days I could lie back and enjoy the sort of sybaritic life that is more difficult to find. Yet here the luxury on a wider scale than one had ever imagined. Twenty grouse was the dinner grub on Saturday night, and as a night cap, bitter mints and Dom Perignon. Esmond [Rothermere] is a gentle, delightful aged boy. My heart goes out to him in his declining years, and Mary is a good wife to him, extraordinarily attractive and intelligent. It is great good luck for each other that they met.

I telephoned Gladys Cooper on the spur of the moment. She had pneumonia and couldn't go with *The Chalk Garden* to Canada. I sympathised. She coughed, sounded less strong than usual, but full of the old fight. 'It's such a *bore* being ill. I've never been ill all my life.' She was pleased I'd called.

I had had an exceptional lunch. I had been invited to my old friend, Honey Harris,[3] whose company I adored at the beginning of my career. I still admire her, but [we] never meet. It was a treat to go to a completely different milieu. It was a leisurely lunch. We gossiped, or discoursed till three. Then Mary Hutch [St John Hutchinson][4] and I went to the Ottoline Morrell scrap show[5] and I, on my way home, dawdled to look in a modern furniture shop. I saw John Gielgud's shining head reflected in the sun, coming up to me. We talked. 'Isn't it awful, all our dames are on the way out – Edith [Evans], Sibyl [Thorndike][6] and now it will be Gladys who's the first to go.' 'But she's recovering, isn't she, from pneumonia?' 'No, she has cancer of both lungs. She doesn't suspect a thing, but that's what it is.'

Gladys – I could write a book about her. She is one of the recurring enthusiasms in my life. She has meant a great deal to me. I was influenced by her when I was her 'fan', then later full of admiration for someone who could be *utterly* herself on all occasions. Few people have had such strength of character as she. Few people have faced the rigours of old age

---

[1] (Sir) Roy Strong (b. 1935), then Director of the National Portrait Gallery, and his wife, Julia Trevelyan Oman.
[2] David Hemmings (b. 1941), actor, and his second wife, Gayle Hunnicutt.
[3] Honey Harris, daughter of Sir Austin Harris and sister-in-law of Sir Osbert Lancaster.
[4] Mary, widow of St John Hutchinson QC (1884–1942). Mother of Jeremy, Lord Hutchinson of Lullington.
[5] Lady Ottoline Morrell (1873–1938), Bloomsbury heroine.
[6] Dame Sybil Thorndike (1882–1976), actress, married to Sir Lewis Casson.

as she, for her having been such a renowned 'beauty' it must have been more difficult, yet Gladys always discounted her beauty, took it for granted, never paid any attention to it. But when horrid things happened, such as her being given non-star roles, and Hollywood starlets took her place, she was never sorry or sad. She became a remarkable actress only in old age, but every phase of her life she has lived to the hilt. She has had great tragedies, her son [John Buckmaster] being mad is a terrible scrounge, but she accepts everything with wide-eyed courage. I'm very loath to accept the fact that she will soon be a thing that no longer is with us.

TV

I came up to London to see the Bailey TV on me in Patrick Procktor's studio. It is an entertainment certainly. It is a Bailey view of me and he does not know me. But for me it is quite unlike the way I feel myself to be. It is a picture of someone who leads a velvety life, no work, no strain, no drama. It is all completely on the surface and very silly. I like the way he has photographed me in my garden against the grey stone walls with the japonica, and superimposed me with hyacinths and spring village scenes. But the waste of time spent on Twiggy and Justin,[1] Lord Lichfield,[2] and Shrimpton[3] is maddening. It makes me angry that it could have been so good if they'd kept in the serious pieces instead of the 'with it'. A waste of Audrey Withers, who really had something to say, of D [Lord David] Cecil and Cyril [Connolly].

But after bleating like this, I ask myself if anyone else would have asked to do a programme on me. Beggars can't be choosers and Bailey, with all his faults, meant well. As Ali F [Forbes] said, 'It was meant to be an act of piety and so he must be forgiven his few blasphemies.'

Khrushchev[4] has died in humiliation. How awful it is that these tyrants and monsters still exist. One gangster is thrown out only to be succeeded by another. The misery and suffering caused by Russia continues today just as foully as ever. I shall not see the day when the 'occupied' countries are liberated, but oh, how wonderful for the world when there is the inevitable uprising against everything that I loathe and am terrified of.

---

[1] Justin de Villeneuve, then married to Twiggy.
[2] Patrick, fifth Earl of Lichfield (b. 1939), photographer.
[3] Jean Shrimpton (b. 1942), model and former girlfriend of David Bailey.
[4] Nikita Khrushchev (1884–1971), President of the Soviet Union 1958–64. He died on 11 September.

28 October 1971

We have got into the common market. I don't realise its ramifications, but it is obviously a great step forward.

Telephoned throughout a sleepless night to Kin in SF [San Francisco]. He was out, but I enjoyed hearing the bell ring in the various rooms of his house (and garden). It brought him nearer and I still feel he is one of the most important influences in my life.

Terrible suspense. We have put in a bid for the Bundys' cottage next door. It would make *all the difference*, if we could feel this was part of my domain, and it will open up Lake Smallpeice to the Downs. But I'm terrified that there may be some last-minute snag, and although the Barclays Bank has accepted our offer, they may find an eleventh-hour bidder, or refuse, for petty reasons, to allow the 'scourge' into their home. 'The suspense is killing me.'

6 November 1971

Alan Tagg brought a box of fireworks with him as a house guest gift, and when the D. Cecils came over for drinks, the small party had their own firework display. It was very pretty and private with about six figures running around silhouetted on the lawn and sloping hills. The crackers and waterfalls of golden rain lit up the distant row of spurs and we noticed that because of the long sunny autumn, the prunus tree was in flower. The urn looked romantic as it was silhouetted against great sudden pink flames. The Smallpeices peered from their cottage windows (she terrified her thatch roof would 'go up'), Ray from his, and we in the comfort and luxury of the winter-flower-bedecked drawing room, through the rose chintz curtains. It was a delightful little interlude, and in great contrast to the grand and exciting bonfire, 'float' procession and great display at Wilton.

Total exhaustion. The lecture I had to give to the V & A audience took its toll. I felt I couldn't talk nonsense so gave almost a week to preparing the three-quarters of an hour long piece on fashion photography (a subject I've never spoken on before). As much as possible of the day of the talk was spent in bed. I felt in good time when I got to the place, and delivered the speech without a falter or tripped word. But the audience, though intent and concentrated, never reacted in any degree. Not a giggle, or titter, not a change from one buttock to another. It was quite a serious talk that had taken years of experience to produce and at the end Wingfield-Digby[1] (who had introduced me in the absence of John P.-H.,[2] who was dining with the King of Sweden) said he had heard one woman tell another she thought the talk was charming! I did not consider that phrase enough to repeat. I came away from an evening of utter boredom (ending with a man who had given me a present of 'C. B.' in a Victoria drawing) with a headache, altogether down.

I felt let down by the V & A. They have taken everything I have given them with the minimum of thanks, and still the frustration of their incompetence continues. No one is in charge of maintaining the exhibition, with the result that there are lots of legitimate complaints. I have had my first baptism of the Civil Service mind, and it makes me *disgusted* that the taxpayers' money is spent on squandering so much by lazy people whose energy is reserved for preserving their lot, and proving they are never in the wrong. All creative effort goes into showing they could never make a mistake.

I have come to the country, utterly limp and rather depressed, and wondering what the next thing will be to do when all the pin pricks and mosquito bites have no longer to be competed with. (Lord Mountbatten's[3] complaints to be coped with, Princess Mary's dress to be docketed.) I feel I have become very unpopular at the museum but I find they are smug, self-satisfied and deaf to complaints, the director being the worst of the lot.

Dicky Buckle

I was able to telephone him and tell him that he would be able to walk up the lane at Gutch Common to collect the Sunday newspapers with an aerial tread, for Raymond [Mortimer] had written a rave on his vast *Nijinsky*. (It transpired Rebecca West[4] had also.) Dicky later called in on his way to London and Alan [Tagg] and Charles [Colville] observed that he was tense and rather ill at ease with me. 'This odd in view of the fact that I've tried so hard to be good and kind to him on his recovery from the megalomania and illness that he went through earlier this summer.'

Yet he didn't have complete calm. Eileen said he had to pull himself up to take a deep breath every time he started on a new topic, and it was he

---

[1] I. G. F. Wingfield-Digby, Assistant Keeper, Department of Textiles.
[2] Sir John Pope-Hennessy (1913–94), Director of the Victoria and Albert Museum (1967–73). He arranged the exhibition.
[3] Admiral of the Fleet Earl Mountbatten of Burma (1900–79). Murdered by the IRA.
[4] Dame Rebecca West (1892–1983), real name Cecily Andrews, author and senior book reviewer for the *Sunday Telegraph*.

who did all the talking. I had the greatest difficulty when telling him that his suggestion of trying to get old clothes from Karsavina had met with success, and that I had a 1920 black sequinned sack and a pelisse (1860) that belonged to her mother, now in my possession for the V & A. Perhaps it is that Karsavina is Dicky's possession. He is going to do a book about 'conversations' with her (a good idea) and he told us how elegant, grand and witty Karsavina could be. About Sokolova[1] she said, 'Lydia has a very good memory, but she relies on it too much!'

Dicky left with his silent ghost (Dossé)[2] yes man, chauffeur etc., and as we all saw him out, I said, 'I can't wait for the post-mortem.' It is sad that Dicky, almost a genius, just does not 'make the grade'. He is basically vulgar and has a quality that makes it difficult to be intimate with him. One cannot love him and maybe this is one of the basic troubles.

Cecil had long vexed himself over whether or not to publish volume 3 of his diaries, The Happy Years, *which contained the story of his love affair with Greta Garbo in 1947 and 1948. After much soul-searching, he decided to go ahead. He wavered. Having accepted an advance from Weidenfeld, he sent it back. Then he changed his mind once more. For this reason, there is an eight-year gap between volumes 2 and 3 of his diaries.*

The decision to publish was to cost him some degrees of agony for the rest of his life. He tried to convince himself that Garbo would never read it, that she had behaved badly to Mercedes de Acosta and thus deserved no pity, and even that, since he was publishing the diaries of his life, it would be incorrect to omit such an important phase.

As publication drew near, so the serialisations began to appear and Cecil succumbed to a deep feeling of foreboding.

Broadchalke   *November 1971*

This piece is written as catharsis. Perhaps if I get some of my *angoisse* down on paper I will feel freer to go about everyday existence without a care. As it is I am suffering those awful qualms that send one's bowels panicking for release, and one's stomach positively aches. Bindie Lambton, the angel, has telephoned from London to send her love, to say she knows I must be suffering, but that I must not explain or complain, that things will get worse before they are better. The cause – *Newsweek*

---

[1] Lydia Sokolova (b. 1912), American ballerina.
[2] Philip Dossé (1926–80), director, Hansom Books, founder of a series of arts magazines, including *Books and Bookmen*. He killed himself by an overdose of drugs and alcohol, fearing debts he could not cover.

has made an item about my *McCall's* instalment from diaries about Garbo.

I imagine it is pretty sensational, and the London *Daily Mail* have got first wind of it over here, and I suppose hell is breaking loose with gossip everywhere. This is something I expected would have to be faced. My heart-searching about publishing and being damned have continued for a very long while. The book was recalled from Weidenfeld after they paid me a thousand pound advance. Then I wondered, what am I waiting for, my own death or Greta's. Then I decided, since the following volume was nearing completion, that I would go ahead.

Now that this bombshell has exploded, all my comfortings about a seven-day wonder, and 'what is an article in a newspaper anyway?' seemed quite ineffectual. I am disturbed and deeply so. I know it could have been avoided and I am to blame, but I decided to be brave and damn all. But now the crunch has come, it is difficult to know what is best to clear the matter from my mind.

If I continue with my garden sculpture the figure becomes the embodiment of my troubles. If I start a painting in the studio, likewise that becomes part of the general malaise. It is a feeling that used to dog me more often in early life. When I published a photograph that I knew shouldn't be published, there was an outcry and God, how I suffered. Lately, perhaps because I have grown more careful, these crises seem further apart, mercifully, for I believe in spite of experiences with the press, I am more sensitive and easily upset than ever before.

I have asked Eileen to try and ward off from me all unpleasantness, but it's going to be difficult. Meanwhile I am here quietly in the country with the intention of getting on with my work, but perhaps a drive in the car or a change of scene would be of help. Perhaps it is like a death, and that with time's healing properties, one will recover, but will wounds always remain?

The awful feelings of guilt and anxiety continued to dog me. I had headaches and felt very rotten. I couldn't sleep without waking to think of some further detail in my diary as published in *McCall's* that would offend Greta or a great number of friends. Then when I thought the excitement had died down, I opened the *Telegraph* and saw a photograph of Greta and myself. Oh, no! My stomach went to water. I rushed to the loo. I could not wait 'til Eileen would arrive at the house to ask if I should take a train up to London or a plane to Tangier in order to escape my own self-recriminations.

Eileen as usual came up trumps, light, airy, girlish, cheerful. Yes, she'd seen it. 'Don't worry. Have a glass of champagne.' When I told Ray not to tell any reporter that I was here because there'd been a nonsense about me and Garbo in the papers, he made me laugh by saying, 'Yes, Mr Isaac (the wonderful part-time gardener) had seen something in the papers.'

Still worrying, but a bit more cheerful, Eileen telephoned early the next day. There was some very good news in the post. A formal letter offering me a knighthood.[1] Oh, this was almost too much to take in. I felt this poor human brain was at bursting point. The last days the cup has been overfilled. Of course this was very pleasant. Secretly I had hoped for such an honour for many years.

Although knights come down low in the scale, it would be a great feather in an industrialist's cap to be thus rewarded. It is not as a result of having friends at court (Weidenfeld with Wilson) or being gradually upgraded in some huge organisation (Fred [Ashton] at Covent Garden Opera House). This was a question of 'Alone I done it'.

I was sad my mother had not known of it, or even my Aunts Cada and Jessie. But I felt suddenly a good deal more elderly and eminent. Still it is a very nice tribute and I feel I have deserved it, not for my talent, but for character, tenacity, energy and wide-reaching efforts.

Yet, now that it has happened (or will it be taken away from me because of the Garbo article?) it is strange how little the elevation occupies my thoughts. The day goes by just as usual, and just every now and then I think, 'How impressive.' Then I think of other knights – Redgrave, Rattigan and Helpmann,[2] and then I'm not quite so impressed. But I am happy about it and must try to enjoy it as the culmination of a long span of work and I must enjoy the fact that a lot of people are going to be very happy about it too.

21 November 1971

Yesterday I got up early to join Henry Pembroke in the forecourt of Wilton, then to go with his shooting party to Grovely Wood. It was a very cold, sunny, wintry morning with a lot of colour still on the trees, and the group of 'guns' and beaters made a formidable array in their dark grey and green colouring. We set off in Jeeps and soon the line-up was in formation in a valley between two wooded hills. In the distance the sounds of the beaters were nearing, tap-tap, cooing, bird noises. It seemed very medieval, nothing like the sounds that the town people of today make. Nearer, a pheasant flies out in panic, a terrible report – it is

---

[1] There was a letter from 10 Downing Street offered Cecil appointment as a Knight Bachelor in the New Year's Honours List of 1972.
[2] Sir Michael Redgrave (1908–85), actor; Sir Terence Rattigan (1911–77), playwright; and Sir Robert Helpmann (1909–86), dancer.

hit. Plop. Among the bushes there is a rustling. More and more birds fall, more smoke, more sparshot, more fluttering in the branches on the ground. The sound is of crackling as if the undergrowth were on fire.

I watch a particularly beautiful bird fluttering its wings, twitching its legs. It is as if [it] were given electric shocks. I hated the slaughter, yet I love eating roast pheasant. The 'guns' were delightful. Henry, in a beret, so utterly charming and smiling and being very much in command of the traditional proceedings. It was a large organisation, with dogs, game carts, Jeeps, beaters and loaders. The loaders had a subservience to the lord and masters which is something one did not realise still continued today. Touching forelock, good manners on all sides, servant enjoying being servant, this was something that one thought had died out at the turn of the century. It was all very ritualistic and medieval. The technique of driving the birds to their doom was damned clever, and perhaps not unduly cruel. But everyone set about their jobs with great unction and enthusiasm and happiness.

Suddenly I felt how much of the English joys of the countryside I had missed with all my town guests, when we will stay at home or at most wander around the garden. These young men were so jolly and delight-fully fresh and natural. Perhaps there were snobbish elements about them with their references to shooting at Windsor and being each considerable favourites of Royalty, but one young man with longish hair, a spiky nose and crooked teeth, called Tryon,[1] struck me as being utterly delightful as he described how beautiful this wood was at all times of the year and how sometimes he and Henry came here at dawn in early spring, when the mist had not dispersed, and the antelope were out and the buds had just burst.

I love the picture with the old retainers so smiling, the dog woman ebullient with six perfectly trained setters.

I motored into Pewsey, a rare lunch so far away with Mary and Philip Dunn[2] at Stowell, and here, from the tall late-18th-century drawing room windows, we suddenly saw the local hunt. It was an English Pisanello with the hounds racing in a frieze, then the very smart-looking huntsmen in black or 'pink' hurtling over hedges in pursuit. It all looked so healthy and clean, and we did not think of the horror aspects of torn-to-death fox. It was all so formal and polite and courteous. Something completely foreign to the world of TV, newspapers and politicians. It is perhaps still a very important structural part of British life and it is wonderful that it can still remain. Long may it last.

---

[1] Hon. Anthony Tryon (b. 1940), later third Lord Tryon.
[2] Sir Philip Dunn (1905–76), Cambridge colleague of Cecil's, and his wife, Lady Mary Erskine (1912–93).

I came back through rain, wind, a tremendous storm that has done the usual widespread damage. But, undaunted, the shots continue (though blue with cold) and the huntsmen (fortified with cherry brandy out of silver flasks) go hurtling over hedges.

Went to two excellent plays last week. Or I should say one good play, *Butley*,[1] and one wonderful entertainment, *The Changing Room*. Storey,[2] who wrote the latter, used to fly up to Manchester at the weekends to play football while working at the Slade. He is now not only a successful novelist, but also playwright. His interest is about behind the scenes at a football match. An enormous cast, I can't think how it would read well, but Lindsay Anderson[3] had made individuals of each character and has made it into a sort of choreographed play. The effect is stunning, for Storey also knows just how to make his theatrical effects. The evening is an effective *tour de force*.

Butley is a most articulate play, in fact one I would like to read, and is made momentous by performances by Alan Bates and [Richard] O'Callaghan. Bates has invented a most original sense of humour. It takes a while to realise what he is up to, but by degrees one is overcome by his tongue-in-cheekiness and self-mockery. What a marvellous prospect in the new theatre he is. He came in on the new wave of Osborne and has gone from one peak to another. A real artist, modest, determined and utterly charming as well as having a most beautiful face. He has grown his hair terribly shaggily long. This is obviously to compensate for the width of his neck which has now become almost inhumanly large and almost freakish.

Yesterday I fainted. It was quite an interesting and invigorating experience, the only drawback being that I hit and bruised a knee and my head. Otherwise no ill effects as far as I know.

The German woman who has been giving me massage in Salisbury had miraculously cured me of my headaches. She discovered the tension at the back of the neck and on the shoulders was such that no blood could get to my head. In five treatments, she has liberated me. The first time she shook my head violently from side to side I felt dizzy and perhaps almost lost consciousness. Yesterday, at the end of the treatment, she twisted my head violently from side to side with such force that suddenly

---

[1] *Butley* by Simon Gray, with Alan Bates, Richard O'Callaghan and Michael Byrne, had opened at the Criterion in July.
[2] David Storey (b. 1933), novelist (*This Sporting Life*), as well as playwright.
[3] Lindsay Anderson (1923–94), influential film and theatre director. He made films such as *If...* (1968) and *O Lucky Man* (1973).

I found myself in a strange world of stretching, striped whip-cord carpet. I thought I had died.

'Where am I?' I asked. I was baffled and, by degrees, I could hear myself breathing rather fast and I was conscious of someone asking, 'What happened? What happened?' The nice little masseuse was crouching, terrified, over me. I was too stunned to realise what had happened and could not move for a bit. When my head had hit the floor the neck had received a jolt, and hurt. Otherwise I was in no pain.

Annie was alarmed. 'That's never happened to me before.' I had fallen first on to my knees and then on to my head. I was worried that I'd be late for meeting Michael Duff at the station. I hurried out with grazed scalp and big limp. I had not the headache that was expected and went through a busy day without troubles. But I kept thinking about the experience and wondered if instead of regaining consciousness and continuing with the ritual of my life, I had died, what a very easy end it would have been, and what instead of dinner with the Trees (Decca, Moucher, Billy, Frank[1] etc.) the alternative, if any, would have been.

Marie-Hélène de Rothschild, wife of Baron Guy de Rothschild, was famed for the fantastic and imaginative balls that she gave at the chateau de Ferrières, not far from Paris. The chateau was built by Paxton and restored by the Rothschilds in 1959. One year she gave a Surrealist Ball there.

1971 was the year of the centenary of the birth of Marcel Proust. On 2 December 1971 Marie-Hélène gave the 'Bal Proust', inviting 350 for dinner, and another 250 for supper afterwards. The men were summoned in white tie, the ladies dressed as Proust's grand heroines from A La Recherche du Temps Perdu. *The guests were served Château Lafitte by scarlet-clad footmen in a scene of extravagant elegance.*

Cecil attended the ball dressed as Nadar, to photograph the guests for Vogue.

Sunday

I went to Paris for various reasons that coincided with the date of the Guy de Rothschild party – *A Côté de chez Ferrières*. Then *Vogue* asked me to take photographs, and, since they would pay expenses, it seemed worthwhile. So indeed it turned out to be, though the jaunt became one of business rather than pleasure. It meant a journey to and from Ferrières, a huge Paxton home 1½ hours out of Paris, and it meant working very hard instead of spending time out, possibly trying to escape

---

[1] Jessica Mitford (1917–1996); Mary, Duchess of Devonshire (1897–1989); Billy Henderson and Frank Tait.

bores, in the crowded mêlée of the party. Ugly salons, untouched since the furnishings were first placed in their present positions.

The ball was a wonderful setting for a Proust affair, but few of the guests had read *A la Recherche*, and certainly not Marie-Hélène who is probably the most spoilt woman in the whole world today. She has every resource to keep reality at bay, so rich herself and her husband is the Head of the Rothschild Bank. The evening comprised 350 to dinner, then 250 afterwards for supper, singers, bands, unbelievable food, orchids everywhere, pale mauve branches of orchids, darker mauve cattybras.

The guests were café society rather than *gratin*, and a lot of newspaper celebrities were treated with importance. *Vogue* wished particularly to have Eliz Taylor[1] as they find that every issue carrying her picture is a sell-out. I have always loathed the Burtons for their vulgarity, common-ness and crass bad taste, she combining the worst of US and English taste, he as butch and coarse as only a Welshman can be. However, at the end of a long line of beauties being posed in attitudes of the time (I was dressed as Nadar), the hostess, foul in white satin and hair down her shoulders, a superannuated Cinderella, brought down the chip-on-shouldered pair who were both extremely embarrassed and self-conscious.

I treated her with authority, told her not to powder her nose, to come in front of the camera with it shining. She wanted compliments. She got none. I asked her to hide a shoulder, lean forward, and went forward to this great thick revolving mass of femininity in its rawest, and put her in position. 'Don't touch me like that,' she whined! For a split second I wondered if I shouldn't say, 'Right, that's enough, that's all for tonight!' But I felt I must be professional to the last ounce of energy and continued, but not with anything but disgust and loathing at this monster. Her breasts, hanging and huge, were like those of a peasant woman suckling her young in Peru. They were seen in their full shape, blotched and mauve, plum. Round her neck was a velvet ribbon with the biggest diamond in the world pinned on it. On her fat, coarse hands more of the biggest diamonds and emeralds, her head a ridiculous mass of diamond necklaces sewn together, a snood of blue and black pompoms and black osprey aigrettes. Sausage curls, Alexandre, the hairdresser, had done his worst. And this was the woman who is the greatest 'draw'. In comparison everyone else looked ladylike.

Princess Grace [of Monaco], very pretty and soft of expression, a big bull puppy now, but lovely clear complexion (unlike the hirsute Taylor).

---

[1] (Dame) Elizabeth Taylor (b. 1932), actress and film star, then married to Richard Burton and at the height of her glory, as Burton bought her numerous great diamonds. They were, for a while, part of the *beau monde*.

The Duchess of Windsor[1] came in and behaved like a mad Goya. She is more than ever a personality and character, but God, what she looks like, her face so pulled up that the mouth stretches from ear to ear. She was galvanised, as if high, her body and arms and hands so thin that one feels she cannot last long. (The Duke too ill to be present,[2] was quietly 'entertaining' Mona and her new doctor husband[3] to dinner.) Several women were ravishing – Hélène Rochas,[4] in black velvet with three white roses on the corsage and a huge simple loaf of bread-coloured hair was the best. Maria Gabriella,[5] a marvellous Winterhalter in dark red and black silk; Victoire de Ganay (Montesquieu)[6] a Sargent in dark plum and pink bows, a ravishing display and I enjoyed my evening taking over thirty sittings and over five hundred pictures.

Back at four a.m. to the Crillon, to worry about the return to England next day. Mercifully the pictures were technically perfect and I was able to come away from Paris having the feeling that now at last I could afford to have a cold and go to bed for as long as I liked. In fact this was not entirely so for I had my friend, Michael Duff,[7] to stay and look after. But that is only a pleasure.

11 December 1971

A dull patch. Never before have I felt so grateful for the fact that I have work to do. Without it I don't know what would have kept me going in the last weeks. The work has been absorbing, not exciting, lots of articles and reviews, and a bit of rather careless painting, but it has been a way of keeping at bay a feeling that nothing is very exciting. I have been fighting off colds and 'flu. I haven't felt full of vim. My body has ached.

Mercifully the little German masseuse in Salisbury has, with her strong fingers, broken up the tensed muscles in my back and relieved me of my headaches. This is the greatest mercy and it will mean that apart from my writing I can do a little gentle reading. For this I am thankful. I

---

[1] The Duchess was already suffering from arteriosclerosis.
[2] The Duke of Windsor was very lame, and soon fell victim to cancer of the throat, from which he died the following May.
[3] Mona Bismarck and Dr Martini.
[4] Hélène Rochas, of the scent family.
[5] HRH Princess Maria Gabriella of Italy (b. 1940), then married to the property developer Robert de Balkany.
[6] Victoire de Montesquiou (b. 1934), married Michael de Ganay. Author of *Je suis née un Dimanche* (1990).
[7] Sir Michael Duff Bt (1907–80), bachelor owner of Vaynol, in Wales, who relayed royal gossip with an engaging stammer. Author of a wicked spoof, *The Power of a Parasol*, privately produced.

am not, however, thankful enough for the female hormones I must take to ward off any coronary troubles, for although they have simplified my life by taking away any sex interests, they make me quite disgusted with my own body.

When I have become restless, I have not discovered anybody that I am really terribly keen to see. Ray has to have one weekend off per month. I have found that those with whom I'd quite like to stay are not available, and when I go through alternatives, I wonder if really I do want to see them enough. Perhaps this is symptomatic of my state of health. I feel very much in need of a break, fresh environment, snow or sun, something to give me some zest, a quality I have not often before lacked.

11 December 1971

I have not imparted the news to anyone that I have been 'recommended' for a knighthood and feel that if I do, some missive will arrive saying that after all, possibly on account of the Garbo revelations, I will not be thus honoured. It is a long time to wait 'til the New Year, and I feel it would be a great crunching blow if I have to find myself 'left out'. For although I know it will not mean anything serious, and after all other knights are very small fry, yet it does give me a feeling of pride and a certain self-importance, and I look forward to the fun of the announcement. With fingers crossed I am biding the time patiently.

As feared, Dame Gladys Cooper died aged eighty-two, on 17 November 1971. Cecil was among those who attended her memorial service at St Paul's, Covent Garden.

Sunday, 19 December 1971

It is very seldom that I am in London at the weekends but I wanted to go to the memorial service for Gladys Cooper. We wondered why it was arranged for a Saturday morning, then when Irene Worth and I got to the church, discovered that had she lived the extra weeks she would have been eighty-three this day. The first person I saw arriving (we did not realise that the entrance to the St Paul's Covent Garden Church is no longer through its colonnaded portico, and we were late), was an old man in black cape with longish white, carefully brushed [hair] with tall collar and big flowing tie, hurrying in front of us. He created a marvellous atmosphere of the theatre that no longer exists. I don't know who he was and the journalists at the new doors did not know either, but he had an aura of the theatre in the days that Gladys was its great ornament of beauty. He was of the ilk of Sir Squire Bancroft, or Allan Aynesworth,[1] he augured well for the service that we had come to attend in a rather light, matter-of-fact way.

Suddenly, to find a packed church full of yellow flowers and a little winter sunlight was to be struck with an emotion that brought the usual tears to my eyes. It is awful how easily I weep. Why have I not any self-control? I was caught unawares this morning and the tears poured, and I felt self-conscious about using my handkerchief, as John Buckmaster, Sally Cooper,[2] were all containing themselves with wide-eyed wonder.

The service started with a short introduction from the cheery, sympathetic vicar, then a psalm, then poor old Stanley Holloway,[3] who is eighty years old, stepped rather falteringly into the pulpit to read from *The Pilgrim's Progress*. This was a tremendous and marvellous shock, for in my abysmal ignorance I have not read Bunyan and not only did the beauty of the writing overwhelm me, but the incredible goodness of Stanley's delivery gave me tremors. 'Death, where is thy sting?' and then when the Pilgrim went over the other side, the trumpets sounded and I, sitting in the front row under the pulpit, was reduced to a pulp.

The service was beautifully arranged, a Shakespeare sonnet on love was read by Celia Johnson,[4] a serenade from *Hassan*, a comic and evocative address by Robert Morley,[5] which gave great relief to the congregation and prevented the atmosphere from becoming too morbid. He changed the mood to one of gratitude for her life, a wonderful life in so many ways.

Her success as a beauty and as an actress had spanned an incredible amount of time. She had setbacks, and grave responsibilities. I believe she looked after her deaf sister and suddenly her beautiful, intelligent, accomplished son, John, went violently and incurably mad.[6] But Gladys never complained, never, as Robert said, sought pity for herself any more than she felt it for others, and we must each do what we can to cope. She had coped with so much so valiantly, right up to the last, when she never allowed anyone to know if she knew she was dying.

A prayer, a blessing, then two minutes of silence in which we were all

---

[1] Sir Squire Bancroft (1841–1926), actor; and Allan Aynesworth (1865–1959), leading actor and director of his day.
[2] John Buckmaster (1915–83), Gladys Cooper's wayward stepson; and Sally, her daughter, then married to the actor Robert Hardy.
[3] Stanley Holloway (1890–1982), actor. He played Alfred P. Doolittle in the play and film of *My Fair Lady*.
[4] Dame Celia Johnson (1908–82), film actress, best remembered for *Brief Encounter*.
[5] Robert Morley (1908–92), rotund actor. He was Gladys Cooper's son-in-law.
[6] See Hugo Vickers, *Vivien Leigh* (1988), p. 213.

to remember in our own way our friend, Gladys. Surely such concentration of thought from two or three hundred people must create a force that somewhere could be felt? Would not Gladys, in whatever life afterwards must be, somewhere receive such vibrations?

For myself I remember Gladys since, as a faltering schoolboy, I went up to her when she was having lunch at the Carlton restaurant with Gertie Millar.[1] I remember the sweetness with which she acceded to my stammering request and said I must of course also ask for the signature of her friend. Her complexion was of a white marshmallow perfection with pinkish cheeks, fair, silky fluff of hair, and the bluest eyes. Perhaps as the draped figure in *The Betrothal* as she uncovered her face, she was the most beautiful of all. The expression in her eyes was of wonder and such compassion that I shall never forget the vision. But there are so many stage memories of her, Paula Tanqueray, Mrs Cheney, she became the target for my first caricatures, and then when I got to know her well, I broke through the façade of almost too great an honesty and a frankness that sometimes hurt. Once I went up to her and asked, 'Would you like to buy a programme?' 'No, I'd hate to,' she said.

During the filming of *My Fair Lady*, I got to know the way she really liked to live, almost out of doors, with the birds flying in through the doors. She lived quite alone and was unafraid of being attacked by the loathsome marauders around Los Angeles. I remember at a lunch, given by Warner, how the press were only interested in Rex and Audrey, but this in no way concerned Gladys. She never felt any jealousy or bitterness, and accepted 'bit parts' with great dignity and eventually became quite a figure in a new vein, both on TV and screen.

Up till the last she had this remarkable sense of reality. She said, 'A man stopped me, coming out of the co-operative store in Henley-on-Thames and said, "Congratulations on being eighty-two," and I could have killed him.'

During the two minutes, so many photographic pictures of her came through into my brain, so many impressions of childhood, adolescence and grown-up life in NY and Hollywood and back here to publishing lunches at the Dorchester.

Now we were saying our fond farewells, and saying them happily, as was evident in the gusto with which the final hymn was sung and the Handel anthem.

Then the trooping out into the court and the exchange of kisses and smiles. So many forgotten beauties from the stage who have those bright blue eyes, good noses and chins, and rugged classical looks that have gone, so many alive octogenarians – Cicely Courtneidge asked Phyllis

---

[1] Gertie Millar (d. 1952), second wife of second Earl of Dudley.

Monckman to introduce me to her. It is true we have never met. She is a marvel. Jack Hulbert,[1] from being a caricature, has become a handsome old man. All the friends – Bobbie Andrews,[2] once the most beautiful boy in the world, on a stick, his sister, John G [Gielgud], Alec G [Guinness], Enid Bagnold, her few remaining hairs dyed red and fuzzed, Cathleen N [Nesbitt], Joan Greenwood,[3] Binkie B [Beaumont], John P [Perry],[4] John Merivale,[5] very sad being, his beard, Evelyn Laye.[6] Outside the sun shone quite bright and everyone was cheerful and chatty. Sybil Thorndike was driven off in a car, waving and smiling. I told her how beautiful she had become, more so now than at any time in her life. 'Don't be such a fool. Don't be so silly!' she said, but she was pleased. Then she said, 'I hope my service will be as gay as this one. It won't be long. You know I'm nearly ninety!' and waving and leaning back and cackling, her companions drove her home.

    Irene [Worth] and I walked laughingly through Covent Garden, and John G., looking very debonair and boyish, asked us in for a drink at the Garrick, but I don't hold with men's clubs or spontaneous invitations, which is silly, and I was quickly back into my rut and enjoying the lunch that Ray had prepared, the first solid meal I've had, due to stomach troubles, for some days. A sleep afterwards and then a journey to Badminton to stay with Caroline and David [Somerset] and to find myself with Daphne Fielding[7] in a completely new and refreshing and altogether delightful atmosphere of jokes, expensive cosiness and simplicity, dogs, children and white-haired local women to tend one like nannies. It was like going back to the womb.

Chez Somersets

The weekend was quite a success for although I didn't feel very strong, managed to rest a lot, sleep quite well and gradually forget myself.

---

[1] Dame Cicely Courtneidge (1893–1980), Phyllis Monckman and Dame Cicely's husband, Jack Hulbert (1892–1978), actor.
[2] Robert Andrews (1895–1981).
[3] Joan Greenwood (1921–87), actress, heroine of the film Kind Hearts and Coronets.
[4] John Perry (1906–95), early boyfriend of John Gielgud, who later worked for and lived with Binkie Beaumont. A director of H. M. Tennent Ltd.
[5] John Merivale (1917–90), actor, stepson of Gladys Cooper, still mourning the loss of Vivien Leigh (1913–67), with whom he lived for seven years. Later married to Dinah Sheridan.
[6] Evelyn Laye (1900–95), sprightly actress.
[7] Daphne Fielding (1904–97), daughter of Lord Vivian, married sixth Marquess of Bath, divorced, and later married to Xan Fielding, the travel writer. Again divorced. Author.

Caroline, very highly strung so that she is continuously flicking her fingers and throwing back her hair, has become quite a marvellous character. David, though attractive, funny, in many ways kind, has been a difficult husband but Caroline has learnt to cope. She has learnt much in fact about life, and is a studier, all the time learning about gardens, cooking, herbals, illnesses, houses. Daphne, who says she herself is a hypocrite, which I don't believe, said that she wouldn't change anything if she had her life again. Since she is now so poor, it shows the value of love, for her love of penniless Xan [Fielding] is overwhelming, no regrets for being the Marchioness of Longleat.

We had a glimpse of ducal life on our Sunday walk, when after a great rain storm, we went for a walk around the park at Badminton. From a distance I spied Master[1] who was doing the rounds of the horses, giving them in his naked hands the chunks of carrot from a basket. Every now and again a yelp, as a horse got his finger. Then indoors to have a drink, Master explaining, 'We're very short staffed,' did the honours and considers vodka the new drink. I spied Mary Duchess[2] coming in in a downpour. The rain had come in the roof and she had had to place *pots de chambre* at all the necessary positions. She gives off pathos. Her high, squeaky voice and sad eyes make me cry. Talk about the awful Royal Christmas cards, the BP family group is appalling, and the QM is worse than ever. Talk about the hunt (about demos yesterday), the neighbours.

A quiet weekend with David flying off to London early Sunday afternoon, people to dinner, and when I left I felt refreshed and pleased at having had such a 'different' time, looking at other people's books and possessions, and being with people who, though sympathetic, are brought up in a very different way and fundamentally have other interests and convictions than my own.

The return journey to Broadchalke was delightful. Motored to Bath and caught the train to Salisbury and suddenly realised how pleasant a country train journey can be. One sees so comparatively little as one drives in a motor. This is one of my favourite parts of England. Bath is always a surprise treat and today, although mid-winter and bad, grey weather, it looked quite as beautiful as ever in the silver mist, and the countryside around Bradford-on-Avon is more feathery and sylvan than any I know. The stone cottages among the undulating hills so beautifully harmonious in the landscape. A real delight to wind along in the slow-

---

[1] 'Master', tenth Duke of Beaufort KG (1900–84), Master of the Horse and owner of Badminton, who wrote in memoirs that he neither wrote nor read: 'Obviously the hunting of the fox has been my chief concern.' Cecil spent a difficult night at Badminton in 1964.
[2] Mary, Duchess of Beaufort (1897–1987), niece of Queen Mary, wife of tenth Duke.

moving train, with the river near at hand, with lots of white birds, swans and all manner of duck. Even at this bleak time of year, the willows were beautiful and the cottage kitchen gardens had patches of brilliant green among the grey. I was in a good holiday mood, coming back to my house for a long spell (two weeks?), having done and completed a great deal of work.

Smallpeice met me with the news that the Wilton hunt had met at Broadchalke, and suddenly, as they were about to do their last Christmas shopping in Salisbury, saw a fox rushing towards them from our new winter garden. The fox leapt our new wall, ran through the wrought-iron gate into the garden and straight up the paddock with the hounds in full pursuit. No damage was done and Claire Pembroke[1] was acutely embarrassed, but we all thought it so inconsequential and unexpected as to be very funny. Hearty laughter on all sides.

New Year's Day drawing nigh, and I am thinking more about my being given a rise in life and wondering if, at this late stage, after all, they won't say they've made a mistake. I haven't told anyone the news for the fear that it will bring the letter of change of mind. For unlike Francis Bacon, who says he couldn't think of anything worse happen to him, I am very much looking forward to all the excitement.

A week of hard painting in the warm but airless studio made me very weak and anaemic. A glance at my white face frightened me. But I slogged on with the pictures, which, unlike others I have done, were done in order to be sold. I wouldn't want them to be exhibited in London or New York, for hard as I have tried to do my best, they are to the taste of less sophisticated types. Water lilies, still lifes, and my rose trellises and close-ups of clematis and Caroline Testout on the terrace wall. I worked a lot from magic lantern slides and this in some instances gave me very unusual compositions. It has been quite an interesting phase, and later when Eileen was shown them, we counted that altogether about thirty pictures have been accumulated for the Vigorioux Gallery.

The only drawback to this phase of work is that I have been suffering a great deal of unrest in my mind about the Garbo diaries, and when one is quietly at work, one's mind goes round and round on the same subject. One small pair of 'waterscapes' made me think all the while of Truman Capote's nasty TV account of me,[2] and of his intonations that I made

---

[1] Countess of Pembroke (b. 1943), wife of seventeenth Earl of Pembroke. Divorced. Married Tertius Murray-Threipland.
[2] Truman Capote spoke waspishly in the *Beaton by Bailey* film, in conversation with Diana Vreeland in her New York apartment.

enemies with his friends, the Paleys. But it was the Garbo indiscretions that kept coming back to haunt me. Apart from the fact that she will be so distressed (though I am convinced she will not read them), I begin to feel that certain bits that the newspapers have and will concentrate on could have been cut. However, I have made the bold decision to publish and even now if I were given a second chance as to whether they should be printed or left out of my diaries, I still think that as a writer I am justified in publishing something that may strike a lot of people as ungentlemanly.

But who knows how in the future people would think about a man's 'kissing and telling'? Manners and modes of behaviour change so rapidly, and possibly nowadays the young would consider my indiscretions quite innocuous. However, at the moment I am suffering quite a bit and no doubt should find a more active way to spend the time. But this is a quiet phase in which I am able to work, undisturbedly, and I must continue. But each day I wonder if word will come that, owing to pre-publication scandal, my knighthood has been rescinded.

Eileen laughs when, on the telephone, I ask if this has been so. Yet no word has come since our acceptance. Would our reply perhaps have been lost in the post? I telephoned at Christmas time (quietly here by myself, suffering not only from a sort of 'flu, but worse from the effect of a 'flu shot, administered by Dr Brown) to Kin and told him the news. He was full of laughter and delight. I then telephoned my sisters, but I felt that if I told anyone else, so superstitious am I, that surely the offer would be taken back. As each day approached I felt more anxiety.

On the day before the announcement should be made, Michael Duff[1] sent me a telegram congratulating me on my honour. Was it really a knighthood? Alan, Charles and Eileen arrived exhausted for the weekend, and when after eleven o'clock I switched on the TV, the programmes were so dreadful that we decided to go to bed. Just as I had started to lose consciousness, Dr Brown and his family, in high excitement, rang to say that they had heard the news on the late-night bulletin. I dare not ask if it was a knighthood. I slept well but was awake to hear the eight o'clock news, and there my name came out first and foremost as being a knight. Thereupon the bedroom door opened and in came Eileen, Alan and Charles, wreathed in smiles and bearing branches of laurel.

Then the newspapers brought further proof, my name large on the front page of the *Telegraph*. Yes, there was no denying, and then the telephone, Diana Cooper pleased to be the first, followed swiftly by John Julius [Norwich], and then a flood non-stop all day, Jakie Astor, David Cecil, John Sutro, the Heads, the Pembrokes, Irene Worth, Lee R

[1] Sir Michael Duff was Lord Lieutenant of Caernarvonshire and would have had advance notice.

[Radziwill], Nancy [Smiley], now in high elation, and the cousins too. I could not stop laughing at being called Sir Cecil. It sounded so unlike me, so much less personal than Mr B. and when envelopes appeared with the Sir on them, it seemed to take away some long applied individuality.

However, I was pleased with myself, pleased that here was a day devoted to accepting praise from friends, via the telephone or cable. Within an hour there were messages from Malta, Hong Kong, Florida, Melbourne. It seemed so strange that this had at last happened. A few years ago I believe Lord Goodman[1] suggested I should be honoured, but, someone 'higher' had vetoed it. I thought it would never happen, but as Jakie said, it was 'high bloody time', and that time had come.

My only regret, and one voiced by many, that my mother was not alive to enjoy the accolade. How proud and pleased she would have been, and the aunts too, and my father so baffled, but no regrets. This had happened and now I must enjoy all its aspects and I was in a laughing mood, and the household was a very happy one.

---

[1] Lord Goodman (1913–95), lawyer and international fixer.

1972

'Sir' is a romantic title. It is much easier on the tongue than Duke or Earl. A Knight at best is something of literature and chivalry. Hugh Smiley wrote an excited delightful letter of praise but said 'Sir Cecil was difficult for people with false teeth'. (I was reminded of an early joke: 'Which switch, miss, is the switch for Ipswich?') Many people describe the excitement of the scene of the variety club benefit when at midnight the news came through of the Honours and mine was the first to be read out, but more astonishing was the fact that Desmond Shawe-Taylor,[1] hurrying to catch a train at Waterloo, had seen my name flashed in lights on the running news bulletin!

The *Sunday Times* sent a photographer down to Broadchalke and astonishingly the picture, an excellent one – in which, all the family agreed, I looked exactly like my mother – was on the front page. This resemblance to my mother is one that pleases me. As I became middle-aged my sisters were apt to remark how I was becoming so much like a Beaton, that on TV I had seemed to be an uncle 'Barley'. I prefer to look like my mother in her old age – for she was noble and distinguished – and lately have felt that I was becoming like her in many other ways – that I sat listening to others with the same caustic amused look on the face – that I moved around the house and garden like her – which brings me to another observation – and that is that I did not realise until recently that the male Beatons are not in general a long-lived family – the Sissons make old bones – but not the healthy-looking 'Barleys'.[2] Perhaps this is as well – I don't want – at this present stage – to endure the disadvantages – the slowing down and the tiresomeness of living to be 80. One never knows if at any given point one would say 'this is enough', but I would have thought another 10 years would have been more than enough for me.

The Knighting – this great dignity conferred – has made me feel that much older and I wish very much it had come earlier – for the reward for achievement would have felt so much greater. As it is I feel it has been given partly for endurance, partly because I couldn't be left out much longer, and at this age I couldn't be expected to get into serious trouble...

---

[1] Desmond Shawe-Taylor (1907–95), chief music critic of the *Sunday Times* (1959–83).
[2] Cecil was always a bit disparaging about his Beaton ancestors. 'Barley' was a family nickname for them. He was conveniently vague about his mother's ancestry – the Sissons family. Her father was a blacksmith.

Dinner party *January 1972*

Pauline R [Rothschild] is a very remarkable eccentric woman. She is of a very rare and rarefied quality, with the strength of character, now backed by Philippe's fortune, to lead just the sort of life she wishes. That this is due to her present circumstances alone is not true, for when she worked as a dress designer for a tough woman in New York (Hattie Carnegie[1]), she dictated her terms – no arrival before 12 o'clock – a vast salary – and she spent the evenings alone in bed reading poems and surrounded by camellia trees which the florist kept for her until they were in bloom. When I stayed with her in Holland it was a wonderful rest to be in bed until 1 o'clock, to return to it after lunch and a short walk until 10 o'clock when dinner would be served.

At Mouton when there are large parties, Pauline is never hurried; her nerves must be in wonderful condition and she is invariably the last to put in an appearance when the guests assemble for the next meal. But I had not realised when as a result of a congratulatory call from Mouton and learning they were soon to come to London I asked them to dinner this time, that Pauline brought her unpunctuality with her. The result a rather wrecked evening.

To meet P. and P., I had asked Enid Bagnold (to whom I was offering the complete olive tree, not just a branch[2]), Diana Cooper, Peter Eyre, the intellectual actor who has not yet had the success he deserves, and the Stephen Spenders, they for the first time as I've never really been very partial to either of them, but they are friends of the Rothschilds. And we became matey and exchanged presents last New Year's at Mouton.

Enid had written several times to accept the invitation with joy but fear. She had no clothes, no hair and very little native wit. She had not been asked out to dinner for years. She would have to leave early, as she is in great pain. The operation on her hip has not been successful, she is living off morphia and has become an addict. She arrived punctually accompanied by the faithful Diana, looking wild and ashen, her eyes made up, a kaftan, an 18th-century paste necklace (a mistake though), which kept falling off.

Champagne brought colour to her cheeks and as the evening wore on she looked as Diana said, a beauty. She spoke in this unexpected little-girl high voice and was in quite stalwart form. The others arrived. Natasha Spender is a really plain woman, such a shapeless nose, such clumsy

---

[1] Hattie Carnegie (1886–1956), retailer, owner of dress and hat shop, designer of jewellery.
[2] Cecil was putting aside the old row over his sets for her play, *The Chalk Garden*.

hands. Stephen in blue velvet looked benign (and he looked a lot at the pictures on my wall). Peter Eyre in a décolleté turquoise shirt and the biggest check I have ever seen in my life made a splendid ornament. But no Rothschilds. Enid asked, 'Why are they so important that we wait for them?'

This was rather typical of Enid's *à côté* side. She can be very snobbish in a *démodé* way. I explained, 'It's not that they're important, but it would be so rude to start.'

Diana said, 'It's unbelievably rude of them. They are an hour late!'

I kept conferring with Ray. He looked up at me with wide eyes from below. The green eggs would be alright and the duck he'd been boring and stuffing and sewing up for the past 2 days would not be overcooked but the vegetables would be ruined.

At after 9 o'clock I thought I heard a door bang and I expected an effusive entrance of apologies. After a minute or two I went up to the hall and there, calm and unhurried, was Pauline arranging wisps of very untidy hair. She looked perfectly terrible in the tightest pink silk trousers and a white silk shirt that revealed too much of the low-hung undercarriage. Philippe was silent and white. 'But I thought you were never coming, we were afraid you'd had an accident, we nearly rang up the police.'

Very few apologies except in a mild *sotto voce* from Philippe who said, 'You've no idea what it's like – Pauline can't be on time. I've been ready on the dot but she can't be hurried and the day has been a bad one for her with the furniture not arriving for the new Albany flat and everything going wrong.'

In answer to why she was late Pauline just said, 'Philippe expects too much of me.' I tried not to show a frozen façade but I did not really thaw towards Pauline for the rest of the evening. She said she thought my fashion exhibition very striking but in no uncertain terms she said we had made a mockery of her Balenciaga – 'Mouton Noir'.[1] Enid on leaving said she liked Philippe but didn't think much of Pauline. She did not get beyond the affectations, the manner that has become completely natural. Perhaps Pauline said nothing that gave of her true essence. Enid told me she was suffering very much from the effects of old age. She could not write. The blank page tortured her. Inspiration had gone.

She did not say that the drug was responsible but she was only able to be partly courageous. Perhaps to get back for another shot, she left early in a mini cab. In the hall she said, 'I haven't worn shoes for months. I must take off these high heels' and on one of the wettest nights of a

---

[1] 'Le Mouton Noir' made for Baroness Philippe de Rothschild in 1960. A full-length semicircular lace-frilled evening coat entirely covered with flounces, worn wrapped across to one shoulder.

London January she walked out across the marble hall down the stone pathway to the pavement in her bare feet. 'I'm like an ox, you can't get through to the bone of the hoof, I don't feel anything.' Diana agreed: 'She's like Doggie.'

By degrees the party took off. At 11 o'clock I was getting tired but more champagne was passed around and the tall goblets filled. Then Stephen started reminiscing about Evelyn Waugh[1] and how some young things, friends of Francis Bacon,[2] had stolen the large old-fashioned watch that Evelyn had entrusted to Stephen while he went to Africa. I told of my first day at preparatory school when Evelyn was leading the bullies – singled me out for persecution. Diana wistfully said, 'I loved him!'

Then, why I don't remember, but she started reciting *Browning*. Suddenly she was extraordinary. She quoted by the quatrain, unhesitant, beautiful in her royal blue with the one pearl in an ear (her maid had forgotten to give her the second one – she doesn't notice things). More champagne, more poems, this is so unlike a present-day London dinner party. Reading and recitation of poetry has long since passed in favour of the radio or telly. Diana was marvellous.

At 1 o'clock she made signs to move. I took her to her battered white car. She should not drive but she is so game for as she told us tonight she is about to be 80 years old. She feels no cold and when I returned saw her fur wrap on a chair. She had driven off oblivious of the climate in royal blue chiffon.

Pauline eventually said, 'I arrived late, but I hope I have made up for it by staying for so long.' It had been an interesting evening. I can't say one of the most agreeable, but perhaps all the better for the undercurrents and electric currents. The one who had shone most brilliantly was Ray with his egg, duck and then the most refreshing melon and lychee compôte, so beautifully presented in 2 half-melons, both beautiful dark jade green.

Pelham Place – Felix Harbord   *January 1972*

Felix Harbord is a most generous good-natured old waffler and behaves like a most chivalrous knight. But although he is continuously clearing his throat as he suggests taking me out to dinner or, to see his 'new' flat – he must have been in it 2 years – he never gets around to being positive and generally has a bite with me before going on for a movie. This time a

---

[1] Evelyn Waugh (1903–66), novelist, who stuck pins into Cecil when they were both at Heath Mount School, Hampstead.
[2] Francis Bacon (1909–92), artist. He once painted Cecil, and Cecil destroyed the result.

difference. He asked me to meet him at the gold and red baroque room of the Café Royal and here he ate oysters.

It was such a rare occasion for me to go to a restaurant in London that I was fascinated to watch the waiters at their subservient jobs. We then went to see the film of Solzhenitsyn *[One] Day in the Life of Ivan [Denisovich]*,[1] a film made in Norway to represent the sufferings of the political prisoners under Stalin in a camp in the wastes of Siberia. Such horror and misery knocked me backwards from the moment that the pictures of those doomed creatures flashed on the screen...

The film was well directed though could not be called a great film for it had no directional strokes of genius to match the writing of the story. It was most realistically photographed and Tom Courtenay[2] always admirable, never overstressed and expressioned...

The brilliance of Courtenay. Not only was he able to create this extraordinary effect in this dark tragedy but simultaneously he was appearing on the stage in Shaftesbury Avenue as *Charley's Aunt*.

How *anybody* in England can be pro-Soviet is beyond belief. What *can* they think? The Soviets are the scourge of the world. A few people say that Russia has always been a poor, cruel, primitive country but however terrible conditions were there was never this terrible lack of freedom.

Weekend at Reddish   *January 1972*

Have been almost a month alone at Reddish, and I have enjoyed the long stretch, and have been able to get on with a great deal of painting. These canvases done especially for Palm Beach. Some I like very much but it was not till Hal Burton[3] came down with Baba [Hambro] for the weekend that I was able to see them in perspective. Hal is not entirely generous though he tries to be fair. He said he was amazed at my vitality, that it was astonishing that I had been able to turn out so many pictures and he thought that I had here a 'little fortune'. That was nice.

But he was non-committal about many of the paintings though later he wrote and said he liked the flowers. But his criticism of certain of them was very helpful and after the departure on Monday I had a busy day in making many improvements according to his suggestions. I am still undecided in my mind as to whether any of the pictures are any good or

---

[1] *One Day in the Life of Ivan Denisovich*, directed by Caspar Wrede (1971).
[2] Tom Courtenay (b. 1937), then a lean young actor. Appeared in *Billy Liar* (1963), *Doctor Zhivago* (1965) and *The Dresser* (1983).
[3] Hal Burton (1908–87), collaborator with Cecil on many projects connected with the theatre.

whether they are merely decorative. One of a white seat in the rose garden is idyllic. It has really come off, and it is one of those flukes that one cannot copy.

Baba was very sympathetic about the house, recovering from a swollen face, eye trouble and worse, the loss of her 25-year long-standing lover. Poor Baba has been not at all clever about this relationship. She has got absolutely nothing out of it and now at the age of 60 is beginning to feel lonely. We are very far distant in most ways and the weekend, though relaxing, would not have been all that fun while Hal and I talked about theatrical productions she had not seen.

But at any rate, it gave her an opportunity to have breakfast in bed, and to notice the various ways in which I have changed and managed about my own house. It was a weekend of non-stop rain and darkness, so that none of us were able to see the greenhouse or the water garden. On my 68th birthday (Friday night) we had a small dinner: Hal, Mary P[embroke], Frank Tait, B. Henderson, Duchess Ashley-C[ooper][1] (which Baba missed) and the only other social activity was the arrival of Raymond Mortimer and his 4 guests (Glenway W [Wescott][2] and Monroe W [Wheeler])[3] for egg sandwich and Christmas cake at tea on Sunday.

Cecil wrote six profiles for Plays and Players *– Irene Worth, Richard O'Callaghan, Fenella Fielding, Isabel Jeans, Alan Webb and Paul Scofield. Isabel Jeans wrote to him: 'I am so deeply touched and so happy about it. I really don't know how to thank you. You have so understood and caught my moods and thoughts, anxieties, and difficulties, about my own particular feelings, both per-sonally and professionally ... Having had my full share of kicks, your article now is a wonderful recompense and a healing balm.' Irene Worth commented, 'Nobody tried harder than Cecil to make me a star.'*

Plays and Players

God I wish I had H. N. [Harold Nicolson]'s facility. He wrote his articles and reviews in a few hours. He finished some of his books in 6 weeks. One evening at Reddish, neighbour Dicky Buckle brought to dinner his chauffeur (!), Philip Dossé who runs all those magazines, *Films and*

---

[1] Lady Lettice Ashley-Cooper (1911–1990), daughter of ninth Earl of Shaftesbury, sister of Viscountess Head.
[2] Glenway Wescott (1901–87), American man of letters, of whom Gertrude Stein wrote: 'He has a certain syrup but it does not pour'.
[3] Monroe Wheeler (1899–1988), friend of the above.

Filming, Books and Bookmen, Plays and Players etc. etc. and I suggested I'd like to air a few of my grievances about London theatre managements.

Why wasn't Irene Worth treated as the *great* actress that she is – (Olivier is much to blame). Why is Fenella Fielding,[1] who was a star leading lady in Henry James's play, *The High Bid*, not given anything but burlesque TV parts. Why is Isabel Jeans[2] out of a job for 10 years? I would also like to praise a few who are accepted but not honoured, like the underestimated Alan Webb,[3] and the brilliant Richard O'Callaghan[4] who was so marvellously touching in *6 Months Gone* and holds his own against Alan Bates[5] in *Butley*.[6]

Dossé was thrilled at the idea – of course, no money could be spared and I liked the idea and set upon it without realising the work involved. The number of times Sheila Feeney had to woodpecker away at new drafts was enough to send her potty. I thought the Fenella Fielding would be easy, although she proved as delightful and intelligent a person in life as I imagined, the piece I wrote was, according to Hal B [Burton], too generalised.

He was right, a lot more rewrites, and as I am taking photographs of most of them, Isabel excepted (as I have such a good one and there was such a to-do about who could pay for a wig for a new picture), it has been quite a big job. And as I have got into it more thoroughly, I realise how easy it is to criticise from the sidelines and how much luck and how circumstances can make a man or reputation. However, it will be nice if through these features some bright youngster will click with an idea and give Fenella Fielding a star part or bring out Wendy Hiller[7] and others who spend most of their time 'resting'.

Following his rest cure, Cecil had an appointment at Buckingham Palace.

9 February 1972

Well, it happened. The sword has been on each of my shoulders. My cystitis has cleared miraculously and my fears of having to run to the

---

[1] Fenella Fielding (b. 1934), velvet-voiced actress.
[2] Isabel Jeans (1891–1985), actress much liked by Cecil. She played Aunt Alicia in the film *Gigi*. She spent her last days as a complete recluse.
[3] Alan Webb (1906–82), splendid character actor. In old age he was forever trying to lure Lady Diana Cooper to lunches he could ill afford in smart and expensive restaurants.
[4] Richard O'Callaghan (b. 1940), actor.
[5] Alan Bates (b. 1934), actor.
[6] *Butley* by Simon Gray (1972).
[7] Dame Wendy Hiller (b. 1912), actress.

Buckingham Palace toilets every few minutes proved unnecessary. The train from Salisbury arrived at Waterloo without the feared delays by strikers. I had for once tried on the clothes I was to wear (grey tailcoat and trousers, black silk hat) and although old they fitted. Nancy and Baba arrived in high spirits in a hire car and were sent off to get lilies of the valley for me to wear in my buttonhole, and then with a lot of high spirits and giggling and the 'staff', Eileen, Ray, Sheila, Karen, waving on the doorstep, we set off.

The rules and regulations started in the Mall when we had to join the queue with others going to the Investiture.

But the long tail behind us prevented feeling of panic. On arrival the recipients were separated from their families and sent to different rooms to be briefed. Huge lights were everywhere for it seems that the Investiture was being televised as part of a programme connected with the pageantry of the monarchy. Everything gleaming, shining, everything under control. What a great feeling this is! In the Palace one feels there is no anxiety, flurry, havoc or disaster. Everyone has such perfect manners, and this makes life so pleasant.

About 30 'Knights' had assembled in the room of striped green silk where so often I had tried to find a new angle for my photographs. One woman present, Cicely Courtneidge,[1] very decorous, about to be made a dame, but a relief for me to latch on to her. We were birds of a feather, and was I right in thinking that some of the older men disapproved of my appearing so extra smart in grey while they were all blackbirds? Dame Cicely talked of her early days, how she started as a soubrette, then when she was alone while her husband was at the war and she had no money. She went on the halls and became a Connie. 'Yes, Jack was here today, and their daughter but oh dear, she felt so alone here, was she the only woman?' 'Yes, but think what a male chorus you have!'

A most attractive, kind, good, gentle soldier (Penn[2]) gave us our instructions and demonstrated the way we should kneel on the fall stool but reassured us, 'It's very simple. Don't get flustered. The Queen may say a few words to you but when she shakes hands it is the signal for you to retreat 6 steps backwards, to bow, then make your exit.' It was all a bit like the first day in the army, or boarding school, but why be difficult? This was to be a great honour and pleasure, and no good ruining it by carping or being difficult.

---

[1] Dame Cicely Courtneidge (1893–1980), created DBE (1972), wife of Jack Hulbert, revue theatre and musical comedy actress, who established herself in the legitimate theatre in later life.
[2] Lt-Colonel (Sir) Eric Penn (1916–1993), Comptroller of the Lord Chamberlain's Office.

We then went in alphabetical file to the coulisses of the Throne Room and from my advantageous position of B could see the Queen at the end of a long enfilade walking towards us with a posse of courtiers behind her. She wore a pale dusky egg-blue dress, short, low sensible shoes (champagne coloured) and neat as ever hair, inevitable pearls and a prettier brooch than the usual knuckle-duster, and a loosely hanging [brooch] full of pearls. No other jewellery, no wristwatch, nothing to get in the way of her job about which she immediately set up unfolding the ribbons of various orders, stretching them with a tight jerk so they would not crinkle as she placed them over the recipient's shoulders, then flattened them well at the nape of the neck, all done very thoroughly. She would make an extremely good hospital nurse or nanny.

Her smile is reserved for the moment when, with met eyes intensely peering into the opposite number, she then asked a few questions as she raised her eyebrow. Dame Cicely looked from behind extremely old and hunchbacked and her curtsey was a small one. But my sisters later said she was marvellously professional. Her stage timing stood her in good stead and she looked extremely pretty in the arc lights.

Then my turn. I cannot say I felt nervous. I felt quite confident that this was surely the least of my troubles and I looked very piercingly at Her Majesty as she wielded the sword on to my shoulders. But what was she saying? Was she saying anything? I have a theory that she feels she knows me well enough not to have to say a few words. I did hear her, however, say, 'This is a great pleasure!' Since she didn't have anything to impart to me I felt bold enough, after she had shaken my hand, to say that I never thought taking her photographs in the little girl's pink taffeta dress would lead to this honour. 'It's a pleasure!' She seemed anxious to get rid of me as fast as possible.

Why do I feel this? My sisters say that they saw her talking to me yet I cannot believe she did. I admire her so much in so many ways, never more than today, but I feel we just cannot communicate. The moment of triumph over, we then were marched left and right into the empty seats at the side of the Throne Room. Here I watched the Queen give honours to 250 people, 3 a minute, so real a personal word (except to me!) that will live always in the recipient's memory. A smile, an intense curiosity, a question asked, nod, smile, handshake, and never a missed opportunity. I asked the Knight next to me if she had said anything he could remember. 'Oh yes, she asked how long I had been at St Thomas's Hospital. How she knew I worked there, I don't know. It was not in the citation – how could she know?'

Medals pinned on firmly, ribbons stretched, the rather clumsy-looking hands never faltered. Smile, eyebrows up. Yes it was automatic but real. No fake could go undetected. I looked about, Gurkhas stiff to attention, like ramrods, old Beefeaters [Yeomen of the Guard], one of whom fainted in the heat of the lights, the Queen never turning round at the thump. My sisters had so much of our mother as they sat taking in every delicious moment ('It was bliss,' Nancy said, running up the steps home) and I spied Princess Anne[1] with her lady-in-waiting, watching the proceedings with avidity. I was surprised at her being there but imagine she has her mother's sense of the correct, and as the proceedings continued it was apparent that they both realised that here in many instances were the backbone of the land, not the heads of industry and the successes, but the heroes who had shown bravery in attacking an armed gangster, or rescuing a family in a fire, or having had the initiative to sail the world alone.

Easy to smile at the matron's windmill ribboned hat, but if one had close acquaintance with her, one would know of her strength of character. And not only did the Queen seem to be perhaps even more interested in the people (of lesser rank) but Princess Anne also. She was getting in training for what might be a regular part of her future work.

Then without any drama the final medal was in place. On a click of steel 'God Save the Queen' and the monarch was at the end of a very concentrated hour and 20 minutes stretch. Great relief as we all shambled out. Great smiles, TV and camera laughter, the outer courtyard a milling mass of amateur photographs, out with the Polaroid and Instamatic.

One little soldier with Chinese eyes stood smartly 'at ease' in his gold gallon swags. Next to him was his duplicate – his 16-year-old son with the same Chinese eyes wearing a blue suit and very, very, very long hair. The Dame doing 1000 faces under the same hat. N. and B. very happy. I relieved, non-emotional, went back to Pelham for a wonderful lunch of fish fritters and sauce tartare, duck cooked in honey and orange, a bottle of a good champagne supplied by Hugh [Smiley]. Tecia curtseying in the hall, the Ellerts,[2] Eileen, all giggly and happy. A lovely celebration and Tecia said, 'How I love a family party!' For once I did too.

Kitty Miller during a dragging conversation said, 'I knew Proust.' Suddenly everyone was on the edge of their seats. 'Tell us, what was he like?' Kitty confined herself to one word: 'ghastly!'

---

[1] HRH the Princess Anne (b. 1950), later Princess Royal.
[2] Tecia Fearnley-Whittingstall (1907–92) and Tess Ellert (b. 1910) and her husband, John (1906–89). Tecia and Tess were Cecil's cousins, daughters of his Aunt Cada.

20 February 1972

We have been going through a black patch. I am not generally influenced by weather or general news but while I stayed getting on with a lot of rather dreary canvases in the country, everything seemed to conspire against me, and by degrees the television news filtered into one's pores.

The miners' strike[1] has not only caused great suffering and deprivement but it has unleashed appalling hatred. Everyone loathes everyone else. Seeing these ugly men, violent and belligerent, on the TV has made me feel horribly remote in my ivory tower. But even I have had heat and light cut, although I have not suffered any great inconvenience and, when the power was cut, could go out into my garden and keep my circulation going with work. But the feeling of hatred unleashed has affected me.

I feel I would like to do some harm to the union leaders. Only the communists and Gormley[2] with ridiculous hairdo are unpatriotic, nonetheless they been responsible for all this bitterness. Whenever aged people have complained to me that they feel the sands are running out, that they do not want to live in the ugly age of the future, I have felt that they were going through a bad spell that would pass. But not any more. I feel that there is now real class hatred and that 'things' are going from bad to worse, not only materially but spiritually. Violence, murder, black-out muggings, beastly-mindedness and meanness, lack of pity are on the increase.

I was sad when Diana Cooper, disconsolate at the death of her little Doggie, came to have an in-home evening with me. She arrived looking beautiful, quite young after her holiday in Africa, but she for the first time said she was quite 'ready to go', that death had no fears for her, that she was content to 'opt out'. She is generally so full of enthusiasm, verve, curiosity, so full of adventure, and certainly she rallied. I suggested we go to see the movie *Gumshoe*.[3] 'How beautifully everything fits in,' she said about the arrangements, and full of spunk we set off.

But during the evening she revealed how pleased she was I'd asked her out. She needn't be in her beastly house, and when I dropped her home, she said, 'Oh this horrid house, I hate it.' No doubt this was a tribute to 'dead Doggie' but it was the first time I got the feeling that she was grad-

---

[1] Edward Heath, the Prime Minister, confronted the miners in the early months of 1972. There were numerous power cuts. In early 1974, the three-day week followed, and there was a General Election in February on the issue. The result was a stalemate ending with Heath's resignation and the return of Harold Wilson as Prime Minister.
[2] Joe Gormley (1917–93), President, National Union of Mineworkers (1971–82), later a life peer.
[3] *Gumshoe* (1971), with Albert Finney, directed by Stephen Frears.

ually getting ready to give up the fight and one knows what happens in these circumstances. 'I am going to turn my face to the wall. I am very good at that,' she said.

Brighton   *February 1972*

Have come back here for the weekend while Ray is on holiday. Brighton is a recurring song in my life. My associations go back so far, since my father brought me here to get rid of a cold or recuperate from measles. I have had many experiences here (my play – bad, filming – not bad), visits with Peter [Watson], the Pavilion, the Lanes, under the influence of Viola Tree.[1] When Ashcombe went, I took Dale Cottage from Enid Bagnold. Now I was here once more among old things I knew so well, the familiar against the unfamiliar. But as always happens with me the spell fades fast. Suddenly the lure of Brighton is gone and I am never sad to leave.

Nureyev, London   *February 1972*

How he has changed since the day of his great leap to freedom and stardom.

He was then like a wild animal to deal with. One never knew how he would behave and I tried to hide my terror and show my admiration which amounted to infatuation. He came to lunch and slept in front of the fire as soon as he had eaten enough.

Now he is very sophisticated, but he has realised there are younger dancers of great promise and he behaves in a more disciplined manner. Yet when he turned up in swaggering kit to be photographed by me in many fashions (for *Vogue*) he showed his displeasure at certain garments which he either refused to (advertise) or else be used for purposes which they were certainly not intended, a blouse sleeve used as a scarf, a pair of trousers as a rug for his cold feet. In appearance he has also changed. His eyes deeper, perhaps closer together, he has lost the quality of youth. But his body is much fitter, muscular and strong and graceful. He gave me a look of boredom at the way the Jewess *Vogue* Editor 'carried on'. He rolled his eyes in disgust at some satin outfit costing many hundreds of pounds.

He did not feel the sitting was going well, that I had not inspired him.

---

[1] Viola Tree (1884–1939), actress.

For the purpose intended, I considered we were doing splendidly, though I was keeping the exciting shots for when we need show no clothes, only 'him', and he was very pleased to pose half nude, though too cold for complete nude. But he said, 'Perhaps we are both too old to do anything exciting like we used to.'

He was enigmatic about most things to do with the dance, very reserved in his criticism, and when I asked him if, on my return from Egypt, I could not come and photograph him in his Richmond house he did not want people to see where he lived. (The style in which he is able to live is very high! And the Soviets would obviously be furious.) It was not the occasion to ask him if he still had suggestions or even threats that he should return home. But I feel that although he has never absorbed anything of Europe and is still completely Russian in every way, he is here for his life, and in some ways he is very disorientated and sad, though knowing full well that he would have none of the advantages he now enjoys even if he went back as a star of the Soviet ballet.

In March 1972 Cecil visited Egypt, touring it properly for the first time. He enjoyed inspecting the ruins and historical sites, but found the country frustrating. In Luxor, he met Peter, the only surviving guide who remembered the opening of Tutankhamen's tomb.

Peter the Guide   March 1972

Sam Green wrote, 'Book in Cairo through Thomas Cook before going to Luxor a guide called Peter (real name Tadros Botros) for your entire stay. Take no other, most guides are awful and obstruct the beauty of what you are seeing. Peter is a most intelligent and beautiful old Copt. Do everything he suggests, listen to every word and hang the expense which isn't much.'

I checked at the local Thomas Cook office. Yes, Peter would be along on Tuesday at 9.30. But on Monday they pretended he had been booked for later in the week. Fury in my eye made the man promise Peter would come to us on Wednesday morning.

Peter proved to be a little elderly Egyptian Jean Cocteau. He was remarkably thin with the skin of his face stretched tightly over beautiful bones – an unusual Cocteau-esque expression in raised eyebrows conveyed also resignation and sorrow as well as fun. The mouth a most subtle little arrangement of pursed thin lips, big hooded eyes. He used his hands to great effect and they became beautiful in movement, as he demonstrated a point or wielded his cane, and he was a dandy. He wore a tarbush, a white djellaba, but over it a natty brown jacket of smart

European cut but showing a great deal *à la Cocteau* of white djellaba cuff influences. Well-made leather brogues.

I mentioned several friends who had recommended him to me, but he did not pretend to recall them. Yes he took so many people around it was difficult to remember. But yes he did work with Howard Carter[1] as a boy and he was 14 years old when they made the discovery of the treasures of Tutankhamen. He remembers it so well, the excitement of first seeing the alabaster jars. 'Mr Carter and Lord Carnarvon[2] were both so high-spirited, it was a joy to work for them. They were always so full of jokes and enthusiasm. And they were very kind. There were 200 helpers, and when Mr Carter opened the door to this great treasure, he then had a metal door put in its place, locked it, took the key and waited for the arrival of Lord Carnarvon who had been summoned by telegram. It took 2 months for him to arrive. There were guards on the door but those were the days when the British were in control and there was no danger of pilfering.

'Mr Carter had a house nearby on the West Bank and Lord Carnarvon had part of it, and here Mr Carter lived and worked for several years before he died. It was ridiculous to say that the curse of the Pharaohs killed him. He himself was so alive. It was just newspaper stuff. Soon they were going to put all Mr Carter's furniture in the Museum at Thebes. He had several things in his house that he had been allowed to take from the Tomb.'

Peter spoke in quite perfect even rather precious English. He said that some of the more brash American tourists had difficulty in understanding him. For a man who is a serious scholar it must be a terrible burden to have each day to escort the ignorami to the beauty spots. I am sure he realised my own lack of knowledge, but his face showed the recognition that comes with wisdom. It was a way of living and it gave him time to study, for he was still interested in knowing more about ancient Egypt. He looked very pained when he said, 'But I fear that many of the secrets of the Ancients have been lost for ever.'

We walked in a leisurely manner to the Temple of Luxor. In the morning light it appeared more magnificent than when on arrival at dusk it had been dusty and unimpressive. Peter with his walking stick drew plans in the sand of the construction of the Temple. First the colon-nade with one remaining obelisk and two huge figures of Rameses II inside the first court with a double row of papyrus columns with capitals,

---

[1] Howard Carter (1873–1939), archaeologist who made the sensational discovery of the tomb on 5 November 1922.
[2] Fifth Earl of Carnarvon (1866–1923). He died in Egypt before they reached the sarcophagus on 3 January 1924.

which is half occupied by the mosque of Abdul Haggagg, with white minaret.

Then on to another hall celebrating the Miraculous Birth of Amentrop to the holy shrine, the supposed repository of the Sacred boat of Ammunka, then to the Romanesque church built by Alexander the Great. Alexander in wall carvings being represented exactly as any of the Egyptian Kings of the previous 3000 years. Peter was amused to point out various felicities with his walking stick, the mixture of style – obelisk, minaret and Roman arch all together within the same outer walls.

It is true Peter is exceptional and he gave a delightful ending to our sightseeing expedition, for now we were to take the plane back to Cairo. But nothing is as expected in Cairo. By the grapevine we heard that the aeroplanes to Cairo were unable to land on account of a sandstorm.

We visualised all our plans going to six. The guide, Maude Belliras, the trip to Nicosia. (I am hoping to stay with Mickey Renshaw.[1])

I did not enjoy the afternoon. After lunch I got into the hotel lift (Raymond [Mortimer] remained outside making conversation with a stranger – in this way he is indefatigable). With no attendant but 2 married French, a Russian and a German couple. The man particularly unappetising with half his jaw cut away, great gaping gaps among his yellow tombstone teeth and a heavy air. We pressed the buttons on the indicator according to the floors we wished to stop at, and once on our way the German leant back and with an asinine smile on his face extended his arm and kept a finger on the alarm button. To my horror the lift stopped. It was the moment of total despair and terror, the moment before the crash of an aeroplane, the end, or at any rate a moment extended out of time when one realises utter despair and panic. I clapped my head in despair. I wondered if I should do as when the Dakota crashed in the war, just lie on the ground. I was quite transplanted from my legs and lower part of the body.

Suddenly I shouted, 'You silly arse!' and knocked the smiling Hun's arm away. The French wife pressed another button and another. The Russian woman walked through the mêlée of shouting people. We started fighting. 'You silly arse! Yes, you silly arse!' yelled the French. More buttons pressed. Still the lift would not move on. Perhaps the door was not properly closed. I found I could get my hand inside the gate and the wall. I pushed the door back. The metal door facing would not open. 'Shut the door,' the others shouted.

We shut the door, pressed more buttons. No movement. All the

[1] Michael Renshaw (1908–78), son of Lady Winifred Renshaw and grandson of fourth Earl of Leitrim. His father owned Watlington Park, Oxford. He was a godson of Lord Kitchener. Worked with *The Times*.

incompetence of Egypt sprang to mind. They could never make things go smoothly but surely they would never be able to repair a situation like this. We might be here for days. I was too sick to pray. Then, since nothing else was happening except a roughhouse among the trapped guests, again I pulled the sliding door. Then with the force of my body, or most of it, to keep it open with my feet, banged the outer door. It made a good noise. I banged, and banged, and banged, and banged, and banged. Shouts about the noise. Suddenly the scarlet-liveried attendant swung open the doors and we belched out. The French and I shouting 'Silly arse!' at the retreating German. Raymond came into my room. 'My dear this hotel is really *not* what it sets out to be. I had to come up by the service elevator.'

While lying on my bed, trying in vain to forget the past experience, the telephone announced that if R. and I could be ready downstairs within 5 minutes, we could be put on the Prime Minister's plane to Cairo. Until the very last second of our protracted panic we did not know whether tourists would be off-loaded, but more exhausted than we have ever been, we managed to return to the hideous city of Cairo where, once we stuck with Madame Belliras, we felt we had a chance of survival...

Cecil was relieved to escape to Cyprus and to find Mickey Renshaw awaiting him at the airport to motor him to 'his green and idyllic arcadia in the hills'. Mickey Renshaw had built himself a house at Ayios Giorgios on the northern coast of Cyprus 'with seven baths to seven beds', as the actress, Fabia Drake, noted appreciatively.

Nicosia, Cyprus   *Tuesday, 21 March 1972*

The joy of finding myself in this hugely civilised house in the most basically beautiful landscape of a high range of jagged and wooded mountains, groves of coral and olive, and tall pale bush-green grasses, was beyond anything I could have hoped for. And the joy of remaining in the same bedroom for an indeterminate stay was also balm to the battered traveller, who most unfortunately must have picked up a germ in Egypt, for the cold that had been threatening for several days now came out in full force. It became one of the worst colds I have had for many years. Generally I go to bed for a day or two, and am then recovered. This cold, with gobs of phlegm from throat and nose, continued for a week. A dreadful guest for Mickey who took everything in his stride, but then he is a man of phlegm himself!

Mickey, as chatelain, is amusing to watch, so well-bred and English as he goes about his garden, doing very hard work for long hours, but never becoming hot and sweaty. With his gloves and lanky figure he moves unlike any other gardener and you cannot believe he can do any good, but the result it here. Although only a beginning you could see what he is going to make of the devastation with which he was surrounded when the workers had finished building his house (according to his specification) and a large swimming pool.

The sight from my bedroom windows when the shutters were drawn in the early morning sent a stir through my heart. It is a miraculous landscape of every sort of blue and green, and the hills are dotted with gorse, broom and mustard all in bloom. No wonder Mickey took the great gamble of giving up his very mundane life in London and at what seems to me to be an exceptionally early age (he is younger than I am) decided to retire. The gamble has worked in every way. Lots of friends come out to stay with him, a well was found miraculously, and the value of the land has already gone up enormously.

His servants give him an attention that is very rare today. His excellent cook, simple, good nursery fare, is like a nanny and treats him like a child. Like a child he is often moody and snaps at her, and she loves it. Mickey took me to the nearby village high in the hills called Mardi, where the piazza outside the pretty little white Romanesque church is nothing more than a yard where a few cars are parked and hens walk around under the blossoming fruit trees. It did one good to see such gnarled shapes as the trunks of these old trees, after the soft, slithery contours of palms in Egypt. I do not wish to end my days in Cyprus, but I do see the great charm and this is a most felicitous and unexpected bonus to my holiday.

The expedition into Kyrenia with Mickey was delightful. The market full of the most appetising-looking fruits, all oversized, limes like gourds, oranges and tangerines, and the vegetables not only beautiful but exotic. Vast artichokes, the first asparagus, pale, ivory balls of cabbage. Mickey, a hard bargainer, does not approve of the English tourists being vague about prices, as this puts up the prices. We meet the locals, two majors are coming to dinner tonight. 'They're very military in manner but they're rather fun and they found this great love for one another when they were in the army during the war and they've lived together ever since.' Imagine my surprise when the majors turned out to be two elderly ladies in fur tippets.[1]

There is Lady Barnes[2] (the widow of the Vanbrugh sisters' brother, a

---

[1] Major Betty Hunter Cowan, WRAC (1912–91), and Major Phyllis Heymann, QARANC (d. 1990). Also known as 'The Cavewomen'. She was a friend of Lawrence Durrell and said of him, 'Little men are often very aggressive, aren't they?'
[2] Daphne Graham (1903–?), acted under the name of Mary Sheridan. Officially the daughter of Sir Richard Graham, fourth Baronet, and his wife, Lady Mabel Duncombe, daughter of first Earl of Feversham. She married Sir Kenneth Barnes (1878–1957), Principal of RADA. His sisters were the actresses Violet and Irene Vanbrugh.

bastard of the Portuguese Marquis de Soveral of Edwardian Society fame and Lady [Mabel] Graham, sister of Lady d'Abernon), living off the royalties that her lover Margaret Irwin[1] left to her in her will. She reminded me of Georgia [Sitwell] but had not much to offer that was not grimacial, Mrs Pemberton, the great gardener of the island, like Margaret Rutherford, Charlie Birkin,[2] who entertained us in his non-committal house and seems very much a 20s dated figure in his Prince of Wales tweed and constant use of cigarette case and lighter, Fabia Drake,[3] a name to me since the day when I stopped going to the English theatre, this lasted seven years about, so I don't know what she has appeared in, but she is a name much bandied in Coward, Binkie [Beaumont], Juliet [Duff] circles.

She lives on the port in a minute dwelling, is delighted to relax and settle, and is a powerful figure. She could become overwhelming.[4] But I was drawn to her, and if I lived here, she would be my buddy. We called in on an old racy relic, the oldest inhabitant, a Mrs ——, whose polo-loving husband was hit on the head by a mallet and never recovered. She is poor but gallant.

So Mickey's social life continues here and it is not at all bad going, and soon one becomes absorbed in the gossip. 'What was the rout at the Patrick in Davey's last week? Have they sold their house yet? Who are the Leslies that are arriving? Is it Anita and her brother?[5] Was Anita ever married?' And then of course we all must add fuel to the flames of the row between Lady Barnes and Lady Fanny Burney (Tom Parr's mother). Mickey gave Lady Burney a body blow by telling her that the Queen Mother alluded to Daphne Barnes as 'Daphers'. She then wished she had not said she was very common and a bad actress in the back row of the chorus.

There is this sort of thing to keep Mickey amused when after the hours in the garden he feels in the mood for relaxation.

And I have enormously enjoyed listening to the gramophone, Britten, Mozart, Mahler, Strauss, Delius and Burt Bacharach.

Have been stricken with the worst cold since childhood. In my overtired

---

[1] Margaret Irwin (d. 1967), historical novelist, author of *Royal Flush* and *The Proud Servant*.
[2] Sir Charles Birkin, fifth Baronet (1907–85), brother of Freda Dudley-Ward.
[3] Fabia Drake (1904–90), stern actress, remembered by the present generation for appearances in *Jewel in the Crown* and as a garlanded old lady in *A Room with a View*.
[4] The archaeologist, Sir Mortimer Wheeler, to whom she took rather more than a shine, certainly found her so.
[5] Anita Leslie (1914–85), Irish writer, and her brother Desmond (1921–2001), pioneer UFO author.

state I must have been prone to any germ going about and there is every sort to choose from in Egypt. After two days in Mickey's clean sunlit air, I had to take to bed. After several days I was no better. When I thought improvement was noticeable relapse set in. A doctor coming to dinner said I must have antibiotics as I was suffering from bronchitis.

How lucky to be caught here and not in some sleazy or expensive hotel. Here every comfort and delicious Mrs Ratcliffe to look after me and supply healthy food. Mickey tactful. Sad that I could not read without headaches, but of all madnesses I embarked upon a rewrite of the Gainsborough play.[1] I started this twenty-five years ago and still I am stubborn enough to think it will work. I have written it (as a result of rereading Willie Maugham's strictures about the style of the first draft) in a more modern idiom. It gives it more life. And I notice so many things can be dovetailed and altered. How did I not notice before? I am enthusiastic and only wish I could manage more than 1½ hours in the morning without getting a really very tough headache.

It has been very quiet. Yet the time goes quickly and when after I'd been here a week Ann Fleming and my godson Caspar[2] arrived I felt the occasion so momentous that we heard many false alarms as we waited for Mickey to bring them from the airport. Ann rather dazed with the flight. When she said, 'Last night I saw such a bad play' (Gielgud in *Veterans*[3]), I couldn't, in this remote fustiness, believe that such things could ever be.

Reddish   *April 1972*

Long shadows and sun stripes on the bright grass with first tree blossom and daffodils to greet me as I pulled back the curtains. It is good to be home. Over a month ago I left and having caught a germ in Egypt spent almost two weeks in Cyprus recuperating. The lure of home becomes stronger. No matter how much I was enjoying the sun and flowers in Cyprus, it was the first signs of spring in Wiltshire that I had in mind so much of the time. (How I ever endured that 10 months in Hollywood I do *not* know!)

But my Cyprus experience was a success. In few places have I ever relaxed and recuperated in such comfort. It was a joy to wake up to a breakfast tray of crisp French bread and see the olives and blue

---

[1] Cecil was yet again rewriting his ill-fated *Gainsborough Girls* play, first staged in 1951 and again in 1959 as *Landscape with Figures*. It floundered both times.
[2] Caspar Fleming (1952–75). He committed suicide.
[3] *Veterans*, by Charles Wood, with John Gielgud and John Mills. The language caused a stir particularly on the pre-London tour.

mountains as the very English Mrs Ratcliffe opened the sunshine from the many roof terraces.

Although my cold became bronchitis and I was as weak as an invalid, I enjoyed listening to the music of Mahler on the record player, the food was enchantingly mild and plain English. Mickey looking like an officer in the Lancers went about his day leaving me to my own devices. (I started to write my Gainsborough play again, and very excited too, but bad headaches continued in spite of the help of the Rev. Sir Patrick Ferguson Davey who has the gift of faith healing and gave me a treatment which failed.)

I enjoyed seeing the wild flowers and other people's gardens, the English colony shopping in Nevocles in Kyrenia. We went on expeditions to Salamis, Morphou, Vourni, and to the remains of a rich Persian's palace. We took my godson to excavate at Neolithic sights. (Once he was held in custody by the Turks for 3 hours.) I enjoyed the Durrell countryside of Bellapaix, with the marvellous remains of a Romanesque monastery. This seemed to be real whereas Mickey lives in too 'new' a colony and garden (no cypresses) and in fact Mickey's house needs another 4 years to mellow. The fight against nature is too uphill for comfort at the moment, and the rough roads to be endured each time one goes out and back are too uncomfortable. However, Mickey is gallant. His gamble will pay off and he is pleased with his *train de vie* in a home that has all the good taste of a Juliet Duff, and which is something that I no longer have any urge for.

I left feeling much recovered, forgetting the awful film of mucus that had caused me to use up boxes of Kleenex and rolls of lavatory paper. I forgot the awful salt water cures up nose and down throat. I forgot the perpetual feeling cold.

It was when I came back to a stormy springtime in England that my recovery became complete. The rest and relaxation had put me into a much calmer state of mind than I have known for a very long time.

Between 11 and 14 April 1972 Queen Juliana and Prince Bernhard of The Netherlands made a State Visit to the Queen and the Duke of Edinburgh at Windsor Castle. Cecil was invited to the evening party following the State Banquet on the first night.

Soirée at Windsor Castle   11 April 1972

The disruption to London traffic whenever a head of state comes on an official visit has been much criticised in the press and everywhere: 'Why doesn't the Queen entertain at Windsor?' This is what she has done for the visit of the Queen of Holland[1] – a banquet the first night, a dinner followed by a musical evening & a tour of the castle treasures. And, on the third night, Queen Juliana herself gave a banquet at the Dutch Embassy.

Ava Waverley[2] was not invited to any of the functions & when she did not see the names of her thorn-in-the-flesh Droghedas as having been invited to the dinner before the soirée, remarked to them, 'I suppose you were the *cure-dents*'.

I too was a *cure-dents* and very impressed to be invited at all, and I loved the evening which started off under the auspices of Sybil Cholmondeley, who had corralled three escorts, Steven Runciman,[3] Francis Watson[4] and myself. The dinner as always at no. 12 KPG [Kensington Park Gardens] was excellent but Sybil has been away a lot, had not turned on the heating and I froze. How mean the rich can be! Sybil was very tenacious throughout the evening and I felt I was not my usual free self to circulate, but Francis was a wonderful cicerone showing us all the beauties of the castle with a great knowledge, and relating the history of every piece of furniture or how an object came to find its way on to this particular mantelpiece or commode.

But to go back to the arrival. We tore through the night on the newly opened M4? or 2 [M4] or what? and might have been anywhere in the world where there are autostradas or freeways, but in the distance, a magical illuminated fairy-story tower showed us that we were at Windsor, and excitement stirred the blood. The castle is at its best at night and on this very special early spring [night] it looked more roman-tic than at any other time with the floodlighting touching the hanging branches of the trees freshly in bud, casting great shadows on the crenel-lated walls, silhouetting statues & picking out the planting of the dotted spring flowers. Near the entrance that we had to take, a tall bank of grass mounted steeply to the castle wall & it was a mass of daffodils.

The slow approach to the castle only made the joy of anticipation the more acute, and one saw through the illuminated windows the party already in progress with people wandering round rooms that were lined with green or dark red silk and hung with huge Carolinian silver mirrors and full-length portraits, the Gainsborough of Captain Tarleton being recognisable at a great distance. Once inside these rooms the view from

---

[1] HM Queen Juliana of The Netherlands (b. 1909).
[2] Ava, Viscountess Waverley (1896–1974) widow of first Viscount Waverley (formerly Sir John Anderson).
[3] Hon. Sir Steven Runciman (1903–2000). He attended Cambridge with Cecil.
[4] Sir Francis Watson (1907–92), Surveyor of The Queen's Works of Art 1963–72, Director of the Wallace Collection 1963–74.

the other side of the windows with the lit-up trees and castle walls was equally beautiful.

Fellow arrivals were all rather anonymous, middle-aged and elderly worthies, but few of the usual society aristocrats. Looking at the Holbein drawings on the way to be received, it was very pleasant to see Paul Scofield and his wife. He is just the sort of person who should be invited, and was typically modest and meek. No show-off about him. The queue, just long enough to raise one's sense of anticipation to the highest, and suddenly without any fanfare or length of carpet, at the top of the stairs, the Queen and the Duke.

She was positively dazzling, the light so soft gave her an incandescent look. Her eyes flashed like crystal, her teeth dazzling, her smile radiant. Something has happened to her that has made her a great star. Her dress was not particularly becoming, her hair as dowdy and stiff as ever, but none of these things mattered. She was at the peak of her looks, and they are looks that work. One would not wish to change any detail, the neck straight and long, the poise, the healthiness, the sharpness so something that has become part of a work of art. It was good to be thrown into such a good mood by the encounter with perfection that one went on to enjoy the other interests of the evening with great relish.

The air was filled with delightful music and unexpectedly one saw, as in some seventeenth-century conversation piece, through several door-ways, in a room by Grinling Gibbons, and painted by Verrio, a most delightful youthful quartet, young men with long silken hair playing violin, cello, oboe and harpsichord the music of Sully, Purcell, Handel and Boyce. For those who did not wish to sit and listen, the tour of the apartments was the chief attraction with special additions brought from the Royal Archives to be exhibited for the pleasure of Queen Juliana and all the other guests.

Many of these exhibits, such as the letter from the future King William III of the Netherlands thanking the Prince Regent for granting him the rank of Colonel in the British Army, the letter from William V of Orange telling George III he has attained his majority, a letter from James I revealing the habit of smoking, an original score by Mozart, an early folio of Shakespeare, and a diary, photographs of visits to Queen Victoria at Windsor. All of these accompanied by captions written in Dutch specially for today's visitor.

Every detail most beautifully thought out, and as for the flowers Patrick P [Plunket] and the Windsor gardeners had performed wonders of beauty, with one vast white obelisk as the culmination of all white and pink blossom. Caroline Somerset and I discovered that it was made up with branches of white cherry and prunus, and rhododendron placed in

Enid Bagnold,
author of *The
Chalk Garden* and
National Velvet.

Kenneth Clark, art historian, and the suburban-looking glass window at the Garden House,
Saltwood. Even Cecil took a photograph out of focus occasionally.

George ('Dadie') Rylands, Fellow of King's,
in a room of his own, at Cambridge.

Sir Nicholas Henderson, British Ambassador,
and his wife Mary on the Rhine.

The Earl and Countess of Avon at Reddish House.

The Earl of Pembroke at Wilton.

Irene Worth, actress and friend.

Bianca Jagger in the garden at Reddish.

Cecil supervising Bianca's make-up
in the guest room at Reddish.

Diana Vreeland in her 'garden
from hell' room on Park Avenue.

Victorian buckets, and slop pails from early bedrooms. The mixture of grand and simple flowers was as I like it.

Gradually it became apparent that the guest list was quite different from the usual, for at last the arts and particularly the theatre were represented in good measure. There were lots of composers – Lennox Berkeley, Willie Walton,[1] and writers [Stephen] Spender and painters, the G. Sutherlands (she told me her dress had cost £500 seven years ago), Pipers, sculptress Dame Barbara Hepworth,[2] who, it seems, has cancer. And masses of stage personalities – the Peter Daubenys, Albert Finneys, John Mills, John Clements and poor darling Kay Hammond more crippled by polio than ever, Flora Robson in a terrible wig and the R [Ralph] Richardsons. He looked like a well-behaved baby sitting up at table in a tall chair with a bib under chin, taking notice of the cornices, the chandeliers and the paintings.

In fact all the theatrical profession had just got it right in a show-off of vulgarity. No acting. All were impeccable except Lord and Lady Olivier [Joan Plowright]. There was something so cheap and second-rate about both of them that they stood out like sore thumbs. He, overfamiliar, over at ease with Royalties, she like a deficient house-parlour-maid. Even Olivier's walk gave him away, with a back sideways flick that was all part of a miscalculated insouciance. I was going through a door with Princess Alexandra when he greeted her with overenthusiasm and yet a certain intimate disdain.

The evening developed into more of a conversationing one. The supper was welcome after so much standing, and we were joined by the delightful young Herberts [Pembrokes]. The Royals looked at their best and even Princess Margaret managed to create a solid, clean, well-sculptured simplicity of line and colour. She wore harsh white and hair scraped back like a wealthy seaside landlady. Queen Mother, in terrible pelisses of gold sequins, wore the only tiara, and Queen Juliana looked nice and cosy and sympathetic in spite of her ugly little face with unseeing small eyes and pig snout. Her hair was fluffy and pretty, her dress – dark, sequined flowers – unusual, her ropes of pearls magnificent (I believe her dazzle of diamonds the night before was blinding – what would have happened if an aeroplane bringing them had been hijacked).

David Westmorland[3] 'introduced' me for a brief moment and the Queen remembered my visit to photograph her in Holland, saying 'That was a long time ago, the years fly, it was *more* than ten years! A lot more!'

---

[1] Sir William Walton (1902–83), composer.
[2] Graham Sutherland (1903–80), painter, and his wife, Kathy (1905–91); John Piper (1903–92), artist, and his wife, Mary Evans; Dame Barbara Hepworth (1903–75), sculptress.
[3] Fifteenth Earl of Westmorland (1924–93), Lord-in-Waiting.

She is a great lady, never thinks of herself as a queen, is utterly natural. She has the nicest aspects of the Dutch. Lots of people I did not see though I knew they were there, but came home satisfied that the evening was over, and I was pleased to be back at what they call a reasonable hour, though after my early nights in Broadchalke, seemed very dashing.

Broadchalke   *April 1972*

None of the three little ducks survive. They had merry lives while they lived. The cause of death is not known, but the many messages of condolence from villagers say that the mortality among young ducks and geese is always high, that no married couple should be allowed to have a family until they are 3 years old, that the mother takes the young too soon into deep water, that they are too cold, catch pneumonia or die of exhaustion, battling with a chill against the current of water. The result of these deaths is that I have rather turned against the parents, who seem quite oblivious of their loss.

The garden was 'open' last Sunday. Such an anxiety lest the afternoon should be wet. The weather for the week before had been appalling (we have had no spring sunshine) and the weather report bad. However, although the rain sprinkled down at opening time, the afternoon was bright with sunny spells, and 300 people enjoyed the garden, the Smallpeices most of all. He lost 15 years in an afternoon. He was working anxiously each evening till dusk over a long period, felt the garden was not tidy enough, became neurotic.

Then compliments and smiles, and both he and his wife were talking to each other as if they had just met and fallen in love. They were amused at the various things that were admired. The trestle tables for the roses to climb over, the grandeur of the greenhouse, which one woman could not get over, the spinach. How could she grow hers as big & beautiful. Grateful thanks all round. And now it doesn't matter how much it rains...

Ray and I have now decided to have cheap fish instead of prohibitive meat. We are threatened with another rail strike and so inconvenience and rise of prices continue.

Reddish   *6 May 1972*

Always great activity in the country. Blick to see about putting the grey stones from the tall wall he has pulled down (an improvement) into a wall adjacent. Decision to pull down the white railings now that they are out of proportion with the new low wall. A pump comes to get rid of the silt from our water garden. Colonel Clark's premonitions have materialised. All the village gives advice, and is critical of others. What to do about carting away the compost heap now the old kitchen garden is abandoned in favour of a green sward opposite. Trees blown down must be sawn off in blocks, but David Offley undertaking the job leaves it half finished. Blick's men work for a day on the job. I try to make a bonfire. No luck. Better success with the weedol. The stinging nettles crumple.

But the great excitement had been that the Muscovy Duck has laid 4 eggs. Will they be brown? I tell Eileen that I'm much more interested in their hatching than I am that my nephew John is about to have another child. Three very pretty little birds are hatched – one all yellow, two yellow and black. During their first day in the world, they walk a long distance to the river, where they swim in circles, fight successfully the current and clamber up the river banks. They are a delight.

Then the awful news that the piece of yellow fluff has been seen floating upside down, dead, relentlessly without life. All sorts of theories. Ducks are known to be bad mothers. They shouldn't take the newly born into deep waters to catch pneumonia. They shouldn't allow them to overexert themselves and die of a heart attack.

The villagers say the Sykeses' dog snatched it, brought it up to Mrs Sykes's feet and that she threw it into the river. Then another little piece of fluff is dead. Everyone says the drake stood on it and suffocated it. Then people say that these ducks should not be allowed to have offspring for 2–3 years, that they then may have an instinct to look after them, that they must be penned in for several weeks after being brought out of the egg, that only 3 out of 70 young have been known to survive. It is very depressing.

But it shows again how one must know about everything, learn the snags before embarking on a new project in complete ignorance. Apart from mistakes, the water garden is a great success and a wonderful joy as well as an improvement to the property.

Cecil toured North Germany with Connaissance des Arts in May 1972. During his tour, he met Andy Warhol.

Friday, 19 May 1972

We had an hour to prepare packing and be ready for dinner at the Haenkels. He makes some sort of commodity and employs 12,000 men and the same chef cooks for the farm as our dinner. We were told the chef was very nervous and we must not be late. I did not expect the Valerian Rybar[1] decoration of the home to be as inoffensive as it is. The flowers, a lot of wild 'rape' yellow mixed with deutzia and pink mar-quarelés, were lovely and the food terrific. A whole salmon cooked in pastry and sliced like a pâté, chervil stuffed with pâté, a raspberry sorbet. The hostess really very bright and I think it hard of me to have judged her as being so pushy. She is full of vitality.

The joy of the evening for me was the surprise appearance of Andy Warhol. He is here to publicise *Playboy*. He looks very young and very healthy under his make-up, a 'new' boy from the dying ghost of last year. He is very original and tonight he talked a great deal. He said we should all go on his tour of the hotels of Europe. He asked who of the group was doling out the dope. He took pictures with a 10 dollar Polaroid. The evening was gay and fun, and I'm glad we were able to enjoy something so unlike the more formal German welcomes.

Cécile de R [Rothschild][2] has joined the group, having stayed on in Paris to go to the Ball for the Queen at the British Embassy.[3] She is obvi-ously very 'narked' with me about the G. G. [Greta Garbo] articles and asked if the snaps I was taking were for *McCall's*. She is rude and rough but I must be tough and take it. After all she is right to be annoyed. I feel guilt myself, and there is every reason why she should feel I have behaved badly, especially as she is one of Greta's 'victims'. However, it makes the 'bus trip a bit less pleasant and as it is one has to fight hard enough to enjoy oneself on it.

But today quite easy and I'm not as tired as I was before I learnt to sleep in the bus.

Later on the same trip   *Sunday, 21 May 1972*

A late lunch at the hotel and Cécile attacked me about the money I had made out of Garbo. 'Let me ask you an indirect question,' her eyes blazing, she looked 30 years younger and in typical Jewish vein prodded and probed, though it took a long while for me to have a chance to give my answers, which in fact were quite honest. Perhaps I should have refused to answer. She will not treat my answers with the respect that I gave to her and she will brag that I told her. However, I thought it best

---

[1] Valérian Stux-Rybar, fashionable decorator who married Aileen Plunket in 1956. Divorced 1965.
[2] Cécile de Rothschild (1913–95). She entertained Garbo whenever she came to Europe.
[3] The Queen and the Duke of Edinburgh made a State Visit to Paris as guests of President Pompidou between 15 and 19 May. They visited the ailing Duke of Windsor at his home in the Bois de Boulogne.

not to bring about her wrath though now I realise it would have been better to change the subject.

Cécile, on this trip, has apparently recovered from her latest nervous breakdown, but she is still vague and peculiar, and can be extremely rude. If she is not interested, she leaves one in mid-sentence. This is a Rothschild trait. But on the attack and on the subject of money she no longer became frittering or vague. 'Let me ask you how much you made out of Garbo on the *McCall's, Times, Oggi* etc. world circulation. I mean how much with *Vogue* photographs *et tout ça* during the past 20 years have you made?' I had not thought. I totted up the *Vogue* pages which amount to 8 at the most, and thought that to date with the serialisation of the diaries, I would have made £4000. She translated in a flash to dollars, to francs. 'Not bad, is it. I mean I wouldn't mind being given £4000 to spend, on the kitchen.' She laughed that nasal choking noise. 'Not bad, eh? For someone who didn't need the publicity. Even Stokowski[1] didn't sell his story to the papers.' She had the figures. She said, 'You know when they did that film about us we were very touchy about lawyers…'The subject was eventually dropped when in a hurt voice, she of *all* people said, 'Money, money, money!'

Near the end of the trip   23 May 1972

I was very tired and went to sleep listening to schmaltzy music on the radio, which gave me my first contact with my former life by announcing the news – Ireland, Rhodesia, Nixon in Russia, and the deaths of Margaret Rutherford and my friend, Cecil Day-Lewis.[2]

The bus trip

By now people are beginning to get tired and to hate one another. I have had enough of the Rothschild bad manners. They only listen if it is worthwhile, otherwise will suddenly turn their backs. So I have adopted a defence mechanism of avoidance.

This has been noticed. The women talk incessantly. Maude Bergerat is always running 'haunted' in the opposite direction, her squeaking husband, walking with head turned round, almost back to front. Mrs McKay arrives late on the scene, hunched but never tired. Marquesa

---

[1] Leopold Stokowski (1882–1977), conductor. Actually, he did sell his story.
[2] Dame Margaret Rutherford, the actress, died 22 May 1972, aged eighty; and Cecil Day-Lewis, the Poet Laureate, also died 22 May 1972, aged sixty-eight.

Merlini 'creates' if she has not got on the right shoes in which to curtsey to Royalty. She will be forbidden further Connaissance trips. Dominique Barret becomes a little less imperious and shows that in spite of her porcelain appearance, she is quite human.

Nancy Lancaster[1] never stops talking but she is good-tempered and excellent company. Perhaps Lanfranco Rasponi[2] takes the prize for self-ishness. When there is a buffet in the offing he is the first to help himself, then go to a hidden corner and, by himself, tuck in as fast as he can. The French doctor, so sexy, is a PC counter hogger and Mrs McKay complains he is always in her way.

Thursday, 25 May 1972

Later we 'went on the town' and walked down the broadway area, where all the sex shows and bordellos are situated along and off the Reeperbahn. It was fascinating to see the tarts at work, plucking one by the coat to come in, 'Just for information. No money, just for information. Look at live fuck show, fuck films, don't be chicken, look just for information! Woman with four men, woman with duck.' It was a long while since I have had any sort of interest in such things and the smell of fried food was anti-sexual in the extreme. But it was something not easily to be forgotten, and a relief from the early cathedrals.

The actual end of the tour   *Friday, 26 May 1972*

The company of the tour has now become a nightmare. I hate most of my fellow travellers with their particular foibles, their selfishness, competi-tive spirit. The Rothschilds more Jewish than one realised. Cécile slowly counting her money in the bus is like Shylock. They do all their home-work in the bus, and Cécile today was trying to remember all the menus of the journey. 'Where was it that we had that leg of lamb and that duck pâté?' Even the nice ones are difficult to pin down to talk to as the others interrupt. 'What? What?' says Liliane [de Rothschild][3] and as one starts to explain the topic she turns her head and is off. By which time someone else has appeared.

After dinner a certain end of term feeling, with a few goodbyes.

---

[1] Nancy Lancaster (1897–1994) interior decorator and gardener, of supreme taste, mother of Michael Tree.
[2] Lanfranco Rasponi, author of *The International Nomads* (1966).
[3] Liliane de Rothschild, wife of Baron Elie de Rothschild (b. 1917).

Lanfranco [Rasponi] and I again went on the tour, and indulged in seeing a live fuck show and a French movie. It was fascinating to see how the 'live' show was performed as a ballet. Of course there was no 'real' performance, but the choreography stylised. As for the movies they have become violent and I was quite disgusted by some of the 'butcher shop' sights and came away eventually rather disgusted, and feeling that only the real sentiments can make such contacts attractive. It was in a way a terrifying experience and made me a bit resentful of the hormones that I have had to take since my operation has turned me into a neuter being. Back for the last packing of the trip and I am so thankful that the ten days are over.

Cecil was in Paris when he heard that the Duke of Windsor had died. The Duke had been visited by the Queen ten days before, during her State Visit to Paris, after which it became clear to the world that he was dying. Cecil had known him for many years, had photographed and sketched the Duchess when she was Mrs Simpson. In 1937, he had taken a series of photographs of her at the Château de Candé and had taken their official wedding portrait photos, the day before the wedding in June 1937.

Paris – Death of the Duke of Windsor Sunday, 28 May 1972

The trip already very remote and I wake to hear Lilia [Ralli]'s[1] familiar chirp announcing the death of the Duke of Windsor.[2] I felt callously indifferent. No pang of nostalgia. Certainly he had been a great figure in my adolescence, so full of charm and dash, so glamorous and such a good Prince of Wales. Then the sensational Abdication and marriage. As a photographer, I came on to that scene in a big way, but throughout the years the Duke never showed any affection or interest in me, in fact rather presumptuously I felt he disliked me.

It was only at the last meeting when I went to have a drink with Darby and Joan, and all his men friends were dead, that he thawed towards me and talked about the 'old times', the old tunes, and the old 'stars' like Gertie Lawrence.[3] He was cold in his friendships, cut them off overnight. Freda Dudley-Ward,[4] when asked what he was like recently, said, 'That

---

[1] Lilia Ralli (d. 1977), Greek-born early girlfriend of Cecil.
[2] HRH the Duke of Windsor died at his home in the Bois de Boulogne, in the early morning of 28 May.
[3] Gertrude Lawrence (1898–1952), actress.
[4] Freda Dudley-Ward (1894–1983), born a Birkin. Long-time mistress when the Duke was Prince of Wales. When Mrs Simpson appeared on the scene, he refused to take her telephone calls.

silly little man? I didn't know him!' Certainly he was silly. When James P-H [Pope-Hennessy] told him he was writing about Trollope, he roared with laughter and turned to Wallis saying, 'He's writing a book about a trollop!'

Well, it is good that she did not die before him. What will happen to her is not of interest. She made no friends. She will have less now. She should live at the Ritz, deaf and a bit gaga. It is sad because age is sad but her life has not been a commendable one, and she is not worthy of much pity. But still I liked her and will try to be loyal, for she was always good to me. Another milestone passes.

I went early to avoid the crowds to see the [exhibition of] Latours, not early enough. The fug was terrible, but I was deeply touched by the paintings, the infants, wrapped like a parcel in swaddling clothes and cap, the brightness of eyes in candlelight, the hands thieving or blessing, the understanding of hair, the drapery, of gold coins. It was extraordinary that for 200 years he should have been in total eclipse, and that still so little is known of him as a man. I spent a long while in the Orangerie, determined to take this opportunity to feel at leisure, and to treat the day as a holiday.

Lunch with a friend from the 'voyage', Jacques Delmas,[1] in his very original and delightful apartment off the Place de l'Odéon. Old oak-beamed ceilings, a clever mixture of old and new, and a tremendous lunch. The first dish of fillets of sole on a bed of chopped mushroom and covered with cheese sauce was as Nancy L [Lancaster] said, 'The best thing I've ever eaten.'

After so much culture I went back to my old vomit with a visit to the Casino de Paris to see Yves St Laurent's clothes. They were no better than they used to be forty years ago. The vulgarity of the show, the noise of the bad orchestration, the poor songs and even Zizi Jeanmaire are not up to standard though the star has a certain glamour & although monstrous, does move her sexy legs in a very alluring manner.

Paris   *29 May 1972*

Each time I come to Paris I rush off to see the 'temporary' exhibitions, never go to the museums, so in the spirit of the Croissière decided to keep up the sightseeing by going to the Louvre, the biggest and best museum of all. The scale is vast and so seldom does one find one's way to the things one wishes. Today I even went to the information so that I should find a certain Gainsborough portrait. On the way I passed such

---

[1] Jacques Chaban-Delmas (1915–2000), Inspector General of Finances in France.

beauty, Rembrandts, Ter Bosches, Chardins, Le Maître d'Avignon, Raphael (a sensitive portrait) such incredible historical jewels, such objects, bronze decorated precious stones of all delicate sorts, a marvellous giant bottomless collection. After 2 hours I felt replete and enjoyed lunch with Mizza Bricard.[1]

She is one of a dead race, cocotte, femme du monde. She delighted me by telling me that of all the pre-war cocottes, actresses, Forzanne, etc. she considered Gina Palerme[2] one of the most remarkable when she saw her lunching at the Savoy. 'What did she wear?' 'Oh, the sort of clothes cocottes wore so much better than the ladies who copied them – draped skirt, huge hat on one side, great muff…'

She extolled also Régine Flory who had been Cochran's mistress while Delysia had been Derval's of the Folies Bergère.[3]

But Mizza's talk was not by any means confined to fashion. Although she talked of the death of Balenciaga[4] and what a terrible time it had been staying on with him and taking his corpse 600 miles back to San Sebastian. As a result Mizza became herself very ill and looks much older and witch-like, having lost a great deal of weight. But she was fascinating in her big blue collie hat talking of the Brunswick family and all the northern German princes she knew well. It was a lunch of interest, followed by a visit to Fellini's *Roma*, more of a documentary than his other films, with some marvellous things in it, but too long.

An evening party at a young man named André Oliver, who designs for Cardin and it made me realise that if you want to make money, go into dressmaking. But his apartment showed what taste and originality he has and I have never seen flowers arranged in such a remarkable way as his, a huge altarpiece of separate bunches of white iris, sweet peas, orchids, anemones, foxglove, all white and marvellously bold and simple, nothing splayed, everything soaring like a forest of trees, very impressive, and such an amusing group that I was loath to leave when Lilia grew so tired she looked like a half-dead ortolan.

Back in England, Cecil was summoned to Windsor Castle.

---

[1] Mizza Bricard (d. 1978), worked for Doucet, Molyneux and Dior. She said 'When a man wants to send you flowers, say my florist is Cartier.'
[2] Jacqueline Forzanne; Gina Palerme, French actress, singer and cinema star.
[3] Paul Derval, director of the Folies Bergere, author of the *The Folies Bergère* (Methuen, 1955); Régine Flory (1895–1926); Alice Delysia (1889–1979).
[4] Cristóbal Balenciaga (1895–1972), couturier.

The Duke of Windsor's Funeral   Monday, 5 June 1972

Very surprised to receive a large, black-edged envelope with the invitation, and life would have been much easier if I'd decided not to go. The Duke didn't really like me, and only when all his friends had died did he call me by my Christian name, and the funeral was on the following Monday, the worst day for me as I try to be in the country to get on with my work as long as possible, and this meant a bad bite into what was in any case a short weekend.

Yet I decided to go because I thought that the event had a minor historical interest, and if I'm becoming a serious diarist, this might be a day of interest. Neighbours Mary Pembroke and the Heads were not summoned and too late did I realise that the Avons were motoring up and back from so nearby. I made arrangements for the local garage to drive me in my car, and the anxiety of being on time hung over me like the Damocles Sword all the weekend.

Mercifully, the sun shone from between rolling ominous clouds and the countryside looked particularly green and fresh and glistening after the perpetual rains. At Windsor a not very large crowd were sitting on public seats outside the castle walls to see the guests arriving, but there was little else for them as the service was 'Private' & even those of us who were 'friends' were placed in the congregation of St George's Chapel, while the Royal Family and activity took place in the Choir [Quire].

Diana Cooper took matters into her own hands and when we were shown to side seats in a great draught from an ever-open door, moved to the Nave. Here we were almost able to touch the 'procession' as it passed, and I with the eyes of a lynx could even see various silhouettes of the leading participants in the far distance. Poor Diana not so fortunate. Her eyesight is such that really she should not drive a car.

Waiting for the service to start, one winkled out the old friends present and it was nice to see that Bruce Ogilvy,[1] who used to be ADC to the Prince, was there, and other contemporaries, Biddy Monckton,[2] Esmond Rothermere, Foxy Sefton[3] (now about the richest widow in England and looking as poor as a housemaid on her day out), Peggy

---

[1] Hon. Bruce Ogilvy (1895–1976), equerry to the Prince of Wales (1921–30).
[2] The Dowager Viscountess Monckton of Brenchley (1896–1982), widow of first Viscount and close friend of the Duchess of Windsor.
[3] Josephine Gwynne (1903–80), second wife of seventh Earl of Sefton (1898–1972).

Munster,[1] Rose Bingham,[2] and looking marvellously cool and beautiful under a huge black straw hat, Baba Metcalfe,[3] who later said, 'Do you realise that you and I are about the only survivors of that wedding at Candé?' There were a few Americans, flown over specially, Winston Guest, looking a real gentleman, but his wife,[4] cut-witted and dreadful in all senses, wore a champagne coloured hat. The French Frogs, the Cabrols and d'Uzeses were furious that the grocer (Fauchon) Bory and his wife Margot[5] had seats in the Choir while they were with the goats.

The vaulted chapel rather beautiful and the music good. Then a clank as the trumpeters arrived. Then the louder clank, clank, clank could be heard as the procession started with the governor of Windsor Castle and the Military Knights in their scarlet uniforms, medals clinking, all marching with a loud stamp-shuffle. The slowness and the muffled metal sound was very impressive, and the fact that these Knights were all aged with clear pink skins under it all quite remarkable. Then the church parade. The Archbishops of York and Canterbury, the Moderator of the Church of Scotland, the Dean of Windsor and verger – then the coffin borne by eight sturdy Welsh Guardsmen, arms linked and heads bowed. On the Duke's personal standard a huge, trembling mass of Madonna lilies, followed by a group of male Royalty – the King of Norway,[6] extra tall, the Duke of Edinburgh, very grey and drawn, and yet exuding strength and a rather ugly vitality, the delightful, charming, wonderful young Prince of Wales, and then so sad to see the young Kents and Gloucesters all past their prime, their hair thinning and their bloom disappeared. How quickly it has happened. As for Lord Mountbatten[7] he has become deformed, a hunch on the shoulder, the head is put on sideways, the neck like a bad ventriloquist's doll. He looked green in the face.

The coffin passed in front of the altar, the service began with the hymn, 'The King of Love my Shepherd is'. Some of the verses seemed rather poignant: 'Perverse and foolish oft I strayed', followed by a prayer and the marvellous psalm 90: 'For a thousand years in thy sight are but as yesterday when it is past, and as a watch in the night. Thou

---

[1] Countess Munster (1905–82), wife of Count Paul Munster.
[2] Rose Bingham (b. 1913), first wife of seventh Earl of Warwick. Divorced 1938; twice remarried.
[3] Lady Alexandra Metcalfe (1904–95), daughter of first Marquess Curzon of Kedleston. Married 'Fruity' Metcalfe, equerry to the Duke of Windsor. The other survivor of the wedding was Sir Dudley Forwood Bt.
[4] Winston Guest (1906–82), American and his second wife, C. Z. (Lucy Cochrane), enduring American socialite.
[5] Baron Fred Cabrol and his wife Daisy; Duc d'Uzes and his wife, Peggy Bancroft (d. 1977); Edmond Bori and his wife Marguerite (b.1902).
[6] King Olav V of Norway (1903–91), grandson of Edward VII.
[7] Admiral of the Fleet Earl Mountbatten of Burma (1900–79), murdered by the IRA.

carriest them away as with a flood; they are as sleep: in the morning they are like grass which groweth up; in the evening it is cut down, and withereth.'

Then the lesson from Corinthians: 'No wonder we do not lose heart', an anthem, prayers, another hymn, then perhaps the most dramatic moment till now when Garter read out the styles and titles of the late Duke – Knight of the Garter, Knight of the Thistle, one-time King Edward VI [sic] of England, Ruler of India. It seemed incredible that this man should willingly have given up so much. It made one realise that he had little appreciation of his great heritage, which today's service made one realise was such a wonderful, historic legacy. It is a truism to say how well we do these occasions. But it is always just right, restrained and perfect. The service was short, and entirely noble. It even gave a departed nobility to a young man who once had such charm that everyone considered he was the ideal choice. But he lived on to keep his charm and little else, and one wondered how lucky we all were that even for such an unsuitable reason as the hard, brash and wise-cracking American, he had stepped down to make way for the Queen Mother, and now the very admirable and remarkable Queen.

Wonderful as the service was, I was not moved by the death of this man who for less than a year had been our King. History will make his love story into a romance. In fact, for us so close, it is hard to see that. Wallis has been a good friend to me, I like her. She is a good friend to all her friends. There is no malice in her. There is nothing dislikeable. She is just not of the degree that has reason to be around the Throne.

During these days of death, she has behaved with extreme dignity. She has by the simplicity of her silhouette made the rest of the Royal Family appear dowdier than ever, but she made me marvel once again that she should have ever become a figure in such a drama.

Clarissa [Avon] later told me that when Wallis appeared in the Choir with the Queen, she seemed very strange, that she did nervous things with her hands and kept talking. 'Where do I sit? Is this my seat? Is this my prayer book? What do I do now?' And all the time her frown of worry and distraught bewilderment gave the impression which the Frogs have lately reported that she has become 'gaga'. The last time I saw her she never stopped talking and if you never stop you are apt to repeat yourself and she churns out the same theme like a stuck record. But Clarissa said the Queen showed a motherly and nanny-like tenderness and kept putting her hand on the Duchess's arm and glove.

I missed all these vignettes and had to comfort myself with the dark shapes of the family, Princess Anne in a huge cowboy hat, Princess Margaret likewise, Tony Snowdon with a high mop of ugly yellow hair and a long face, the Queen Mother with veils flowing behind her head,

Mary Morrison[1] in waiting, a giant Pixie in a tall pointed hat, Grace, Lady Dudley,[2] very neat, but strangely out of context in such a gathering.

The procession out of the Choir, Heath, very calm & healthy, Douglas-Homes, Buccleuchs, Courcels,[3] (their last appearance – they are leaving tonight for ever), no Labour, no representatives of the arts.

Then great relief when outside everyone could greet one another. Edwina [d'Erlanger][4] in a cavalier hat, looking very self-conscious, the Frogs furious about the grocer. We looked at the funeral wreaths lying on the grass, dying quickly, in the wind and sun. Some marvellous tributes as well as the charming pathos of all the gifts of the poor, a hydrangea in a pot, three dead roses tied with a sad ribbon, a child's offering, all placed to make a parterre of flowers.

The cars with crowns on the windscreen passed off down the hill. I bid bon voyage to Diana, so bravely to drive herself to London in her mini, and I with the suddenly local-looking Ivor to drive me back to Broadchalke where the relief of my return made me realise that all weekend I had been subconsciously worrying about the difficulties of getting to the church on 'time'.

Footnotes

Freda Dudley-Ward absentee – quite rightly – he behaved so badly to her and her daughters and she never encouraged the publicity.

The most moving sight was to see carried on cushions the orders that he now in death had to give up – the diamond embroidered Garter.

These of such inherent grandeur, such dignity, that one was reminded of Shakespeare's Kings and Princes, and they made one feel that the fair-haired Prince had not been of the stuff of history, that he was the perfect young Prince of Wales, with charm and a smile for all, but that his tastes and life were not of a high quality and that it was inevitable that he should fail in his duty.

At no time during the service did I feel pity for the dead Prince, only a great emotion that the strength of the monarchy was something that could not in spite of all today's rebels be overthrown. It is as important an ingredient in the life of Britain as ever it has been, or so this simple service gave me the conviction.

[1] Hon. Mary Morrison (b. 1937), Woman of the Bedchamber to the Queen from 1960.
[2] Grace, Countess of Dudley, widow of third Earl of Dudley.
[3] Sir Alec and Lady Douglas-Home; eighth Duke of Buccleuch (1894–1973) and his wife Mary (1900–93); and Baron Geoffrey de Courcel (1912–92), French Ambassador to London (1962–72), and his wife Martine Hallade.
[4] Edwina d'Erlanger (d. 1994), widow of Leo d'Erlanger (1898–1978), banker.

Madrid   *15 July 1972*

After many delays and much rearrangement of plans (with Derek Butler as assistant) to photograph the Brit Embassy under the care of the Russells.[1] The weather worse than ever in England, dark, rainy, terribly cold, no garden.

The household very Oriental, with only John as English as could be. Aliki a dervish, Georgiana a plump little partridge with lisp and Latin lateness. Embassy ugly beyond even Aliki's recall. Dinners – their Spanish servants have caught up with the times insofar that they are now only a century behind instead of four! They still have an enviable knowledge of cuisine. They seem unworried and this is why they can do with so little sleep. Hostess said, 'The hospital complains of the noise of our dog kennels, but they didn't have to put a hospital next door.'

The Russell dinner was an interesting mixture of the contrary, backed by painters, sculptors and writers. Interesting to see how the Embassy runs on comparatively few but hard-working servants. Aliki has a talent for organisation. The height of the town, the change of air, made me very tired, and I realised what a lot of work I have been doing in the country, and how it was only understandable that I should find myself able to sleep late into the morning.

It is sad that at Broadchalke I can't take things more easily. Few opportunities to see Madrid but it is a town that needs some. Rather grand, with avenues of trees, but instead of the usual heat the trees have drawn the rain and I am an ape in a white suit while everyone else is dressed for the elements.

No new impressions. Old friends overcoming any difficulties there might be under the Franco regime. Louis Escopan older, as nice as the Goya he looks like. Visit to Prado. Goya of a hunched old woman with puff hair and blue bow a miracle of paint. I realise how little attention I pay, how little pains paid Velasquez's remarkable feats of the art of paintwork. I don't like Rubens, not mad about Tintoretto. Weak on Italian Renaissance, I much loved the Patiniers, Memling, Bosch. Altogether a pleasant little excursion but I am not in need of another for some long time to come. Hopefully to return and get rid of a chest complaint and to rest my eyes which have looked so strained and tired that I cannot understand how people can find me as the Spaniards have said 'handsome'. I have a true hatred of my head and all that it proclaims.

---

[1] Sir John Russell (1914–84), British Ambassador to Madrid (1969–74), and his wife Aliki, formerly the wife of Commandant Paul-Louis Weiller. Their daughter, Georgiana, was mooted as a girlfriend of Prince Charles.

Buckingham Palace Garden Party   *July 1972*

I have never been invited before. It rankled rather. I knew that it wasn't really a feather in my cap to go, but now that the pasteboard arrived, I was completely oblivious of the honour, and felt it only as an appalling chore that took me up to London when I could have had a week in the country getting on with my writing.

It turned out to be an event that I will always remember, but will not participate in a second time if the occasion arises. I went straight from the train to the Palace by which time most of the crowds were on the lawns scattering about in semi-sun, with gusty clouds and aeroplanes above. It was not a pretty sight, the colours garish and the women's fashions of an abominable drabness, the girls particularly awful in long-flowing Victorian nightdresses, clumsy sabots and floppy crinoline straw hats. Just how dowdy the English are was seen to the best advantage here.

But then the Queen, whom I respect and admire and am fascinated by, is as dowdy as anyone. Today I caught a glimpse of her standing talking quietly to a very moth-eaten couple. She was relaxed, at ease, and occasionally glanced at the sky to see an aeroplane roar past. She wore a really suburban white straw hat, a white, white coat flecked with turquoise, sensible white shoes, a terrible glacé white handbag.

As I tiptoed to catch further glimpses through the flanked crowd, I thought how like my cousin Tecia Chattock the Queen was, the white and rose complexion, the same button pearl earrings, the hair cut too short and waved tight behind the ears, so neat and orderly and suburban. I was greatly amused by my thoughts when I noticed Patrick Plunket, on duty as equerry, had spotted me and when we caught each other's eyes he nodded his head in mock seriousness.

The whole garden party was suburban. The gardens laid out with less than taste in the municipal manner, bloodshot roses, yellow and red mixed, liver-coloured and retina irritant scarlets. Everything well-grown and sweet peas to take a prize for size. It was for me a feeling as if I had arrived on another planet, or at any rate in New Zealand, for in the crowd I knew no one, not a familiar face. I wandered lonely as a cloud. It was not a pleasant feeling. But there was much to amuse me and also to touch the heart for these people were all so admirable, the salt of the earth, they had done good deeds, worked for their country, they were the country's backbone, and I feel that the Queen knew this well.

The Mayors and Mayoresses of so many great cities were with Bishops, with great groups from India or Africa, people who work on TV I recognised, others were totally anonymous. Many very simple poor folk who were tucking in to the Royal tea with a fervour that would last them a lifetime. The cakes were good and plates were piled with three fish mousse croquettes, two macaroons, a meringue, a piece of rich fruit cake, a sponge finger and an éclair. The balancing feat a marvel. I enjoyed a cup of delicious iced coffee.

By degrees I became quite at ease in my anonymity and walked down to the lake and watched the RAF band, the military band, all playing 'Hello Dolly' or other well-known musical hits of twenty years ago. The exit was a long projected ordeal, but I was in no hurry. Went home amused and impressed by the country in another of what I pray to be one of its edifying aspects.

14 August 1972

Kin came to spend a week with me on the way to a Swan's Hellenic cruise. He was intent on seeing the places that he and Gene taught at their university. I have not counted the number of years since Kin and I were last together,[1] but we have communicated on the telephone and he has even sent me a few letters. But one always wonders if one's friends have changed, if one has changed. But on seeing Kin on the doorstep of Pelham, with beard, deep chestnut, long hair, and larger and broader and fatter than ever, the regard of goodness and understanding in his eyes was completely reassuring. There is always something for me to learn from Kin and on this visit he said he now knew a lot more about me from having read and studied books on England.

We have a wonderful rapport. He is exactly the opposite of me yet we complement one another so well. His brain is an analytical one, mine instinctive. We can criticise each other's work, and are of great help. But Kin's great attraction to me is that he makes allowances. When one tells a story against oneself he switches the sympathy and makes one's failings into pluses. He puts one on one's metal, at the same time as making everything seem so much easier.

We went to museums, theatres, shops, then to the country. He approved of all the alterations, the new water garden, and he gave extra significance to an ordinary social encounter, to the motor trips. We were called by the telephone at six o' clock and drove in a heat haze to London, the fields of cut corn were a wonderful yellow and other fields deep cocoa, and the distances so hazy and blue that they were pure Monet. Then a rush to do proof correcting and hurrying over last-minute chores and Kin was off without regrets on either part, but grateful to each other for the pleasant encounter, Kin to Greece and me to Majorca.

---

[1] Cecil visited Kin in San Francisco in January 1970.

Chez Chiquita – Majorca   *August 1972*

This would be the ideal holiday if only I could spend three to four hours a day reading. But since I have had to be so careful to keep headaches at bay and have not by any means succeeded, it has sometimes been a bit difficult to know how to fill in the time, especially early morning and post-siesta. There are so many books I want to read, but have had to make do with short reading aloud sessions given by Tess d'Erlanger and my hostess. I have enjoyed the little pamphlet about the Gerald Murphys,[1] bits of Harold Acton, 'Life of Wilfred', and P [Peregrine] Worsthorne in *Sunday Telegraph*. I have even found I suffer from drawing unless I am careful to arrange my drawing block in a manner so that my nape is straight and not locked in a downward position. This brought on a bad spell when the old Goyaesque gardener was sitting to me.

So the days have been spent mostly helping Chiquita [Astor] in house and garden, preparing for the day when order is made of the present chaos. We have been to a delightful nursery garden and planted spar-rmannia, pampas, reeds, rosemary, santalina. I have painted windows and doors to get rid of the bright ginger polish that mars the general effect. This job lasted several days as it was hard to get the right colours and so many had conflicting views.

Chiquita is basically Spanish, splendid, earthy, without any affectation, vulnerable, sweet, and sometimes ugly, sometimes beautiful. There are few people with whom one could spend so much time alone and not find talk limited or jokes exhausted. From Jakie she has learnt wit and she was born with wisdom.

It is a simple, carefree life with little from the outside world to disturb one. We motored an hour around a side of the island to dine in their romantic and rusticated farm, miraculously placed overlooking the bay, when reality *did* encroach, and directly on arrival, Mary [Dunn] gave me stick about the awful inclusion ('unnecessary to the book') about her friend Heber Percy.[2] She said, to my surprise, that it had shattered him. I was surprised how quickly I recovered from the attack and thought myself lucky if worse does not befall me.

---

[1] *Living Well is the Best Revenge* by Calvin Tomkins (1971).
[2] In *The Happy Years* (1972) p. 130, Cecil wrote, 'Pathetic Gerald! When he returned to Faringdon life was made no easier for him. He was not even allowed his breakfast in bed. It was not long before, in desperation, he turned his face to the wall.' There was also a footnote which read, 'Robert Heber Percy, a young friend who disappointed the Berners' family relations when it was discovered he had inherited Lord Berners's house and possessions.' Heber Percy would take his revenge. See p. 360.

The evening in company with Asa Briggs,[1] completely charming and so bright one forgets his non-good looks. A model dinner, yoghurt and cucumber soup, a stew with pears in it, marvellous fruit and wine, and a cigar under the moon, and a deep admiration for the simplicity of the way that M. and P. [Mary and Philip Dunn] live. They have always been without any conventional ties and their mode of life is very much in the spirit of today.

Today the sun pours through the windows. We are to lunch at Marita Mouton's house, said to be the best decorated. We have plans to see various aspects of the island but miraculously the time has flown so that at the back of my mind is the fact that before long my quiet sojourn, so long needed, will be over.

Au Revoir to Majorca and arrival for Diana's 80th in Zell   August 1972

Although this summer has been such a rotten one so that one feels one has missed out a whole year, still the end of the summer holds up as a sad time for me, and I had the same old *angoisse de départ* in good measure on leaving Chiquita's ultra-serene atmosphere. The stone steps and bald garden were something I had had enough of – a further two quiet weeks was just about '*assez*'. But I hated leaving nonetheless, and knowing that I was now going into autumn (in Austria) and the fact that I had a long and elaborate journey starting soon after 7 a.m. did not make me as light-hearted as I have been lately.

However, much of my anxiety was heedless, the plane changes turned out to be smooth and eventually a man with my name on a card presented himself at Munich and drove me for a very long way to Zell-am-See. The new autobahns make distances comparatively short, even so this was a two-hour journey. I had not been in this part of the world since the war and I was tremendously impressed by the beauty and grandeur of the lush countryside, incredibly shaped mountains, brilliant velvety slopes. I had remembered the pretty spires or domed pinnacles of the churches, the painted façades, and the petunias hanging from window boxes.

But suddenly to be back here after nearly forty years brought with it a great emotion and I found myself reliving so many instances connected with my first associations with Germany and Austria when Peter [Watson] introduced me to these countries. I remembered our motor tours and the intensity of our feelings for each other, and as I

---

[1] Professor Asa Briggs (b. 1921), later Lord Briggs, Chancellor of the Open University from 1978.

remembered the poignancy of the situation I started on my overdone habit of blubbing once more. The driver was quite oblivious of my tears and I indulged myself to the full.

It was a beautiful sunny day and the time of year we were always here, when the sunflowers were out, and the harvest being gathered, and apples ripening in the orchards. At last, replete with beauty and sadness at the memories of the past, we turned into an overgrown drive to the little shabby Schloss Zell, a tall white building dating back to the 14th century. There to expect the welcome that I had not had at the airport. But no hollow echoing shouts reverberating through the corridors and vaulted ceilings from Diana, no laughter from Raimund [von Hofmannsthal], no mellifluous calls from Liz. A German woman servant showed me up to my brightly perched bedroom at the top of uncarpeted stairs (the house is very bare and poor, but in its surprising, very Austrian way, charming). I asked if the *Frau* was *zuhause*, 'Yes.' But still silence.

I opened the first letter I have had for two weeks from Eileen and in it the information from Miss Peggy Ramsay[1] that although she'd enjoyed reading my play, she had asked managers if they felt like running it and they all felt that although it had not come in to London before, it had received such enormous publicity that it stood little chance now.

I had wasted six more months on the work. I had literally given myself hundreds of headaches. I had thought it would be the culmination of my wishes if, in the case of this play, three times proved lucky, and I had started the last rewrite six months ago in the hope that the play would be published, and I supposed this could be done, but I was quite shattered with unnecessary disappointment now that I was told the play stood little chance.

It was while I was reading this letter that at last Liz appeared. She had been gardening and had not heard the dogs bark to announce my arrival. She was with Jason Cooper, 13 years old, and very distant. She would ask me a question and interrupt the reply. She bullied Jason. Where was Raimund? Rai was obviously ill and very nervous. He looked so thin and old. I was sad for him. No sparkle left. It may be that he and Liz had had a major row earlier in the day. Certainly they were now sparring, and Liz was merciless. She meant to be nice to me, but nonetheless gave the impression of being a termagant and her beauty was suppressed to her ill-humour.

By degrees a tea, interrupted by the arrival of an electrician to mend a light, and lots of dog scenes, was staged with Madame N. trying to make a little sense out of chaos. But it was a horrid tea party, and both Liz, Rai

---

[1] Margaret (Peggy) Ramsay (1908–91), theatrical agent, who looked after Joe Orton, Alan Ayckbourn, David Hare, Robert Bolt, Stephen Poliakoff and others.

and I were annoyed that Felix Harbord had arranged to have a long-discussed picnic today and not after Diana's birthday. Half the party were out all day and by 7 o'clock had not returned. I came up to my bedroom to try to gain a little vitality and to change my mood, but I could not sleep, and only by very slow degrees did I feel I was recovering from the shock of my arrival.

The shock continued. When I came down from sleep to join Diana, Liz was exasperated beyond belief. Jason [Cooper] interrupting as Diana gave a description of the disastrous Harbord picnic. It had been too elaborate, with grouse and lobster from England, too far away, and when the party arrived, the Prince of Hanover[1] said, 'Are you Lady Diana Cooper? Well I am Ernst August and I have been waiting for you an hour and a half.' Diana rejoined with a left and right, 'I don't know why you have, but I am ready for a drink.' Felix had put the emphasis on all the wrong things, gold service brought out especially from England and no jolly jokes, too much to eat, smoked salmon, lobster, grouse, *boeuf à la mode*, a birthday cake, an Esterhazy cake etc. After lunch the party had motored on to see a hunting lodge, belonging to the Prince, filled with stags' heads. Diana pointed to the jewel in her hat and said, 'I collect unicorns.' The Prince imagining her to say this in the spirit of his collecting stags said, 'But they don't exist any more!'

At dinner in the nearby gasthaus I was amazed at the noise made by the Paget/Cooper family and sat silent while all shouted and interrupted. Suddenly Liz, furious with John Julius [Norwich] for saying 'non swanks' (as a joke) gave him a resounding smack on the face: 'Oh don't be such an arse. Come off it. Lend me your ears, silence! ! !' 'Will you listen to mes' reverberated through the whole dining room, Diana in a bad state and looking awful, the children drunk with high spirits and delightfully raucous. Then mercifully the day came to an end. Dreamless sleep.

Diana's 80th birthday   *29 August 1972*

Breakfast downstairs always a shock, but this the rule of the house, then to Diana's dark-panelled bedroom where the birthday presents were offered to Diana, lying very flat in bed in a position that made her chin double, nay triple. However, in a deep, crackling voice she took a long time to open each present ('Why not prolong the joy! It's my upbringing to open everything very carefully, and preserve the packing paper') and said just the right thing, not putting on a high-powered act, completely at ease and not emotional. Only once as a joke she said, 'Just what I wanted.'

---

[1] Ernst August, Prince of Hanover (1914–87), head of the House of Hanover.

The grandchildren gave her delightful home-made presents (Artemis [Cooper] had painted a unicorn on a pebble to look like a medieval miniature). A crowded bedroom, those present: John Julius, Anne, Jason and Artemis, Liz, Rai, Arabella [von Hofmannsthal], Ali [Forbes] and myself.

Diana looking through the album of photographs of herself I had given her, kept saying, 'It's the pains you've taken that's so touching.' I had wanted to give her a good present and this was the right occasion. Going through the album John Julius supplied captions. Towards the end: 'There's life in the old girl yet.' Diana said of the photographs, 'They go back such a long way!' Then she had John Julius sing a ribald song about 'I want to be violated in violet time'. The birthday had been a huge success. Ali took some flashes. ('Very common,' remarked Diana.) By now it is 10 o'clock. How will the day be spent? Of course the nearby mountains are almost invisible in the rain.

The rain stopped. The party went to the village of Zell, the population classless, all the same class. It was lovely to sit at a café and watch but Diana allowed me to take photographs of her and now that the local men had mended my colour camera, I enjoyed Diana's posing, an old trooper, or fire horse champing to get back to the scene of the fire, while quite a large crowd gathered.

D wearing a birthday burnouse of brown with a hood, like a Capucin monk under her picture hat in splendid fettle, reading out birthday telegrams from faithfuls, Judy [Gendel], Enid [Bagnold] ('What a run! Fifty years of superb performances and still running strong. What a miracle!'), Raymond [Mortimer], Patrick S. T., Rhoda B [Birley], the [Isaiah] Berlins (a surprise). Lunch a gala family affair, Diana launching the conversation on Greek mythological characters: 'Who's been to Troy? What did Iphigenia do to save the fleet?' The grandchildren responding with gusto. They are brought up in the Diana tradition – their huge brain boxes used in a superb running condition. No toasts; sausages, dill sauce, blueberries out on the terrace until the sun gave way to rain.

A siesta with no need to hurry downstairs. I have got into the habit of lying and thinking by the hour. I have got accustomed to the rowdiness of the household, Liz knocking back the ball with greater gusto than anyone, a contradiction in terms. Afternoon reading aloud by J. Julius, who had fractured a leg playing tennis, of H. Nicolson on Adolph and Benjamin Constant. Diana rambled on about Madame de Staël and her brain is as acute as a poignard.

Family confidences from Liz, the troubles with her children etc. picture books (Copley, a surprise), great laughter, Ali Forbes immensely funny, well-informed and tough. I love his company. The children very bright, Artemis at dinner telling me about her preparations for Oxford, having given up restoration of Tintorettos in Florence. Her brain goes off like fireworks. Raimund a bit piano – I was worried about him. He looks old and ill, hang-dog, pathetic. Retirement does not suit him. His effervescence was part of his great charm. The night's sleep came as a shock of suddenness, a day of idleness filled with interests. Tomorrow, if fine, sightseeing around Salzburg.

Thursday, 31 August 1972

My last day here. We spent it motoring a terrible distance almost to Linz to see St Florian's and the Altdorfer paintings there, Diana in the motor keeping the conversational ball rolling, stimulated Jason's historical curiosity by asking him all sorts of riddles. It has been a remarkable education that her mother gave her and which Diana has passed on to her child and grandchildren. Mama Rutland's habit of throwing out all her preconceived notions if she came in contact with something good of its sort was also seen in [her] not allowing her children to go to despicable musical comedies, only opera and Shakespeare were their entertainment until Lily Elsie appeared in *The Merry Widow*. Then the children were encouraged to go as often as they wished to study the grace and beauty of the heroine and to try to copy her effects.

Diana later gave an extraordinary description of her going to a Foyle's luncheon for Barbara Cartland[1] and she pulled her own hat over one ear in imitation of the authoress of trashy novels (the favourite reading of Clemmie Churchill) and when I remarked on the inaccuracy of Cartland's last 'memoirs' and surely D never had black sheets, she said, 'No, but I had a black bedroom at Belvoir' then proceeded to give an hilarious description of the Renaissance influence showing itself in the decoration of Crivelli swags of leaves, the marble washbasin and the Punch Ball in the centre on which she tried to get rid of endless weight, as she and Iris [Tree] played 'punch Ettie' (they hated Ettie Desborough, later learning to like her). Then on to the lengths to which they went to try and lose a few pounds, asking a Boy Scout to go into the chemist for an emetic, and drinking gallons of mustard and water. Dinner followed by gramophone records of Anna Russell rotting *The Ring*, then excerpts from *Götterdämmerung* with Diana interrupting and looking for lost spectacles, Liz in a state of misery, Rai very sad. The break-up of the holiday, the party diminished. Another summer holiday over, a summer that has had very little impact for me.

---

[1] Dame Barbara Cartland (1901–2000), prolific romantic novelist, invariably clad in pink.

Diana's departure, by expensive taxi, where the traffic for Olympic Games [in Munich] was at a standstill. However, after a long wait in the fumes of modern traffic, I arrived at the airport with over two hours to wait. Hence this excerpt.

Returned for five days home. Did those good long mornings of work (still on the 'unwanted' Gainsborough play) and to stop the British men wrecking the dining room with their hideous paper all around the skirting, then back to take a plane to Noël's in Switzerland. I had suggested the visit to him since D. begged me to 'help her out' and felt I wouldn't chuck. It would have been much easier to stay put and from the moment I saw Diana, Artemis, Cole Lesley, Graham Payn, Lilli Palmer and her husband, Carlos Thompson,[1] sitting round a little table in the airport café, I knew I had been foolish. Diana was in no need of me. She was her own star and so full of her recent visit to Berchtesgaden, so incapable of not shouting through everyone's talk, that I soon became put out and mopey. If I tried to talk in the car to Lesley, we were interrupted by Diana in the front seat.

At dinner Diana was projecting and furious if the conversation was not general, i.e. all listening to her. The same old stories – Paul Getty, Penelope Betjeman's[2] TV appearance, the notes she leaves to traffic wardens on the window of her car. Yes, we've heard them so often. Artemis still smiling. After dinner Diana, unable to hear Noël on account of her deafness, interrupted, switched and hogged the talk so that I became very angry. I know it must be terrible to have been the most sung-about beauty, to get old, I know how plucky she is, feeling she must keep the flag flying.

My heart goes out to her. That only makes it all the worse for me to suffer and see her being, of all the things she dreads, a bore! It was a terrible evening for me until she went to bed.

Noël at Les Avants

Of course I've heard about Noël's Swiss retreat from taxes. It's very typical of him, comfortable, lots of signed photographs, a house that might have been brought from Eastbourne. I had often talked about visiting it, but this had not happened until this evening when I found Noël in

---

[1] Cole Lesley (1909–80), Noël Coward's secretary; Graham Payn (b. 1918), Coward's boyfriend; Lilli Palmer (1914–86), previously married to Rex Harrison, and her husband, Carlos Thompson.
[2] Paul Getty (1892–1976), oil millionaire; and Penelope Betjeman (1910–86), wife of Sir John Betjeman, Poet Laureate.

a scarlet jacket, hunched and crumpled in a chair, looking very old and resigned. He even seemed a bit surprised to see me although, no doubt, as he later said, he'd been so looking forward to my visit. A glass of brandy and ginger ale was in reach and the cigarettes at hand. He seemed fatter, more crumpled.

But soon I realised his brain and intelligence are in as good shape as ever. He was just as quick on a 'comeback' as before and within a few moments we were each enjoying our jokes and laughing a lot. But Noël is only a bit more than 70 and until the last ten years still had his marvellous stripling quality, but he has aged terribly quickly. He might now be 85. He suffers from a bad leg. The circulation can't be relied upon and if he walks he can be in great pain. As a result he doesn't walk and spends much of his time in bed. This is not good for anyone.

But Noël has aged into a very nice and kind grand old man. He is really a darling, so trim and exact, his memory unfailing. You know that when he gives an imitation of someone else's talent or personality he will be absolutely on the ball and never prejudiced. There are certain types that he despises. He has no time for amateurs, or people that tell lies or are phoneys. But he is incredibly generous in his appreciation of most people, particularly those who have succeeded in his profession. When you ask him a question, he respects you by answering, perhaps with a moment's slight pause, but at length, until he feels he has given you what you asked for.

Naturally we reminisced, about the first times we met, how he gave me a deserved 'going over' during a return journey from America, and more recently about the production of *Quadrille*. He complimented me on my professionalism and said I was the most direct and workmanlike person to have as a designer. He laughed about a dress that, after many delays due to post-war difficulties of getting any fabrics, arrived for Lynn Fontanne and she looked awful in it. Noël very timidly said he thought it was a mistake. I answered, 'Yes, so do I. Let's give it to Marianne Spencer.' And we did, and she looked fine in it.

He praised Lynn Fontanne's performance, how she read with complete lack of sentimentality the line, 'Yes, I had a son, he died.' Yet you know it was one of the great tragedies of the character's life. Then Noël recalled how Lynn, on stage, looked at herself in a mirror, plucked a rose from a vase and caressed it tenderly against her cheek. Noël gave a great moan, 'It was so beautiful, it broke my heart.'

He praised Lynn's recent TV performances as the Barrie old lady showing her medals. He praised Barrie, said the first act of *What Every Woman Knows* was masterly, quoted *Dear Brutus* as one of his most favourite plays. But this brittle-looking youth had loved so much, had had a capacity for being so deeply moved by so many plays, operettas, poems, books and histrionic performances.

It was later in the evening quite wonderful to hear him singing in a quiet but musical voice, the songs that meant so much to him as a 9-year-old boy. He remembers still all the lyrics, having at the earliest age the love of rhyme. He wrote a book of poems at the age of 12. He now sang Vesta Tilley songs (a great star whom we'd love if she were performing today), Albert Chevalier, Albert Chevalier in a terrible Jack Hulbert musical called *The Light Blues* in which Noël had learnt to tap-dance.

He sang little snatches of songs from forgotten musicals (*My Lady Fayre*), a number of Cecily Debenhams, a great praise of Maisie Gay, whom Noël considered more of a brilliant character actress than a comedienne. For each revue sketch she stretched the part as if it were in a Chekhov play. He eulogised her in *The Bus Rush*, less praise for [Beatrice] Lillie, who never characterises.

I asked about the stars he had seen from the pit when taken by his mother on birthday treats – Lily Elsie, the way she moved, very slowly, but with such incredible grace, those long arms and never a coy gesture. 'She was such fun too – a darling! One laughed with and at her and she was so beautiful, her voice true, even when she came back to the stage in *Pamela* and was no longer young and strong but very true and pure.'

Of Gertie Millar: 'Oh, she could dance like a wisp, with those tiny legs, and she was a star, and like all stars she had vitality. No one without any vitality can have any glamour.' Only once did I think it silly of him to say that no one but he and Cole Porter had ever written such good lyrics, but maybe this is true. He talked lovingly of Gertie Lawrence as someone with whom he could never quarrel for she was such a perfectionist.

It was an interesting experience, worth the air journey, to find oneself in this house, so unlike anything that has been part of my life of late. The theatre has lain dormant for me. It was like a return to a former love, to be here where the walls are lined with stage books, where every old theatre magazine is still to be found, where all the old-time records are stored.

Coley and Graham are delightful companions to Noël. They don't agree with everything he says, but they are impressed with him, and look after him in admiration as well as adoration. It is interesting to see the way the end of a life of such success is ending for him. He spent such fortunes until he had a fright and realised he must make a 'nest egg' and preserve it in this country. He lives quite comfortably, lots of entertaining of friends, many cars, a huge Swiss servant cook-masseur, a flowing grog tray. It is all he wishes for and in his mind he is as active as ever, though probably no longer creative as a writer. He makes a 'thing' about being old and Coley tells him to shut up. But when we came up to bed (in the recently built lift) Noël plopped himself down on the stool and said, 'It's awful, I'm so old.' He was very misshapen, bending forward with head bowed as he went along the corridor to his very sparse bedroom. But he did turn round and say how pleased he was to have me stay with him.

September 1972 [Wednesday]

Noël says he reads for half an hour before going to sleep, then remains unconscious until 10 o'clock. He then realises how nice it is to be asleep and turns over for another hour and a half. This morning his tea tray was brought in at noon. By 1 o'clock he tottered down to the purple sofa downstairs, was in excellent wit at lunch and went back to bed immediately after. The rest of us went shopping.

Noël still in his room until dinner time. He does not write any more. Perhaps he reads, but I doubt if he does. It is difficult to ask the 'boys' what he does. He certainly won't take any exercise. The blood does not get pumped to the brain and he has complete lapses. Yet he is in so many other ways remarkably quick...It is extraordinary to see someone so 'gaga' physically remain so alert mentally and one wonders why he does not write any more. Is it that the hands tremble? The knife and fork quiver and he often puts them down without eating. He seems not a bit interested in food, but then he never was...

Cole Lesley takes care of all the accounts, and a file is copied, so that the Swiss tax people have his earnings sent to them by the time they go to Jamaica, and when they return in the spring, the bill is presented and paid. The money situation is obviously excellent though Cole said he felt queasy today for writing out a cheque for £8,000 for the lift in the house; this comfort for Noël so he should not have to walk up and down, has cost altogether £20,000. Noël is by no means in the Sinatra class but his visits to Las Vegas were the nucleus of his nest egg. N. himself does not have any money 'sense'. He got scared when he found himself in debt, but he has not much interest in gain, and does not realise that others may not find this part of life as easy as he does. Throughout his grown-up life he has been able to earn, and he takes it for granted that he should travel first.

It is a happy household. Cole said he thought 'Master' was more contented here than in any of his other homes he had created and likes Switzerland, and since his arrival 13 years ago, many friends have come to live in the neighbourhood.

Elizabeth Longman[1]

Elizabeth Longman, being brave after her husband, Mark, had died, met a tearful Raymond Mortimer at the opera, and in an effort to show her bravery said, 'Everything's happened at once. Mark went, then the boiler went.'

October 1972

Ray has insisted on having one weekend off each month and since Mrs Smallpeice does not really like to work in the house, it is best for me to make this weekend a means of going to other houses. Michael Duff's invitation to Vaynol was readily accepted as I had reached a point of exhaustion in my writing, I felt a break would be helpful, and not only would I enjoy to see Vaynol again after so long, but perhaps was even doing Michael a kindness as he finds several of his friends are not able to afford the journey for a weekend and loneliness is something he has to contend with.

Vaynol used to be the centre of much frivolity and inspired gaiety: charades, improvisations, elaborate dressing-up, practical jokes, youthful gaiety of all sorts. Now about thirty rooms in two wings have been pulled down, the Trustees who run the estate have become more and more difficult, and now Michael has difficulty in maintaining the place under very different conditions.

However, because Michael was at some meeting, and he has a very busy life attending to his various responsibilities, we were met at the station by the old chauffeur in a new-looking car; and an old butler came out of the front door as we drove up, made a little speech regretting Sir Michael's absence, and then said that the first time he had seen me was in 1936! Patrick Procktor on hearing this was staggered, as it was the year of his birth, whereas I could not believe that forty years had passed since I first came to this house. So the visit took on the colour of a journey into the past.

Here were so many bibelots and pieces of furniture that had belonged to Juliet [Duff], here so many memories of events that had been entirely forgotten by me. Soon Michael appeared and all was changed by the readiness of his interest, his curiosity, his humour. For someone who

---

[1] Lady Elizabeth Longman (b. 1924), daughter of tenth Earl of Cavan, bridesmaid to Princess Elizabeth, married Mark Longman (1916–72), publisher of the eponymous firm. They lived at Bishopstone House, near Salisbury.

started as a backward child, he has achieved great things for on his own he has made a very interesting life. He has fulfilled his responsibilities alone (Caroline[1] no help to him whatsoever). He has kept amazingly up with the times and become more and more of a character. He is in no way an eccentric of the past. But since he and I have shared so much of the past together (I felt that being a part of the Vaynol group I had found a niche into the life that I wanted) we necessarily veered towards subjects that we had both shared.

Juliet's albums and scrapbooks were brought out, and I was staggered that the well-remembered events here recorded had taken place so long ago. It was unbelievable that 40, 30, 20 years ago seemed just as yesterday, and that even now I couldn't see myself as anything but a stripling.

Michael gave me a feeling of strength. He has survived well, so why shouldn't I? He had no regrets, so why should I feel sad about the passing of so much, rather than gratitude that so much had been fitted into life? It had been frivolous, but it had been a creative frivolity, and it must have taught one so much about certain aspects of life. Anyhow, it was no use sighing. It was with a haunted fascination that one looked at these old milestones with a fresh eye. People that, at that distant time, had seemed so old and decrepit, appeared quite young, and even beautiful.

I had always thought of Juliet, twenty years older than oneself, as an elderly lady, but in these snaps she was a good-looking young woman of 50. These days are utterly remote and one would not wish them to be the same but the snapshots and press clippings made one realise how much life has changed within the short space of a lifetime, and indeed how much shorter some of the life spans have been of contemporaries long since dead.

Vaynol (continued)   *October 1972*

Am not really happy here. The house is still comfortable enough but it is not what it was and I am rather depressed at finding that so many years have passed since Michael and I knew one another. Patrick and his harmless, but nonetheless tiresome, girlfriend (how I hope he won't marry her) make the age syndrome more acute and so many of the people we mention are dead since long past. The weather is appalling, a gale blowing, the house has no open fires, and it is not quite warm enough, the food tasteless and, in this condition of general malaise, I came across a paragraph in a Sunday paper in which Deborah Kerr[2] said that for me to write as indiscreetly as I had about Greta was 'revolting'.

---

[1] Lady Caroline Duff (1913–76), daughter of sixth Marquess of Anglesey.
[2] Deborah Kerr (b. 1921), film actress, friend and summer neighbour of Garbo in Klosters.

I try to be tough, to ignore the censure I knew would be inevitable, yet after an interval of not thinking about my bad behaviour, this came as such a shock that when I went by myself for a long walk through Michael's beautifully planted park, I had no other topic in my mind. Neither did it leave me during the waking hours. I had hoped that time would heal any wounds, but I know I have done wrong and the fact that I could, if given the choice now of doing or not doing the same thing, I would not change. So perhaps I will continue to be punished for a very long while for what is an inexcusable act of 'ungentlemanliness' even though fundamentally I still feel I had to do it.

New York   *21 November 1972*

I have been in a daze for about a day and a half. Long wait at airport before take-off, then eight-hour flight. Complete exhaustion on arrival so another ten hours' sleep or half-sleep. I now begin to feel readjusted, and have taken in, at last, the fact that I'm back in my rooms, now redecorated, and yesterday's excitements and dramas seem very far away. After a nightmarish winter dark stormy rain journey from Salisbury, torrential rain, train broke down, I went to see Baba in the London Clinic. We are all in a terrible state of anxiety lest she has some form of cancer. She seemed more cheerful than last week, but perhaps because she is well cared for.

On 20 November 1972, Cecil had attended the special service of thanksgiving for the Silver Wedding of the Queen and the Duke of Edinburgh, at Westminster Abbey.

Early call for preparations to go to the Abbey for the 25th anniversary service for the Queen's marriage. Ticket to Dean's Yard, saw Sybil [Cholmondeley] and Moucher Devonshire[1] kiss one another. Lucky to draw up behind a busload of Beefeaters, all old, some with pince-nez, a contrast to their ruffles and beautiful finery. These old men nanny one another, putting on the swords at the right angle in scabbard, preening, gloves on. Church already filled. Sat next to Jakie and a clutch of Astors and some Greek relation of Princess Marina, who with her husband looked to see what Royalty were invited. 'Holland hasn't sent anything. Denmark hasn't sent anything either. Which door would Paul and Olga

---

[1] Mary, Duchess of Devonshire (1897–1989), Mistress of the Robes to the Queen 1953–66.

[of Yugoslavia] go in by? Michael of Romania looks very Hanoverian, the Greek King's put on a lot of weight.'

I spotted lots of old Palace has-beens. That awful John Colville,[1] his mouth now turning down like a croquet hoop. Never seen such a caricature, like a Dickens, Philip [Hay], once so good-looking and his battered wife, the Fords,[2] a nice old body came up and chattered – Miss Lightbody,[3] the children's nurse, a very great help and need in times of trouble years ago.

Marvellous Orlando Gibbons music, fanfares, anthems, hymns were part of the service that we know so well to do. We've had generations of practice at pageantry, and today everything was clockwork. The arrival of the Royal Family was well worked up and each wearing brilliant colours like stained glass – the Queen with flattering ostrich feathers in turquoise blue, Princess Anne in Tonga green, puce and magenta, Princess Alexandra likewise, the Queen Mother brilliant viridian, the sad Duchess of Gloucester,[4] brave in deep crimson, and Princess Alice,[5] older than anyone, a historic figure of withered skin in a huge fox bear-skin. Princess Margaret, a set smile on a well-enamelled face, made a fatal choice of putting on a black coal heaver's hat with a dark red dress, but the Queen's enamelling was marvellously successful, her complexion so good that maquillage goes on it like cream on a peach. In the strong lights the skin very wrinkled around the eyes, expression dazzling, happiness, fun and gaiety.

The procession always very dramatic with Beefeaters, Men at Arms (so old, with helmets and halberdiers, like a Fernando drawing),[6] and the clergy, with crosses and brocades, very impressively brought up by a seven-feet-tall Dean of Windsor. Service mercifully short. We flocked out into the sunshine and chattered with neighbours, Liz Longman, Mollie and Robert Salisbury, and widow Betty[7] – Mollie, dressed in a huge and voluminous highwoman's coat with a vast hat sprouting a waving tail of pheasant's feathers, and Michael Duff, badly dressed, not at all for the occasion, Ava [Waverley] shuffling on tiny feet, very decrepit

[1] Sir John Colville (1915–87), Private Secretary to Princess Elizabeth (1947–9), and to Winston Churchill (1940–1, 1943–5 and 1951–5).
[2] Sir Edward Ford (b. 1910) and his wife Virginia (1918–95).
[3] Miss Helen Lightbody, Prince Charles's nanny.
[4] The Duchess of Gloucester's son, Prince William had died on 28 August, in a pointless aeroplane accident, turning too sharply while taking part in the Goodyear Air Race.
[5] HRH Princess Alice, Countess of Athlone (1883–1981), last surviving granddaughter of Queen Victoria.
[6] The Yeomen of the Guard and The Gentlemen at Arms, Body Guards to the Queen.
[7] Lady Elizabeth Longman; sixth Marquess and Marchioness of Salisbury; and Elizabeth, Marchioness of Salisbury.

in a medieval bowler, that loathsome Duchess of Westminster like a policeman in drag, 'Tortor' Gilmour,[1] pretty horrid in a borrowed mink coat.

And then a return to home life, packing, last-minute SOS, and Nancy [Smiley] from hospital worried about Baba's condition. Lunch off the sweetbreads ordered for Baba before she went to the clinic, alternately talking of Royal festivity and terror of cancer. And then the staff waving goodbye, Eileen admirable, cheerful, game, courageous, Ray, and Nancy and my hating to have to face up to the strain of New York life after nearly 2 years' interval.

New York   November 1972

Ten minutes after my dazed arrival at the hotel, Sam Green, bright as a star, rings to tell me he is in a state of shock, that his friend, Mrs Barbara Baekeland,[2] about whom we had both spent much time writing a play, or a novel, has been stabbed to death by her doped son. 'That's terrific!' I said, perhaps rather unsympathetically. Sam had been asked to be executor of her will. 'She still hounds me after her death but I don't know if I'll accept. Matricide is a messy business!' We perhaps can now proceed with the story project. We had not been able to decide on a suitable denouement. Is it here? Could be a thrilling book.

Rather a strain. First day. Yet no headache! This very good news. Sitting with M [Minna] Wallis (she two hours late or more). Looked as if it would be good.

Gladys Parr very sympathetic about my 'diaries' – a nice Fleur Cowles-like woman, and then in the evening an honouring at Raffles on my knighthood with a framed medallion certificate of honour from John Lindsay, Mayor of New York. Quite an honour – I am secretly bunched

---

[1] Victoria Gilmour (1901–91) ('Tor-Tor') Cadogan, married (Sir) John Gilmour, second Baronet. Mother of Sir Ian Gilmour (later Lord Gilmour of Craigmillar).
[2] Barbara Baekeland was stabbed to death by her son Antony in a penthouse in Cadogan Square on 17 November. When the police arrived he was on the telephone ordering a Chinese take-away. He was tried at the Old Bailey in June 1973, and because it was argued that Barbara had been trying to cure him of homosexuality, with a strong hint of an incestuous relationship, he was found guilty of manslaughter. He was sent to Broadmoor, but discharged in 1980. He went to live with his grandmother in New York, but attacked her. He was confined in Riker's Island, where he committed suicide on 20 March 1981. The Baekeland family had made a fortune from plastic, and Tony ended up killing himself by smothering himself in a dry cleaner's bag. This inspired Sam Green to suggest that a more felicitous title for the best-selling book, *Savage Grace* might have been *Plastic to Plastic*.

but it goes off me like water off mummy duck's wings. But grateful, so far New York turning out to be so much nicer than expected.

Thanksgiving   November 1972

No half-measures in NY. Today is the great cranberry sauce holiday and the city is as if dead. Those that have not gone to the country are asleep. The silence is unnerving. Whereas most days it takes half an hour to get my breakfast after ordering it, today the room service is waiting for my call and the boy comes immediately. The telephone is silent, all very agreeable, but not what I came to New York for. One has to be on the go. One could easily become neurotic, feeling one is no longer needed. However, the respite is a short one and is salutary to the physical system.

Diana Vreeland

Diana Vreeland giving a great performance before lunch about how the Italians destroy themselves every hour on the hour, yet they survive. 'You can't get to Rome. It's cut off. And if you should strike it lucky and arrive by air when there's not a strike, then you'll never again be able to communicate with the outside world. There is no telephone, no maintenance, the Colosseum is falling down. No one repairs the Forum, which is not even safe for cats any more!'

A shock at the Metropolitan Museum. About to pay for an entrance to the Kings Book of Persian Miniatures, I was asked 'Are you a senior citizen?' 'When does one become a senior citizen?' 'At 65!' I had no idea that at 67 I would be recognised as anything more than the galvanised middle-ager I feel myself to be. The free entrance did not compensate for the body blow.

Baba

New York. St Regis. Breakfast just begun when telephone rings unexpectedly early. It is my brother-in-law Hugh, from England, with a note of anxiety in his voice. Obviously he was very emotionally het up. 'It's about Baba. You know they examined her and thought it gall trouble.' 'Yes, yes.' 'Well they've moved her from the London Clinic to Sister Agnes.' 'Ya, yes.' 'Where she's had an operation, but they find she has cancer of the pancreas and they can't do anything about it. She may last another two weeks, but they are going to keep her under sedation. But they are going to tell her. We all think she would prefer it to us all telling her a lot of lies.'

How terrible! Oh, how terrible! My frivolous life changes abruptly to basic reality. I now know what we had all feared and it is worse than we could have imagined. Baba is still young. She has never been ill for a day, so strong, but she has been sad, her life never really a happy one. Her husband killed so early on and never a recovery, and much of the time being brave and making excuses for her loneliness.

Now this abrupt development. I don't know if I will be able to go home for the terrible end and I feel too stunned to feel anything, but the tears that are always so near the surface have begun to pour. So much about my life is now about to disappear, so much of childhood, so much of shared family existence.

When the visual pictures of Baba faded, I thought of her as a strong, quite serious character, much more difficult than Nancy, more profound, but difficult to get on with, secretive and tight-lipped, stubborn, courageous. Most vividly do I remember when I called on her with some Reddish late-autumn flowers and found her unnerved by pain and suddenly letting down and weeping. 'You've got me at a bad moment,' she said, starting to be brave again. It was a rare moment and now I think of what she must have suffered, I am filled with the deepest pity.

But I must think of her, the last time I saw her, in the London Clinic. She was so relieved to be taken care of. She suddenly looked so much less tired. She was in good spirits, her fair hair newly arranged for her visit, her bedclothes terribly becoming. She looked thin and her hands were scrawny, but she seemed to be rallying.

Dallas   *26 November 1972*

Still haunted by unhappiness. Most of the day I am dogged by this feeling of the sadness of Baba's impending death. Less than a week ago she was so cheerful in her hospital bed, she looked so pretty, and was delighted to know she was in good care. Now this awful blow has changed everything, and I keep remembering the various phases we have been through. It was she who waited up till the late hours for me to return home and be told of Reggie's death. She was the right one to do so, for she was calm and wise. She had always been the favourite of her nanny, and everyone agreed she had more depth than Nancy. She was not so spectacular, but she had courage, and she was the one to ride well and turn cartwheels and find life at school without its difficulties. And I remember her so well by the snapshots, and now she is being eaten by this tragic disease, her body being wasted away in an agony that we trust is chilled by all the dope known to medicine. One can only hope that her suffering will be short.

New York seemed rather more unreal than I have ever known it, probably because the 5 days were spent without much work to do, and many people were away for the Thanksgiving holidays, and the strange air illness that I get when flying over the Atlantic made me feel particularly on edge. I felt too that New York had changed and that my friends were no longer on the crest. Around was illness, death, or retirement. I found Diana Vreeland extremely erratic, incapable of sticking to the point, and taking in less than she should. My great standby was Sam Green. I found his life delightful, always original and adventurous. He has become much calmer and more profound, altogether the nicest person I can now feel to my NY link.

Dallas

Chapman Kelley,[1] whose gallery was to exhibit my paintings, turned out to be an extremely pleasant sympathetic guy with a beard, a scraggy wife and the extraordinary knack of doing his old-fashioned thing in terms of modern art, for he is a painter about to be acclaimed by the great collector Hirshhorn. He liked my paintings (more than I) as he felt they had an affinity to what he was doing. It was interesting to see how awful his paintings of nudes or figures in fields of flowers were, but how when the figures were abstracted, the fields became quite lyrical in terms of abstract art.

The private view of my pictures was agonising. A self-conscious, inept, fat young photographer made us all embarrassed and was slow at his job. People who looked as if they haven't an oil mine to their name tucked in, and no sign of a red tag. In fact, all through the evening only one ted tag was stuck to the typed list, although I believe about 4 others were sold before final lights out. What a contrast to the wholesale buying at Palm Beach! I was appalled, also tormented about whether or not the pictures were of any merit.

New York   November 1972

Partly due to the Thanksgiving holidays, New York seemed like a week of holidays, and I felt that it was a bit difficult to fill up the time (any rest I could have was beneficial for I felt ill as a result of the inevitable cold

---

[1] Chapman Kelley, Texan artist and painter of wild flowers and sailing boats.

caught in the transatlantic trip here). But by far the greater reason for my feeling a bit lost was the fact that Margaret Case was not there to welcome me, to help me with so much information and to make me feel in touch. I mourned her death very much, and more than ever the manner of it. I am convinced that it was her treatment by *Vogue* that caused her utter dejection and drove her to jump that terrible height. I found few people to talk about her, they had dismissed her from their minds. Life must go on.

But I made Diane Vreeland, against her will, talk about the situation at *Vogue*.[1] It seems a state of desperation has set in, Penn[2] the great is being dismissed and there is still general guilt about the way they have behaved. This only makes them the more aggressive. But they were a sinister bunch. A few days after Margaret's suicide, the papers reported that she had left a large sum of money. This could not have been true and certainly not ratified at short notice.

Then the letters that Margaret left for her friends were seized. Diane had to get her lawyer to get her letter. She was told, after a great delay, that she must go down to the Condé Nast lawyers to have the letter opened in front of them. This she refused to do. Her lawyer would go. More delays. Months passed. Where is my letter. Eventually, Diane's lawyer was told 'There is no letter'! This is real Mafia horror and the implications are that in this non-existent letter Margaret must have mentioned the appalling behaviour, not only to her, but also to Diane, who has now decided that the only thing to do is to 'Forget it'.

Cecil organised a ball for some 'tough women' in Dallas before flying to San Francisco.

San Francisco   *November 1972*

Kin. I know that he is important in my life and good for me, and the chances of meeting are rare, so although I was 3 and a half hours away by jet [from Dallas], took the opportunity to fly to him. He looked very different at the airport, bigger, taller, wider, a bit broader in the face, and the beard and hair rather wild.

But I was touched to see his marvellous clear-glass bright eyes again and he seemed equally pleased to bring me back to his house where we sat side by side with my luggage in front of me, as if one were in a train, and so much to hear and tell, of his Greek cruise and visit to Salerno and

---

[1] Alexander Liberman was responsible for Diana Vreeland and others.
[2] Irving Penn (b. 1917), renowned photographer.

Syracuse, his work, his closeness to Plato and all the ancient philosophers. This level of intellectual talk is what I need. I lap it up even if I do not comprehend it. He is brilliant and has become more mature in his approach to life, but it saddened me to hear him say that although he had chosen to live the way he does, and would like no other form of existence, he does not think that he would want to go through it again, that he had not ever been really happy, did not consider his life worthwhile.

At lunch at a Bay-side fish restaurant, he said he thought Margaret Case, suffering from a cancer, was quite right to jump. It would be a painless death, and life was only worthwhile if pleasant. He had no feeling about suicide being wrong. It was a sensible way of getting out of an impossible situation.

The rain poured as if in London. We went to the *Ruling Class*[1] film which Kin explained a little to me, but the author had too much to say on too many subjects and the whole thing was extremely taxing. Then back to a coarse steak, cooked by Kin, and eaten in a home rucked by the wind. To dam up a howling draught, he got a towel and shoved it in the side of the badly fitting window. I wager it will remain there for a great time to come. I was terrified of catching a worse cold and a stove starting to smell made me realise how vulnerable to wooden fire I was in a home.

Kin had to leave before daylight, to talk almost incessantly and over-conscientiously to his students. He loves to work, but it has become too great for him and he looks overtired. His complexion very white and the skin lilac around his eyes. It saddened me to see how, in the 10 years I've known him, he's become so much older. As he ate some yoghurt out of a carton he looked like a very old, bearded eccentric, and no longer the glorious young student I discovered under such strange circumstances, and who became the most important thing that entered my life during the filming of that great epic.

It saddened me too when I woke and went round the house in daylight, to discover how incredibly dirty, dusty and overcrowded, and full of refuse the house has become even since my last visit. No one has dusted it, he throws everything on the floor. The mess is unbelievable, indescribable, old newspapers a mile high, broken glass, cracked pots, empty bottles, cartons, old bits of worthless junk, the accumulation is beyond a joke. It worries me. It is as bad as the accumulation of the Collyer brothers.[2]

I long to start to clean up but the job would be endless and he would be furious if one threw away an old rusty nail. It is becoming quite unhygienic. Ants are over everything and even some mice are about. Instead of

[1] *The Ruling Class* (1971), based on the play by Peter Barnes and starring Peter O'Toole.
[2] The Collyer brothers – Homer Collyer (b. 1881) and Langley Collyer (b. 1885) were two eccentric bachelor brothers who lived together in a three-storey brownstone at

it being the home of a philosopher, a stranger would think it was the hide-out of a madman. I found it terribly depressing and the less time I spent looking around it, the better. But my eyes could not rest. In every corner more rubbish. I dare not throw away even the empty lavatory paper roll for fear of it leading to a wholesale clean-out and I was thankful to leave the house to go to lunch with Whitney Warren and on to the de Young Museum. For without Kin to attend to the various worrying noises from the gas or Frigidaire, or some unseen contraption, the house becomes quite spooky.

Kin's presence makes it all part of his atmosphere, but when he is absent, the various W. Heath Robinson contraptions take on a rather sinister aspect. The huge Frigidaire, which no doubt he bought at a thrift shop, has tubes leading from it that drip like the saline drip into jam pots. The door, in order to close it, must be hit low down.

If anyone were to take an inventory they would be working for months on end, and they could not imagine who or why the owner had pinned to the wall 'instructions to all persons of Japanese ancestry issued by Western Defence and South Army Wartime Civil Control Administration'. Or why he had exhibited terrible 1912 advertisements of ladies with frizzy hair, cats and peaches and pears. There are, lost among the displays of gardening and building tools, the snorkel, goggles, the half-empty cartons of 'Bug-geta', floodlight lamps and dried, dead verbena and fir, and his mountains of old clothes, some very nice pieces of pewter and silver, and even Kin admits that somewhere, completely lost amongst the mounds of rubbish, are the helmets and epées of the days when he fenced for the Olympic games.

By degrees the overwhelming dust got on my nerves and I snapped at him when I remarked that he had scratched his nose and should put some ointment on it. When he rubbed the dining table with a finger, and then put some cortisone on that dirty finger, I said 'You must wash your hands. That table is filthy!' He took it well, but it was a dangerous outburst. Likewise when I gave him some flowers he opened a cupboard for 2 blue glass vases, and rubbed the dust off with his hands – 'Now do wash' – he excused the dust by saying, 'My flower vases don't get used as much as yours do.'

But all is worthwhile when he is talking about his works and beliefs,

2078 Fifth Avenue, a run down part of Harlem in New York City. On 21 March 1947 the police were called. The house was piled high with junk. The police spent some hours getting through a honeycomb network of tunnels to discover both brothers dead. Langley had killed himself in a booby trap he had set against burglars, bringing a pile of garbage onto his head. His crippled brother had died of starvation. Amongst 136 tons of rubbish were found fourteen pianos and two organs. The house was pulled down as a health hazard.

when he is talking on any subject he is pure gold, and my heart went out to him more than ever when, tired on his return from a day's teaching, he took a short nap then read my slight play through and wrote a very brilliant and helpful analysis of it. This gave me the opportunity to work all the following morning for 4 hours on it, and I am sure with beneficial results.

San F. has much to recommend it, but I suddenly decided to quit. Kin has too much on his mind to look after me, has to get early to sleep, so I bought a return ticket to London.

With a very early morning departure, I started off on the 12-hour 'Jumbo' flight, through a day and night, to arrive at some unconscionable hour to face up to the reality of Baba on borrowed time and to hear the latest pronouncements on the state of her health.

Baba in fact was, as Tecia [Cecil's cousin] said, as 'bright as a button'. Her personality at its best, vital, energetic, funny. But maybe the incurable illness causes this euphoria. She has obviously faced the fact that she may die, but she has only spoken of the cancer to friends, not to family. She has lost a great deal of weight, is yellow from the jaundice, but she looked beautiful, and made me feel happier in these horrible circumstances than I could have believed possible. To my amazement her old lover was visiting her when I arrived, and she was glad to be rid of him. She said casually, 'You know, I haven't seen him, and do you realise he's married his secretary, a girl 25 years younger than him. Of course it won't last, he must have gone mad!'

There was no gloom of impending death about her. It is strange how quickly one takes for granted the worst news. Nancy, stunned by the bad news, shook and trembled for 10 days, until she decided she must take a pill. Now, like all of us, she accepts the terrible fact and goes about it with as much calm as possible.

I am glad I made the journey home. I am happy now to be back in my house in the country, with so much to do, with Roman hyacinths and paper whites in bowls around the room, the white cat asleep at the foot of the bed, and the winter sun streaming over the frosty lawn and hill through my windows.

Baba, now safely ensconced at Hawarden,[1] is living for Christmas and the celebrations with her grandchildren. What will happen after does not bear thinking about. She said to Andrew Elphinstone[2] that she did not want her girls to know how ill she is, while they pretend to her that they don't know what the future must hold for her. But Baba is too weak at the

---

[1] Hawarden Castle, Flintshire, home of Sir William Gladstone Bt and his wife Rosamund, Baba's daughter.
[2] Rev. the Hon. Andrew Elphinstone (1918–75), nephew of the Queen Mother.

moment to take the trip back to London and to face going to the dreaded Marsden Hospital for rather unpleasant treatment (cobalt), neither will it be of any use to her, so says her doctor, so I am once more about to leave for the US, but with the comforting knowledge that Baba is not suffering unduly and that she is surrounded with loving care.

In fact, I have now realised the extraordinary qualities of her favourite Rosamund who showed me what a bright, intuitive and nice person she has become, a fit companion for her brilliant husband and a credit to Baba. She can be relied upon to make the right decisions and no matter how difficult the situation I was very moved by her straightforward summation of the status quo, and knew that whatever she decided would be best for Baba, was the only right one.

Royal Gossip   December 1972

The *Daily Express* shows a huge photograph of a great bruiser woman in the hunting field. She wears her hard-hat low on her rock-like head, a stern regard in her eagle eyes, and her legs bursting out of the tightest britches. She is said to be the woman who will become Princess Anne's mother-in-law.[1] Certainly Princess Anne has such a strong will that if Phillips[2] is the man of her choice, there is no stopping her.

Dalí[3]   December 1972

He spends 2 months every winter in the St Regis Hotel. I went to see him for a quarter of an hour. He is a great personality and really very delightful, clever and funny, and it was remarkable to seen him converting the 'French' suite into something of his own. It looked like a Dalí décor.

I was surprised on the night of my arrival to find on my bed a circular disc of silver-paper-wrapped chocolate, placed on the pillow. Was this a joke of some friend? (If Sam had been around, I would have guessed he was responsible, but he is in Egypt.) Next night, two chocolates, one on each pillow. I then realised that this was a *petit soin* invented by the hotel as a nicety for each guest.

On arriving at Dalí's sitting room I saw hundreds of these chocolate

---

[1] Anne, wife of Major Peter Phillips. Born Tiarks. She frequently wore the outfit chosen for Princess Anne's wedding at subsequent Royal meetings at Ascot.
[2] Lieutenant (later Captain) Mark Phillips (b. 1948). Olympic equestrian. They were divorced in 1992.
[3] Salvador Dalí (1904–89), surrealist artist.

discs placed in a row and running like a line of ants all over the flat sur-
faces of mantelpiece, commode, television etc. He does not eat chocolates, as he has a weak liver, and had preserved these to count the days he
has spent here. (Other strangenesses included an invalid chair with an
umbrella and a top hat over it, a huge black cabinet with dark glass paintings on it, and a strange and inexplicable picture of a beer advertisement
added.) Also the TV was showing a static picture of a beautiful young
man. The knobs were taped so that they could not be moved and with a
'Sony' lamp trained on to the chair, placed on the TV screen, he could
avail himself of everything in front of the screen that he wished to study
at length.

He showed me drawings he had made inspired by the shapes of
newsprint, and then (which he hurriedly explained were as good as
Raphael) were shown on the screen. He was very in earnest about his
tricks and jokes, and I loved him for being such an original individual, but
today was terribly put off by his really appalling bad breath which made it
almost impossible to regard the things he wished to show at close quar-
tets. On the way to the lift he regretted that with the modernisation of
the hotel they are getting rid of the wonderful art nouveau brass gates to
the elevators. But he had made a deal with the hotel and they had already
discarded two from each floor so that he was now able to buy 40 of these
gates and was having them shipped to Cagnes for his swimming pool.

Reddish – the cook that went   December 1972

The new cook – he has been here 10 days – has done a midnight flit on an
early Sunday morning. I did not find the violet-coloured note until a
quarter of an hour before 3 people were coming to Sunday lunch. The
joint bleeding in the refrigerator which had been unaccountably turned
off. The man, hippie type and unattractive, had seemed so contented,
liked the cottage, said his mother would be visiting him. He talked up his
future here, and the larder was full. Suddenly no trace. He left in his car
as soon as he had brought in my breakfast.

The shock makes one sick. Not only that such leaving should be the
reward for our consideration to him, but that someone who seemed to
approve of our way of life should see fit to disappear and in such a
manner. It makes me suspicious that he may have appeared here to find
out what we were about, what he could discover about Garbo or the
Queen Mother. Maybe he is just a tiresome, feckless creature of moods,
who quite suddenly decided to quit, his excuse being that he had to spend
more time in this house than in his cottage.

But whatever the reason it has given me a horrible jolt when there is so much else to think about, and it is too awful to have to ring up Eileen on a Monday morning and to tell her that she has to go through this heart-breaking procedure of interviewing dud servants and then hoping for the best, and in the kindest way, showing them the ropes. And it is these sort of jolts that upset one's equilibrium and if carried to a greater degree could make one want to pack up oneself.

New York Gossip   *December 1972*

John Gielgud had the idea that not only might he make a great deal of money by directing a musical over B'way but would also have a lot of fun. He has now returned a sadder man, and it is up to [Arnold] Weissberger to see that the thugs who made his life so miserable on the production will fulfil their contract. After a while, John realised that the leading lady for this revival of *Irene* was none other than the aged film star, Debbie Reynolds.[1]

Terrible troubles when in Canada where they were touring. A terrific snowstorm overtook the country, winds, blizzards. No one would be able to get to the theatre even from nearby let alone the huge buses that tried to come from some distant town. The management called to stop the buses as the performance was cancelled. But, accustomed to storms, the Canadians had left at 6 o'clock instead of 11 in the morning and had started by the time the cancellation was phoned through. They would have, after all, to play the matinée, but then it was discovered that Debbie Reynolds had severe laryngitis and could not appear. The understudy refused to go on. She had had no time to study, did not know the part. The management begged John to come on and read a synopsis of each scene while Debbie Reynolds would go through the movements of her part. The theatre filled up. Debbie gyrated as John in his *voix d'or* recited,

> In my sweet little Alice-blue gown,
> I was both proud and shy
> As I saw every eye,
> In every shop window I passed by.[2]

---

[1] Debbie Reynolds (b. 1932), Texan-born film star, specialising in 'girl-next-door' types. Married the singer Eddie Fisher (later married to Elizabeth Taylor). As her film career faded, she turned to Broadway and starred in a revival of *Irene*, which was a hit. Gielgud directed, but it was not a success as he knew nothing about musicals. He was fired but nevertheless netted £40,000 from the run, most of which he gave to fund a fellowship to help young directors work on the classics.
[2] This is Cecil's version.

The audience was furious: 'Outrageous!' they shouted. 'Money back.' They stomped out. 'Ridiculous! Speak up! Nonsense!' Catcalls.

Suddenly Debbie Reynolds regained her voice, rushed to the footlights and squawled, 'Shut up, all you bums. I'm not here to be insulted. I should never have turned up for a lot of hoodlums like you. I should have remained in my home with my seven maids.'

1973

Baba's Birthday   21 *January 1973*

Will it be her last? Oh dear, how sad her case is! She is a skeleton, terribly weak & yet her spirit rises above her awful illness and she is not depressed. She talks of future plans. Meanwhile her daughters have come up from their distant homes and rallied to cook a festive lunch at Baba's little house and bring her from her hospital room to eat turkey and drink a bottle of wine with the closest members of the family. It must have been a very sweet, tragic little party for the chances are very small against the disease being dissipated or cured, and Baba (although 60), the youngest, seems so young to die.

Reddish   *February 1973*

In a way I am superstitious, no hat on bed, spit if you see one magpie, don't go under a ladder etc., yet I don't give much credence to the thought that bad luck goes in threes, or that 'This is not my day!' But in fact I have to admit I have been and probably am still in the middle of a 'bad patch'.

Last weekend I was in a foul mood. I was cursed with a violent headache as a result of writing too long on two successive days. The weather at this bleak time of year made everything ugly outside and the beginnings of spring could not be seen anywhere. I was horrid with Eileen and by the time Tuesday came along was content to give up my work and go to London to indulge myself in pleasures, to take time off to go to the exhibition of drawings at the BM and at the Queen's Gallery.

Time to go to plays. But it was not to be. My 3 folders of Vol. IV of Diaries came back from Weidenfeld with a great many queries and suggestions for alterations. I often complain that the publishers don't do enough to aid me in correcting the final script, and I was thankful that with the arrival of young Mr Buchan the post of editor had been most meticulously filled. But it was agonising, unnerving, slow work and the time went by so quickly and my mood was one of exasperation. On arrival from the country, my desk was filled with disappointments.

My short story had been returned by the weekly *Telegraph* and nothing in the mail did anything to raise my morale. Among the telephone messages, one must be answered immediately. 'Please ring Miss [Sheila] Lemon.' But why not wait till the morning? Things might be in a better vein by then. But no. I grabbed the receiver as if asking for further punishment and I got it in good measure. The verdict this clever little agent gave me on the 2 plays I'd sent her, and for which I had been waiting so long for a reply, was as bad as it could be. Neither play did she like. I have worked off and on, headache on headache as a result, for months on the latest rewrite of the Gainsboroughs, and for 2 months on my return from my summer holiday, and the chickens come home. My expectations were high. I am furious that Alan [Tagg] and Charles [Colville] were depressing in their verdict. I had a big blow when Margaret Ramsay said it wasn't stage-worthy, but I improved it and yet not enough. Miss Lemon was very forthright and bright and asked, 'Am I depressing you very much?' She knew the answer by my voice.

There were other things to make me downhearted. Baba's spirits are so good that she prevents us from worrying about her being so ill. Her 'discomfort' is sad to watch. If only she could just doze and sleep instead of being made to suffer. The money situation is not very encouraging. Every day becomes more and more expensive. News is squalid and horrible. Cruel war in Ireland. Shocks at home. And yet one must be thankful that one is not as some of those disabled or destitute old people one sees on the TV. Anyhow, by Thursday, I was begging to get back to the country from which I had fled two days earlier.

A rushed visit to Baba, a return to Pelham and Ray, a cook who did not show, a quiet arrival at Waterloo and then through a chain of unfortunate circumstances by mistake I got on the wrong train. My peace of mind was shattered. It was a nightmare experience. But eventually I arrived home, slept and was feeling quite cheerful at the start of another morning's work on the photograph book and on bits of the 'Index' and most fortunately I was not visited by a blinding headache in the afternoon.

Hawarden Castle   *March 1973*

The inevitable has happened. As the doctor predicted, Baba's condition has slowly deteriorated. She has come up to her beloved Rosamund for the last time. She is desperately weak and during the last days it has been felt that she could die any minute. But she has rallied, made an effort, and though her strength is ebbing it seems to me she might linger for several weeks. In a way I hope she won't, for she has not given in. It makes her angry that she is not strong enough to come down to lunch, that she cannot write her name, or light a cigarette.

The amazing tenacity shows that she does not realise that she is dying. She talks of going back to her cottage and seems to have resigned or forgotten the fact that the doctor told her that she had cancer and only a few weeks or possibly months to live. She seems to think that the deep ray treatment and the injections have been successful. She is a bit exasperated, critical, and bullies her nice nurse, but she is not sorry for herself. She is not even depressed, at least she hides such feelings from us. She has always been good at keeping things to herself. Even when Alec [her husband] was killed, or her lover left her, she told nobody. A dark horse, she may be playing her last game now, but I rather doubt it.

But terrible as her predicament is and it is heartbreaking to see her, I do not think she is suffering more than general discomfort. Perhaps after all the deep rays have prevented her being in real pain. But she cannot feel well, looking the way she does, for her body and her head have lost that sulphur yellow of jaundice and her head is now less yellow than grey. I have never seen anyone dying in this way and it is unbelievable that anyone can live while looking like this. It is particularly strange to see her lying propped up on the blue and white striped pillows as she is tended by Nurse Sheridan, who is a pink and white peroxide blonde. Looking from the one to the other increases the shock of seeing my sister who, three months ago, was also particularly pink and white of complexion, now grey as a lizard, and yet after the first shock the effect is very beautiful.

It is a comfort to all the family that Baba looks incredibly beautiful. She is so thin as to be hardly recognisable, the flesh is wrinkled and sagging, her neck, one doesn't look at it, but her bone formation of face is quite marvellous, high cheekbones, noble nose and brow. Her forehead is without wrinkles. Her lips have become thinner and new lines have appeared at the corners of the mouth, but the general effect is homogenous. The fact that she lowers her eyelids a lot and occasionally one sees that the eyes themselves are watery and red somehow only adds to the strangeness of her beauty.

Rosamund and Willie [Gladstone] both remark upon the uncanny resemblance to my mother in her last illness, and Baba is more than ever like my mother in the things she utters in her clipped quiet voice. She is caustic, she is definite: 'Yes this is a very good pineapple' – Re the mother-in-law: 'I keep away. I don't cross her path. It is better so.'

Although so weak, she is still very alert: 'You must see Willie's possessions – the Italian Renaissance treasures and the French clock in the Library, I love it! And you must put on your overcoat and go and see the drawing room. Willie will open the shutters, and get him to show you his drawings. He's collecting Lear.'

At supper last night Baba was so weak that she could not remain propped up on the pillows for more than a few minutes. She seemed to gasp a lot and the nurse looked worried, and the pulse was beating twice its normal rate. This is a sign that the heart is feeling the strain and it will be the heart that goes. Baba lay back and after a few seconds was asleep. I wondered if perhaps it was not the final sleep. But she rallied and later talked to Rosamund who is torn by indecisions from one hour to the next. Was she right in advising her sister [Alexandra Lamb] not to go to Rhodesia and what would Baba feel when she was told that Mickey Lamb, her son-in-law, was flying back tomorrow?

Personally I doubt if Baba now has the capacity to reason. She seems to accept everything as it appears. No energy to reason why, and yet I may be wrong. All I know is that I am very sad. I know that Baba is over sixty years old now and her life has not been an unhappy one though I don't think it could be considered a fulfilled life. But I am somewhat comforted to see that death need not be as terrifying as one feared and that, in spite of her ghastly illness, she is not suffering as my poor darling Aunt Jessie suffered. The sedatives make the withering away less tragic and unless Baba has to suffer some horror such as fighting for breath and air, her fading out will be like that of a plant which suddenly becomes sick and is a hopeless case that one watches die by inches. It is sad but it is part of the general scheme, and if I am told that the same fate is in store for me, I don't think I'd jump from the window, unless of course I was in great agony and doctors would not give me enough penicillin to relieve the agony.

This is necessarily a strange weekend in a strange house 'with strangers'. But it is a trust that for however much longer I am spared, I will not forget.

Sunday, 11 March 1973

The best spring day so far, sun all day long in a huge sky that one knew could never be clouded over. A marvellous feeling. I read and wrote a bit too long in bed, without any feeling of pressure, but it gave me an afternoon headache. Perhaps I was very tired by the emotion of seeing Baba dying and the encounter with her nice nurse, Mrs Sheridan, outside my door was deeply disturbing. Although we are all deeply aware that Baba is dying, the fact that she had deteriorated enormously during the night came as a horrible shock. 'Yes, her pulse is even faster that it was. That means that her heart is feeling the strain. Yes, yes, you can go in and see her if you wish.' I steeled myself.

Baba has been very careful to see that her hair should look well and when I first saw her two days ago, I remarked upon how nice it looked, so silvery and shiny. She was pleased and repeated my compliment to Rosamund. Last evening I had watched her while the nurse propped her up for the ritual of the rollers which Baba used to perform. But now she is far too weak even to hold a cup to her lips, so she submitted to the ritual. The first thing that struck me on entering her room, and I saw her lying asleep with her face turned towards the window, was that her hair had fallen on to her forehead. This somehow added the final touch of poignancy to the picture and it affected me deeply. I stared at Baba. Her mouth was slightly open in a sort of ecstasy, but she was breathing badly and I knew it would be unkind to talk to her. She lay a small steel-grey piece of sculpture. And I left the room in a state of complete breakdown.

I came to my room and sobbed. I did not want the others to see me red-eyed and went out for a walk in the marvellous spring sunshine, up to the remains of the old castle. But still I wept. It was the sight of the hopelessness of someone who had been so close to me when we were all young that 'dissolved' me. I tried to reason with myself. How much worse for Rosamund losing her mother. But still the sight of her lying there caused me to lose control.

It was a difficult day to get through. It was good that there were so many children about, to give a sense of continuity. They were so noisy and badly behaved at lunch. Rosamund taut and exasperated. She has much to cope with. Willie is smiling and good-humoured all the while. Later in the day I went in to see Baba several times. She had regained consciousness and was even giving her nurse a bit of sarcasm. 'Dear, dear, dear, we are in a bit of a state,' she said. Her face seems to have shrunk even more and her eyes are stretched and she reminded me of photographs of newly born babies.

In a monotone she made a few remarks about the subject I brought up at random. She said about Charles,[1] her grandson, 'Yes, I adore him,' but sometimes it was difficult to understand. She was confused about the time of day and kept asking if I had had my breakfast. In the evening Xandra [Lamb] arrived. Her breezy manner was a help. During a quiet spell downstairs, I asked Rosamund about the funeral arrangements. Baba asked to be cremated and her ashes put with the Beatons at Hampstead, but they had made no arrangements yet. It was extraordinary to hear the two daughters being so businesslike about the plans: 'It would be awful if we go to get that donkey tomorrow and Mummie pegs out.' Yet they are just as upset if not more so than I am. Xandra said that, when she first heard the news, she was shattered.

I went in to see Baba before going to bed. She was propped up, a tiny marmoset on the sheets. She may linger for 48 hours, but no one here wishes that the end should be prolonged.

---

[1] Charles Gladstone (b.1964), Rosamund's elder son.

Monday, 12 March 1973

An early morning of anxiety as I had planned to return home and the union of train drivers has made travel havoc, and I did not like the idea of bidding adieu to Baba. The nice, cheerful Mrs Sheridan had said that her duties as nurse would probably be over by tomorrow and, since Baba's condition yesterday seemed so very weak, I feared the worst when Xandra brought in my breakfast tray. But the cheerful bright-eyed waitress said Baba's condition was much better, and so it was with a lighter heart that I went in to take my leave. Packing and diary had made me rather short of time and I was surprised to find that Baba, lying back facing the door (her face tragically yellow in the dull morning light) was in communicative mood. Her voice was deep and low, but quite clear, and her brain was alert. 'Have you been comfortable? Has the bathroom been warm enough? Have you seen the drawing room? It is pretty, isn't it? It's really the library and the room where the books are is really the drawing room. I don't like Mr Gladstone's Palace of Peace, but I'm glad they've kept it intact.' This was amazing. After yesterday an astonishing revival. Baba continued, 'I've heard – someone told me that Sharples[1] with his aide-de-camp has been shot in...' – she fumbled & got the word wrong – 'Bermuda – yes, Bermuda. Nancy and Hugh will be upset. He was a neighbour. How terrible, and it might have been John Smiley[2] who was shot with him.'

I said I was going out in the garden for a walk as I did not want her to know I was leaving the house, but she seemed to want to talk some more. Yes, she was sorry Nancy was ill, but did not give her much sympathy. Perhaps instinctively she knew how much more seriously ill she was herself. When the cheerful little nurse came in, I kissed Baba for the last time. So many remembered childhood kisses were brought back, the youngest of the family always coming in for the maximum of kisses. Because Baba appeared so much less vulnerable, she prevented me from collapsing as I had done yesterday. I felt quite matter of fact and hard-hearted. I knew this was the last time we would talk to one another, but I had done all my suffering at the poignant sight of her upturned head on the pillow and her tired very grey face.

Today she helped me to 'be a man'. I marvelled at her courage, her

---

[1] Sir Richard Sharples (1916–73), the Governor of Bermuda, was shot dead by an assassin, walking in the evening at Government House, Bermuda. He was a former MP and had been Governor of Bermuda since 1972.
[2] Sir John Smiley, baronet (b.1934), only son of Nancy and Hugh.

strength. It was the same determination to battle on that had kept my mother and her sisters alive so long after others would have given in. Goodbye Baba, Baba who was always so independent, so lithe and grace-ful, always with a pet dog, so athletic and country-loving, who loved against family wishes and was sadly widowed, so brave and defiant, carry-ing on with the upbringing of not always easy children. Goodbye, my most beautiful, first, home-made model, and goodbye to so much of my own life. Goodbye to Baba.

Almost a week later

The doctor had given Baba forty-eight hours to live. Four days later she telephoned Nancy. She wanted to make what was perhaps she knew a last call. It was tragic. Baba could not talk properly. Her speech too slurred to be comprehensible except for a few sentences. Nancy said how much I had enjoyed my visit. Baba said, 'I'm afraid I wasn't very good company for him.' I waited to hear further news, not wishing to telephone the Gladstones. They have enough to do. Then yesterday morning early, Rosamund telephoned. Baba had suddenly suffered a good deal of pain. She had had strong injections to send her into unconsciousness and this morning, at 4 a.m., she died.

Although we had known this would happen and were rather hoping it would happen quickly, the news came as a horrible shock. When later in the morning, Nancy telephoned me, she had only time to say 'How sad this is', when we both broke down.

For Nancy the break is even worse than for me. The two sisters were so close, but I was very overwhelmed with sorrow. It seemed so awful that Baba should have to undergo so much painful and disturbing treatments during the last months. They may have protected her from pain, but the doctors knew her case was hopeless. So alone and without anyone able to help, she had to suffer, perhaps to buoy herself up against what she knew was a fatal illness. But she would not let anyone know what she thought. That was typical. She was very self-contained in her private thoughts. We will never know.

Now I have the picture of her, after all those early pictures, a little wafer, grey-faced, but beautiful, lying there near the window.

End of March 1973

The Queen Mother, so naturally affected, was mincing out of the dining room at a dinner at Lady Doris Vyner's[1] when the hostess whispered it would be so marvellous if the Queen would say a few words to the woman who had been responsible for the repast they had all enjoyed. So the Queen with fingers of one hand touching her ample bosom said to the good woman, 'How lovely to be a cook!'

Terrible dramas with the Muscovy ducks, incest, cruelty, jealousy. Mistress daughter attacking mother, drake attacking new brood. It is as horrible as the way the union leaders and Northern Irish are behaving. The latest from Ireland – three tarts lure three young soldiers to a house – one goes out to bring in the murderers and the three soldiers are shot. A cripple crosses the street slowly. The bus conductor puts on brakes. IRA members lob a bomb into the bus full of old people.

At this time there occurred two major theatrical deaths, Binkie Beaumont, impresario and a monster in his own way, died on 22 March aged 64, and Noël Coward on 26 March, aged 73. Cecil had an ambivalent view about both of them. Cecil was disparaging about Beamont's visual taste. 'See his Essex cottage,' he once wrote, to make the point.

Binkie Beaumont

Binkie Beaumont has died in his sleep. He had been drinking lately and smoking all his life. Looked like a death's head at the awful concert (K [Kenneth] Clark/Joan Drogheda) last week at St John's, Smith Square. Early in my career Binkie had ruled theatre-land. He did well by me (and I by him) when he agreed that I should design *Lady Windermere* [in 1945]. I should have affection for him, but I do not. He was a cold, calculating character, always having quarrels. He was devious and Machiavellian. Serpent-like, one never could trust him. He had much to be said for him.

He was good to old friends, was a master over detail and a brilliant businessman. (It seems that recently he nearly went bankrupt.) But the

---

[1] Lady Doris Vynor (1896–1980), second daughter of eighth Duke of Richmond. She found the Castle of Mey for the Queen Mother.

emotion on hearing of his death is not one of sadness – just that he had a good life according to his terms – and an easy, quick death.

On the other hand I am very sad that the great figure of my early life, Noël Coward, has died in Jamaica. He had an agonising last half-hour and it is as well that he has gone for he was a burnt-out case. He had drained his body and mind of all its strength and a sad old man remained, who had only a few little sparklets of the old wit and bonhomie.

As the years advanced – and how can there have been so many years packed into such a short span of time? – Noël became nicer, more kind, fairer. He was a benign, mature old man full of wisdom. His intellect has never been his strong point, but throughout his life he has been determined to learn, to learn more and more, and he had a library large with the books he had read. His taste was never good either and his writing could make one writhe.

But what remarkability, what professionalism, what strength and courage in face of defeat, what depths of experience! His natural and intrinsic talent was no doubt remarkable, but it was backed by such strength of character that if he had not succeeded, he would have exploded. A man that I became very fond of, and our last parting was very poignant now that it has been proved that I thought it was the last at the time. We both told one another how we loved one another.

Once more the awful journey to NY and this time due to a nervous fidgetiness and vibrations from everywhere the trip seemed to take for ever. Horrible storms while circling NY, but no disaster and without too much trouble or difficult readjustment of time, back to my bed at the St Regis.

It was here that four months ago I heard on the telephone the news that my sister Baba had only a short time to live, and now she is dead and I think a lot about her character, courage, independence and her young beauty. I think a lot about the friends who so suddenly died in the last weeks. Poor Nancy Mitford should be the next to go. I hope she will be spared further agony, and altogether my waking thoughts were rather unhappy ones – so unaccustomedly early I ordered my breakfast.

Dared look at the advertisements for my book in the papers. Though the publishers have done me proud, am dreading the exploitation. Flowers from the publishers. This has never happened before, and also from the Sonnabend Gallery who are to have an exhibition of my earliest photographs.

---

[1] Lord Rothschild (1910–90). He ran the Think Tank for Edward Heath.

I told Lincoln Kirstein Victor Rothschild's[1] joke about the American dream being that thirty million blacks would swim back to Africa with a Jew under each arm. He laughed extravagantly and said, 'How true!'

My first NY day. Awake (natch) much too early but it gave me a good start for all the business telephone calls I had to do for my publishers, Sonnabend Gallery, and in search of History of Photography number by G. P. Lynes.[1] Mostly successful. A large advertisement for my book in the *Times* gave me a bit of a shock but I turned the page quickly and Weissberger said it was very good. Anita Loos said à propos the publicity tour, 'Writers have to do it. Critics aren't read. It's the only way to have people know of your book' ...

Evening, arranged by Sam, spent at Mrs Staemphli's[2] large dinner for Niki de Saint Phalle.[3] I took Diana who was more engrossed in Andy Warhol on her right. Andy now very talkative and healthy, but his business manager, Fred Hughes,[4] is the one I like. I found him absolutely entrancing, so unselfconscious, aesthetic, lively, bright, easy, funny. I adore his company, and his looks, which Diana says are those of the Rocky Twins. She urges him to make a film about them, ending up with a shot of them high-kicking up the stairs of the Élysée Palace in the arms of Hitler. Mrs Staemphli, an invalid, with creeping paralysis, in a chair, was seen after much talk from Sam on the subject of Mrs Barbara Baekeland, now dead of knife wounds inflicted by her son (about whom we started to write a story) for the first time. She is non-vulgar thin (contrary to expectations) but looks untrustworthy, sly.

Andy was taking polaroids for *Vogue*. How much farther can a name take you. The pictures were awful, but Andy's enthusiasm and energy boundless. At midnight he went off to another party, while I hoped my approaching headache would vanish in slumber. A very pleasant day, nothing to grumble about. In fact, the clear bright sunshine and the company I kept put me into an energetic frame of mind.

Next, Cecil went to Chicago for more interviews.

---

[1] George Platt Lynes (1907–55), a photographer much admired by Cecil.
[2] Emily Staemphli, art collector and friend of Marcel Duchamp and Mme Pierre Matisse, who advised her. She was a McFadden by birth and entertained exotically in her Fifth Avenue apartment.
[3] Niki de Saint Phalle (1930–2002), artist and sculptor.
[4] Fred Hughes (1943–2001), Andy Warhol's business manager and later executor.

Friday, 13 April 1973

The day was not without its setbacks. Whether or not it was out of malice a commentator, after a radio interview, gave me a review of my book by – of all people – Auberon Waugh,[1] the son of my old arch enemy. He seems to have inherited the spleen of his father. A devastating attack aimed to reduce me to a shred. It hurt. Then a horrid little woman journalist, referring to it, said, 'You're supposed to be a marvellous person, but they say your book is awful' and she handed me Waugh's review. Of course I knew this tour would not be all milk and honey and, if worse doesn't happen, I'll feel I've been lucky nonetheless.

I do feel terribly guilty about exposing Garbo to the public glare. Even though those things happened thirty years ago, my conscience has been pricking me terribly. Yet I know that if I had the option of not publishing it, I would still go ahead – and suffer. I only trust Greta can rise above it in the way she did about Mercedes's book.[2] But I long to get back to water garden and try to forget all these things, and concentrate on my work, that will not necessitate personal relationships. I realise now how very dangerous these diaries are – and how, if there are to be future volumes (and I read between the lines that Auberon Waugh would wish for my death) I must be very careful not to overreach the bounds of decency, taste, tact or be unkind in a way that I fear I have been in this present volume.

Beverly Hills Hotel   *April 1973*

Alan Kellock,[3] with very long strides, dark flowing silky hair, thick wiry black beard, is the 'Rep' from McGraw [Hill] looking after me. He is nice and gentle, likes nature, mountaineering, fishing. He keeps me from bleak loneliness, and gets me to impossible places on time. TV and radio stations awful. [Irving Paul] Lazar and the Berksons[4] have entertained me, kept utter boredom and loneliness at bay. But my conscience ruins the whole day and night, and particularly the waking hours. I cannot now think why or how I ever reasoned that it would be possible to betray Greta.

---

[1] Auberon Waugh (1939–2000), mischievous writer and son of Evelyn Waugh. Founder of the *Literary Review*.
[2] *Here Lies the Heart* by Mercedes de Acosta (1960). Mercedes revealed much about her love affair with Garbo and left provocative portraits of many women.
[3] Alan Kellock, New York publisher, later with Viking.
[4] Seymour Berkson and his wife, Eleanor Lambert.

When some rubbery little woman explains how much she loved this or that (and she quotes from the book about Greta) I am aghast. How could I have done it? I think of Greta with such remorse. I try to imagine her not reading the book, but even so. I feel I have committed a murder even when someone comes up and says, 'I'm so glad you wrote the book.' I know I will be paid out for having made this mistake. I know I will be punished, apart from what I have already suffered. I long to escape in order to forget.

But will I be able to forget? And the second volume is yet to come. I need someone who could give me a bit of strength. I poured out my troubles to Kellock. He was sympathetic, made no comment. Kin will understand, but will he offer comfort? I wonder if he will understand my predicament? I telephone him. He is so quick to understand everything...To have someone who can clarify situations for one is very rare. I am impatient to see him and try to unburden myself on him.

Betsy Bloomingdale[1] sends me roses from her garden. They are enormous, stout, like gaunt artificial roses. The leaves are polished and wonderful. They are the biggest one could find anywhere. They are Hollywood roses and they have no scent. And they last only a day.

San Francisco   *April 1973*

So much that has been eventful in my life has happened here. Now after 12 years of friendship with Kin the tour brings me within range of him, albeit for only a short glimpse. But he comforted me with his opinions that I am worrying unnecessarily, that the qualms I had been feeling on this trip were unfounded, or at any rate greatly exaggerated by the pinpointing of the Garbo story in my book. 'You couldn't leave out such an important event in your life from your diaries, which are your life's work, and after all she cannot expect to be the private person she would wish to be if she has made her career in films.'

Kin would never say anything that he would not mean just to assuage my pangs and anxieties. He has such a quick clear brain, it is always like being with some kind of diviner of truths when he is around. In spite of the noise and bad food in the San Francisco restaurant, we had a pleasant evening together before a 5.30 a.m. call that was to prepare me for a TV appearance, sandwiched in between advertisements, Martha Mitchell and the Watergate Scandal.[2]

---

[1] Mrs Alfred Bloomingdale, rich socialite and friend of Nancy Reagan.
[2] Martha Mitchell (1918–75), garrulous wife of Senator John Mitchell, who took to

Had a 5.30 a.m. call in order to get to a TV station. Who can *look* at TV at that hour? People telephone in and ask questions. One man: 'Why, since you tell us of Miss Garbo's sensitivity towards self-exposure, have you devoted 2/3 of your book to her?' A difficult one to get out of. I'm wondering if I couldn't become a politician. In NY on a similar programme, some woman telephoned: 'Didn't you once write that the Jewish people were fossils?' It was lucky that I could deny that, but how long people's memories are. I'd thought that after nearly fifty years...[1]

Back in NY, the loneliness and anxiety of the early wakenings are forgotten. It seems as if the gruelling trip had never been. I'm convinced it cannot have sold any books and yet the country is so vast.

I had a most dreamlike, extraordinary macabre experience in one of the aeroplanes during the past week. Strapped in my seat ready for take-off, I found that the woman in white next to me was exactly like Garbo. I could only see the tip of her nose protruding from her long bobbed hair, but she was in all respects like a Garbo of 30 years ago. Her clothes, natural, woven, homespun, beautiful sandals, and her sunburnt hands were exactly like Garbo's. I could not imagine how two people could be so alike. The hair had no grey in it and was not dyed, so I knew it was not Greta, but what was even more extraordinary was that this woman exuded the same ambiguous sex attraction – half boy/half woman – that Greta had when I first met her.

It was quite alarming and I wondered if my hallucination would continue when suddenly the steward asked if the woman next to me would move so that a man and his son could sit together. The woman proved to be Scandinavian, her face unlike my love's, but the aura had been extremely disturbing.

On arrival in NY, Pat O'H.[2] tells me he had seen Garbo in an Italian grocery store this morning. She had two bags in which she put the vegetables she was buying. She wore dark glasses but was full of smiles and everyone very solicitous of her though respectful of her wish for anonymity. The proprietor spoke Italian to P. as he pointed out *la donna*

calling the press during the Watergate scandal, hoping to clear her husband's name, but succeeding in incriminating him.

[1] In 1938, Cecil was fired from *Vogue*, when a newspaper column picked up some minute writing that he had inserted into a drawing, which contained anti-Semitic material. He did not work for a year and a half. From time to time, he was dropped from designing a stage or screen production, when someone recalled the incident. 'He was punished,' said Irene Selznick, one of those attacked in the drawings.

[2] Patrick O'Higgins (d.1980), a bachelor friend, who worked for Helena Rubinstein. Author of *Madame* (1971).

incognita. Somehow it made me feel a little less guilty to know that she was smiling as she bought her carrots.

Nice exhibition at Sonnabend of my early work. I am quite proud of my beginnings as a photographer. To the young generation I have become an old master.

Easter Sunday   *22 April 1973*

Mrs Cornelius Vanderbilt in a Queen Mary flowered toque, used to be photographed at church parade. Now, after the Easter Sunday service, Fifth Avenue is blocked off to become a jostling mass of humanity garbed in the most incredible fancy dress. Negroes are the most preponderant but they are put in the shade by the drag queens who appear in crinolines with vast paper hats, or with sunshades and paradise feathers. Another sign of the deterioration of taste and standards. The few respectable people look like dodos.

Broadchalke   *Early summer 1973*

I am in a state of ecstasy. The spring beauty of pale green, the trails of narcissi and the first blossoms are at their best. We are blessed with continual sunshine. Nothing in the world could be more beautiful. It is everything I've been dreaming of while in those dreary American hotels.

Dicky Buckle came to dinner and ruined the evening. He can be so delightful, funny, witty, brilliantly informed and good company. I have pity for him as he's very unhappy at not being the success he ought to be, and try to be kind. Sometimes it's difficult because he is jealous of me, of my garden and the improvements. He longs to spend money on his 'hovel' but he is never solvent.

I arranged that Billy [Henderson] and Frank [Tait] should bring him to dinner. They arrived at his cottage at the appointed time to find Dicky entertaining the Jimmy [Sterns]. He made no move to dislodge them and when they went, Billy said he must telephone to tell me they'd be late. 'No, don't do that. I can't bear people who have servants, and you know you have to be on time for the cook.' Billy said it was only polite to warn a host of impending lateness, whereupon Dicky went upstairs to dress.

Froideur in the car coming here. Froideur from me knowing Dicky was the culprit. Instead of the evening being the success it would have been without him, he was one big personality too many. He held forth with turkey-cock face and changed subjects in midstream. Everyone exasperated, determined that he should not hog the show. Electric atmosphere, contradictions, discussion too felt for comfort. My evening was a failure. I hated it. No one enjoyed it and as Dicky left, I heard him say, 'With all this paving I feel as if we're crossing a courtyard of the Vatican.' A big failure of an evening. My 'kindness' not to be encouraged.

Stephen Tennant – an extraordinary recovery. After being almost blind for 2 years, has had 2 cataract operations so that now he can see properly. His spirits are high, he diets on melons, is now a possible shape and has bought new clothes. His brain is incredibly flexible. He remembers everything he wishes. He quotes passages of prose and poetry, he is witty. He talked of the disadvantage of brittle nails: 'Oh! I'm now always breaking a nail, and of course that means immediately breaking social engagements.' He has a poetical side and talked of the 'lazy glitter of sun on a stream'.

24 May 1973

How lucky I am to have this beautiful house. It is a day of sun, blue sky, long shadows on the lawn, daisies, buds everywhere, and my garden is at its best, the beginning of summer. The lilac is out, the roses beginning, and I spent much of an afternoon picking flowers to put around the house in honour of my guests. All this beauty strikes me afresh because Enid Bagnold is here for the first time and I am seeing what she sees.

We had a terrible quarrel. I thought I'd never make it up with her, but after a dozen years, it was agreeable to hand her the olive branch, and now I am enjoying her pleasure at the beauty of the countryside and the comforts of my home. And when Diana [Cooper] arrived, I realised how lovely it was to have her here again, how she embellishes the scene and even at 80 is so full of youthful enthusiasm.

A packed week in London. Headaches drove me to abandon my book a day earlier and go up for the garden Chelsea Show. Crowds thinner. I bought yellow delphiniums and striped tulips. On arrival at Pelham, was treated to a scene of appalling rage and bile, spleen and jealousy from Ray. He has a great jealousy of Eileen and now this outburst was caused by her trying to save me money. The situation hung over me. Eileen equally upset, almost said that it was either a question of Ray or her. I got 2 more headaches.

Noël's Memorial Service called a Thanksgiving. Capacity filled St Martin-in-the-Fields. No question. John Gielgud reading a beautiful Shakespearean sonnet was the best, John Betjeman in second gear, but

Olivier quite embarrassingly bad, telling a long story about a French film which had *no* bearing on Noël, and reading an embarrassing dirty schoolboy poem about Auntie Jessie farting in the Underground. What a coarse creature he is!

All the old girls were there, Phyllis Monckman looked like a blush rose, after years of pain. She is a good old girl.

A Wrightsman evening. All went well. Ray gave us a splendid little dinner before Bennett (Alan) *Habeas Corpus*.[1] In spite of bad tickets the entertainment was witty, contemporary, in fact of the minute, for so much of it seemed to be about Tony Lambton,[2] who has been photographed having sex with call girls, and his career wrecked, and a scandal to drive Watergate off the headlines. Poor Bindie.[3] Poor Tony. He's too intelligent to have this happen. But it shows on what thin ice we all skate.

A dreaded talk with Ray before leaving for the Friday early morning train. I had to look away from him as I delivered the speech about everyone working in harmony together. Such a situation as existed could not go on. If it came to a choice between him and Eileen, it was obvious who would have to go. Ray looked very white. When I told him there must be no more reports like this, let's forget it and start again with a two-quid rise, he shook my hand.

Eileen reminded me of the day that the young Duchess of Kent, Kate Worsley, married in Yorkshire. The Queen and all the Royal Family were on the lawns with the thousand wedding guests and when Eileen went into a library to telephone the press about my photographs, she discovered that Father Worsley[4] had sneaked off to watch the cricket at Lords on the television.

Stas Radziwill   *June 1973*

Stas Radziwill[5] sits silent throughout dinner party in S. of France. Mrs Kellock, rich American, turns to Stas and says, 'Do you realise you have not addressed one word to me the whole evening?' Stas replies, 'When I sit next to women like you, my best friend is potato.'

---

[1] *Habeas Corpus*, opened at the Lyric on 10 May and starred Alec Guinness.
[2] Viscount Lambton (b.1922). Parliamentary Under-Secretary for Defence (RAF) 1970–3. Renounced the Earldom of Durham 1970. Resigned 1973.
[3] Viscountess Lambton, formerly Belinda Blew-Jones. Married 1942.
[4] Sir William Worsley Bt (1890–1973), Lord Lieutenant of North Riding of Yorkshire (1951–65) and father of HRH the Duchess of Kent.
[5] Prince Stanislas Radziwill (1914–76), Polish nobleman.

Jerome Zerbe, photographer, asks Stas if he will give him a lift to country club. Stas: 'Yes, and when we get to the club I *kill* you.'

Meanwhile it is June 16th 1973 and the summer weather is so unbelievably beautiful that I only wish my sense of delight and enjoyment were as great as it used to be. Perhaps after a day or two's rest I will regain my zest. Already I feel less tired and have been out on the dew-coloured lawns. The birds are having a fine time (the pigeons too destructive!) and the doves seem to have made a haunt of the place. We saw a kingfisher down at the water garden and there are chaffinches, yellowhammers and the garden is at its peak.

Just *before* its best Clarissa [Avon] came and had tea under an awning on the terrace and thought she liked the garden best now when you could see the 'shapes' before all the colour. The terrace is a mass of roses and I only trust the summer will continue till next weekend when the garden is 'open'.

Lunched with Sybil Cholmondeley for the Queen Mother. The Graftons[1], Betty Salisbury (very mean and tiresome, wanting me to advise her about a *cheap* camera to give to her grandchild[2] on his 21st birthday. 'But Betty, you can't give him an Instamatic. You can't give him less than 50 quids' worth!' – Betty giggling nervously). Also present Raymond M [Mortimer]. (Why oh *WHY* did this dear nice man keep one hand in his pocket as he bowed to HM?) We don't want *any* evidence that that swine, Evelyn Waugh, was right in accusing Raymond of being second-rate.[3])

Also present Arnold Goodman, who turned to me and said, 'I heard someone saying they didn't get on well with you.' I got free advice as to whether Cukor had libelled me by saying on TV that I had pickpocketed him, that I had tried to strangle him and that I was a forger.[4] Arnold said it was said as a joke, that I might get the BBC to give me a thousand pounds and an apology, but that I'd better go off and make a thousand elsewhere. It would be only a boring horridly drawn-out bore.

At first Ali Forbes and a stranger rang up in a state of shock saying they thought it was disgraceful, not at all a joke, that I could claim great damages, but after a lot of wasted time I fear I will get nowhere. Arnold was very perspicacious, saying he thought Cukor resented having a

---

[1] The eleventh Duke (b.1919) and Duchess of Grafton, close friends of the Queen Mother. The Duchess was Mistress of the Robes to the Queen from 1967.
[2] Lord Valentine Cecil was born on 13 May 1952.
[3] Evelyn Waugh's diaries were being serialised in the *Observer*. Waugh quoted Mortimer saying to someone he admired, 'If I caught a cold from you, I'd treasure it.'
[4] George Cukor made some ill-thought and exaggerated references to Cecil on a television programme, and Cecil consulted his lawyer.

designer that got all the notices, that it had never happened to him before, that he was a jealous man.

The Queen Mother in blue, a hat a solid mountain of forget-me-nots, the sort of things that used to be put on children's hats, is very quick off the mark for a joke. Her brain is very clear and à propos of the Nigerian State Visit,[1] I said, 'Surely these black visits were becoming somewhat ridiculous and unnecessary. Next we would be entertaining Amin.'

Queen Elizabeth was vastly amused when I suggested they'd like nothing better than to be given an afternoon 'off' for shoplifting at Harrods.

Summer 1973

The [Lambton] scandal has almost replaced the Watergate muck-raking from the front pages and it is impossible to get any society friends on the telephone. They are gossiping as never since the Profumo case.

Bindie is able to laugh. She laughs at some of the letters from irate clergymen and patronizing people like Lord Scarbrough[2] who write that Tony's brilliant TV talk [with the political interviewer, Robin Day] somewhat mitigated for his having plunged the name of the British aristocracy into the mire.

June 1973

Profumo[3] appeared at the Coward Memorial Service. He was a changed man and his face, from having been aquiline and brilliant, is sagged and baggy and half asleep. Poor man.

25 June 1973

A ball galvanised the neighbourhood. House full everywhere, including mine. (Eileen, Christopher Gibbs, Victoria York[e][4]) and the garden

---

[1] President Gowon paid a State Visit to Britain 11–15 June 1973. Later, after being overthrown, he studied in Britain.
[2] Eleventh Earl of Scarbrough KG (1896–1969), Governor of Bombay 1937–43, Lord Chamberlain 1952–63.
[3] John Profumo (b.1915), Secretary of State for War 1960–3. Resigned as a result of an affair with Christine Keeler.
[4] Christopher Gibbs (b.1938), wild youth of the sixties, antique dealer and adviser to the Rolling Stones and Paul Getty, who matured into a respected establishment figure; and Lady Victoria Yorke (b.1947), interior decorator.

open for the nurses. This the high point of the garden season. A marvellous spell of sunshine was shattered by the much needed rain. But it rained for too long, and would it stop and dry up in time? It did, a marvellous day, Smallpeice grinning from ear to ear, his years and fatigue forgotten. A great crowd and they adored the garden for it is now very beautiful. Alan Tagg who has helped so much said it reached a new peak, and the scent alone was worth the 10 pence admission. The terrace a mass of damask roses, great fronds all smelling divinely, and the knot garden lavender was just coming out, the syringa (philadelphus) and cherry vying with one another in clouds of scent and then the pastry garden at its best, one mass of white and pink sweetly scented balloons. It was a day for white suit and children almost naked, and old people, and everyone was forgetful of their troubles.

This day out of time was a busy one for us at the house. A relay of guests and it was such a joy that the younger generation so enormously appreciated Ina Claire[1] and that her old buddy, Michael Duff, came over from Wilton to greet her.

Ina looked trim and spare and pretty, and she won all hearts by her frankness. 'Someone told me the other day that I must have a lovely present for Katherine Cornell[2] as it was her 80th birthday!'

'But it can't be. She can't be that age!'

'Oh yes, she was born in 1893.'

'Good God, so was I!'

Ina clapped her had to her forehead. She is the youngest, most effortless 80 I've ever known (and there are some amazingly young ones about, D [Diana] Cooper included). It is marvellous to see someone who was a great stage star and probably America's best ever comedienne being neither spoilt nor theatrical. She is *dans le vrai* and absolutely on the level. She holds people up if they exaggerate or miss the point by even a little. She is fair, and square. She had on her mind the fact that there were few people today who remembered her.

'Perhaps I underplayed. Perhaps that's why they remember the Lunts and I'm forgotten, except for the 5 movies I appeared in and I was never any good at movies. In fact I had to be in a play for 6 weeks before I really got into the part. But I never appeared in a Noël Coward play. I didn't like them. They wouldn't have been right for me. I needed something with a little more depth.'

---

[1] Ina Claire (1892–1985), silent film star, who appeared in *Ninotchka* with Garbo. She married a rich lawyer and thus gave up her stage and film career. In later life she lived on Nob Hill in San Francisco – a curious man called Roger, more or less at her permanent beck and call.

[2] Katherine Cornell (1893–1974), actress.

She described how Pauline Potter Rothschild had helped her with the fittings of her clothes at Balenciaga when she was about to appear in the Eliot *Cocktail Party*. 'When the clothes were finished, I asked Pauline what I could give her – not flowers, or books – what could I give to show my gratitude? Pauline said, "You could give me that Louis XVI Cabinet we found in Paris and you now have in San Francisco."'

(Ina gave it.)

'It cost an *enormous* sum of money!'

But Pauline, says Ina, is always asking for great presents. She would ask for a house. Yes, she got several houses.

Prompted by me, Ina told of how Vincent Astor[1] at the time she was appearing in *The Quaker Girl* in NY asked her to marry him. The romance had been a very youthful affair, he perhaps thinking that a young actress would teach him the facts of life, but she, not having had any experience, was as naïve as he. In any case, Ina said, 'No, I have my career to think of. If we married and it didn't work out, you could marry again. You're very rich, but I couldn't go back to the stage.

'He used to come and see me in the flat that my mother and I had, way up on 100th Street. It was a terrible place, but we were so proud to have got out of lodging houses, and it was there that Vincent heard of the sinking of the *Lusitania*. He knew his parents were on board and he kept telephoning for news, and then he decided to telephone to someone very high up in Washington and he was told the news was bad, that almost certainly his parents were drowned. And they were.'

And Vincent became the head of the family and never saw Ina again. 'In fact,' Ina laughed, 'he never even paid for the long-distance telephone call.'

David Herbert rushed over from a Wilton ceremony to 'remember' Sydney [Pembroke]. Going round the garden with me, said about P. Coats,[2] 'And he's such a snob, an unconscionable snob. And it's so odd he should be for so long. It is becoming interesting because there are so few snobs, now that it's unfashionable. They're becoming a dying race. There's him, there's Betty Salisbury, and the Crawleys.[3] It would be worthwhile making a study of them.'

Later in the day Cyril Connolly thought this quite untrue, that the South of England bred a particularly English form of snobbery and, if the

---

[1] Vincent Astor (1891–1959), American real estate tycoon.
[2] Peter Coats (1910–90), widely known as 'Pettycoats', he was a garden designer and wrote a column for *Homes and Gardens*. Had run Viceroy's Lodge for Lord Wavell and was the long-time boyfriend of the diarist and MP 'Chips' Channon. An intensely social man.
[3] Aidan Crawley (1908–93) MP and his wife, who wrote biographies under the name Virginia Cowles (1912–83).

young did not have these inclinations, they now acquired them later on. That snobbery was induced by the insecurity of one's parents, of oneself, and that only with strong applications of 'Peers Poultices' did the disease die out.

Cyril, at dinner with the Hobsons,[1] was angelic. He looks really quite pretty now he's so thin and healthy, and he was a martyr of patience, for Deidre [Connolly] interrupted and talked across him each time he started on some flight of literary fancy. He can be wonderfully good company and tonight his performance was splendid.

Talking of wits, how Coward went back to Wilde, Wilde to Rochester and all had this reversal of logic and stand-off attitude that made their jokes. I suggested that wit was always something said from a pedestal and quoted Leonora Corbett[2] ('Say it with Sèvres' – at an upturned wine-glass), and Noël having this high flight even when of lowly origins. Yet the cockney defies me with his quick wit.

Cyril liked Coward very much as the years advanced, though he was horrible about him in his early stages. Noël at a reconciliation trapped Cyril into writing in one of his own books: 'To N. C. whose writings are better than anything in this work'! Cyril despised most of Noël's plays, did a very funny imitation of Coward – Mountbatten and the cowardly sailor (who of course had to die) in *In Which We Serve*. But he thought Noël's quickness of wit his greatest asset, and Cyril would have loved to have made the joke à propos of Ian Fleming's house in Jamaica (which was always full of hypochondriac illness): 'It should not be called Golden Eye, but Golden Eyes, Nose and Throat.'

Much discussion about E. Waugh's diaries, which C. called 'a fart from the grave'. C. always under the misapprehension that E. liked him, challenged E.'s agent, saying he would give her £50 for any favourable allusion to him among his whole life's diary. She could only find unpleasant ones. Deidre squawked, 'Oh yes, you remember you nearly had a nervous breakdown when you first read what Evelyn wrote about you?' Cyril said that E. was so hated by the men in his battalion that a guard had to be put on his tent at night, just in case . . .

Cyril came up with a lovely suggestion for the title of my big work on photography – *The Ghost in the Machine*. This fits.

Each summer Kitty Miller, rich, worldly and ruthless, gives a five thousand pound party at the Savoy. She is ruthless in discarding old friends and is expert as a brilliant proprietor of a brothel might be in arranging

---

[1] Anthony Hobson (b.1921), Head of Book Department at Sotheby's, and his wife Tanya (1929–88).
[2] Leonora Corbett (1907–60), theatrical director.

people who pass her test to appear in their best clothes and hairdo. The result is that she gets the cream of café society. This year was one of her best efforts. She even got the Duke of Kent.[1] But maybe I enjoyed it because, having slept so long in the country, I am not feeling tired.

Also I was fortunate in being able to avoid all the leech-like widows who are apt of latch on. Also I was fortunate in sitting next to Liza Maugham Glendevon,[2] who gave me, in her unaccustomed tipsiness, a detailed account of her visit with John to Windsor Castle for Ascot week. Naturally she had adored it, in spite of the other guests being dull and very young. There'd been wonderful tours of the castle, and in the evening they had had Menuhin or even Joyce Grenfell,[3] and a marvellous traditional banquet.[4] But fascinating was Liza's description of the Snowdons... After dinner on the first night, Princess Margaret suggested games. 'No,' said the Queen. Princess Margaret's lower lip shot out, and the party went for an hour-and-a-half, marvellous moonlit walk around the castle, the pie crusts most romantic and beautiful.

Nancy has made a deal and bought Baba's car. It has been standing in my Pelham Street garage for 6 months. When the car was delivered Nancy, full of emotion, broke down when she found in it Baba's headscarf and shopping list, and in the boot, her very small green gum boots.

Nancy Mitford died in Paris, after a long illness, on 30 June 1973.

Nancy Mitford has been spared at last. For five years she has been in intermittent torture. The French doctors gave her up, could not discover where the cancer lay, the young men at the Nuffield in Portman Square located the disease in the spine and it responded to treatment, but broke out elsewhere, all over, in fact, and poor Nancy, shriller as well as swollen, went back to Versailles to die. Even so it took a long time. Now she is out of her agony and one feels grateful that my sister Baba's suffering was comparatively short.

Poor Nancy Mit. She was so plucky and gay, but I don't think she had a happy life. As a girl she was without sex appeal. She was unrequited in

---

[1] HRH the Duke of Kent (b.1935), cousin of the Queen.
[2] Liza Maugham (1915–1998), daughter of Somerset Maugham. Married Lord John Hope, later Lord Glendevon. She had known Cecil since she was a little girl in New York in 1928.
[3] Yehudi Menuhin (1916–1999) had used the state rooms at Windsor for the Windsor Festival, which he directed between 1969 and 1973. This was his way of saying thank you. Joyce Grenfell (1910–79), comedienne, appeared at the Festival in 1971.
[4] The Waterloo Banquet in the Waterloo Chamber, when the Duke of Wellington presents his annual pennant as rent for Stratfield Saye.

her love for Gaston Palewski and had to rely on her writing for success. She was very conscious of her fame (in the hospital she said, 'It would be a feather in these boys' caps if they found a cure for me, for I'm very well known, you know!'). She laughed readily, chuckled, gurgled, was a bit governessy in personality (the dry lips, the tiny mouth) and I could never trust her not to sacrifice one for a joke (beastly of her to laugh at Duff [Cooper] who had been so hospitable, calling his *Operation Heartbreak* 'Operation Sickmake'). But she was witty and one laughed a lot in her company. It is awful that the ranks are closing in. But genuinely I cannot *really* admit that my heart went out to hers, but then her heart was a very peculiar one, and not at all like other people's.

Old Vic

God, I am prejudiced against Lord Olivier. He can't do right by me and he's made yet another howler. As head of the National Theatre he is responsible for such a bad production of *The Cherry Orchard* that for once I was not moved by what must be my favourite play. I have seen it at least 14 different times, and always came away with a glow, this time only with anger in my heart that anyone should have allowed an American to play Madame Ranevskaya in an English production. Constance Cummings may be alright in *Long Day's Journey*, [O'Neill] that most boresome play, but why, for God's sake, *pretend* she could be this lazy, lovely, silly lady? She has no style, no class, as Dr Burroughs would say. Her gestures are hideous, gauche, her mouth is never at peace. She has a boxer's chin and heavy, ugly hands.

The production is a disgrace. The governess is given a 'glamorous' make-up and her tricks made into a major feature; Quilley,[1] as the Virginian, appeared aristocratic, 22 'misfortunes' (calamities now much too butch and lively to be clumsy, the maid Dryaska flat and grimacing and Anya mandible Vanya amateur; only Michael Hordern,[2] a lovely actor, was good as the brother). But worst of all the last scene, of being left alone, was played to a revolving change of scene.

I go to the theatre so seldom nowadays, it is awful to have one's treats destroyed. I hoped for a lot of this for Alan [Tagg] had done the décor – even this a disappointment. Luckily I can enthuse about my two visits to see *Habeas Corpus*. Alan Bennett[3] has real wit and literary style. This is his funniest, a variation on Feydeau. It is full of glorious jokes and impeccably acted throughout. Even Alec Guinness seems to have got rid of his

---

[1] Dennis Quilley (b.1927), all-round actor, with good voice.
[2] Sir Michael Hordern (1911–95), actor, best remembered for 'bumbling' roles.
[3] Alan Bennett (b.1934), originally *Beyond the Fringe*, later dramatist and actor.

mannerisms and lets his teeth go without pursing them. A delight. How I would like to write in this vein.

Stephen Tennant has made a great comeback. His eyes and teeth have gone. He can hardly waddle along, he is so fat, his hair, white going to beetroot, is shoulder-blade length, yet his mind is as clear as ever it was and he is quite brilliant at times.

We have been treated to some splendid repeat performances about Queen Elizabeth, Willa Cather and Sarah Bernhardt, and some really boring repetitions on Martha Eggerth and partner, Jan Kiepura (and yet stylised curls, face lifted so smoothly, but in a deep resonant voice, he has been singing at the top of his lungs, reciting poems of Anna de Noailles and talking brilliantly of the malice of Lytton Strachey).

Of Anna de N. [Noailles] he described her in bed with her rope of black cobra hair, banks of flowers and her misery of love unrequited. When Jean Cocteau asked her if she believed in God, she chased him down a corridor saying, 'If he existed, I would have been the first to know!'

He described, as a boy of 11, seeing the staggering beauty of Gladys Cooper, her doe eyes and heart-shaped face, and yet she sat on a chair like an ordinary woman and spoke in a clattering voice. He has great love of nature, birds, of insects and flowers, and makes the garden alive.

Patrick Procktor ran into Stephen in the Salisbury art shop and begged him to come to the opening of his exhibition. In the middle of a purchase he said to the owner of the shop, 'I'm being kidnapped!' He sat in the middle of the gallery in TV arc lights and would not be moved, said Patrick's pictures were amusing but didn't think he knew about green. Dicky B. recoiled from the effigy. The audience laughed. Someone said they liked the curtain colour of his suit. Stephen, exiting, said, 'I've been paid a compliment. At my age, a compliment!' and, turning to Patrick said, 'Thank you for kidnapping me.'

Reddish   24 August 1973

Have been here for two weeks on end, and now the summer is drawing to a close. (Surely we will have some more hot weather. There is an autumnal look to everything, the dew is thick. Most of the summer garden flowers are over and it seems they have died so quickly this year. Is that another sign of growing older?)

Over too is the Festival. Considering how mismanaged it was in many ways, it has been a success. From a musical point of view the standard was very high. Kirkpatrick gave three harpsichord concerts and Handel's

Alexander's Feast in the cathedral was a glorious event. There was perhaps too much running around for me to do without being responsible, but we managed, without rows, to compete with the last-minute hitches and disappointments (Princess Alexandra was stricken and unable to leave her bed), and plans are ahead for another Festival next year.

Another milestone is that I've finished the bulk of my photograph history book. The relief is wonderful. It has kept me to the grind for over seven months and that is too long for such a book. At one point it became a chore, but one had to bang on. Now I'm delivering it into other hands.

I have also remade my will. Since Baba and so many people mentioned in the former one are dead, it is necessary to alter it. But the sad realisation is that there are so few people whom I feel I can make happy by leaving them anything of consequence. It seems that Nancy is likely to fall heir to my riches and, apart from Eileen, there are few who I feel really warrant more than a pleasant surprise.

If I were to leave Kin a large amount, it would mean little to him. It makes me realise the unimportance of wordly possessions, and perhaps mistakenly makes me feel that it is silly to bother about economies. All these 'terminations' put me in a curious mood, the sad mood that I always feel at the beginning of the summer holidays, when I know by my return the long autumn and winter will be upon us. However, I feel no longer under pressure and this seems to make my head feel clearer.

One summer I let this house to the Americans, Mr and Mrs Carey. After 7 years, Mrs Carey telephoned to ask if she could come down and look around. So I invited to lunch Mrs C. (I discovered Mr C. had meanwhile 'passed on'), her nephew and niece and Alys [Countess of] Essex, who became a friend. Alys is in such a frightful state of mind that Mary P [Pembroke] volunteered to bring her and take her away.

The lunch was an essay in the macabre. The nephew turned out to be a ghoul, Mrs C. , perhaps because deaf, won't try to listen to anybody. Her voice trails off and is inaudible, and Alys, making a stab at helping on the conversation, repeats herself all the time. It became a farcical tragedy when Alys became a sort of Gertrude Stein and kept asking, 'Is Zia [Wernher] still alive? They used to be so kind. They took me to Newmarket.' Enough 'kindnesses' for the moment. Let's have some young ones around.

Marlene Dietrich[1]

The TV gave a repeat of Marlene's successful performance staged at Drury Lane. It showed the best that TV can do – the quality of the photography was extraordinarily exact and one saw more and heard more truly than if one had been a part of the wildly enthusiastic audience (dead Binkie Beaumont seen applauding frantically – a rather macabre and unexpected glimpse, but he looked young and his enthusiasm gave him a beatific expression!). As for Marlene, aged 70 (actresses are always said to be older than they are), she was quite a remarkable piece of artifice.

Somehow she has evolved an agelessness. The camera picked up aged hands, a lined neck, and the surgeon had not been able to cut away some little folds that formed at the corners of the mouth. He had however sewn up the mouth to be so tight and small that her days of laughing are over. She cannot stretch the lips more than a very short space so that none of the old folds are visible. The teeth are no longer intact and the good forehead, the deep-set eyelids are useful attributes, and she does the rest. The 'make-up' with too much eyelash so that the rather hard pupil of the eye is never seen, is perhaps too exaggerated, but it is a wonderful alibi, and the huge canary-yellow wig and the colour chosen to cover her skin and the dress is quite triumphant.

Not much of a never musical voice is left, but her showmanship is intact. She has become a sort of mechanical doll – a life-size mannequin. The doll can show surprise, it can walk, it can swish into place the train of its white fur coat. The audience applauds each movement – each gesture – the doll smiles incredulously: 'Can it really be for me that you applaud?' Again a very simple gesture, maybe the hands flap, and again the applause, and not just from old people who remembered her tawdry films but the young find her sexy, she is louche and not averse to giving a slight wink. Yet somehow avoids ugly antics. Marlene is certainly a great star, not without talent, but with a genius for believing in her self-fabricated beauty, for knowing that she is the most alluring fantastic idol, an out-of-this-world goddess, or mythological animal, a sacred unicorn. Her success is out of all proportion, and yet it is entirely due to her perseverance that she is not just an old discarded film star.

She has created another career that has lasted forty years or more, and with so little. Her songs are rubbishy, not old-fashioned, but like herself, of another sphere. She magnetises her audience as she has mesmerised

---

[1] Marlene Dietrich (1901–92), film star and diseuse, icon of the twentieth century. See also the Introduction, pp.8–9.

herself into making them believe in her as being the great phenomenon that she is. She is Cocteau's sacred monster in person.

Even for a hardened expert like myself it was impossible to find the chink in her armour. All the danger spots were disguised. Her dress, her figure, her limbs, all made to appear like those of the youngest. When one thinks of this old doll rattling on and coining in the money, and then when one thinks of Greta, lined, grey, unhappy, never doing anything to stave off boredom, one wonders that they are of the same stuff. I sat enraptured and not a bit critical as I had imagined. The old trooper never changes her tricks because she knows they work, and because she invented those tricks she must be given credit for being a virtuoso in the art of legerdemain.

'You know me,' Marlene is fond of saying. You don't. Nobody does – because she's a real phoney. She's a liar, an egomaniac, a bore, but she has her points. She's never late, she's generous and she's, as a performer, on a grand scale in a period of pygmies.

After a lapse of 25 years, I have heard from that little monster, Charlie James.[1] He is up to his old tricks of abuse. A short note arrived telling me that a long letter, part of which I won't like, was on its way. It has arrived. Rather than be upset while I am gardening (it is then one remembers the horrors), I have given it to another mutual friend, Mary Hutchinson, who will tell me what she thinks about facing up to its venom. Such a pity he is so difficult because I would like to like him and feel he is a genius manqué. When I saw in Houston the coloured walls and furniture he'd designed, my heart went out to him.

The Watergate scandal goes on from bad to worse. It doesn't need this sort of skulduggery to make me anti-American. (How is it I admire and love Kin so much?) But it certainly exaggerates it, the lying, the devilish wickedness makes me despair that a nation can be so rotten to the core and my guess is that Nixon, though despised and ignored, will continue in power and be just as crassly self-satisfied as ever.

Mary Hutch [Hutchinson] and Felix H. [Harbord] and I looked at Julian Jebb's TV programme on Virginia Woolf, one of the best of its sort I've ever seen. It was surprising to see Raymond [Mortimer] coming out about V. W. fantasising about his grand social life, non-existent, but the sort of thing V. W. would in a way have liked, how she made up her versions of what a person's life was like and got annoyed if they said it

---

[1] Charles James (1906–78), brilliant dress designer, with a character flawed like that of Francis Rose, or Stephen Tennant.

wasn't in fact like that. Dadie Rylands was excellent, so articulate, true and funny and it was altogether a real picture that came across.

Mary said V. W. was not a nice person, was very malicious, but *did* think she was a genius. The parties were Greek or Roman, in an antidote to the Victorian prudery, and very outspoken. But no one drank or ate much, most didn't bother about food or drink when they were young. Mary, connected to almost all the Bloomsburys, has been badgered to write her memoirs but even refuses to let her letters be published in her lifetime.

It is now the holiday time, so lovely to be at home in one's own setting rather than battling with travel and other people's ugly houses.

Towards the end of August 1973, Cecil went to stay with Diana Phipps at the Villa Abruzzi in Esté, Padua, taking Sam Green with him. Heading towards his seventieth birthday, Cecil examined himself – thinning hair, paunch, paleness of eye, and noticed that young people offered to fetch things for him and asked if he was tired. Lady Diana Cooper had been there for ten days. At first she was 'calm, dignified, beautiful', but when the other guests left, she had 'recourse to the vodka.'

Diana Cooper – Esté   *August 1973*

Sam Green said I looked at her critically, appalled but without pity. This is not true, yet perhaps it is true to say that my horror and revulsion were even stronger. For Diana to blur her words and to look with bleary unseeing eyes, to stagger, to wave her arms in grotesque gestures, was something that one would rather forget. And in this state, the decline in beauty and strength had become much greater than it was a year ago. She could hardly stand without lilting to the left. Her legs were on almost back to front, her feet in terrible great black clogs, swollen and useless.

The 'Last Attachment'[1] was mercilessly attack[ed]. Diana was easily offended, easily shocked with a jump (she would jump out of her skin if one walked in on her without warning) – this all as a result of the strong liquor stimulus in her system.

At a mountain bistro one night, she was sitting next to Sam, who was unable to put food in his mouth, for so sheer was his concentration on this remarkable woman he had met for the first time. (She turned and spluttered about Sam, 'Marvellous man.') We were all very sad, and I said

---

[1] Nigel Ryan (b.1929), Editor and Chief Executive, Independent Television News 1971–77.

that, although she had the constitution of a tank, the end was in sight and I for one would have lost one of the great figures of my life.

But next morning Diana, with her companion, was to drive right down to the Hofs at Zell (they had been awaiting her for two days). The departure was to be at ten o'clock. She looked startled, appalled as I bade her good morning. 'I'm an hour out,' she said in shock. Then she discovered the loss of her red bag, in which she puts all her oddments. The Last Attachment *must* go to the hospital where she had left it yesterday (she had made a date with a dentist but instead went to the hospital for the strongest laxative they have).

I steered away from the room until with my new book of Diaries under her arm, she emerged. She had been terribly touched reading her letter to me about Duff's death, but imagined people would ask why she had allowed it to be published. 'Anne will understand. Pam won't.' But she didn't mind what people thought. She liked the bit she'd read about me and my mother.

Diana was dressed in dark blue and white, a white muslin collar and she wore the big white felt hat she bought for the Duff Cooper prize-giving to Quentin Bell for his *Virginia Woolf*. Suddenly she became the great beauty again, alabaster, periwinkle eyes, cool, calm, a great personality. In a mood of calm she made funny gestures, reduced everyone to laughter. She said something fine to each of the guests. To Howard Stern, whom she called 'elevated, a character of Chaucer', she named 'Stranger'. 'Well, goodbye, Stranger,' and her embrace of hostess Diana and her little one was heartfelt, but in the grand Sarah B [Bernhardt] manner. She gave us the bewildered Nun's look of wistful surprise and drove off in a haze of legendary loveliness.

I was so happy. Later I asked Sam what he thought of her. 'Terrific.' He loved her generosity, her warming to people and animals and ideas. He loved her enthusiasm. He was obviously bedazzled for they don't make women like that in his country.

Even for me this had been a revelation, for under these strange conditions, she had shown the freshness of her mind, her appreciation of beauty: 'And to think that the outdoor dining room was built only for occasion!' (the marriage of the owner's daughter), 'And what is a Basilica?' and her quotes from early learning of the poets ('We were never allowed "Pretty [Little] Miss Muffet sat on a tuffet"') and not being timid about 'slurping' the soup, of economising but expecting a grand style in others, a strange mixture of lack of taste in certain friends (perhaps it's just that she has a weakness for the rich), but the highest standards of behaviour and taste. Fair to the most extraordinary pitch of exactness, incapable of telling a lie, always reacting in the truest way, she is a proud and courageous creature. Although a noble, good woman, who may resoundingly exasperate one, but whom one knows to be many cuts above almost anyone else.

Esté

It does one good to heave oneself out of the rut, but I am always sad at leaving my house at the end of the summer. August is the month I love the most in the garden and this year the wrench was particularly strong because of the beauty of the long sunny span. For weeks only one storm and then more sunshine. Why leave? Yet others were having holidays and one couldn't suddenly change all the carefully arranged dates. Again reluctantly, I left behind the memories that go back to schoolday summer holidays when in one's nostrils was the acrid scent of phlox, and it was the time of the new apples and all fruits, plums, and pears and greengages. And one's eyes were wide in wonder of the poetical strangeness of the Japanese anemones, and the butterflies turning the buddleia. I hated to think that all the convolvulus and bluebell and poppy life would be over on my return.

Esté   *August 1973*

A day's trip to Mantua in the great heat knocked me out to such an extent that for several days we remained at the villa, idling. Very 'familiale' and remote from the outer world, it was like a bolt from the blue when George Weidenfeld arrived hot from his latest romance in Venice (TV Evelyn ? Walters ?[1] – tough, intelligent) via Israel and the S. of France, with all the international news and gossip of which we are all completely ignorant.

It seems the pound has gone lower than before, that England is considered as a faded, leisurely, old-fashioned country, as Italy was considered by Henry James, that the Austrian Germans have the strongest currency, that Germany and France are loathing one another, and Germany threatening to continue financial aid and become a separate power like Japan, and George told us that Kissinger[2] was now Foreign Secretary and bets 5–1 that Nixon will survive, and that so clever was his recent press interview in which he said the account of bugging he did was nothing to that

---

[1] Barbara Walters (b.1931), ABC news presenter.
[2] Henry Kissinger (b.1923), Special Adviser to the President of the USA on National Security Affairs.

in the days of his predecessors, that Nixon's unpopularity had turned, and that he would survive to be even a popular president.

He told us of the new horror generation of rich young people, the sons of multimillionaires, who have rubbished the money placed in their care to avoid death duties, who are far worse than their fathers, who at any rate had the distinction of making the fortune. He described their parties in the S. of France, that appalling smile, of the pimps and gigolos at the 'Golden' Ball, graced by Mrs Lasker[1] and her guests all looking like mummies, the 'boos' when some Jews gave a 'Bavarian' Ball near Monte Carlo.

George's vitality, curiosity and intensity in all sorts of worlds is unquenchable. He is very good value and very shrewd but fair. He makes me feel rut-ridden and sluggish. Little wonder that he has swept all before him and from England branches out to have the best of so many worlds.

Arriving at Vicenza – Villa Lambert   August 1973

Sam and I drove from Esté arriving at the above on time. The rewards of travel are sometimes so great that they do compensate for much of the discomfort and anxiety. Sam is of a wonderfully impervious disposition so that unlike me he never worries. But although as usual we set out without maps and only the haziest ideas of how to arrive, the journey soon made Esté slip into the background of memory and suddenly America in its most modern, aesthetic tastes was substituted.

Wild sculptures and paintings and odd decorations greeted us, and a large party assembled to celebrate the 75th birthday of Peggy Guggenheim.[2] God she is ugly, and gauche, and not at all appetising. She can be mean as hell, but she is a serious person and it was quite a dramatic moment when her friend Roloff Beny,[3] the photographer, with white pulpy face and marmoset hair, got up in a purple suit, his neo-decadent face lit by a candle, proposed the toast to my oldest and youngest friend. Peggy almost swooned, so shy and vulnerable is she. The dinner was ruined by the non-presence of two guests, the evening a mess, and luckily the travellers were allowed to slip away to bed.

---

[1] Mary Lasker (1900–94), philanthropist.
[2] Peggy Guggenheim (1898–1979), art collector.
[3] Roloff Beny (1924–84), Canadian artist and photographer.

Venice   *1 September 1973*

Unexpectedly found myself here after an interval of at least 5 years, and there were moments of beauty at sunset and later by artificial light, with the dome of San Salute lit in a greenish brilliance, reflected in the morning water of the current, which alone justified the visit. Venice is a place that has played an extraordinarily important part in my life, and once more memories of forgotten events and people flooded back, and as with the last visit, the effects appeared differently. There is never a monotony in this most evanescent and ever changing masterpiece.

The object of our visit was the Volpi Ball. Perhaps there will never be another one. This was to celebrate the 18th birthday of Olimpia Aldobrandini,[1] given by Lily Volpi's son[2] in the Volpi Palace, the façade of which was hung with crimson velvets of great antiquity and beauty. And inside there were between 700 and 1000 guests, far too many, and the heat unbelievable. But for me the evening was fascinating. So many friends from the past appeared and it was a game to recognise them in their self-made disguises or else the changes made by time. Some who had been very dark had yellow hair.

Tragic to see was Donatella Hercolani,[3] who had been famous for her mysterious beauty, had become a scrag with chipped hair bright yolk-yellow and a nose like a snipe. Lily so short-sighted that she could see no one, and therefore left alone. The usual bulwarks like Marcello,[4] the Fascist, her protruding teeth, like a dirty old comb, now replaced by a modest row of enamel. The Foscari,[5] heavy as a great safe, teetering on wire feet and legs, in a dress that had not enough authority, her trademark a Mozartian bow at the nape of her gold and pepper coiffeur.

On the whole, the Italian women age well, and the men seem to be indestructible. The youth very good-looking and the dresses far grander and [more] ambitious than any one would see in England. All less hippie, more conventional, even embroidered. One could not feel that the Communist party had made much progress when such an evening as this was possible. Emeralds, diamonds, sycophantic, well-trained servants, huge *pièces montées* of lobsters, obelisks of stephanotis and lilies, tuberoses by the ton.

---

[1] Olimpia Aldobrandini, married 1974, Baron David de Rothschild.
[2] Countess Volpi, famed for her balls in Venice. When she ceased to give them, few bothered to visit her.
[3] Donatella Hercolani, Italian jet-setter.
[4] Countess Marcello, friend of Mussolini.
[5] Countess Foscari. The Foscari are a prominent Venetian family.

It was interesting to see the influx of the new stars. Andy Warhol in a silk dinner jacket, Bianca Jagger with a swagger stick, Helmut Berger, very German and Marlene Dietrich-esque, his hair dyed yellow, and the latest girlfriend of David Rothschild[1]. The usual American vermin were reduced to a minimum. Earl Blackwell and Eugenia Sheppard[2] also succeeded in lowering the tone of the evening.

With sharp black Japanese hairdo and a dark blue and red dress, my loyal friend and wonder, Diana Vreeland, who had called about someone to iron her dress, was squashed in the throng and her efforts to be impeccable could not be appreciated; Princess Grace, more made up than usual, really quite pretty and only a slight suggestion of Mr Rittenhouse about her; using ghastly old-fashioned English slang...

Audrey Hepburn[3] greatly admired. She wore pink Givenchy ruffles, her hair in curls. Great animation, but my eagle eye spotted a certain amount of grimacing, which is fast making her into a caricature. She will not be a beautiful old woman, but through her photogenic qualities, a rich one, for she has accumulated a fortune from films. Though she is not likely to leave husband and children to make another, she has not announced her retirement. Her young husband, a doctor,[4] does not get credit for being a serious character, but Audrey, trying frantically to keep up with his younger friends, finds herself having to have a far more social life that I know she really likes. When I asked if her husband enjoyed such an exhausting evening as this, she said, 'Oh yes. It amuses him as a contrast to seeing so many people who are ill.'

It was a hard night's work for me. But it gave me one of the very rare feelings that I had succeeded in making many good friends. They rallied loyally and had not forgotten old times, which had completely escaped my memory, while so occupied with the excitements of my ceaseless work.

The others went off to Venice to watch the Regatta (I, arriving in late evening, saw the best, the return of the boats, in the apricot Canaletto light) and I had the day to myself. It was like a purge.

---

[1] Bianca Jagger (b.1943), then married to Mick Jagger; Baron David de Rothschild (b.1942).
[2] Earl Blackwell (1913–?), and Eugenia Sheppard, founders of Celebrity Service International. Blackwell kept tabs on 100,000 names. Sheppard organised a best-dressed list and was thus known to 'watch the chic by night'.
[3] Audrey Hepburn (1929–93),Cecil dressed her as Eliza Doolittle in the film *My Fair Lady*.
[4] Dr Andrea Dotti (b.1938), psychiatrist and playboy. Married Audrey Hepburn 1969. Divorced 1982.

Valentina Schlee – Venice   *September 1973*

It is a strange experience when wearing dark glasses to see someone one knows a little coming towards one. Will they recognise me? Will one recognise them, or cut and pass on? This morning a tall bore of a woman, who is a friend of Lilia's and works at Dior, hove into sight. Through the dark glasses we stared at one another and then passed on.

Then later who should I see, also dark spectacles, but Valentina Schlee. This was the first time I'd encountered her since the publication of the diaries with so many allusions to the 'Little Man' (her husband) in them.[1] Would she slap my face? Would she give me the cut direct? We passed nearer and nearer. She eyed me coldly. As we passed one another, I, very exaggeratedly, doffed my straw hat.

'Ohh, my Dahlink – Ceesaile. Oh my heavens!'

We kissed, laughed, made banal observations. Was she having a holiday, I asked.

'Are there any holidays any more?' she asked.

Then on leaving my hotel a few hours later, there was a message from the concierge. 'Mrs Schlee wants you to send some vaccine against the cholera, as she cannot get the doctor here to give her an injection.'

Meanwhile the cholera panic spreads, a minor form of *Death in Venice*. It was civilised behaviour on Valentina's part to pretend to ignore my diaries, for it cannot be possible that she has not heard of them.

The summer holiday in Italy came to an abrupt end. Sam and I had packed a great deal of movement and variety into the two weeks since arriving at Esté. In fact, that part of the holiday seemed charming but remote. The chance of the almost unknown lady from Dallas, Evelyn Lambert[2] turned out successful. She was high-powered, art-struck, society of all sorts struck, but warm and human and kind, and only her – to me – artificially cultured voice could be faulted.

Our visit to the very advanced modern arty Villa Lambert was broken by a beneficial jaunt to Florence (Harold Acton in his best Mandarin style; John P. H.,[3] surprisingly smiling), Piero della F., Donatellos, Magdalene, then the Volpi Ball in Venice, the Accademia minus (for repairs), the Carpaccios, and suddenly Sam decided, since I was nervous to get home, to go on impulse to Egypt. Instead, I have one long

---

[1] Cecil did not identify Georges Schlee by name in *The Happy Years*.
[2] Evelyn Lambert, Texan hostess, who took a house on the Veneto.
[3] Sir John Pope-Hennessy, Director of the Victoria and Albert Museum, who spent his last days in Florence.

purgatorial day of travel. I was extravagant enough to give up my free ticket, pay for a new one and the trip from Venice took no longer than for me to write a page of a new entry into a short story and to eat a meal.

Arrival, to do a great afternoon's work feeling fiddle fresh. The news on my desk is not as inviting as generally. Proofs of all sorts had arrived and the evening was spent correcting a lot of stuff from Weidenfeld. It seems the summer weather has been consistent all the time I've been away and it has not broken now. I woke to a great expanse of blue above.

Imagine the joy of waking to a haze heat. One knew it would last for ever. It was so wonderful to feel well and refreshed, and to come back to this enjoyment and to know that for a day or two there would be no interruptions. I was alone to enjoy this rare and delicious treat all by myself.

I went round the garden in my bare feet in the heavy dew. In spite of the heat it looks natural but I am not anything but happy to have this extra present of hot sunshine.

Another delicious day followed. A young neighbour, Peter Lamb, came to be drawn and is as beautiful as a young fawn, though no one would admire him as much as I do, or see that he is beautiful. I read my play, pleased with the 1st act, disappointed with the 2nd, but encouraged and enthusiastic to do a lot of work on it. Then a bit of gardening, a sauna visit, the globules and nodules have increased alarmingly but Margaret thinks she made progress in breaking them down. Then through the evening sunlight of Tippit Wood to Cranborne and David Cecil. (Rachel a late arriver, saying to Hugh, 'What's that?'

'Tonic water, Mother.'

'But we've got some. Oh well, no. Lovely.')

David telling of his dislike of Evelyn Waugh whose loathsome diaries are now coming out in book form, and the lovely day was over. But another one followed at once, or so it seemed, so deep was my sleep.

Again glorious heatwave, haze on the lawn sloping in front of me. A Piero di Cosima of wild life, ring doves, fat pigeons, a long-legged pea pheasant and a fat young rabbit, eating and pecking together. Later, after a great morning's work on my play, I came to the terrace, where at the close of the day, I am now sitting.

The sun gives an apricot yellow glow to everything and the green is still fresh, and the scents are strong, thyme, rosemary, roses, nefrita, verbascum, grass, lizards, hay. The birds are the only thing that makes sounds. No traffic, no aeroplanes, just terrific birdsong and a clop of horses' hoofs as the doctor's daughter rides up the lane at the top of the paddock. The birds at the river's edge are enjoying watching the fish, as did Mrs Eide, when suddenly an orange and turquoise kingfisher alit on a bank near her. It is the time of year I love best, Japanese anemones, phlox, fruit ripening (I cut away some leaves round the peaches to give them a chance), the new trees planted for decoration have become greatly productive. I am on the terrace writing.

The cat Timothy White is asleep on the warm flagstones and a mouse like a toy has skedaddled across the path, unmindful of the sleeping danger. The doves coo – and they remind me of my mother, but I am not sad and although I hate my diaries being in print (I've had to hide the *Sunday Times* from myself today), I feel really more contented and reassured than I have been for years. Perhaps it is the high point. It is certainly a perfect moment.

Cyril's 70th Birthday   September 1973

It was been Cyril's apotheosis. His first book in years, collected reviews, has come out (with my jacket – it gave us all such heartache – *The Evening Colonnade*), and his publishers gave a warming party for it at Brown's Hotel. Fifteen-yr-old Cressida, incredibly precocious, asking people who they were and, if celebrated, photographing them, tottering on high heels, smoking cigarettes. Cyril calm and enjoying the celebrations, writing delightfully witty *dédicaces* for the various friends.

A difficult group. Sybille Bedford, Duncan Grant, (Lord) Robin Maugham, horrid, Iris Murdoch, Jane Howard, horrid (I realised how much I disliked her and her husband). Edna O'Brien, Sonia Orwell,[1] and so many others that if it were not for the great heat of a London heatwave, I might have delayed going to the country where I could only stay till the Tuesday as Cyril was then being fêted with a big lunch by the *Sunday Times*.

Cyril had not been told the <u>venue</u> until the last minute as the car turned into Regent's Park and went into the zoo.[2] The heatwave

---

[1] Sybille Bedford (b.1911), author; Duncan Grant (1885–1978), painter; Viscount Maugham (1916–81), writer; Iris Murdoch (1919–99), novelist; Elizabeth Jane Howard (b.1923), writer, then married to Kingsley Amis, 1965–83; Edna O'Brien (b.1932), writer; and Sonia Orwell (1918–80), widow of George Orwell.

[2] The *Sunday Times* published an account of this party in its *Atticus* column (written by Allan Hall). *Atticus* reported that Connolly celebrated his birthday 'with radiant aplomb'. Other guests included Lady Diana Cooper, Robert Kee, John Lehmann, John Russell, Dilys Powell, and it was presided over by the Deputy Editor of the *Sunday Times*, Harold Evans. J.W Lambert said that 'the hour and a half Cyril passed in the office each week correcting his copy was an eagerly anticipated high point'. At 5 p.m. on the day of the party, the telephone rang in the Literary Editor's office at the *Sunday Times*: 'He had lost his wife and where, he enquired plaintively, had everyone gone? We got him home safely, our Palinurus, wily navigator of life's storms, only briefly and pardonably becalmed.'

continuing, the friends gathered outdoors in the Members' Yard, drinking champagne. John Betjeman with trousers too short walking like a toddler on the sands. He only lacked a bucket and spade. Anthony Powell, Hamish Hamilton,[1] 8 people from *The Times*, Raymond Mortimer, in old age looking beautiful with long, wavy silver hair.

To comfort those of us who are reaching the age of 70, R. said that he had been happier during the last five years (he is 75) than at any other time of his life. He certainly looks contented, calm, serene, unworried. He has no ambitions and his calm shows. He is more beautiful than he has ever been.

Philippe de Rothschild, Ann Fleming, Anthony Hobson and Tanya. I sat next to Deirdre who kept saying breathlessly to Jack Lambert[2] (the host), 'But what a wonderful *menu*! Such a *menu*!' Saddle of lamb, raspberry ice etc.

Deirdre told me how Cyril reads in bed almost all day. He hardly ever goes out and at Eastbourne they see no one. His life is entirely centred round his books. He is about to give up the Book Department at Sotheby's as the Texas world and US slump has knocked the bottom out of his activities. But it seems an interesting, satisfying life. He is without ambition, lazy, acclaimed. He knows he's good and somehow there's enough money to keep going in his own way (which is to buy an occasional object of beauty).

Cyril looked calm, pretty as a celluloid cupid in a bath. Cyril in such spitting-out form that one wondered if he was going here and now to settle old scores. The apparent nervousness, and although he says he has never made a speech, did in fact deliver himself of a spontaneous piece of brilliance, a typical piece of Cyril embroidery, about his growing up, only son, unhappy childhood with ill-assorted parents, how he won a scholarship, went to St Cyprian's, where a younger boy, Beaton – he was only called Beaton and he's sitting over there – taught me about painting, and we ate raspberries together. When the black ones were finished, we ate the green ones.

Then the unhappy only son of ill-assorted parents went on to another school. Here he attained puberty and he admired the shell-like ear of a boy with black hair, Noel Blakiston[3] (shock) – and he's sitting over there. And then I won a scholarship to Eton, and I became friends with K. Clark – and he's sitting over there – and then worked in J. C. Squire's office and

---

[1] Anthony Powell (1905–2001), novelist; Hamish Hamilton (1900–88), publisher.
[2] JW Lambert (1917–1986), Literary Editor of the *Sunday Times*.
[3] Noel Blakiston (1905–84), ran Cambridge Public Record Office 1928–70, Hon Fellow of Eton College 1974. Edited *A Romantic Friendship* (Constable, 1975), the letters he received from Connolly, most of which were written between 1923 and 1927.

was helped by J. B. [Betjeman].[1] Sensation – and he's sitting over there! And Tony Powell helped me – and he's sitting over there! Sensation.

And then here we were to alleviate the hell of this birthday. We thought he might be going through the whole 30 (odd?) guests and make of it a 'This is Your Life' but it was perfectly timed and not a sentence too long.

It was funny, pithy, satirical, well-dramatised, Cyril at his best. A lovely celebration and rounded off in hilarious laughter as Ali Forbes, in the best possible form, gave me a lift home.

Cyril said he felt like a retiring ambassador, a statesman who leaves the Palace and is determined to lead a dignified life tho' living in a small room.

He had read so much and came to the conclusion that his resolutions were that in future he would say only what he meant and would do only what he wanted to. He discovered La Fontaine had said this, so he had no opinions of his own. He said a 70th birthday was like crossing an imaginary line, like the Equator, that in fact it was the state of the chassis which was real.

Visit to K. & Jane Clark   September 1973

'Come down for lunch. I'll meet you at Folkestone. You must see where we live. Kelley (Colette) always says the *mot juste*. [She] says I should be called Lord Clark of Suburbia.'

I liked the idea of seeing Folkestone, of laying ghosts of my past. I always enjoyed my childhood visits there and have not been for so many years, and I was curious to see what sort of a house a man of such taste as K. would build for himself when he decided that Saltwood Castle [near Hythe] was too difficult to 'run', had too many staircases for poor Jane to manage, and was altogether unsuitable for two elderly people to live in alone. In an effort to avoid death duties, the castle was given over with a considerable sum to the elder son,[2] while the parents live in the grounds in a small plot that was formerly the apple orchard.

K. said he gave the architect a rotten time for he supplied the rough

---

[1] According to Atticus, what he said was, 'And in London he had been lucky enough to work for a demon editor with fire in his belly, a commanding figure who wouldn't even let him smoke in the office, invariably referred to by his initials J. B.'

[2] Alan Clark (1928–99), MP, self-confessed womaniser, driver of fast cars, historian (*The Donkeys*, *Barbarossa* etc) and diarist, whose account of the fall of Mrs Thatcher remains unchallenged.

plan of a slightly straggling Japanese one-floor building and even told him the size of the bigger rooms: 'I want this to be the size of my carpet.' Admittedly the drawing room is rather beautiful and it shows off to great advantage a fine Turner and Degas, the colours, all tobaccos and browns, are beautiful, but Kelley was right. As we drove down a road with worse and worse villas each side, we turned off and bang in front this, another suburban bungalow, had a rather horrid picture window and red brick low garden walls, while the windows on the far side looked out on to a backdrop of the silver-coloured castle they have left.

K. and Jane say they have no regrets at leaving the castle, that they have no affection for it, yet they gaze at it all the time though, in part through tact and a wish not to impose, they seldom visit the children and grandchildren.

I feel the move is a great mistake and it was difficult to enthuse.

But the visit was interesting for after lunch (a bit of nonsense talked about how brilliant the cook was – he was Margot Fonteyn's chauffeur for 17 years, a dreary meal with the main course, veal, covered in sizzling chewing-gummy cheese, and how we, Irene Worth and I, should go and thank him in the kitchen. 'Don't tip him,' said Jane, 'but he'd be so pleased to be thanked'), we went to the sitting room for coffee and cigars, and K. with the minimum of interruption from Jane, held forth in a most delightful way.

His mind is as clear as ever (the preface he's writing to a book of H. Moore's drawings was on the floor in his study, a lesson as the most perfect calligraphy with only about three slight corrections on the whole of the first long foolscap page of script, I thought of my 9 rough copies!). He never forgets a date, a name, a sum of money, his interests are worldly as well as artistic. His parents were without aesthetic interests, rich and heavy, dawdling. The young K. was very shielded and he was appalled when the Empress Elisabeth [Eugenie] in old age asked him to kiss her. 'I'd never been kissed. My nanny never kissed me, nor my parents. When this huge elderly woman whom I loved asked me to kiss her goodbye I fled from the room.'

K. talked on many subjects, but not merely flatteringly, he talked of how, in nearly every case Ingres portraits were of people he posed in the attitudes of classical sculpture, that he refused for many years to do the portrait of Madame Rothschild, but on meeting her realised she was humble and meek, and so liked her but painted her low down the canvas to show her humility.

Some of the portraits which seem as easy to achieve as the daguerreotypes which intrigued and influenced him so much, were so difficult that he could be heard groaning and even yelling in the night, bemoaning the fact that the painting was not as he had wished it. Sometimes the sitter had to wait so many years to be painted that the face had to be stylised not to show the passage of time.

K. talked of more mundane things – who was the most destructive wife? K. considered Lady Radcliffe:[1] 'her husband the most brilliant man in England has had his career ruined by rudeness and tactlessness.' Kathy Sutherland was another cited: 'But in the old days, we used to keep them, but have only been rewarded with bitchiness.' It's true.

Who were the hostesses to compare with Colefax and Cunard? He was putting the record straight about Sybil C. in his autobiography, for he felt she had been grossly misjudged. How well she had managed on only a little money, with her meals so well cooked (scrambled eggs and gooseberry fool) when so many interesting people met one another for the first time.

I warmed to K. He is the best company even if one has reservations about his point of view, his idea of the truth. He is a cold-blooded fish and one feels that he has a heart, otherwise how could he put up with Jane's continual drunkenness? Jane was sozzled by lunchtime and took a long while getting to the dining room, but she is one of the nicest drunks for her goodness and benign attitude come to the surface. She must be a very Christian creature for in her cups she becomes only sweeter.

I enjoyed seeing the quality of the objects, the 'precious stone' dishes, the Chinese pots, the china, the modern pictures and the gloriously bound books in specially built cases, and I felt the atmosphere was real and not for show, that this was a place where people worked and read and listened to music. But I felt the locale was a disaster and how much better if they had bought a 'dreary little period house' which they described. 'Here we've a sun trap for our old age.' It suffices, but I'd rather have one of those delightful Victorian and Edwardian seaside houses with white-painted balconies that Irene and I passed on our quick journey back to the station for a train taking us back to Cannon Street.

Critics   *September 1973*

I wouldn't look at the reviews of *The Happy Years*, because I was so terrified of what the critics would say about my revealing a relationship with Greta. *The Strenuous Years* is out this week, and Eileen is away, so unable to shield me from my onslaughts. However, the *Observer's* Maurice Richardson[2] has

---

[1] Viscountess Radcliffe (1903–82), Hon Antonia Roby, married first, Major John Tennant, and secondly, Cyril, first Viscount Radcliffe (1899–1977).

[2] Maurice Richardson (1907–78), wild Irish critic, reviewed television for the *Observer*.

praised me so highly that I glow with pleasure and feel that I can now take minor mosquito bites in my stride.

However, it does seem extraordinary that so many people feel sancti-monious about me confessing that there were bad times as well as good. God knows one doesn't want to brag about one's being unsuccessful in career or that one's peace of mind is disturbed. Of course one doesn't welcome the approach of old age. Yet some people don't think it right that one should air these truths, and others are harping and beastly. Osbert Lancaster,[1] the greatest bore in private life while being one of the funniest cartoonists ever, has shown his spleen, jealousy and envy (the knighthood rankles a lot), but even kind friends have been horrified by the blurb:[2] 'How can you denigrate yourself thus?'

There are those who continue to put me in a very high level of superfi-ciality (O. L. included – jealousy again – I'm a better stage designer than he!) and point out that Diana Cooper's letter is the best thing in the book (I've always known that it is, but what a wonderful ornament to have). But, nevertheless, the criticism is minor. It is said that I am not able to rise above bad reviews. In fact, the skin becomes thinner with the years and, when faced with the displeasure of some whom I have written of, Eileen says; 'Surely we take that in one's stride!' But no, I don't. Likewise my stride diminishes with the years.

Betty Somerset   *September/October 1973*

[Cecil had already written two pieces in his diary, worried that his friend, Betty Somerset, was likely to die. He also took it upon himself to write and warn the Queen Mother of Betty's impending demise.]

Betty didn't want to live. The world had become so rough and violent, ugly and unlike that which she loved. She wanted to opt out and her death is a release for her to 'join her Bob'. But the funeral service was nonetheless extremely upsetting. My emotions are so easily roused, but I never realised how upset I'd be until the family trooped in, Caroline so tall, her children even taller, David so effortlessly distinguished. I believe, given a chance, I could fall in love with him. And just a few friends there singing banal hymns, hearing a ridiculous parson propound sentiments of which Betty would so disapprove.

---

[1] Sir Osbert Lancaster (1908–86), cartoonist, writer and theatrical designer.
[2] The blurb began: 'The carefree days are over. Moving into middle age, Cecil Beaton is beset with anxieties and doubts.'

I had forgotten to bring my glasses so could not read the John Donne prayer, and only heard in the lesson: 'if these be of my virtue, and if there be any praise, think on these things.'

Betty said, in an effort to be whimsical, 'I don't think God likes me, and I don't think I like him for all sorts of reasons, for doing such cruel things to people and being so badly dressed. I hate the brown Jaeger dressing gown with a rope around the waist. We wouldn't want him like that at a dinner.'

Yet here the usual baby hymns and nursery sentiments, the flowers from Gullivers of Salisbury that Betty would have hated. It was cold, and bleak, and I blubbed. This made me embarrassed because David, who is deeply sad, was clear, blue-eyed, smiling with a wonderful, frank regard. It was sad in spite of it being an easy death and one that was welcomed.

Sad, selfishly, because it was a treat to go and see her in the round house, a particularly long treat when the garden was at its pale yellow and white best, but even in winter, when one just sat and talked in the warmth of her room and she, in dirty pinkish colours, looked so haggard, ravaged and yet beautiful, with her star sapphire eyes, full of surprise and wilfulness, her sweet smile, her particular manner of smoking cigarettes, rising above food and being totally contented never to go out of the gate with her notice: 'Please shut the gate', so that that awful old Murdie could not roam. That hideous balloon-sausage dog she loved so much that when it became ill and could not go up the stairs, she spent the night on the downstairs sofa by its side.

It was one of the joys of the countryside that here, so near, was someone so special and rare.

Diana Cooper   *September/October 1973*

I showed her a caricature[1] I'd done of Violet Trefusis, whose love affair with Vita Sackville-West is making sensational reading in the *Sunday Times*.[2] Diana recoiled in horror: 'Yes, we called her the pig, and you've got her powdering her face. She kept dabbing powder on until she looked like a well-floured scone.'

---

[1] For obvious reasons, Cecil never published these caricatures. They were the opposite of the beautiful photographic portraits for which he is famous. It was his way of letting off steam, and he was a brilliant and wicked caricaturist. He did a series of Vita and Violet, and some devilish ones of Anne, Countess of Rosse. There was a good one of Diana Vreeland and one of the Duchess of Windsor, staggering out of Maxim's in Paris, inspired by a newspaper photograph.

[2] Nigel Nicolson had written the story of his mother's affair with Violet in *Portrait of a Marriage*.

Stephen Tennant

Took Diana (and Peter Eyre) over to tea on a last-minute impulse; strangely enough we were welcomed. In fact, Stephen so over-excited at Diana's arrival that he never drew breath for an hour and a half. He quoted verbatim passages from Mrs Gaskell on the Brontës, Agnes de Mille on Pavlova, related the plot of Marie Corelli's rubbishy novel, *Thelma*.

Some of his descriptions were remarkable. Of Diana's eyes he remarked that they were like those of a tiger. Of Gary Cooper that they were quartz, of precious stone found embedded in rock and fringed with ferns, dark and rather sticky.

He surprised Peter (*bouleversé*) by saying that most people's success came less from their talent than by sticking to the job. How could he know?

Have been on a ten days' stretch in the country trying to finish my play *Chickens*. Am excited about it, but will probably once again be doomed to disappointment. While the incessant interruptions go on – two men came over for 2 days to alter the telephone system. Like children they want reassuring, and they have to call out the Chubb alarm man, who has been out three days earlier as a result of an 'alert' in the middle of the night. The yard was always crowded with lorries. I can give little time or patience to these people, but feel I have to pay attention to Brian Blick, the builder, as he knows that things are going to get worse (to the guttering, and the roof of winter garden), if not attended to now.

Thus, at the minute, while sending a mass of bills and notes to Eileen, I put in a memo saying, 'At one moment this morning there were working for me – one solitary person – 2 hedge cutters, 2 sweeps, 2 Smallpeices, Isaac, Mrs Eide, Mrs Stokes, Brian Blick and his Ron, almost a round dozen.' Eileen sent back the memo with an appendage: 'And up here, Ray, Karen, Sheila, me and typist in Salisbury. Interesting, thought-provoking. What caused this comment now? Were you: pleased, appalled, bemoaning, regretting, gloating, self-aggrandising, fearful, sobered. Are you sensible, sure? Solvent?'

The answer is that secretly I do like activity, that I love to get things done, to have the iris planted in the winter garden for next year. But I do not want to spend this appalling amount on upkeep, that with all this 'service' I don't feel I have any comforts (exaggeration), that it can't go on like this and that the day must come when serious decisions must be made. Yet it is difficult to cut down in London, to give up London unless one retires, opts out, and I don't want only to remain here.

Princess Anne's Wedding   *November 1973*

She was a bossy, unattractive, galumphing girl. When about fifteen I photographed the family in a group, celebrating the birth of the latest addition,[1] she was not helpful. While waiting for the Queen to come in I suggested I might take some pictures of the newborn 'if that was in order'. 'I don't know that it would be in order,' opined the ugly girl.

At the end of the sitting, a very unsatisfactory one, I cornered the girl and said, 'I know you hate it, but let me take you hating it in this direction, now hate it in that direction, go on. Hate it! Hate it!' The girl looked at me with a snarl. I don't know if it was supposed to be a smile, or a sign of trapped terror. The pictures were revolting.

I don't know if Princess Anne had remembered this incident. Anyhow it was Norman Parkinson[2] who took the 'breakaway' photographs which, with a good deal of help from *Vogue*, made her into a beauty. It was only natural that Parks should do the wedding pictures and jolly well he did them.

However, I was invited to the Ball before the wedding and Patrick P. [Plunket] said it was the Princess who put the tick against my name. And for this I am grateful for that tick was the means whereby I had a very amusing evening.

I had high expectations of the dinner party before given by the Queen Mother at Clarence House. Unfortunately I was disappointed. The 'glamour' had gone. It is a hideous house & the mixture of furniture makes for a rather sordid ensemble. Some of the pictures are so bad (in the dining room particularly) that it gives the appearance of a pretentious hotel. The Queen Mother wore diamonds & a silver dress concocted by Hartnell that had flying buttresses from the shoulders of pleated white tulle. This pleated theme was in evidence again at the bottom of the dress.

Nice Patricia Herbert [Dowager Viscountess] Hambleden looked like a caricature of a dowdy lady-in-waiting and all the women of the party looked unbelievably drab, none more so than Lady Carrington in gypsy trail plum colour and the lady who sat on my right, Lady Abergavenny. The Salisburys[3] – Mollie who generally comes up to scratch on these occasions, looking like a tired piglet. Her hair too curtained on to her

---

[1] Prince Edward (b.1964). Princess Anne was then thirteen.
[2] Norman Parkinson (1913–90), photographer.
[3] Iona, wife of sixth Lord Carrington; Patricia, wife of fifth Marquess of Abergavenny, Lady of the Bedchamber to the Queen; and the sixth Marquess of Salisbury (b.1916) and his wife Mollie (b.1922).

little tired face and the white ruched dress a real abomination of unro-
mantic dowdiness. Robert as difficult of approach as ever. Mary Soames[1]
was well upholstered and prettily healthy – an apricot in a good condition
– and the others were really very dull: a Norwegian Crown Prince[2] with
his wife. The men were better and Christopher [Soames] has become a
really Johnsonian, Gibsonian character ('fill it up to the top') who comes
into the room like a thunderstorm.

I was even disappointed with the food and found it all too creamy. The
Queen Mother enjoyed her glass of wine and held her head back each
time she quaffed a glass. Pictures admired or not (Martin Gilliat[3] wants to
get the A. [Augustus] John off the drawing room walls and he's right).
The QM couldn't remember the name of the painter of St Agnes
(Millais).

And then 'we mustn't be late!' – the departure. Went with a money
man named Wilcox[4] in his large Rolls. He chastised his chauffeur for not
following the QM's car as we got caught in the mêlée outside the Palace.
Here the cars were jammed into a large yard, a moonstruck Ld Louis
Mountbatten among the fenders directing the traffic. A lot got out and
walked and so did we. No line-up of guests, no reception by the Queen or
members of the family. Do your own thing. Wander. All the rooms in use
and all crowded to the extremity.

Generally, when I go to the Palace it is to take a photograph sitting
and the burden of the job hangs like a sword of Damocles. Tonight I felt
free to enjoy myself and I realised that at long last I have acquired a
certain self-confidence. In my early years it was always a strain to go into
a crowded room and come face to face with people who I knew
disapproved of me. Now to hell. I disapprove of a lot of them.

The ballroom had been invested, by Patrick P. [Plunket], with a huge,
towering wedding cake made of white chrysanthemums, a good idea, as it
appeared festive and broke up the wide sea of floor space. Suddenly face
to face with the Queen. She was walking on her own, looking a bit like a
lost child. She seemed genuinely pleased to see me. Her face lit up,
smiles, and talk for the first time was not stilted, all about nothing, but
the gaiety of the occasion – fulsome compliments from me. This sort of
thing could only happen today in England, a gay occasion, smiles.

Then straight into the thinner arms of Pss Alexandra. She is at the

---

[1] Mary Soames (b.1922), wife of Christopher Soames (later Lord Soames) (1920–87),
daughter of Sir Winston Churchill.
[2] Crown Prince (now King) Harald of Norway (b.1937) and his wife Sonja Haraldsen
(b.1937).
[3] Sir Martin Gilliat (1913–93), Private Secretary to the Queen Mother.
[4] Probably (Sir) Malcolm Wilcox (b.1921), then Vice-Chairman of the Forward Trust
and Director of the Midland Bank.

height of her beauty. She is on the border line of disaster, a few months more and she may appear too thin, too gaunt, too wild and made-up. Tonight it was absolute perfection. She was in Metona turquoise ruffles with diadem and ringlets in the Empire style. She was nervy, funny, gesticulating like her mother. The other Kent family group looked cretinous, ghoulish, a bit Addams cartoonish.

Then on an exploration jog. I suddenly saw in a flash the heroine of the occasion. Princess Anne had become an Aubrey Beardsley beauty. Never more was I astonished. She has become very thin, her figure trim, her neck like a swan's, her nose long, her mouth and eyes beautifully made up, her hair high in great volutes of gold. Her dress a Renaissance – Empire style in yellow satin with slashed silver at sleeves and arms. She appeared graceful, calm and beautiful. Over her shoulder a glimpse of the rather 6 o'clock shadowy chin of her fiancé,[1] and his hair looked like black hay. But how can one really tell in one cinema flash.

Princess Grace too in a flash of raspberry colour and a tiara (recently bought!) as she danced with a Spanish prince. A session with his sister-in-law[2] on a banquette, she the wife of the Pretender to the Spanish throne, she Greek, clever, nice and Jinny Ogilvy[3] a paragon of gaiety & dignity. She never does anything wrong but shows great independence of attitude. The best jewels on the hideous Duchess of Wellington,[4] her tiara like a Christmas cake of 18th century diamonds.

Begum Aga Khan[5] out of kilter, a common model, with too long fingernails. Caroline S. [Somerset] lovely, kissing everyone. Anne T. [Tree] embarrassed, corked up, disliking it, Elizabeth Cavendish in disguise as a distinguished dowager (it cost £17 to have her hair frizzed), Debo Devonshire[6] [with] two vast diamonds like an antenna bobbing down from her ordinary farmwork hairdo. Anne Armstrong-Jones [Countess of] Rosse in emeralds of unparalleled size, looking like a Mazinophan Empress, Peter Ustinov.

Ted Heath arriving in a haze of good health and strength, in spite of the horrors of the world today with a war in the Middle East affecting us all, and rationing of petrol in the offing. It was extraordinary how he has developed since becoming first minister. He has shown such courage and strength and the manner (never being ingratiating, or rather too falsely so) and it seemed has become easier and may I not be damned for saying

---

[1] Captain Mark Phillips (b.1948).
[2] Princess Sofia (b.1938) married Prince (now King) Juan Carlos of Spain (b.1938).
[3] Virginia Ryan (b.1933) married thirteenth Earl of Airlie (b.1926).
[4] Diana, married eighth Duke of Wellington (b.1915).
[5] Sally Croker-Poole, married the Aga Khan. Later divorced.
[6] Lady Elizabeth Cavendish (b.1926), and her sister-in-law, Deborah Mitford (b.1920), married eleventh Duke of Devonshire (b.1920).

tonight he exuded a certain sex appeal. This is more than Macmillan did as he sat complaining that he knew no one any more.

Princess Alice,[1] over 90, going off into hoots of laughter when I asked her to be photographed, Dss of Gloucester[2] moving and twitching out of misery and nervousness, Prince Charles getting very red in the face and rather butch with huge butch feet and legs. D. of Edinb. haggard and awestruck. Jane Westmorland quite pretty and incredibly young in her usual black and white way, the hideous Mrs Wills and the horrid Lady Rupert Nevill who are so pleased to be part of 'the Queen's set', Lord Rupert[3] getting a bit drunk and rowdy. But rowdiness was part of the evening's fun for a lot of the fiancé's friends from the army and the hunting field gave the evening a touch of extra beefiness. The (red) pink hunting coats added to the looks and of course it would be up to that snobbish Diana Herbert[4] to ask, 'Who are all these people?' They were friendly and nice, and let in a breath of countrified air with their whoops and cries, and slips on the slippery dance floor.

It was very difficult to catch sight of many of the people one was interested to see and when, having walked for at least ten miles, or so my feet seemed to say to me, I was bent on going home, I caught sight of Pss Margaret. Gosh the shock! She has become a little pocket monster – Queen Victoria. The flesh is solid and I don't think dieting can reduce a marble statue. The weighty body was encased in sequin fargets, of turquoise and shrimp, her hair scraped back and a high tiara-crown (she bought it for her wedding) placed on top. But the hairdresser had foolishly given her a vast teapot handle of hair jutting out at the back. This triple-compacted chignon was a target for all passers-by to hit first from one side, then another. The poor midgety brute was knocked like a top, sometimes almost into a complete circle.

As I talked, a waiter passed with a tray of champagne and once more a biff sent the diminutive princess flying. Poor brute, I do feel sorry for her. She was not very nice in the days when she was so pretty and attractive. She snubbed and ignored friends. But my God she has been paid out! Her appearance has gone to pot. Her eyes seem to have lost their vigour, her complexion is now a dirty negligee pink satin. The sort of thing one sees in a disbanded dyer's shop window.

The horrid husband was nowhere to be seen. It is said that the Queen would be willing to let Pss M. get rid of him but Tony won't go.

---

[1] Princess Alice, Countess of Athlone (1883–1981), granddaughter of Queen Victoria.
[2] Princess Alice, Duchess of Gloucester (b.1901), aunt of the Queen.
[3] Jane (b.1928) married fifteenth Earl of Westmorland (1924–93); Jean Wills (1915–99), niece of the Queen Mother; Lord Rupert Nevill (1923–82) and his wife Camilla.
[4] Lady Diana Herbert (b.1937), daughter of sixteenth Earl of Pembroke.

Given a lift home by the Ogilvys and Hambledens,[1] very gay and friendly. A nice night out for which I had to pay with a hangover the next day, for the five glasses of champagne I had drunk in self-defence had tightened the arteries and the headache that overtook me lasted most of the following day.

Hatley – Chez Jakie Astor   (*Saturday 15 December 1973*)

Enormous relief. My big photography book is finished. There will be last-minute inclusions and a lot of corrections and we still (Gail[2] and I) have to choose many photographs to accompany the text. But the main slog is over. And it has been a slog. Amusing and entertaining to find what interesting and often eccentric types the pioneers were, and the variety of the subject prevented my being ever bored. But the slog was in polishing the various entries into readable shape, and much of this was done in the knowledge that my morning's work would eventualise into most distressing headaches later in the day. Gottfried says these come from the arteries becoming tighter in age. But it is very unaccountable that I am struck on one day and not on another. If I do a stretch of several days' work, then I know that by the time I go to London with the stuff ready for the typist the headache is going to follow me in the train to the great city and quite possibly the first afternoon at Pelham is being spent lying on a bed with a couple of aspirin inside me not doing the work as efficaciously as they should. However, all this is for the moment forgotten.

One does not remember past health, good or bad, and I am now, bookwork going through a good patch, headaches at bay. Gottfried says I am in better health than I have been since my loathsome operation. (I inveigh against the surgeons who robbed me of my boyish figure and my interest in sex.) The reason for my feeling so well is that I have had long spells at Reddish when I have not only had a siesta after lunch but have slept from ten o'clock at night till eight the following morning. Often I have wanted to carry on with my work in the afternoon but know this is dangerous, so much of the time has been spent doing odd jobs, though alas not reading, for this is one of the major ways of getting eye strain and neuralgia a few hours later, or during the night.

Not only have I been busy for nearly a year on the photography book (when I complained of the length of the chore to Elizabeth Pakenham [Longford],[3] she said, 'But I take five years on each of my books!'), but I

---

[1] Fourth Viscount Hambleden (b.1930) and his then wife Maria Carmela.
[2] Gail Buckland, Cecil's co-author on *The Magic Image*.
[3] The Countess of Longford (b.1906), biographer (Queen Victoria, the Queen, the Duke of Wellington).

have also indulged myself in the writing of a play. This is the greatest pleasure for me, and when I am unable to turn my attentions in that direction, felt very frustrated.

However, in spite of its having most unencouraging opinions thrust at it from 2 agents, and one management, my friend, Hal Burton, said he thought that although it was glittering on the surface and was static and undramatic, the necessary elements could be built into the situation. To do this according to his vague instructions was the greatest joy. Now I am awaiting his verdict on the new draft.

No doubt there will be more rewrites, but if it will eventually lead to a London production, then I will feel that one of my most gnawing ambitions will at long last, at the age of 70, have been achieved.

Although I do not allow myself the luxury of thinking in terms of a stage production, I am tempted to feel that with the practice of so many years, 'my inner ear' tells me whether what I have written sounds right or wrong. I am still very bad at getting beneath the surface.

Equus is on at the Old Vic for only a comparatively few programmes. It seems extraordinary that Peter Shaffer[1] should be altruistic enough to more or less give his play to the disastrously run 'National' Theatre when he could have made so much money with it in the commercial theatre.

I praised his play to him when we met for the first time (at Frank [Tait]'s and Billy [Henderson]'s cottage). I told him how moved and thrilled I had been by something that was a real tour de force in the theatre, or milestone. I said I thought that it must give him the greatest possible satisfaction to read such notices as his play received and to watch the audiences being so completely engrossed and reacting in just the ways that he had planned they should.

He agreed that a successful playwright had a much keener enjoyment than a novelist or some other writer who could never really see how much his work was being appreciated.

Shaffer struck me as being strangely stagy, though why someone who has been writing successfully produced plays for so long should not have been slightly tainted, and using stagy jargon, I do not know. But for so intellectual a writer, it surprised me to find echoes of John Gielgud in his personality and also in his physical appearance. The texture of his white, ivory-smooth skin, his general colourlessness and his large nose were very like John. So too his manner. But he is a far more truthful person. He doesn't indulge in persiflage. He would not make an effort by saying anything that he did not feel. He is not interested in effects, or getting a

---

[1] Peter Shaffer (1926–2001), playwright, wrote *Amadeus* (1979).

laugh. He is always on the search for new ideas, a person to be much admired and respected.

I asked him about various stage personalities. His accounts were never prejudiced, always fair, however horrendous. And horrendous was the word to describe his relationship with Maggie Smith and her husband (at present) Bob Stephens.[1] Although he has written (several?) plays in which Maggie Smith has had incredible success, when he sent her his latest play, one which had taken a year to write, she never replied. He rewrote the play and again (unbelievably) sent it to her. Again no reply.

Shaffer holds Olivier to have genius in the theatre, but as a man considers him nothing. Shifty, unreliable, cowardly, and burnt up with jealousy and envy, he is a disaster at running a theatre. It is up to him to have a success, yet when those who have made a success for him are praised, Olivier turns against them, throws them out. Shaffer tells of the infinite pains Olivier goes to in the study of a performance. He spent hours with a tape recorder in his Brighton attic getting to perfection the country accent for a part to which he then gave no 'soul' or reality.

Shaffer gives him no credit as a director and thinks he missed the opportunity of his lifetime at the Vic when he had playing for him the perfect cast for the *Importance* [*of Being Earnest*], with himself, hold on, as Lady Bracknell. Shaffer is convinced Olivier would have been superb: 'After all, the old girl is camp!'

Visit to Dadie Rylands at King's   *November 1973*

The coldest day of the year at Hatley. Even indoors it was difficult to be warm for long. The fire would die down and the draughts come through enormous windows. My clothes seemed inadequate when in the already darkening afternoon, Jakie took me in his new Mercedes to Cambridge. (He had given me instructions as to how to drive myself, but I would have made a mess of the expedition.) Light was fading when we got to the Backs and you could see the pinnacles of King's Chapel through the black branches of willow trees. Black figures were skating on the river. Undergraduates with mufflers were hurrying off with fresh cardboard cake boxes to fug up and have friends for tea. We were frozen by the time we had instructions from the porter and found our way to the rooms that Dadie has occupied since he became a Fellow.

I saw Dadie two weeks ago at Raymond M.'s at Crichel and was struck by his healthiness, his freshness, vigour and purity. I thought him a wonderfully rare specimen, a creature uncontaminated by the rush and

---

[1] Robert Stephens (1931–95), actor, then married to Maggie Smith (b.1934), actress.

squalor of contemporary life, a creature who seldom took wing from his life of books and study but whenever he made friendly forays, possessed a childlike enjoyment and quickness of eye that few seem to retain in old age.

But extraordinary as it seems to me, Dadie is now over seventy. He still appears to me, even if a bit thinner on top, to be the young bullocky blond that he was when such a figure at King's, when I was unhappy at St John's.

Dadie was, with his pale blue eyes, blue tie, pink and white complexion and canary quiff of hair, a spectacular figure. A great friend of all the Bloomsburys, the names of Lytton (a drawl Lllytton –), Duncan, Vanessa and Clive[1], were seldom off his lips. He was loved and passionate, his reputation was most enviable, and he became the Duchess of Malfi in a production that I should have graced if only I had not been so tiresome and difficult. Truth was Dadie was the best Duchess of Malfi I have seen out of at least a dozen. He was like a unicorn, neither male nor female, dignified, rare.

Now Dadie, in boyish open neck, welcomed us from the kitchen of his spacious rooms that at a glance one could tell were a magpie's hoard of silver, china and twentyish paintings. I have seldom seen anything so ordered in its clutter, and mercifully everything was extremely well dusted and polished. Nevertheless, the effect was very peculiar, a mixture of an old Victorian lady's taste, a donnish severity of mahogany bookcases and showcases (for more china and silver) and a hangover of Bloomsbury décor. Carrington had painted very typical and pretty panels on the doors and cupboards, and his smaller sitting room was liberally sprinkled with dated nudes against a noughts and crosses background.

Dadie made the tea, produced hot buttered buns and macaroons, and showed a wide range of interest and he asked about Jakie's 'arable land', gave information about what all the Cambridge celebrities were doing and how they had achieved eminence in other fields. He was quick and trenchant. His little beady eyes popping, and his lips pursed in a pout as he listened. One felt that time had in no way impaired the sharpness of his brain. He talked about [Thomas] Hardy, quite a close family connection there, about Siegfried Sassoon and Stephen Tennant, Victor Rothschild and Raymond M. [Mortimer], all of which he described in a very true way.

Jakie sat in amazement, I in admiration that Dadie, whom I did not like when at Cambridge (jealousy?) has now sweetened, mellowed and I felt that he must be a very happy man. But no. He is extremely lonely,

---

[1] Lytton Strachey, Duncan Grant, Vanessa and Clive Bell.

feels the lack of grandchildren, finds the hours of waking and early morning appalling and depressing.

He is at his happiest when after seven or eight cups of tea, he lies in bed reading. But three o'clock in the afternoon is a dire time for him, and whisky helps him to continue at six o'clock. But he has said he would like to commit suicide. This is to me, who am, touch wood, of an extremely happy nature, a very great shock. His eyesight is perfect, so he can indulge in his favourite pleasure for the rest of time. But it does not seem to add up to the contentment that one reaches with his later days.

The telephone rang. He answered it in his very poor and small little bedroom with the chamber pot under the wash basin. 'They've called it off?' he asked. The dinner engagement was off. He would cook eggs and sausages for himself on his little Belling, and he would get through the meal and the washing-up and clearing away in ten minutes flat. And then the long evening would be in front of him.

Pelham Place   *November 1973*

Have rather enjoyed a spell of London life. Guilt pricks me when I have a car for the morning but there is little chance of picking up a taxi and I'm no good at buses. And the time goes by so quickly that it is impossible to see half the exhibitions that are so enticing. However, this week I've managed the great Bakst Revival Show, the English Landscapes at the Tate (rekindling my love of Gainsborough), the drawings of Cézanne, which I can't enjoy, the Magritte surrealism at the Marlborough, and I've been to see *The Wolf*, Molnár, not really worth an evening in the theatre, tho' Judi Dench and Leo McKern gave outstanding performances. I was inveigled into seeing two common plays by Rattigan, *Coriolanus*, couldn't hear half the speeches and Nicol Williamson proved himself not a Shakespearean actor. Dignity is necessary. He has little. Production good.

Various people came to lunch, Patrick P. Procktor got away from his dreary Danish-pastry wife, in the last stages of pregnancy, and as usual was an intellectual treat. He keeps a marvellous simplicity and is never guilty of a ready-made opinion. Whitebait, pork, imported raspberry sherbet with ice cream.

On a Monday Fred Ashton came to lunch and altho' I had intended it to be a heart to hearter, asked Diana Cooper and Honey [Harris] (an old friend whom I *never* see). D. and F. were good together, and Honey was amazed to see Diana behaving in her most outrageous, typical way. How when at the Embassy, Bébé [Bérard] came to dinner, Jasmin, the dirty little dog, dropped a turd on the drawing [room] carpet and Bébé, in a panic, picked it up and put it in his pocket. 'Good for Bébé,' Diana roared! She laughed inordinately. Her sort of a joke.

She talked about early days of theatre-going. She had been shocked that Duse[1] used no make-up. The old Sarah B.[2] was a monster. V. Duchess[3] loathed [Adeline] Genée, but was converted to ballet by Pavlova. Diana and family were made to go every Sat[urday] to see her matinée performance.

Freddie told how marvellous Pavlova was in a *Dance à la Nuit*, in which she was wrapped in dark rags and fled terrified at the approach of dawn.

Fred gave a funny imitation of posture, and of the Queen M[other], attitudinising as someone asked, 'Champagne? Whisky? Brandy? Martini?' and then silence and gestures stopped, as if in great surprise, she answered, 'That would be delicious!'

Diana talked more than usual, for she has until recently kept quiet about it, about old age. The *dégringolade*, the getting worse: 'I'm so relieved Duff didn't have to go through the agonies of old age.' It was the loss of zest she minded (not that to see this as having any bearing on her. I don't think her enthusiasm is forced). Lately I have heard Diana laugh more raucously. She used to say she never laughed. Is this a hysterical development. Diana went off in her 'coat of shame' (given by the loathsome P. L. Weiller[4]), very pleased with her lunch. 'I was looking forward to it,' she said, 'and it was every bit as good as I expected!'

When stricken with swollen glands under the ears, and given antibiotics until I felt awful, I telephoned to Diana to know if she would 'let me off the hook' and not be present at her gala *Cockie*, where I'd said I'd be one of the hosts to the supper guests. 'Of course, don't give it a thought. I never mind about these things.' She is a true, good friend. The relief was great.

---

[1] Eleonora Duse (1859–1924), actress.
[2] Sarah Bernhardt (1844–1923), actress.
[3] Violet, Duchess of Rutland (d.1937), Diana's mother.
[4] Commandant Paul-Louis Weiller (1893–1993). Part of his Gnôme et Rhône company was nationalised and became Air France. A man of enormous riches, he was an aviation hero in the First World War and imprisoned by the Vichy government at the beginning of the Second. He lived to be 100, and was still wind-surfing within a month of his 99th birthday. He gave Diana Cooper at least two mink coats, each of which she jokingly described as 'the coat of shame'.

December 1973

The worst national crisis since the war, and one that is partly self-inflicted, makes it all the worse. There is no chance. We have our backs to the wall, but don't know quite who our enemy is. (Russia with Love – of course we will wake to find ourselves like Hitler's Germany, overpowered without our knowing what has happened.) The Arabs have used their oil as a weapon of war (quite legitimately, and have us all held up to ransom), and just as this crisis makes Christmas dark and cold, the miners' and train drivers' unions take the opportunity to inflate their particular interests. No country has national spirit any more. Those who are able to make others suffer do so [with] impunity. This is the bleakest, most dire phase. The Communist unions have the popular media (certainly the press) in their clutch and the *Daily Express* could not come up with a caricature of Brezhnev, arriving off an aeroplane to peace talks followed by tanks. No one seems to know, or be capable of doing anything if they do.

Meanwhile the country is really in the worst phase, grinding to a halt. No wood for windowsills, no gravel for building, no glass. Shortages which will affect all of us. It is an act of faith to go on working on my play when theatres are doing disastrously or on my photography book when paper is becoming short. In every 'walk of life' the effects are beginning to show. The interruptions and the unemployment will lead to more and more violence, and the insurance rates will go up higher. Where is there to go? Nowhere? It is a depressing dreadful time for all, and my antibiotic treatment is not much of a help to the general state of affairs.

Headaches prevent my reading. I am jinxed with anything mechanical and the music on radio or record player thwarts me. Nothing to do by try to sleep and each time to make me feel if the swelling under the ears had gone down. It has not. I look coarse and feel like a bullfrog.

Meanwhile the Communist Daly[1] flourishes, and so do [Joe] Gormley, [Harold] Wilson, the Burtons[2] and all the horrible people who appear in the papers.

---

[1] Lawrence Daly (b.1924), General Secretary, National Union of Mineworkers (1968–84).
[2] Richard Burton and Elizabeth Taylor.

Delysia *December 1973*

I wanted to see this great star of the '1914' war, who imprinted herself so much on generations of revue and musical comedy audiences, and whom I thought, as a young boy, the quintessence of French naughtiness and glamour. I heard she was coming to stay in London and I telephoned. But we could not arrange a meeting and she returned to France, a sad widow of 3 years, her husband, a cousin of de Gaulle and a consul general all over the world, having died of a heart attack. She has been left badly off, as when her first manager and lover, who had made her a star, got into financial difficulties, she tried to save him by selling all her marvellous jewels and her life insurance. Unfortunately, Cochran[1] had not behaved well to her at the last, although she would be the last to complain, or be bitter, as I was later to discover. Then I heard Delysia had come to settle in Brighton of all unlikely places. I tracked her down and was rather anxious lest my taking her out to lunch would be an expensive 'flop'. (I remember once when Charlie James said I must meet her and I took her to supper at the Savoy, after enormous *'frais'* with the waiters to be served liver and bacon, the bill for those days was prodigious.)

When I arrived, a little late, having been warned that she was very fat, at the basement flat she has been given by some kind, rich faggot, the appearance of a personage beckoning me at a window was a reassurance. In spite of her now being 86 years old, it was the same Delysia. A very slight bump on her back, more double and triple chins, but the face was softened and the old features remained intact. She was quite chic in a crimson velvet raincoat, imitation Chanel suit, poor gold jewellery, well-washed and dyed hair and well-preserved hands with pointed pink nails. She walked carefully, but in no way showed her age in the way she deported herself and she got into the taxi with alacrity.

She had suggested we lunch at Wheeler's and she knew she would like a glass of sherry and smoked salmon, then to follow lobster and mayonnaise, but she changed her mind to have the Dover sole meunière that I had chosen. She chose strawberries and cream, while I had a sorbet. Bill £11, not bad, as it was a great treat for her and she furnished a treat for me.

---

[1] Sir Charles Blake Cochran (1872–1951), theatrical producer.

Christmas 1973

The festivity passed off with the minimum of embarrassment, pain or sadness. As a result of my mumps, I was still very weak, and obviously from the reaction of others, looked as pale as a ghost. But Nancy, suffering from the nagging emptiness of Baba's recent death, was calm and cheerful, and we had the right proportion of sociability and rest. My arrival at the little church service on Sunday morning was bright and full of colour, and the hymns were less embarrassing, in fact the Rosetti – 'In the bleak mid-winter' – quite delightful and instead of an address, topical allusions to the world's troubles all the while.

Billy and Frank for Christmas lunch and dinner at the Trees, a very gay evening with Anne T. trumping her own ace for inadequacy as hostess by forgetting to order toast for the pâté or smoked salmon, giving Hugh a smoked turkey that had started to go mouldy, and forgetting coffee and liqueurs.

On Boxing Day the neighbours came a hundred-fold for mulled burgundy. It was very hot and spiced. The columns in the hall had been trimmed with garlands of greenery, extremely pretty, and the first bulbs were out in the pots. The usual mixture, the vicar, the Lord Lieutenant, the Oliviers and lots of decorative young.

When Nancy and Hugh left, I felt more bereft than I have for many a year, for I have no very specific job to do at the moment and have to be careful not to exert myself after the meridian in a way that would give me the always near headaches. However, a spell of another week by myself is something that I should enjoy and, after a long interval, I am making an effort to go to the studio and do a lot of drawing.

1974

A month of Sundays is how Alan explained the last ten days of festivity. Christmas and Boxing Day and New Year's Day continued with the coal and locomotive crisis, has wrought havoc to the life of the country. The few shops that are open are lit by candle. Pickpocketing and shop-lifting rife. Mr Sieff[1] has been shot at close range, Gormley, agonisingly ugly, speaks illiterately on serious subjects, there is every reason to be depressed. Gradually one is conscious of shortages. Paper, oil, shaving cream, paints. Five plays are closing in London and soon my own activities will be curtailed. How long will Weidenfeld want to publish all these books? Who will want my play (if it is ever finished and good enough for the stage)? In an insulated way, I am enjoying myself in the studio, doing a mad series of pictures of, of all difficult subjects, the Queen Mum, and caricatures illustrating the Sapphic relationship of Violet Trefusis and Vita Sackville-West.

But I fear this escape is only temporary, and the doctor tells me I should have a holiday in the sun and I just about feel ready for it. And I was looking forward to a long winter here with no need to go abroad!

12 January 1974

My darling Aunt Jessie's birthday. How long ago it is since she provided so many of the delights of my childhood, but the memory of her is delightfully alive.

I see it is also the birthday (70th) of Oliver Messel, my great rival of so long standing. He has made a wonderful new life for himself in the West Indies, and in spite of great illnesses, shows himself to be a mighty strong character and personality, and I am fond of him.

Yesterday I went to the Imperial War Museum, a place I loathe, to see the collection of my photographs that I took during the war for the M. of I. [Ministry of Information], not C. of I. These negatives have been printed and put into over thirty albums, and to my amazement, [I] find

---

[1] Edward Sieff (1915–1982), President of Marks and Spencer, father-in-law of George Weidenfeld, was shot at in his bathroom on 30 December 1973; his assailant the international assassin known as 'Carlos the Jackal'. One bullet lodged in his mouth and another in his neck. When asked if his teeth had saved him, he said 'Good old Milk Marketing Board'.

there are between thirty and forty thousand of them. It was an extraordinary experience to relive these war years, and so much of it had been forgotten, and most of the subjects were dead. The Arabian Front (where at least 300 of my pictures were lost, incidentally), Burma, India, China.

I had not realised that I had taken so many documentary pictures and that so many were only of technical interest. The amount of work confounded me. I looked at them with eyes of today, and not those of 30 years ago, and saw many things that today are 'accepted' and which were before their time. It is nice to have so many pictures added to the repertoire of my 'Best'. It was a thrilling but upsetting morning, for I felt that I was dead and that people were talking of me in the past. 'The greatest collection by one person of any subject in our service' It was also very disturbing to see how many of the people were completely forgotten. But so many too were brought back to life from death.

It is very eerie to discover at the age of 70 I have survived so many younger people. Here were ADCs and husbands of Wavell's[1] daughters all long since out of the running. And those that have survived are no longer recognisable. It was fascinating to see the scenes in old Imperial Simla, the rickshaws drawn by uniformed servants, the grandeur of the houses, the palaces. It was extraordinary to see the bar scenes, the men on leave, swigging beer and how I had been able to 'frat[ernise]' with such unlikely types. It was a morning of deep concentration and when three hours had passed and I uncrossed my legs and got up from the dark to prepare myself to go home, it was as if I had been living in a completely different world.

I went out into the grey dreariness of Lambeth. It has been a particularly revolting week with strikes, rationing of electricity and fuel, with bitterness spreading, and dark grey skies, altogether the lowest mark of many a long day, and I felt that in spite of all the horror of the worry, much of it had been rather beautiful, in great heat, in places of wonderful natural landscapes, and although I am very optimistic by nature, felt that perhaps my life today has become less exciting, but overwork has covered me like a pall, and that I should allow more time for enjoyment and lack of anxiety.

I came away pleased that I had done such big jobs (I must go back and see the other half – all Egypt and the Middle East, and England at war), and marvelled that I had done it with only one Rolleiflex. How it wasn't broken, I do not know. How I had used no shade, or the lens or light meter. Yet it had worked and some of them are, apart from their historic interest, extremely beautiful. If I had not been feeling so tired and ill (as a result of mumps), I would have been pleased with myself. As it was, I was

---

[1] Field Marshal Earl Wavell (1883–1950), Viceroy of India 1943–7.

relieved to be going off for a change of air and atmosphere, to stay with Tom[1] and Fulco [di Verdura] at Brighton.

Cecil was horrified to hear that James Pope-Hennessy had been murdered at his home in Ladbroke Grove by three thieves, searching for a rumoured £150,000 advance given him by American publishers for a book on Noël Coward. Sean Seamus O'Brien (sometimes called John O'Brien), a train guard, and Terence Noonan, unemployed, were sentenced for manslaughter. Later their sentences were reduced to twelve years and ten years. In an appeal the judges said that Pope-Hennessy had suffered only superficial injuries and died as a result of choking on his own blood from a lip wound.

Death of James Pope-Hennessy   25 January 1974

The various news items on the television come and go so rapidly that one wonders at times if one has heard aright. My heart missed a beat as I learnt that James had been severely beaten up, wounded and stabbed. A photograph of James's poetical face was shown on the screen, and before one could take in the horror that in fact James had died as a result of the mugging, the news moved on to Ireland or to a football match.

I was struck by an overwhelming sorrow and horror that did not leave me during the night. When I woke and the breakfast tray came in with the newspapers and letters, my hopes that the newsflash might have been an aberration were dashed when I saw the same beautiful face in a photograph on the front page. I looked at my letters. Surely this envelope was written in James's hand? I opened it and a most tender, friendly, sweet letter from him (someone I had not lately heard from) pierced me to the heart. James was thanking me for a present I sent him at Christmas, which he had found on his recent return from America where he had been interviewing friends of Nöel Coward for his forthcoming biography, and he longed to meet me again.[2]

James came into my life at the beginning of the last war with such a new and fresh sort of appeal. He had 'quality', was intelligent, and intellectual, and serious, and yet such good company. I became influenced by him and he was a 'highclass' influence. I delighted in him and we became fast friends. We did a book together, he the text and I the photographs, on the bombing of London. Our expeditions to the city were not only dramatic, often tragic, but very enjoyable. Sometimes after exploring the

[1] Tom Parr, interior decorator, with Colefax and Fowler.
[2] The serious purpose of the letter was to seek information about Coward.

still-smoking ruins, we went to the Strand and ate a good lunch in a restaurant. At a time when food was becoming scarce this was an added excitement.

James seemed to be as full of delight and surprise in the things I knew and talked about as he was with the world that had imbued in him perhaps by the redoubtable Dame Una, ever since he was a small boy. James introduced me to Clarissa Churchill (to become a life-time friend), and to many others whom I delighted in.

I remember seeing James from a taxi as he got out of another taxi in front of Batsford's. He was late, he was panicky, his arms full of books. As he descended, his hat hit the top of the taxi, hat and books went flying. I saw in that glimpse myself.

Later James tended to be rather difficult. He drank too much. He made friendships too easily with the 'the lower orders'. This was danger-ous and extremely boring for his other friends, who often said, 'Unless he's lucky, one day James will find himself murdered.' James lost his looks, became bellicose, devilish and impossible. Maybe drugs, as an anti-dote to drink, did improve the situation. 'You do spread your friendships thin,' he once taunted me. I was hurt. Every time I returned from America I brought him a present. I was always the one to ring first. He seldom took the initiative and then there would be a long silence; and now this.

It seems that his murderer was a young Irishman whom James had brought back from Ireland after his long sojourn there writing the life of Trollope. (The Windsors had said, 'he's writing a life of a trollop. Ha. Ha!') The man had stayed in his house, then sent away, went to prison for a beating-up in a pub. Len,[1] James's good Samaritan, a house painter, employed this Irishman, Shaun, to help him, had gone with others to paint Ann Fleming's house in the country. Anne adored him.[2] He climbed up trees and brought down birds' nests.

It seems James at dinner the night before his death said to his servant,[3] 'We must have a carving knife.' Next morning Shaun and his accomplices came to ransack the flat for the enormous advance the *Evening Standard* had said James was being paid for his life of Coward. James had been bludgeoned, gagged and roped to a chair. When the servant, Les, arrived

---

[1] Len Adams, described by Peter Quennell as 'James's confidant, travelling companion, aide de camp, bodyguard, household help and general nanny, even in times of crisis, a limited privy purse'.

[2] Ann Fleming later wrote, 'Of all Len's assistants the one I liked and talked to was Sean Seamus O'Brien; he adored the country, seemed a beautiful woodland creature, found birds' nests by instinct, shinned up tree trunks, was shy and good-mannered. *How* could he have murdered James?'

[3] Leslie Smith, Pope-Hennessy's valet, then aged twenty-five.

back from shopping, he too was attacked, a witness, to be got rid of. Les produced the newly bought carving knife, stabbed one of the men, who subsequently fainted in a no. 88 bus, and a blood bath started. Les, hand almost cut off and face slashed, managed to escape into the street. How the others got away I don't know since James's house is opposite the police station. Blood everywhere, James's flat in turmoil, the three men caught and now up for time. But sadly James's name will be everlastingly smirched and he might so soon have been a reformed character and safe.

For many days I was stricken with the memory of James's charm, sweetness, bright intelligence and high quality. Then by degrees it became rather a solace to remember that for some time now James had no longer been the person I knew and loved. It was the last stage of Dorian Gray that had met the awful, macabre and terrifying death. One shuddered still at the possibility of what the last minutes must have been, and one almost hoped that he had been drunk or unconscious, and one wondered why oh why James with such talent, charm and good looks had gone the way he had.[1]

10 February 1974

A financial blow. Eileen told me that £7,000 in tax is due and that I have not the money with which to pay. I have been living at a rate far above my station and must seriously retrench on staff. And possibly sell many of the things I like. It is an impossibility to know in advance how one's tax is going to turn out. If one had had a good year, then the tax comes in 2 years later, and one is unable to pay after a bad patch. It is disturbing and I have spent the last two years doing things I enjoy (writing books that don't bring in much), rather than battling in Hollywood or on Broadway. It is unnerving, and I'd hate to have to give up Reddish, but there is no doubt that I am behaving stupidly in not saving for the years that may be spared me, and spending more than I make.

11 February 1974

For better or for worse, I feel I have finished my play. Hal Burton, who has been so helpful in giving it a plot, has to read it once again and will doubtless make a few more suggestions, but I feel I must have [come] nearer my goal, and it is a relief to feel, for better or worse, this is it. I see what a folly it was to send it to Michael Codron or anybody in its former state. But one of the difficulties for would-be playwrights is that people

---

[1] Cecil's account of all this tallies concisely with later published versions.

who can give them constructive advice are so very scarce, and one does not know what one has perpetrated.

When he first rang me, Hal said, 'No, no, it is not a play. Nothing happens. No one plays against anyone. It is completely static.' And he was right. He went on, 'It is full of effervescence and witty, bright dialogue.' I asked, 'But can it be *given* the necessary?' A pause. Hal deliberating, then said, 'Yaais' and went on to say he thought it could be given the bones, the structure, on which the flesh must be built. I am more than grateful to him. But I don't know now what to dare to think, who to give it to, or what to hope for it. It is very important to me that it succeeds, ridiculously so perhaps. I long for a production at a small London theatre, more than for my photography book to be a success. It would really give me enormous satisfaction if I could have produced (with Hal's directives) something that could run for six months.

Everything is in the lap of Fate. But I go to Mexico in a spirit of thankfulness that the work has just been done 'under the wire', and that I can have a really restful holiday and build up my depleted physical system.

The Kingfisher   *February 1974*

The winter garden has become one of the most magical places in the garden. To visit this place of rushing water, babbling brook and bird is like arriving in a different country. (To think that all these years I was hardly conscious that a river did go past my property!) Every sort of bird seems to congregate here, quite different from those that come to the terrace. We are surprised often to see a heron or two on the lookout for fish, but the greatest excitement is to see a kingfisher, a rare enough streak of blue was seen by Isaac. Then Hal saw one fly past like a dart. It is said that kingfishers fly so quickly that by the time one says 'Look!' they have gone.

This most brilliant metallic bird is said to have such an unpleasant smell for other birds that it is solitary and safe, yet it is said to be very scarce. Yet suddenly I saw one, and the sight gladdened my fading spirit. Then one day not only did a kingfisher fly past me, but landed on some reeds by the river's edge. Here it stayed awhile, then another came out, and the two flew in opposite directions. I am hoping that a family will be hatched in the spring, and that these marvellous feathers, the colour of a Brazilian butterfly, will give an additional gladness every visit to this lovely scene.

Diana Vreeland   *March 1974*

'Pink is the Blue of India.'
  'Think top lid!'

Bat Stuart[1]

Bat has friends and real friends in every part. Her horizons seem to be limitless. She knows the fantastic stories that have happened in the upper echelons throughout the world. How her best friend, Jane Stewart[2] was made to take Mrs Graham, the wife of the Evangelist,[3] to see her father.[4] On arrival she was told Lord Londonderry was indisposed. 'I must see him. I've come all the way on Billy's account.' So Jane took Mrs Graham up to where the drunken Marquess was lying in bed. 'This is Mrs Graham, father.' Lord L. threw aside the bed sheets and shouted, 'Get in.'

Bat also regales us with true inside stories, of how Stavros Niarchos[5], in one of his blind rages, kicked Eugenie in the pancreas, broke the vital organ and she died.[6] Bat is not only extremely factual, and not given to exaggeration, but is also extremely artistic at getting into the skin of the people she is telling about. With gesture of lower lip protruding, and trying to find the side wisps of hair, she becomes Diana Vreeland, telling us of US housewives wearing nothing while doing their housework, yet when the doorbell rings, they don the 'open the door housecoat'.

Bat also tells of how Diane emphasises things as being 'Blue, blue, blue', or is someone 'totally' innocent, or a 'total' man. Good too are the imitations of Diane with Kitty [Miller] and Margaret Case in Majorca, all drunk before lunch. Kitty, on seeing Diane in a black kaftan, shouts, 'You look like a camel driver!' Margaret, straight and stiff in her chair, nodding

---

[1] Bat Stuart, first wife of Hon. John Stuart, second son of first Viscount Stuart of Findhorn. She was Cecile Barr. She first married George Tonge, then Stuart from 1957 until their divorce in 1958. She was a 'walker' to Kitty Miller. Now deceased.
[2] Lady Jane Vane-Tempest-Stewart (b.1932), now Lady Rayne.
[3] Billy Graham (b.1918).
[4] The eighth Marquess of Londonderry (1902–1955).
[5] Stavros Niarchos (1909–1996), one of the great Greek shipowners in the same league as Aristotle Onassis. He had a villa on Spetsai. When he died, he was largely forgotten and his death did not inspire the publicity that attended him for much of his life.
[6] Eugenie Niarchos (1926–70), one of the Livanos sisters. Her death on the island of Spetsopoula was certainly the subject of some innuendo at the time. Stavros Niarchos then married (1971) her sister, Tina, formerly Marchioness of Blandford, and before that married to Onassis. She also predeceased him (1974).

asleep backwards, is woken by Kitty shouting, 'Why don't you go to bed?' and Margaret saying, 'No, I want to hear what is going on!'

Perhaps funniest of all are Bat's recollections of the life now completely ended that took place for so many years at Vaynol. Here Michael, a great eccentric if ever there was one, would entertain an extraordinary mixture of people, and play tricks on unsuspecting neighbours. Once they were backed all the way up the drive and given the dinner in reverse order, starting with coffee and liqueurs, and ending with soup. Once Peter Lubbock[1] was treated like a horse. His meals were of oat, locked in a stable and when he got to his room, his bedroom was full of hay. The joke ended by PL suffering a terrible attack of asthma. Nanny Thorpe appeared and gave the entire household a great demonstration of how firm she can be. Quite right too. Most of the jokes were harmless as when the D. of Kent was staying and each night they'd listen in on the telephone, and hear, 'Clear the line for the King, clear the line,' and eventually the gruff monarch [George V] would say, 'And how are you? Your mother's got a bit of a chest.'

The change in a lifetime is quite remarkable. Now Michael is very lonely at Vaynol, which is exceedingly run-down, and few people can afford the train fare and so few neighbours are anything but dreary bores.

On 15 February 1974 Cecil flew to Mexico for a holiday. He found that Mexico City had acquired 'the ugliness and impersonality of every huge city in the States.' He drove on 'for many hideous miles' to Cuernavaca ('the City of Eternal Spring') to stay with two Americans that he did not know, Brad Fuller and Jack Kleiser. Though grateful for their hospitality, Cecil concluded 'their life is not mine and it worries me that the niveau *is so different.' Their house was next to a penitentiary:*

One can see the guards in their birds' nests while others prowl the roofs with rifles over their arms. All day long orders are shouted at the incarcerated persons, who are 'said' to be humanely treated. But there are conflicting stories. The guttural rasping is not a pleasant accompaniment to this life of idle society gossip. It makes its futility all the more pointed.

A high spot of the holiday was to visit the prison.

---

[1] Peter Lubbock (1909–1985), travel agent by profession, half-brother to various Tennant sisters, including Lady Eliot of Harwood and Lady Wakehurst.

Visit to Prison   *February 1974*

Was rather dreading seeing what goes on behind the barbed wire walls that are quite near to our garden and from whence the cries and orders of the prison guards can be heard all day long, in fact from 6 to 6. We could hardly believe that the government would allow us to see inside. But, indeed, it proved to be possible to visit and to discover how 'humane' is the treatment doled out to malefactors.

The arrival and long-delayed entry made everything that followed appear more dramatic. Guards stood around with rifles at the ready, others were eating sugar cane with a great crunch. We were scrutinised through a small window for quite a time. We were put to tests, asked to show we had no keys and then were allowed through various heavy doors, painted bright blue. Once inside this bright blue was everywhere to be seen. All the walls of the various buildings, the dormitories, and houses, football confines etc., were white but everything else painted blue. It was surprising to see the men, in all sorts of different clothes, lolling around and talking to their visiting womenfolk, or doing that stirring work, whose name I forget, which is supposed to be a kind of therapy.

The hard labourers were smoking, squatting and breaking stones, not an inspiring pastime but by no means arduous and the young man who showed us round was 'in' for murder. A drunk tried to get his girl, hit him with a bottle, and in return was hit by this young man so hard that his head was cracked open and he died. The 'culprit', awaiting trial – it will come up in a few months – was astonishing looking with the narrowest hips, long legs, high cheekbones, a Genghis Khan moustache and beret worn over his long curly hair at just the right angle. It was a very chic appearance, but his eyes were like darts, coal black, and you would not trust him an inch. He showed us the prisoners making shoes, sandals, pants, handbags, 'wall hangs' and belts.

The prison became, by degrees, almost a sympathetic place in which to work. Roses were growing in neat parterres and huge ficus trees gave shade. Each individual free to do what he wanted (he must work to pay for his keep and food). Most of them confined here had been caught selling drugs. The minimum sentence is three years, can be 20! (An American, whose plane had crashed killing all but herself and boyfriend, when they were miraculously pitched out [was here]. The police found dope in their bags and here they remain unfortunately.)

Some of the women looked quite slick and relaxed, and one wondered how one would feel, if by some misfortune, one were to find oneself here, incapable of escape, and having to find the intellectual resources to remain here with no thought of ever living anywhere else.

It is perhaps easy to say that mankind becomes accustomed to any conditions, but how difficult it must be even for the poorest Mexicans here, who are said to be very lacking in brain matter, to reconcile themselves to their fate. I have been feeling sorry for myself quite a lot of my time here, complaining miserably of the bad food, the boring people and parties, the emptiness. But one is comparatively free, one is able to indulge oneself quite a lot. One is not shouted at, and at the mercy of the sugar-cane-eating guards with their likes and dislikes. It was good to know that a lot of the shouts we heard all day long were not invective, but calls to those other guards to open the next locked door to whoever may be given permission to move from one quarter to another.

I came home low in spirits, but thankful for what benefits there were to be had.

Presently, Cecil was pleased that Sam Green arrived and that they could proceed to Guatemala:

Sam's cheerful voice and infectious smile made all the difference. The last 10 days has been without his sort of appreciation and understanding.

Dinner at a pretentious restaurant after seeing *Jesus, Jesus Super Star* [sic] (no good really), made poignant by the arrival of Queen Marie José of Italy[1] and her naughtiest daughter.[2] Suddenly you *knew* these were personalities. They exuded an aura. They looked and sounded so highly civilised among the incredibly gauche waiters and ghastly tourists.

The General Election   *February 1974*

The General Election is being held today in England. Am terrified of the results. Kin in San Fran. told me the result was not known finally, that it was neck and neck, that Heath had been dealt a terrible blow, and the future looks more complicated than ever. Am aghast, at a distance and disgusted that that little swine, Auberon Waugh, in an article in the *NY Times* continues to denigrate his country abroad. Prospect not bright.

Am longing to leave Mexico with its smug and ugly native colourings, never to return. Am thinking Guatemala will make the whole expedition worthwhile.

---

[1] Marie José (1906–2001), daughter of King Albert I of the Belgians, married King Umberto of Italy.
[2] Princess Maria Gabriella (b.1940), married at one time to the property developer, Robert de Balkany. Enjoyed a flirt with Earl Mountbatten, as recorded in his diaries, a flirt somewhat disapproved of by his family.

The Mexico that I first visited with Peter Watson has vanished, and there are no echoes. The opera dome has been completed, but the city is now built on a Paris design with avenues of trees, but it has no character and America has abandoned it as another country.

Leaving Mexico I saw, on the way to the airport, newspaper sellers rushing around with the headlines 'Panic in London Banks'. My heart stopped.

Guatemala *February 1974*

For almost a week we have heard no news of the Election result until last night the *Miami Herald*, that most incompetent of all papers, gave a story that Wilson had gained the most votes, but had failed to get a majority, and that Heath was being urged by newspapers to resign. So much depends on Thorpe,[1] but the situation could not be more unsatisfactory, or disastrous for the country. I am aghast at the thought of hearing the worst, but must wait till I get to Florida to find out the worst. At the moment I feel like a Mayan at the end of his civilisation.

From Mexico City Sam and Cecil proceeded to Guatemala, visiting Chichicastenango, San Antonio, and then Antigua. Though interested in what he saw, Cecil hated the tourists, but enjoyed observing his travelling companion:

Sam has an extraordinary eye for discovering among the junk in the worst antique shops some object that is beautiful or valuable. He has thus paid for all his trips, and here in the most unexpected quarters, he has found a beautiful Ghirlandaio-esque cameo, a wooden crucifixion, masses of stuffs and embroidery, plate, on which he will make a vast profit, likewise a Japanese coffee set, and a rude crouching carved figure of Christ, which he is most daringly and generously and firmly giving to John Richardson.[2]

Sam, exasperated by his flu-cold, nevertheless took misfortune with his accustomed gaiety. When things are wrong, he becomes a placid martyr, which is strange since he is such a fighter and go-getter at the best of times, and we enumerate the trips abroad we have taken – Peru, Bolivia, Jamaica, Italy, Dordogne, and this one had been well worthwhile, if only that from now, Mexico and Guatemala need not be on our list.

---

[1] Jeremy Thorpe (b.1929), leader of the Liberal Party, 1967–1976.
[2] John Richardson (b.1924), art historian, biographer of Picasso, and author of razor-sharp memoirs and essays.

Palm Beach   *11 March 1974*

The past five days have been spent bathing in the milk of luxury of the Wrightsmans' house. After the exigencies of travel, it has never before appeared so congenial and beautiful. We have done little but rest, talk, look at picture books, read, swim and I have even done a bit of work on my play. It is only now that I am beginning to realise how out of sorts and depleted I have been for a long time on end. Now I am, after being appalled at the reflection in the mirror, beginning to look a little better colour (though my eyes have lost their strength and I'll have to dye my eyelashes if I want emphasis!).

The house, the pool, the garden, have memories for me that go back a long way. It was a high spot for me when I used to gad about here in the days of Mona Williams. Today life is very different. Whereas it used to be a three o'clock bedtime, after a spell at a local nightclub, now we are in our rooms by 10.30 or earlier. It is all very serene and delightful and thus calm is arrived at, at enormous expense.

Jayne has made the place beautiful with the help of the best decorators and highest museum quality furniture. The flowers are arranged with consummate care. Altogether, there are fourteen servants indoors, at least six outside, and Jules, the giant French chauffeur. There are indeed few places left where existence is carried on at such a scale, and perhaps this is the last lap of luxury for me, at any rate until I can return to this country, for on returning from the wilds of Guatemala, where newspapers were sparse and inadequate it has now become known that the worst has happened at home, that that swine Wilson has taken power again, that that good man Heath, with his courage and determination for fairness, has been pipped by a whisker, and that we are now in for a period of wildly rising prices and possible economic bankruptcy.

Esmond Rothermere[1] came to dinner and when asked what he thought of Wilson's return, said, 'It would be very good for inflation.' The miners have been given their exorbitant demands, and already six other unions are on the strike bandwagon. Charlie Wrightsman, who has not made and kept his great fortune by luck, sees the future of the US as extremely gloomy. 'Already we are in the middle of a great recession,' he says, and everyone is having to alter their way of life. 'There will not be any way of having servants and carrying on as we have. A great change is taking place. There will be wealth taxes, and perhaps we have a year left.' A year is not a long time.

---

[1] Esmond, second Viscount Rothermere (1898–1978), newspaper proprietor (*Daily Mail*).

Meanwhile, what will the immediate future bring to me? My resolve and intention is that having now recovered from near exhaustion, I must really try hard to see that I do not overtax myself in the way I have for so long. Perhaps with the play finished there will not be the necessity. I must allow myself time for reading (and keep writing to a minimum). I must draw and paint and do things that do not nurture headaches. As for hopes, there is the play, and as nice Mrs Waugh in the village said, 'How brave of you to do something that always brings with it so many difficulties.' The photographic book is still to be finished, the pleasant part to be done, and then I must do work that is not such a financial risk if I am to compete with the present crisis and keep my own particular wolf from the door.

Chas W.: 'I wouldn't take his recommendation on a can of dog food.'

Return from Palm Beach *March 1974*

Five days living in the void of such extreme luxury as only the Wrightsmans can provide in that most escapist last-call of hideouts, was just about as much as I could endure. These days did me a great deal of good after the strenuous travel, but even so I had my play to work on all morning. When that came to an end, I am faced with a blank day before taking the plane away from the orange trees, kumquats and gardenias, into the basic reality of London under Wilson's minority government.

The plane journey was horrid, much of the night being spent in a degree of terror as we tightened our seat belts against the turbulence (shades of my Dakota crash!). However, arrival was safe, though low cloud had sent all earlier planes to Manchester, and I was soon back at my desk piled high with long letters, feeling wonderfully relaxed and without my usual impatience to get on with the next thing. Eileen told me of the wretchedness of England during the recent election, the messy result and the *un-British* (!) bad manners of booing Heath as he left No. 10 and the poignant photographs of his belongings, piano, pee pot and yachting cap, being taken out of his home as if the bailiffs had seized his possessions.

By degrees, only, will we realise the mess we're in, as when I walked round the water garden with Smallpeice. 'What's happened to all the white irises I've planted?' 'The mice have eaten them.' 'Can't we put down some traps?' 'No good now.' 'All the silt has blocked the entrance to our spring – can't that be moved?' 'Nothing to move it with.' 'Can't we get a long-handled spade?' 'Haven't got one.' 'Can't I ring Woodmans or Brewers?' 'They won't have one. Salisbury doesn't have anything like that.' Frustration set in.

My very quiet return was a bit of an anti-climax for I caught a cold at the Festival committee meeting (icy room, back to window). The financial news of the Festival is disastrous and we're in a great state lest all our efforts will have been in vain and the project cancelled, and spring does not seem any nearer than when I left a month ago. Smallpeice delivered his Parthian shot. 'And we've got the blackthorn winter to come on yet!'

The Mugging

Marilyn Quennell, a rather unaccountable girl, planned an extremely congenial party for Peter's[1] 69th birthday celebration. A dinner to begin with, with lots of old friends, Cyril C., Freddie Ayer, John Betj., Anne T. and Eliz C.,[2] was followed by a scrimmage of people that represented the tastes of Peter, literary and decorative. I sat on a sofa talking to Kathleen Tynan[3] and later Evangeline Bruce,[4] who, knowing that I enjoy leaving an evening as early as she, suggested we should telephone for a taxi. 'Don't bother. I'll get one on the doorstep as people are still arriving.'

Evangeline waited with a large group in the hall while I waited in vain. A group from the dark dining room passed me on their way out. Laura Canfield, now Laura, Duchess of Marlborough, since she was wed to old Bert for about 10 days. I complimented her on her appearance, kissed her, then passed Philip and Mary Dunn, both friends of mine, followed by the 'Mad Boy' [Robert] Heber Percy, who wore his asinine grin. As he was within 18 inches of me he surprisingly gave me the most terrific blow on the chin.

This sent me a few inches further away from him so that he arrived a most terrific, frenetic kick at my balls. The aim failed, or my overcoat softened the pain, but I found myself down the three front door steps on the pavement.

Here the Mad Boy had me in the ring and he shot out punches of ungoverned rage at my face, one on the eye. I saw stars, one on the jaw, one missed my nose, not that soon I knew where the blows were falling. All I did know was that suddenly, in a flash, I was being seriously beaten up.

---

[1] Sir Peter Quennell (1905–93) and his wife Marilyn, formerly Lady Peek.
[2] Cyril Connolly, Professor Sir Frederick Ayer, Sir John Betjeman, Lady Anne Tree and Lady Elizabeth Cavendish.
[3] Kathleen Tynan (1937–95), second wife and biographer of Kenneth Tynan (1927–80), the acerbic critic.
[4] Evangeline Bruce (1914–95), wife of David Bruce, American Ambassador in London, and author of *Napoleon and Josephine*.

My mind flashed to past years. When a boy, one felt one might at any moment come across this violence. In fact, one had had to take boxing at a private school, and this consisted of receiving numbing, painful blows on the nose. Suddenly this fear was a reality, and long after one thought such things possible, for curiously at the back of one's senses, one may have felt that one of the advantages of becoming elderly was that one was likely to escape this sort of violence.

But no, here was the Mad Boy paying off a very old score. There might have been scenes like this at any time in the last 30 years, since I first knew him, and Gerald Berners[1] confessed to me at the end of a weekend at Vaynol that he had fallen in love with him. But this onslaught was the result of my having written and published in my diary the fact that [the] Berners family, much to their surprise and disappointment, had been bypassed at Gerald's death and that the Mad Boy had inherited money, house and all its contents, but that Gerald's last days were not happy ones. The Mad Boy had gone to a lawyer to sue, had been told he had not got a case, so he had waited his chance to take the law into his own hands, break it and give me my comeuppance.

Unfortunately, the circumstances were ideal for him. I am no good at the art of self-defence and only made feeble attempts to hide my face. I shut my eyes, saw nothing, but heard the Dunns and Laura say, 'Robert! Robert! Stop it, Robert!' Then presumably they faded away and left me to my fate.

So this was it! I felt I was in a limbo, not of pain, but of shock and terror, for I did not know where this would end. The blows continued. I hung on to the roof of a parked car. I hung on to some railings. I would not shout for help. I did not utter, neither did I run back to shelter. Some ridiculous pride prevented me from doing anything but suffer silently. Mercifully, although I felt dizzy by now, I did not fall to my feet, for then the maniacal fury of my opponent, my lifelong enemy, would have inspired him to kick my face in.

'Now run! Now run!' I heard him taunt me. Then somehow the mugging was over, why, I did not know! Later I discovered that Philip Dunn had decided to come back to the scene of the massacre and pull the Mad Boy off me. I went into the Quennell house, told Evangeline I'd been beaten up, and sat on the stairs, panting as if I'd finished a mile sprint. My nose was not broken, neither were my teeth, my face was very sore and some blood came from my ear. But I was safe. Eliz C. and John B. were terribly upset, and so too the Tynans, who took me home in their car. 'No, no brandy. I'll have a couple of aspirins and go to sleep.' But of course I did not sleep. The shock kept me awake for hours, and my sleep

---

[1] Gerald, fourteenth Lord Berners (1883–1950), eccentric musician and composer, owner of Faringdon.

was eventually made nightmarish with memories of the 'stars' I'd seen and the sheer violence.

Charlotte [Gaffran] came to give me exercises next morning. When told the story she said, 'You are cold and shivery. That's a sign of the shock. You need to be calm. I'll give you a massage and you'd better go to the doctor as soon as possible.'

Of course the telephone never stopped ringing. Some friends were deeply sympathetic, others really only after a firsthand account in order to be able to relay the gossip. And then the time-wasting talks about whether to bring the assailant to book and perhaps prevent or discourage him from further violence, or to let him laugh to himself that he got away with it.

PS, after a great deal of worry and expense, although the solicitor thought I would have a good case,[1] I decided against facing up to so much worry and bad publicity, and to forget the whole bloody business. Unfortunately it is not so easy to forget, and often I have visions of the traumatic experience happening again, and I have wondered whether or not I am fated to meet with a sticky end.

18 April 1974

Not a very good month, perhaps better than winter, but the beauty of the English springtime, though more marvellous than one had ever remembered it, has been marred by jarring cold winds. Horrific general news & often horrible personal experiences – such as bad temper or 'leavings' in the household. Mrs Eide has been such a prop, such an exquisite French cook for a year, that her bettering herself by going to manage the Maxwell Josephs' chateau in the Dordogne has given us an upheaval.

Worse, a flaming row with my sister Nancy. The Kodak people put on a very good show in Holborn of my life's work and I intended mentioning how happy I was that one of my earliest models was still with us this afternoon. Not only did Nancy arrive too late for the speech-making but when she saw me came up with a pursed grin of pleasure to tell me that I had post-dated by ten years the only photograph of herself. This was the straw on the camel's back, the 'once too often' extravagance of 'knocking me down', 'putting me in my place' etc. I was beside myself with rage, let out a volley of fury there and then, and continued when the Smileys came

---

[1] Cecil's lawyer, Mr W.D. Park of Linklaters and Paines wrote on 16 April 1974, that Cecil would probably have won if he had sued, but was wise not to proceed. 'May I suggest you give a party for all your friends, show them this letter and then forget the whole thing.'

back to the house for dinner. Hugh, like a turkeycock, shouting 'He would not have his wife abused', Nancy in a state of terror of him. A really horrible row. Equally distressing for all. But the result is that I will never give Nancy any of my books or allow her to criticise any of my work in future. I cannot lay myself open to such tiresome and unnecessary and unimportant criticism.

Alan [Tagg] & Charles [Colville] came for Easter. For four days we conversed, went for walks, ate enormously and did only the minimum of work. (Still my play has to go on being retyped!) Alan has a wonderful way of seeing the humour in every conversation and amused me by [relating] Michael Duff's intent keenness on hearing that Byron loathed his mother and loved boys. Michael, who loathed his mother, kept asking, 'And Byron loathed his mother, didn't he? He loathed her. He loathed his mother, didn't he! And he preferred boys, didn't he? He preferred boys to girls, didn't he!' Alan never forgets anything that has amused him in the past.

He relayed to me a scene when Juliet [Duff] and Simon [Fleet] had returned from a visit to Enid Bagnold Jones, with whom I was having a ten-year feud, and hating every aspect of her ugliness from a distance, her thinning hair, her nutcracker jaw, her double-lidded eyes. Juliet and Simon vied with one another to describe how well she had looked, and how well dressed she had been as a hostess. They described her Arabian clothes, her jewellery, her sandals, her skin, her smooth face. When the eulogies were over, I asked, 'And what does she do for hair?'

Mrs Stokes   *April 1974*

Mrs S. knew her husband was dying as he lay in the bed beside her. She rushed out of their new bungalow to get aid, but in the middle of the night was unable to rouse any neighbours. She rushed back to find the door of the bungalow had slammed shut behind her. No key. At last the doctor's locum was roused, [Dr Christopher] Brown being in hospital with badly slipped disc.

By the time help came, Mr Stokes was dead. Mrs S. has taken it badly, doesn't enjoy Bingo any more, doesn't want to go away or go on bus tours. She is off for 2 weeks (the gardener's wife rather complaining about doing the grates), but Eileen says she thinks Mrs Stokes will really enjoy being a widow, enjoy her independence, and 'come into her own'.

Staggering what a quiet life Clarissa [Avon] leads here looking after Anthony. They came to lunch last week and it was an event. They don't seem to 'see' anyone. They are content to keep to themselves and of course Anthony has to preserve his energy. It is due to Clarissa's nursing and devotion that he is still alive and although they are both bad-tempered and shout at one another, they get along marvellously and Clarissa accepts her life as inevitable.

She thinks now that after Anthony's death she will most probably live abroad, possibly in Portugal.

Raimund died   April 1974

He would have been miserable if he'd survived the operation which would have made him an invalid. Rai was not for old age. He died three years later than he should. The zest was lagging, the smile sad, the spring in his gait was no longer there.

He was a life enhancer. He had no ambition. He was good, kind, full of such charm that the first time I met him I could not believe he had not immediately fallen in love with me. But Rai had no time for the boys...Rai loved ladies, England, music, youth. He has enriched my existence a lot. I am grateful to him.

As for Diana, she's bereft. She said, 'I'm tough about death.' But Raimund's death has knocked her badly. It came at a time when she could not get rid of a bad bout of flu. She has aged suddenly. Her appearance has suffered and she no longer seems to care (not that she ever did). Even so she remains an extraordinary machine, a subtle electronic device that knows so much. With her death will come a great loss of understanding of life in its now fast disappearing attitudes, a loss of experience, subtlety, goodness, benevolence (I was surprised to hear her say yesterday about K. Keith,[1] 'Yes, I dislike him intensely and I hardly ever dislike anyone!'), and a loss above all of wit and humour.

Diana walked round my cold garden in the thinnest of clothes. She had come to see the orchard ablaze with poppylike tulips and jonquils. 'Yes, it was worth it. Yes, it's always worth it to come to Sissel's. Lovely present of spring flowers and in that beautiful basket. It's the *basket* that counts too.'

Reddish   3 May 1974

Awful to be so dependent on servants. But the departure of Mrs Eide to her grand chateau (Jewish) in the Dordogne has thrown a spanner in the

---

[1] Sir Kenneth Keith (b.1916), later Lord Keith of Castleacre, merchant banker and businessman, married to Slim Hayward.

works here. Mrs Smallpeice, the gardener's wife, is working so frenziedly for the curtain going up on the opening 'for the nurses' on Sunday that she does not wish to do anything but lay breakfast. Mrs Stokes, the daily lady, has been away, trying to recover from the shock of her husband's death, so I am alone with a cold chicken. This all right up to a point, but it is maddening when there is more than a little washing-up. Eileen came down to stay and found another couple, and we had one of our rare (thank God) dust-ups, while under the influence of champagne. And when the washing-up was going on, Eileen makes it clear that I don't know how to do anything in the kitchen the right way, and the moment comes...

But it *is* sad that at the time of the year when the countryside is so beautiful and the garden begins to look as it should, I am unable to invite friends to stay.

I have rather enjoyed not having them during the long, cold weeks of the past months and it has given me an opportunity to slog on at my photo book and the play. Now both these have been sent off. Also a Lily Elsie for the Oxford University Press,[1] and now all that remains to be finished up from a great number of oddments is an introduction to the reissue of *Three Weeks*.[2]

Meanwhile I'm waiting to hear if Michael Codron[3] is to be the first to deliver a shattering blow by 'refusing' to do my play. He is the person I would most like to do it, and have therefore let him see it a second time. (It was a charade when inadvertently I sent it before.) He is quick to experiment, he is really professional and contemporary, and maybe my play may strike him as being amusingly old-fashioned. Anyhow the waiting period is agonising, and I shall feel quite sick if I see, on my return to London, that tell-tale large envelope.

Meanwhile, while waiting, while doing nothing, I should be enjoying myself. But this does not seem to be a good period. So often in the past week I have been upset (Mary Pembroke by her lack of sensitivity, Tom Blau[4] – his pushing over the abyss, etc.) and this lack of serenity is apt to give me a headache.

I really feel stale, and have been pushing against odds for too long now. I long to have a change, to start off again. But since I am incapable

---

[1] Cecil wrote Lily Elsie's entry for the *Dictionary of National Biography*.
[2] Cecil wrote an introduction to the reissue of this novel by Elinor Glyn. Published by Duckworth (1974).
[3] Michael Codron (b.1930), theatrical producer of Harold Pinter, Joe Orton, Simon Gray, Tom Stoppard, Alan Ayckbourn etc.
[4] Tom Blau (1913–84), an Hungarian who founded Camera Press in 1947, which distributed Cecil's photographs. Sometimes he annoyed his photographers by taking portrait photos himself. Author of *In and Out of Focus* (1983).

of even the simplest form of cooking, I must only hope that someone will come to the rescue, and make life a bit easier in the country, where everything is planned, at great expense, for it to be easy.

Sir Alfred and Lady Beit[1] were robbed of nine million pounds worth of paintings, stolen from their home, Russborough, Co Wicklow, Ireland. They were tied up at gunpoint and Sir Alfred was hit on the head when he dared to look around.

Alfred and Clementine are a gloomy, sad, boring couple (childlessness is one of the reasons), but they both behave with such calm dignity when telling the TV people of their horrible, shocking experience of being bound, knocked about and robbed of nine million pounds' worth. Two kinder people do not exist. It is awful it should have happened to them.[2]

PS, NB   *5 May 1974*

All the 19 paintings stolen have been recovered.

Such odd letters to be answered. One from a man saying he is looking forward to bringing his mother aged 92 to the garden opening on Sunday, and may his mother use my loo.

The stars really do seem to influence me (and one's state of health does also!). It has been a difficult time and I feel even a bit disenchanted with the home in the country. It has been so cold and wretched. I am cook-less and on edge. This week there have been rows with Blau, of Camera Press, and I find nowadays, with age, that the tensions bring on a headache. And I have to resort (though only occasionally) to calming pills.

The morning ritual of Timothy, the cat, coming to my bed, is something I enjoy. He is energetic, sometimes unruly, but lately has been affectionate enough to purr with his paws on my shoulders! I stroke his head, which is touching my neck. The remains of my yoghurt is his reward.

---

[1] Sir Alfred Beit, baronet (1903–94), and his wife Clementine Freeman-Mitford (b.1915).
[2] The gang that robbed the Beits included Dr Rose Dugdale, a girl of respectable parents. On 25 June Rose Dugdale was jailed for nine years in Dublin after admitting receiving nineteen paintings worth over £6 million, taken from the Wicklow home of Sir Alfred Beit. When Charlotte Bonham Carter heard of this incident, she commented, 'I always knew Rose was a strange girl, but I never thought she would tie up the poor, dear Beits.'

Garden opening broke all box office records. £80. The Smallpeices, from being bent like croquet hoops, straightened up and lost 20 years. So many compliments paid them. Smallpeice carries a triumph, but it is in between seasons, orchard dead and lilacs not out. The children ecstatic, so much space and sun. One father and his son run about wildly, other children rolling down the slopes. The 92-year-old successfully went to my 'loo'. Yehudi Menuhin was seen driving away. Derek Hill brought his brother en route to the Avons. God knows how the portrait will turn out. Derek is to paint Anthony. The portrait is to take one week. Derek and Clarissa are already at loggerheads and Anthony doesn't like the idea of someone who avoids tax by living in Ireland and who was a conscientious objector! Derek is difficult, looking for slights and rude to servants.

It will be interesting to see...

Buckle   *May 1974*

Dicky is also one easily slighted. I dined with him in his cottage, which at last he's enlarging and giving a garden. A propos Rai and Liz: 'They came to my cottage for a meal at Broadchalke, but cut me in London.' He is now being 'slighted' by the Salisbury Festival people not telephoning enough to him.

He asked me to leave him in my will the David Hockney drawing 'as you will probably die before me'. Eileen, loyal as ever, was incensed. 'I don't think you *will* die before him. I don't think he is in a good way at all. That bronchial cough is very bad. He may go at any moment.'

Dicky was bitter about having to sell a quarter of a million pounds' worth of pictures as a result of having the privilege of the benefit of working for the Astor Astor. (His way of saying that he was underpaid all his years on the *Observer*). He said he thought he would resign from the *Sunday Times*. I begged him not to lose his platform.

Eileen thought Dicky had changed a lot, had lost his buoyancy and sense of fun, had become pompous. He is a talented creature, with a very good brain, but there's something rotten at the core. He's not entirely a gentleman, and is not a happy or fulfilled man.

Kin   *May 1974*

So extraordinary that Kin, from one day to another, refused to communicate with me. His letters were amusing and intelligent, and a great joy to me. Suddenly a blockage. When I complained on the transatlantic telephone, he sighed, he gulped, he was deeply disturbed. 'I'll write,' he choked out, but he didn't. Not even when I had my operation, not even when I got mugged. No matter what. Yet when I telephone to him, he is highly delighted, and whenever I see him, we are always as we were. It is strange that of all people I wish to impart my news, good or bad, it is to Kin so many miles away and seen so seldom, and this in spite of the fact that although his reactions on the telephone are wonderful, honest, loyal, there is complete breakdown of communication through any other means.

Eden, Avon   *May 1974*

Derek Hill[1] has been painting Anthony all last week. I went direct from London train to the house for lunch and to help out in case of need. Clarissa met me outside the front door. 'He wants to go on and on, and Anthony is absolutely exhausted. He's had to go to bed. He can't stand the weight of the robes.' Clarissa saw the look of shock on my face. 'There's been no row, but he's spilt the oil and turpentine on the carpet, and we haven't got any more.'

The portrait proved to be the usual rough sketch. Derek doesn't even bother to paint the hands. The head is a delightful, charming likeness. Not 'striking' as Clarissa said, but tentative and modest. The pose also slightly tentative. One of Derek's best, but so slight that one wonders why he can't make a strong statement. This is hardly worth the canvas. Still Derek is happy. He is marvellously calm and content. He sleeps a lot, eats enormously and, although 'touchy', has altogether a happy life.

Poor Clarissa. One cannot say the same of her. She is dreadfully on edge, but Derek and I (in Anthony's absence) produced a jovial atmosphere, and the dining room resounded to laughter and that must have surprised the sour old butler, who ceremoniously handed the *excellent* dishes. Clarissa is a perfectionist as *maîtresse de cuisine*. Incidentally, Derek was taken to lunch with Mary Pembroke and given the inevitable shepherd's pie, but without the 'sick' to begin with!

Poor Anthony. I didn't realise how frail he is. He could not possibly survive another operation, so his life is hanging by a very thin thread.

13 May 1974

Rebecca West invited me to lunch. I was delighted to go as I have long admired her quick, sharp brain and have had little opportunity to get to

---

[1] Derek Hill (1916–2000), portrait painter. He portrayed Lord Avon in Garber robes.

know her. Recently she wrote to tell me how much she liked my piece on, of all people, Lily Elsie. In her letter, she further surprised me by telling me such people as Lilah McCarthy,[1] the intellectual actress, had been so impressed by the 'amiable' musical comedy star.

Rebecca West is 83. She has recently been ill, is rather deaf, but in most ways she is astonishingly lively. Very often, when in London, I go out to lunch. It may be a business arrangement, or I may go to see a particular friend, or even, though seldom, to a lunch party. This outing was an exception. Not for a long time have I enjoyed myself so much, and I went off from the house on edge, tired, headachy.

R. W. was a great stimulus. She lives in an impersonal block of flats overlooking the park, and in it are a lot of good paintings, Vuillard sketches, Lowrys, Tchelitchews, Burras, Wyndham Lewis. The furniture is good Regency, the furnishings pale and boring. R. W. in a pant suit and frothy wig was a dynamo. 'This is Rivers Scott, Literary Editor of the *Sunday Telegaph*' (a fresh-faced man with 5 children). From then on, the three of us were 'off to the races'. I felt myself to be in good form, only because I knew that what I said was listened to and respected. (Foolish people interrupt 'til one gives up trying.) She herself was the major-domo and had in her incisive brain all the things she wished to talk about. For me, apart from Lily Elsie, there was a Syrie Maugham link, R. W. being a tremendous ally, appalled that Syrie was so maligned. She talked of other people she liked and admired, either for their work or their character, or both, like Wendy Hiller,[2] the actress, but she didn't mince her words as so many women do when she disliked someone as much as Shaw, whom she found disloyal and mercenary. Of the people she had known to be wicked she put Beaverbrook highest on her list. R. W.'s horizon is very wide. There is nothing 'special' and exclusive in her taste of people. She is an intellectual, but not a highbrow.

R. W. is known to be difficult and can be awful to family and close friends. She is obviously dynamite in the house. But how refreshing to come across someone who gives an added gusto to life and I came away, back to the chores, having felt I was stimulated, having been given a rare treat and I'm sure the smiling, apple-cheeked Rivers Scott went back to his office with the same reaction.

---

[1] Lilah McCarthy (1875–1960), actress, wife of Sir Frederick Keeble (1870–1952).
[2] Dame Wendy Hiller (b.1912), actress. She had not long appeared in the National Theatre's revival of Ibsen's *John Gabriel Borkman*.

Death of a Gainsborough Play   *17 May 1974*

When I was in Cyprus three years ago, I spent the mornings at Mickey
Renshaw's house with a chair propped in front of me as I sat up in bed.
On this I had the latest draft of my Gainsborough play. I had been suffering from rotten headaches – eye strain? If I wore a dog collar to keep my
head erect, I was less likely to suffer later. Yet the headaches were pretty
severe. However, my enthusiasm that I was really making strides with my
play was such that I persevered and in fact worked with the greatest
relish. I felt at last I was bringing the play to life.

My hopes were dunched when two agents were not interested. I let the
play lie dormant. I wondered if perhaps later I would have a 'brainwave'
that would make all the difference. The play was well constructed, so full
of incident and surely the central character was a great prop?

Hal Burton has been tremendously helpful with making my Chickens
play stage-worthy. When he felt he had done as much as he could, I sent
him the Gainsborough play to see if he could come up with as many good
suggestions for improvements as he had with the farcical comedy.

But no. He thought the play had many merits. It wasn't just a question
of polishing the dialogue, he didn't really believe in any of the characters.
He didn't feel Gainsborough came to life.

St James's Palace Lunch

Martin Charteris,[1] as Private Secretary to the Queen, is given lodging in
Friary Court, St James's. He is not given much else and since he has little
private income, his mother Letty having made several marriages, but able
to keep little for old age, let alone sons, Martin and his delightful Gay live
very frugally.

Ann Fleming and I were asked to lunch and this was considered a
beano. Gay cooked the lunch, a sort of cold avocado soup, chicken with
curry sauce, watercress and raw mushroom salad, and cheese. The talk
was pretty frank about the Labour government wanting an immediate
election, the Queen to let it be known she did not approve. Pretty frightening forecast as to Labour's intentions but more as to the intentions of
self-appointed Scanlon[2] and the unions. All rather risky, all rather alarm-

---

[1] Rt Hon. Sir Martin Charteris (1913–99), later Lord Charteris of Amisfield, Private
Secretary to the Queen 1972–7. Married Hon Gay Margesson (b.1919).
[2] Hugh Scanlon (b.1913), later Lord Scanlon, President of the Amalgamated Union of
Engineering Workers 1968–78.

ing, except that our alarm was interspersed with gales of laughter. For it
was a very gay and funny lunch.

It delights me that someone like Martin has been chosen for this job.
He is so unpompous. His sense of proportion just right. He is gracious,
knows how to behave, but is never 'taken in'. He hated to have to fulfil a
lot of appointments at the Palace, and then take the Queen out on a stint,
before delivering her to a banquet, he himself to come back to an egg,
cooked by himself.

Delightful details on the *tenue* on the Royal Train going to Scotland.
The Queen and Prince Philip having their own coach, with bath. Martin
now has a bunk since the train has recently been remodelled. He says the
food on board is marvellous, particularly the breakfasts, with Dover sole,
crisp and crunchy, the bacon, and the breads, particularly the ginger-
bread. The teas marvellous with muffins, tea and cake. All the staff jolly
and glad to be seen each time, one of the few relics of the Victorian age.
As we left, Martin had to unlock the gates, everything very closely
guarded since the Pss Anne Shooting. A delightful, ribald lunch, with a
feeling of doom hanging over the nearby Palace.

John Julius [Norwich] was an early friend, through the TV, of James,
now Jan, Morris, the man who became a woman. Jan's book[1] has created
a furore, and Jan has appeared on TV, as an honest, delightful and quite
attractive woman. She has behaved with enormous dignity in the face of a
cruel and vulgar onslaught from that coarse-grained Robin Day.

When John Julius first asked James-Jan to dinner, his guest rang up to
ask how J. J. would prefer him/her to be dressed, as a man or a woman.
J. J. cleared his throat, and in as casual a voice as possible, replied,
'Whichever is the most comfortable.'

David Herbert

David, here for his annual three weeks from Morocco, has not wasted a
minute of his valuable time. He has seen and heard everything to do with his
vast family. He knows all the gossip and relays it with effervescent candour.
He makes one laugh out loud. He stayed the night in a spell of sunshine and
as we sat on a bench overlooking the village from the top of my gardens,
told me about the humiliation that his grand Paget mother always had to go
through. This tall, stiff-backed, stiff-upper-lipped woman, the acme of
Edwardian conventionality, had the red carpet pulled from under her so
many times that it is amazing that to the end she kept her rigidity. This was

---

[1] *Conundrum* (1974) by Jan Morris (b.1926).

in spite of husband running away and becoming bankrupt, brother marrying unsuitably, sons being homosexual and difficult in so many ways.

David gave a very funny imitation of his aunt Olive (Olive May – Meatyard) [Countess of Drogheda] chiding her children in the most cockney terms to 'splesh about in the sea'.

We decided that the same fate attends his sister Patricia. No one could be more conventional than she. But she too has to face up to the most appalling succession of disasters and scandals...

Stephen Tennant, after a day's rapture in Bournemouth – lobster thermidor and crêpes Suzette at the Royal Hotel – and a walk in the public gardens, his idea of heaven, appeared on my doorstep. He looked like a mad tramp, shoulder-length hair, recently dyed mahogany. 'Have you my bag you promised me from Mexico?'

'Presents should come at the end of a visit.'

When I gave him the brilliantly coloured object, he gasped, 'Oh, it's more me than me!'

The fateful blow fell. Michael Codron rejected my play. The disappointment was acute, like a knife thrust, but the pain did not last long. I set about sending it off to Hal Prince and I suppose now we are at the beginning of the long grind of trying to get the play put on by anyone who will touch it.

George Weidenfeld

Geo. Weidenfeld has for a long while been suggesting he give a party for me. The seventieth birthday was the inevitable excuse and I was only sorry that he should seem so intent that it should be a stunt party. 'Perhaps some sort of fancy dress?' Certainly that would not be a good idea. People are in the mood to go to parties, but not to go to any trouble. Fancy dress is habitual, all day long people dress up, but a fancy dress party is a thing of the past.

However, when I suggested women and men should wear flowers and it should be held at the time of the Chelsea Show, George was satisfied, and I was relieved. I had no misgivings about George giving the party although seldom have I enjoyed his parties. This time the guests would be different. I looked forward to the evening although I felt a bit anxious. Such an added effort to be made. Unfortunately I was stricken with a mighty headache. It seemed to lift in the excitements of the occasion. George, [his] flat done up brilliantly by the talented Geoffrey Bennison, wore a red coat. Jokes that he was hunting with the Melbury were inevitable.

But he was a most excellent host, very middle European in his manner, bowing, kissing hands etc. He had arranged a splendid buffet dinner, a vast Scotch salmon, beef, strawberries, the tall rooms were not too hot, or crowded, a good list of people, who were all in a rarely smiling mood. Diana Cooper arrived late and made a sensational entrance in a huge hat trimmed and over-trimmed with rows of hosta leaves from her garden, a green Walter Crane dress. She looked so freakish, and marvellous. The young beauties were Antonia Fraser's daughter, a Rossetti Ophelia with frizzy hair and flowers in it, Charmian Scott Stirling,[1] a flowered Botticelli, ravishing, delicate, Renaissance flowers sprinkled, and Caroline Cholmondeley.[2] She is garrulous and funny, and beautiful beyond words. Her face, no bigger than my hand, is exquisite in its pearled, smooth, even shiny perfection.

Patrick Procktor and his wife with more flower wreaths on their heads, Freddie Ashton had a tiger lily and lily of the valley buttonhole (I wore a huge posy of gardenias and lilies of the valley), Ali Forbes, a marguerite chain, some women only made the minimum effort. Jayne Wrightsman carried a white bouquet. The party went on till 2. Unexpectedly, Marella Agnelli[3] and the Gérald Van der Kemps[4] from Versailles, and Henry McIllhenny from Washington.

Good friends turned up, Cyril C., Peter Q., Ann Fleming (Lord Goodman too), Loelia,[5] Liza Hope [Lady Glendevon], George's friends, lots of pretty women and tycoons, [Jimmy] Goldsmith, Max Rayne. The sweet Gibsons appeared late, Fenella Fielding outrageous, monstrous, funny, in a hockey girl's hat, Irene W [Worth]. I got bunched with some nice books, and altogether worth coming up to London for.

Whitsun weekend. It is now called the 'Long Weekend', because it does not take place at Whitsun. Another horrible change.

I was waiting for Barney Wan to arrive to work on the final stages of the layout of *The Magic Image*. He did not show up for a day later than expected. For once I found time hanging heavily. The garden could not be enjoyed at this marvellous time, because gusty winds brought icy weather. All the reading I could do was the three-hour rewriting of diary in the morning.

Fearful of headaches, I had to tread water during the afternoon and

---

[1] Charmian Montagu-Douglas-Scott (b.1942), married Archibald Stirling of Keir. Divorced 1977.
[2] Lady Caroline Cholmondeley (b.1952).
[3] Marella Agnelli, wife of Dr. Giovanni Agnelli, Chairman of Fiat.
[4] Gérald Van der Kemp, Curator of Versailles (1912–2001), and his wife Florence.
[5] Loelia, Duchess of Westminster (1902–93), by then Lady Lindsay of Dowhill.

evening. There did not seem to be much to raise the spirits. The news from Northern Ireland is catastrophic and God knows how peace may be regained. Wilson is not only muddle-headed, spending taxpayers' money like water, but is like a mad Roman Emperor and, defiant as ever, has made Marcia Williams a Baroness. Such hypocrisy of the Labour government is outrageous. How the vile Mrs [Barbara] Castle has also been rumbled.[1] Rich friends like Leo d'Erlanger , who has done so much for the country, has to sell up and live in Switzerland if he is to leave anything for his son. The TV and newspapers are full of violence, thuggery, and people who behave like Robert Heber Percy. But where to go? How to escape the reality? One's work is the solution, but if things get as bad as they may, who can afford books or plays?

When suddenly, Barney Wan, smiling and immaculate in Yves St Laurent, arrived at the station with the book layout, all was changed. He's so sensitive, quick, intelligent. He has the Oriental's love of intrigue and knows everything that is going on in the worlds of art and journalism. He had been to a preview of the Wedekind play. He had seen so many people, yet he is never hurried, is quiet and shy, an adorable little creature. He was followed here by Michael Haynes, proposing himself and luckily the sun came out and he was able to lie on a mattress under the trees in the paddock, unlike Barney and I, [who] went through the arrangement of the pages for the last time.

Anthony Crickmay, the photographer, came down to take pictures for *Réalités*, and by the time I got to bed, I was too exhausted to be depressed or to give a damn about Northern Ireland, Ethiopia's famine, or the way the world was heading for doom.

Bonn – Berlin   *June 1974*

It is raining here at Reddish (we need rain as we are undergoing a drought). Liz [von Hofmannsthal], Michael D[Duff], and Ali F [Forbes] are staying. No question of a walk, let alone coffee out of doors. The cook (a temporary, a little misery) is leaving tomorrow and is tiresome today. The papers are full of gloom. (The Price sisters have ended their fast, so the bra howls may be less horrendous), but the Panovs have been allowed to go free to Israel. This is the best possible news as at last the Russians have come to realise how swinish their attitude is to all and sundry, including the artists.

---

[1] Marcia Williams (b.1932), Wilson's Personal and Political Secretary. Created Baroness Falkender 1974; Barbara Castle (1910–2002), Labour MP and a member of successive governments led by Harold Wilson. Life peer 1990.

The tax situation is appalling, coffee, sugar and so many other luxuries are difficult to find. One is piqued by postal delays, but my God, how fortunate one is to be in a free country, how glorious life is in comparison to that endured by the millions under the Soviet heel.

I have just got back from a short visit to the Nico Hendersons.[1] After two days in Bonn, staying in the pretty, white icing sugar *Residenz*, we flew to West Berlin and, on arrival, I was taken on a tour of the 'Wall'. It was an experience that was dreadfully disturbing.

The wall itself is depressing enough, a slovenly made slice of foul concrete, too high to scale, with a greasy, curved top to prevent fleeing hands from getting a hold. Those who take a poor chance on their lives by trying to free themselves from life under the Soviets have to contend further with barbed wire, the border guards high in their dreadful turrets, and at once, the automatic guns that go off at an unknown vibration, the landmines, the potholes and the terrible Alsatian dogs that are meagrely fed so that they remain savage.

From our vantage point of safety it was terrible to look upon what appeared to be a completely deserted city. It was as if a scourge had visited the place and life hardly continued. Bombed buildings and rubble remained from the Armageddon of the last war and now a few distant traffic signals were working. But there was no traffic to be seen. As it happens there is, a mile away, a town that, though meagrely poor in comparison to West Berlin, is more alive to the theatrical arts, where stage productions are lavish and all the personnel required can be corralled, so that when *Traviata* is given, sixty waiters are brought in to serve the *demimonde*. But life in this Russian-dominated prison is tragic and terrifying. No one is free, always the sword hanging over their heads. Poverty everywhere one looks, trains, trams, the vehicles on the road (a foul stench of bad petrol fills the nostrils).

As we were taken (Ann Fleming and myself) to the various checkpoints in our British Military car, I was really rather alarmed at the danger, although no such danger existed. But our guides told us of the continual attempts at escape that somehow quite miraculously continue to be successful, though we do not know how many are shot or tortured for unsuccessfully attempting to free themselves of their shackles. Those who attempt the terrible dare are mostly very young, and under interrogation they reveal themselves to have escaped for personal, rather than political reasons. When they have reached sanctuary, the army give them a rousing welcome and the festivity ends in their becoming stupefied with drink.

---

[1] Sir Nicholas Henderson, Ambassador to the Federal Republic of Germany 1972–5, later to France and the USA.

The British Military Police enjoy their job, convinced that it is the best post going. They love taunting the Russianised guards who are court-martialled if they should let an escape pass unnoticed. In fact, they and their relations may be tortured for not spotting and shooting at an escapee. So when the run is on, the British fire guns in the air to give the Germans an alibi. The Russians, lest the guards become friendly, change the personnel each day. One man is unmarried, another has ties. They are strangers so are not likely to exchange confidences.

One of the most 'inviting' spots for a possible escape is where the river bends and, at a certain point, is quite narrow. But this is treacherously deceiving and the refugees suddenly find themselves in the face of gunfire. Shrines erected to those who have died here are tended carefully, with flowers and lamps renewed. It was a haunting sight.

The wall was erected to stop the millions that defected from the East. But not before the best brains had escaped. It is not good propaganda for any regime that the inhabitants of a country have to be imprisoned within its confines. Even now that a certain freedom of visiting is permitted, those that are allowed to go from the West to the East are so terrified that they are not likely to spend a night in the foreign zone.

The scene at Checkpoint Charlie was really rather alarming, although after all these years there was no real cause for alarm. I heard an Englishwoman express the undercurrent fear that we all felt when her 3-year-old daughter rattled some railings and terrified she shouted, 'Ursula! Don't do anything that will get us into trouble!' The search for escapees or smuggling of any sort was unbelievably thorough. Yet in spite of all, there are still those who have the nerve or imagination to circumvent *all* difficulties and close to Checkpoint Charlie is a small 'museum' that shows man's ingenuity and courage. Of those who have, by brazen cheek, circumvented all difficulties and found themselves free.

But looking across the no man's land of East Berlin, close to the Brandenburg Gate, there was nothing to be seen that was free, except a rabbit, which climbed too far among the rubble ruins of what appeared a dead and deserted and very sinister city.

At another lookout post my far-seeing eyes discovered a man in a mackintosh standing by a wood. The Military Police put up their glasses. The border guards put up their glasses. No doubt he was a guard 'stretching his legs' from his post but, because he was an unaccustomed sight, he became an object of conjecture.

Those who try to escape are often the border guards themselves, for they know the weak points, but often they are shot by their confrères, fearing retribution to their family.

The hatred of the Russians for the Germans for the suffering they endured is only comparable to the hatred of the Germans for the

Russians. However, the West Berliners are extremely fond of the British, Americans and French who are guarding them and the air lift which saved the blockade is not forgotten. There is great rivalry between East and West Berlin Embassies.

My greatest hope is that one day, during my lifetime, the Soviets will crack, that the subjugated 'satellite' countries would regain their freedom. I asked our military guide if he was optimistic. He said, 'Something must change.' Meanwhile he is enjoying his *Boys' Own Annual* fun of helping escapees by acts of humanity and quietly taunting the Russians. He is well-paid and goes for holidays skiing and driving. A very different assignment from being sent to Belfast!

The East Germans are still paying the price of following Hitler and no doubt will continue to do so until some equally terrible madness overtakes either the Russians or some other country. Meanwhile there is no crack in the wall.

The women invited to the dinner party for Princess Alexandra were so dreary to look at that I could not believe they could show any signs of allure. But I discovered my vis-à-vis knew all about D. [Lady Diana] Cooper and the [Max] Reinhardt gang, read a lot, knew about current affairs and plays and players throughout the world, and of course they were very up to date on the cinema, and fell upon any words they could squeeze out of me about the making of *Fair Lady*.

Callaghan[1] came, with great arrogance, to say the Labour manifesto insisted on renegotiating the terms of our entry into the Common Market. In turn he was arrogant, then cry-baby. He is arriving again next Wednesday, and it is known that the Germans will give him a dusty answer, that Britain is now considered a minor power like Italy or Denmark. Pretty shaming, and that we have to be represented by such third-rate hypocrites is intolerable. How sad that Heath lost by a whisker, is now criticised by former loyalists and is not likely to come back.

Stephen Tennant came for pre-lunch drinks, accompanied by two pretty girls, formerly unknown, penfriends of Willa Cather. The shock of arrival at this house and subsequent meeting must have been appalling. Once here he showed to Liz Hof, Michael D. and Ali Forbes his drawings and paintings, copies by the dozen, all the same subject and treatment,

---

[1] James Callaghan (b.1912), Foreign Secretary 1974–6, Prime Minister 1976–9. Now Lord Callaghan of Cardiff.

then showered on us signed photographs of himself, photographed 30 years ago. A visit the friends will never forget.

Maurice Richardson

A new man in my life came to lunch after I'd written to tell him how pleased I was at the review he'd written about my Diaries. He turned out to be a great character, an Irish Randolph Churchill, never stopping talking, imitating, telling funny stories and roaring with laughter. He told me how he'd recently fallen in love with a secretary after she'd worked for two and a half days. 'I proposed we should go to bed. She responded immediately. Her breasts were well-formed, her bush, unlike her hair, which was mouse, was bright red.' They made love three times a day in between pleas from her that this has got to stop. The sort of man I see seldom. Very interesting and such a relief that he did not once ask anything about myself or my work.

Lunch at Martin Charteris for the Queen Mother. Gay said, 'I know you're a non-drinker, and I'm afraid we've run out of tomato juice, unless Martin remembers to bring some from the Palace.' Martin turns up in bowler with brolly, under his arm a paper bag full of tomato juice.

The Queen Mother not at her best, but her eyes are full of life and humanity. I told her about last week's visit of thirty blue-haired American women. I asked the gardener, did they like the terrace with all the roses? All the lawns? What did they prefer? Smallpeice said, 'They showed *most* interest in the compost heap.'

A horrible story

Lord Leicester[1] of Holkham was always tight-assed, a prig, a thoroughly tiresome, conceited man, but he was respectable above all. He had a position at Court close to the throne, his wife a lady-in-waiting to the Queen. Lord Leicester became so ill he nearly died. He recovered. Perhaps his illness was responsible for his becoming so impossible that his very charming and *comme il faut* wife left him.

Recently, Lord Leicester has been very peculiar, but not so peculiar that when he asked on the telephone to speak to the Queen Mother, anyone thought anything about it. The telephone bell rang in the QM's sitting

---

[1] Thomas, fifth Earl of Leicester (1908–76) married Lady Elizabeth Yorke (1912–85), Lady of the Bedchamber to the Queen.

room. 'Lord Leicester on the telephone, Your Majesty.' 'Oh, yes, put him through.' The Queen Mother waited – 'Hullo,' she heard, 'is that you, you fat old cow?' The operator heard the click of HM's receiver being put down.

Caroline Somerset: 'I'm getting more and more fond of Sally, Duchess of Westminster.[1] To begin with she was playing the lady a bit too much, and saying, when she went round the garden with me, "How did you ever know about alchemilla mollis?"'

Painswick

A delightful visit to Glos, laying the ghost of Painswick where we spent one of our happiest summer holidays. I did not realise what a beautiful town it is, in a silver hollow of dark green, forested hills, a miniature Salzburg or Bath, with noble houses, pale dove-coloured, elegantly façaded, decorated with pilasters and porticos, and the churchyard with 99 yews. Seen this evening against a thunder sky, old gravestones, a silver church, and on the outskirts of town, the vicarage, 'private' hotel where we stayed, where we were told the old man in an overcoat was Maeterlinck,[2] who was writing a life of a bee.

The Great Exodus

Healey[3] the Chancellor of the Exchequer, has proclaimed his intention to do away with the rich, and the rich are leaving England in great quantities. It is extremely sad that that good man and great patriot, Leo d'Erlanger, is forced to give up his homes in England and retire to Switzerland. The Channel Tunnel was only one of his big schemes and during the war he was of enormous importance in helping to see that our finances were kept at white-hot temperatures. In the world of banking he has met misfortune with courage but, as a result of this last blow, he now looks a broken man. I fear he will not last long in exile.

I went to his house in Upper Grosvenor Street to collect a great collection of discarded Paris dresses to exhibit at the Guildhall in Salisbury for the Festival and then to give to the V & A. The American Embassy is opposite and there was a queue of 200 young people waiting, as they do every day, to emigrate to the United States, a pretty horrible sight. (One wonders if these people will fare any better in that jungle.)

[1] Sally (1911–91) widow of fourth Duke of Westminster (1907–67).
[2] Count Maurice Maeterlinck (1862–1949), author of *La Vie des fourmis* (1930).
[3] Dennis Healey (b.1917), Chancellor of the Exchequer 1974–9. Life peer 1992.

Edwina's clothes conjured up the past very vividly. Here were forgotten names, hats from Maud at Nano, Suzy, dresses from Hélène Lyrande, flowers, shoes, all from places that had such glamour in the days before the last war.

They are now something that does not exist. There are no silk flowers, there are no artists capable of cutting fabrics like Vionnet. This was part of a Proustian world, of which the present generation knows nothing.

Diana and the Car Wash

Diana and her constant source of irritation 'Nose' Wyndham,[1] 'Auntie Nose', were dressed up in their best to go to a 'smart' lunch party. Both wore large hats for the special occasion. Suddenly Diana realised her old mini was looking particularly shabby and in need of a good wash. There was just time to go to one of those places where you drive in, are shut in your car, as water spurts in all directions, cleaning it most miraculously without human effort. It is an extraordinary sensation to sit in your car while jets of water pry into every corner and nook and cranny. It gives one the comfortable feeling, isolated from outside and blind to the world, of being in the womb.

Diana and 'Nose' were delighted with the experience until they realised that dirty suddy water was pouring down from the leaking roof on to them, water spurting through the windows from the back of the car, and through the leaking doors. The two ladies banged on the windows, desperate that the torrents should cease, but there was no gainsaying the deluge once it had started. They screamed and yelled to no avail, as they became soaked, and the large brims of their hats filled like a basin, caved in and fell over their faces in a sad and sorry sight. I have not heard in what manner the two arrived at the lunch, but Diana will certainly have made the best of the story.

Midsummer Day

It is the supreme moment of the year, the countryside at its most lyrical, and the weather has been the sort that we dream about during the interminable months of winter. The village people in cotton, the men often stripped to the waist, the garden here is at its best.

Yet the whole country is in turmoil. We wait for the worst economic

[1] Violet Wyndham (d.1979), author, mother of Francis Wyndham (b.1924), author and critic.

crisis to happen as if the next war was to be declared. The economic situation threatened to bring about an inflation which will bankrupt the richest and the middle-bracketed. The government is incapable of making bold decisions to stop inflation. Rather do they continue to play party politics. Many staunch Conservatives have ratted on Heath, consider [Enoch] Powell violent and incapable, a hypocrite and a madman, and no one seems to be on the horizon to save our bacon.

Three rotten headaches in a row. I begin to get worried. The specialist told me I was in good order, not to fret, the arteries were tight, but nothing to worry about. Perhaps I will go to another specialist who may tell me how I can enlarge the arteries. Most unexpectedly, after a quiet day, I woke up yesterday morning with another headache, not too bad but enough to make me feel uncomfortable. I could not read or write. So I took myself off to the garden to do last minute tidying up before the opening. Smallpeice slaving away put me to shame.

Nonetheless, I did some strenuous work in the water garden, then started to take the weeds among the Canterbury bells. The afternoon 'turned out nicely' after days of downpour which have wrecked the garden. Last week it was it its peak, now it is sodden! I deadheaded by the bushel, the roses, the iris and cleaned up the terrace. The head lifted after lunch and I went on with weeding. Irene Worth was reciting Shakespeare on the garden seat where the first candidum lily is out. Her devotion to the arts and to Shakespeare is all consuming. Later she did much to help cleaning up the borders and the petals, and the weeding of the rose borders.

It was a pleasant day and I was thrilled when the sun came out, and I thought in error that we should have a fair day for the old ladies and children and the miscellaneous bunch that comes in for the 'Gardeners' Sunday'.

Alec Douglas-Home[1] said he didn't think it would be a bad thing to have a Labour government in for two years. But how to get rid of them after that time and what havoc they would cause in that time.

Diana, terrifying driver, scared the wits out of me going over red crossing. Two minutes later she was booked. Only one more mark against her and she'll have to give up. She arrived at Clemmie Churchill's[2] for lunch,

---

[1] Sir Alec Douglas-Home (1903–95), Prime Minister 1963–4, later Foreign Secretary in Edward Heath's government, Lord Home of the Hirsel.
[2] Baronness Spencer-Churchill (1885–1977), widow of Sir Winston Churchill (1874–1965).

apologising for being late, but saying she had had a furious policeman straddled on her bonnet in Kensington Palace and he would not get off!

The flycatchers are even more frantic than usual. The eggs have hatched and the mother and father birds dart backwards and forwards in a frenzy, trying to satisfy the hunger of the small birds with huge beaks who inhabit the nest above the little woman on the cornice of my window.

The 'Gardeners' Sunday' was not the success of the Easter opening for the rain which had held off had prevented the usual numbers from arriving in their numbers. We clocked up nearly 600 which was good, though the flowers were dashed by three-day rain. The polyanthus roses a pulp. However, the usual praise of Smallpeice and he bared his teeth with the usual pride – it was his Sunday and in spite of falling off a ladder and being in pain, he doggedly trimmed every blade of grass and the tidying up continued until the very hour of opening.

Irene Worth

God, the vitality! She is a blockbuster. Reading, late into the night, all morning, reciting Shakespeare, as if that was not enough, she asks advice from Smallpeice on herbs, how to prune, how to cultivate, how to tell one rose from another, one bird. She is lifting heavy weights across the lawn, deadheading malmaisons and Madame Hardy. She rushed down a little blade, sweating, her boots bouncing over the lawns. She leans out of my window till she is in danger, to spy on the newborn birds. She says, 'You must read Tennyson, George Eliot, you must send a telegram to John G. You must go to Persia again, to Kashmir. You must go to Spain!' I am whacked. Her voice rises like a little girl's. She laughs, giggles, looks a hundred, but the spirit is undimmed . She is a remarkable girl-hag.

A few days after this entry, Cecil suffered his serious stroke, while at home in London.

1978–79

In 1978 Richard Buckle edited a selection from the six volumes of Cecil Beaton's Diaries, and this was published as Self-Portrait with Friends *in 1979. In his introduction, Buckle wrote of the effects of Beaton's stroke in 1974:*

Enforced idleness brought him near despair. Then he asserted his will-power. Before long, with his left hand he began first to sign Christmas cards, then to write letters, then to draw, then to use watercolours, then to paint in oil and even to take photographs again. But the Diary was given up for good.

In a 1978 interview to mark the publication of The Parting Years, *Cecil declared that there would be no more diaries. 'Really, no more?' he was asked. 'No' – firmly 'not even posthumously.' Yet, unbeknown to Buckle or to his friends, Cecil did resume writing his diary. There were times when a name failed him, his syntax was occasionally muddled, but he filled the best part of a volume between 1978 and 1980, writing with his left hand in a black felt-tip pen.*

It would be unfair to reproduce this diary in full, but a few extracts give the flavour of these difficult years.

Sunday, 1 July 1978

It was 9.15 by my watch. A lot of very young girls were in operation (squeals, giggles etc.) by the time I had regained full consciousness. The heat of the mattress was too heavy for me to remain long in the dead-dull day awake. I enjoyed the heavy meal of toast covered with the best marmalade until Grant [his nurse] gave me my morning bath.

I was still buzzing with last night's ware. It had been such a beano! Every ingredient right. In spite of the horrid cold & rain which could not get it right.

The house was glistening. Young persons in a variety of fancy dress were rushing about. The house of the palest pink was double noble.

As it happened, I was on a good wicket. I had called at Buscot where the Ball[1] is being held. Just enough time left to go to my nearby Bay Tree Hotel to make the niceties of the beautification. I was very patient. At about the correct time I joined the '*Bal en Travestie*' which was waiting to go into the crowded rooms. I did not get a chance of measuring the

---

[1] In the summer of 1978, Diana Phipps gave a famous ball attended by the cream of English Society. Lady Diana Cooper attended as the nun in *The Miracle* and Lord Goodman as Friar Tuck.

windows lit up, or of counting the shell-coloured roses adorning the vestibule. A group of terribly congenial persons took me by the arms and offered me to the *Assemblée* gathered already there. From then on the ball consisted of bright lights lit with wider lights from flashlights. It was *féerique*.

So many people came up to me. Diana Phipps as a 'Moderne Marguerite'. Her bosom very sylph-like, her coarse cotton skirt in flounce. She did not appear in the slightest put out that her guests were breaking all rules. Her daughter[1] quite exquisite, with a twenty-ish cut to her fine 18th-century coat and cut. Her hair curved so that nothing could disarray it. She was ideal and we both were sad that her grandmother, her mother's mother,[2] did not come from her house to the ball.

The beauties included Mrs [Evangeline] Bruce, and Diana Cooper. To my regard she looked terrible, with a pair of false eyelashes which turned out to be quizzers. Once she dropped them she became OK – and OK for this play meant a lot! Mrs Bruce looked fantastic, and there were thousands of others I went on meeting until it was past bedtime and I had to get hold of Grant to take me to bed.

Jane Abdy[3]

Jane Abdy came to stay for a short visit. She was met by Eileen, and already by mealtime we'd used up much energy. The afternoon was spent over the television screen and an hour was devoted to sleep, after which we spent time going to comedy, which was forcibly told and already scruffily told, and the evening meal was good.

Next day was wet. We walked in the wild, wet pond, and enjoyed all the elements there. The sun blessed us with its blessing, and after a hurried march, we sat all the afternoon, watching the New Born Child at his third christening. Bjorg brings a freshness to his play. It was impressive to watch. Then a performance of impermanence. The local play was not really felt and the local picture was not of much importance. We talked hard and long. We tried the impossible.

Oliver Messel died in Barbados on 13 July 1978.

---

[1] Alexandra Phipps (b.1959), twice married.
[2] Cecilia Sternberg.
[3] Jane, Lady Abdy, third wife of Sir Robert Abdy, art dealer, who, many years later, bought 8 Pelham Place, Cecil's London house.

Oliver Messel

I went to bed at the usual time and after the lights had gone out for keeps, I heard the telephone. Grant answered it, and next morning (after I enjoyed a sleep full of night) I had the news that Tony Snowdon had telephoned with the news of Oliver's death. This gave me a great shock as I always thought of him as a peerless match to me.

My thoughts went straight to him. Our one day lapse in the book of fame – when to become so very near me in all but growing up. We had shared lovers though I am bound to admit I did not do well in the race. When I took my first house, Ashcombe, I had Peter [Watson] and Oliver to hold it at bay for me. The shock of Peter's love of inferiors, was, for me, a great drawback, and probably realised by Oliver soon enough!

I used to admire Oliver's drawings, his sketches, and his general misdemeanour. He was my friend and my rival. We went about our ways in the best possible manner. We were great friends and only a too frequent row would put us on a special limb. We were again friends. Then Oliver became his nephew's uncle.[1] He went to the Abbey as a 1st in rank ranker. His mother[2] became higher than God! He travelled to Jamaica and stayed with his near friend. He amazed me by having a dozen dark friends to stay while beautifying his house, which soon developed into a 'straight' jacket. He was altogether charming.

And full of jokes! His eye was as keen as ever. I used to enjoy his sudden impersonations. I was said to have been his most 'live' impression.

He wrote me a long letter which I only received a fortnight ago. It did not speak of ill health, though he was more or less incapacitated. It was the last letter I received. It did not acknowledge his age or his inner doubts. Yet everything was there. I shall miss very much not having his very apt cradle of wisdom at beck and call.

Diana Vreeland

Diane has been nearly three weeks here in residence in London and I fear she is less surprising than she used to be. Perhaps her cries of the heart are less vivid. She has become with age the person she has forgotten to be. Only in stunning epigram is she as she used to be. Then she was noble

---

[1] In other words, Oliver's nephew, Anthony Armstrong-Jones, rose to fame, particularly, when, in 1960, he married Princess Margaret, a development which exercised Cecil considerably.

[2] Cecil referred to the Countess of Rosse, always a *bête noire* so far as he was concerned.

and surprising. Now she is no longer surprised. She recognises the surprise and is unburdened by its familiarity.

Saturday

We have a lunch party here today. Clarissa [Avon] is bringing the Moores and Mark Amory[1] today. Thence, after a rest, to go to Ann Fleming. I must not be too 'profound' or everything will get repeated. She is so nice to have as a companion but it is such a bind to have to mend one's ways and give her only that which one longs to leave behind.

I have not written a word in seriousness since I was struck numb with my incurable illness. That was three and a half years. I suppose I didn't want my agony updated. I put down not a word. I would save for my memory book a few nuggets that I enjoyed keeping. The results were pitiful.

A week spent doing nothing much. The diary was completely unattended. I had nothing to write about. Nothing that is above the common rut.

Poor Charles James died 9/25/78

What a sad fellow! My heart went out to him as far as it allowed. He was impossible to use as a friend for misfortune of some strange sort would soon upset the apple cart! However, I have a strange feeling for him. He could be utterly wonderful and then, with alacrity, kill everything by being objectionable.

My memory of him goes back a very long way. At Harrow he bearded me in the snow and made me feel as wicked as he. He taught me much. Then, when I arrived at New York, he continued with his wider scope of knowledge about the seamier side of life as well as the bright side. He influenced me a lot. I took pictures of him and his clothes. I followed his steps with great alacrity. When he came to London he reached a new peak of dressmaking and all it pertains of. But rows followed and I was not remote from them. Oliver Messel and I gave an unsatisfactory showing of his clothes [in 1928] – again an upset. Later he became impossible.

---

[1] Viscount Moore (b.1937), Derry Moore, the photographer, later twelfth Earl of Drogheda, his wife, Alexandra Henderson, TV producer; and Mark Amory (b.1941), biographer of Lord Berners and now Literary Editor of the *Spectator*.

Years passed and in New York we became friends again. His talent was marvellous. His wit bitter! I could not but be his friend. A terrific row fell upon us. We fell apart. The letters he wrote me filled a volume. After a time I became a friend of his again, and so it went on. I never knew if we were 'on' or 'off'.

Now poor Charles is dead. No one could cope with his temperament for long. An absolute plethora of press cuttings have been blown over for me to see. I am terribly sad for him, terribly sad that I could not do for him.

S. Tennant

I have a frantic letter from Stephen. He generally writes more of the spume with sun-flecked clouds on the surface, but now is all hollow and banal. I cannot bear to think of his idleness and wonder what it consists of! I think most of his ideas are sound! It is difficult to know how to answer him! I have sent off a letter full of bromides, but I feel they are not worth sending, let alone his answering. It is an end to an epoch, a very frail one, but still it held forth a lot for me during the time I spent with him when he filled his birthday bright day in London, surrounded by people of his age and temperament. Oh dear!

During this time Cecil contemplated leaving Reddish House and possibly moving into the White House at Wilton. As it turned out, he remained at Reddish. He received a great boost when invited to Paris to photograph a special edition of French Vogue.

A trip to Paris

Imagine my complete astonishment when the telephone rang from the famous Paris [*Vogue*] with a request that I should do for them 40 new pages. I was enchanted, and at liberty! Come hell or high water! I learnt very little about the job, except that all the prices were arranged, that the hotel and all expenses would be paid. Right! I could only think of the vagaries I was up to! My brain was full of new ideas. I worked at my items until I was exhausted! Nothing is more pleasurable than this. I must keep cool and not cool off. I should keep all energy for forgotten ideas.

Meanwhile Cecil read The Face on the Sphinx *by Daphne Fielding published by Hamish Hamilton in the summer of 1978.*

The Face on the Sphinx

How silly I was not to enlarge my feeling for Gladys Marlborough[1] when she was still above board. I could have. I perhaps should have. She was still far and away stone sober! I should have enjoyed her so much and could have learnt a lot from the way she behaved. I saw her at the twilight of her days, but still there were long times of complete rationale.

I admired her beauty and did several interpretations of her but, on reading Daphne's book, I now find her very accessible, and to someone like myself she must have been remarkably 'sensible'. I find her very fluid and, apart from her dog's smell, she must have been very much at home with artists and writers.

[Diana Cooper] said, 'She was so inferior to her sister [Audrey],' but I was able to throw a cloud of coins in the air. They fitted Gladys but were wild in the mark of [Audrey]. Also, [Edith – another sister] was able never to expend money for return of her prints.

Paris

This book has been brought to Paris, where it was left seriously alone. Not till the return from that gay centre has it shown signs of itself. It has been a triumph.

I got along famously. Only did a three-handed troublemaker do me any harm, and that was funny. I shot Princess Caroline, Paloma Picasso, young Rothschilds, and the young Matilde Abdy,[2] and a dozen people I know little of, and enjoyed myself enormously. It was hard work, but I tried to give up one day of the seven. I took pictures until 8 o'clock.

A few meals were taken which, numb from fatigue, at the Hotel Montalembert (a short distance from the hotel) & others were at Lipp, Mona Williams [Countess Bismarck] (looking terrible!), at her house which they say is being sold, and at Maxim's where a grand dinner is given in my honour.

---

[1] Gladys Deacon (1881–1977), second wife of ninth Duke of Marlborough. A beauty and intellect in the *belle époque* of Paris. Cecil had sketched her in the late 1920s.
[2] Princess Caroline of Monaco (b.1957); Paloma Picasso (b.1949); Olimpia Aldobrandini, who married 1974, Baron David de Rothschild (b.1942); and Matilde, wife of Sir Valentine Abdy Bt.

Monday, 16 April [1979]

At last spring has arrived! I am so pleased, as pleased as everyone in the streets & in the lanes. A few more dry & tightly packed days like we have been having, and one imagines all hell will be let loose. It is an extraordinary change for me! I have been infested with gloom. The lighting system went wrong, and one was living in a state of gloom. Each day was affected by the last. The sky was persistently grey. No sunlight affected one. A living mess. One had no plans to get out of the mood!

The days of photography made the weeks go very quickly. There was a dozen people to take.

In return, there was the weekend at Vaynol, gay, carefree, and independent. It was a coarse-grained interval with nothing to do. It started off terribly cold and ended in a miasma. The journey to and from Bangor was my milestone. And again the victory over the weather. It turned quite hot! So hot that people in the South were trapped with heat! Returning to the Dorchester was a cool treat.

It was a sudden heatwave! Passers-by raced at an unbelievable speed. The traffic went at an easy milestone. I found the accepted a bore. I returned to a frenzied night out. A long act of suffering at the Court Theatre, a play freshly acted sent shivers down one's back, and gave one to think a lot of.

3 June 1979

I don't know the dates any more.

Went to London which was very grand and very varied too. This time it was to stay at Brown's which I had never been to since I was born. The price of everything was fantastic, not that the rows of noughts keep anything secret! Photography was my natural habitat.

Patrick Procktor opened his house in [Little] Venice to us. It was wonderful. We went for half an hour to see the new garden room at the V & A. Thence to meet Beatrix Miller [Editor of *Vogue*] at the Caprice. A great trek to the lavatory across the way took about an hour! Next day photographing [Diana Quick] who is unknown to me. She is very well-known & has the central part in [Evelyn Waugh's] film.[1]

---

[1] *Brideshead Revisited*, to be shown on Granada Television (1981).

Lunch at a place in a hurry, then to photograph the Bishop of Southwark[1] who has many faults, but was interesting to take. Then to photograph a post-pop group, who maybe will be famous in a month. Clarissa Avon was the reason why we went to the next haven, where I saw H. Pinter's[2] play.

Now I'm busy trying to forget the original plans & just have to be in time for Queen Elizabeth's visit to Diana's for lunch. What can there be to fill in a frenzied day. Now there is nothing to do. I opened, distrustfully, this diary and fed it a little. What else to do – very few letters. I have no longing to read a diary since my reading of Diaghilev is just finished.

After a stay in Italy with Lord Lambton Cecil met Diana Cooper at the airport.

Diana Cooper accompanied me home. She was really pathetic. I had not seen her in such a state of funk. She looked terrible. Her incredible complexion was now fully reverted in its latent tragedy. The wrists were red and blotchy! Her complexion, now covered with a milky hue, only half hid the blotches of red and white. Her make-up was only half a shell. Her hair was hideous, likewise her clothes. Oh dear. She sat reading the papers like an automaton. Her eyes did not fit the sockets. Oh what a tragedy! I felt at long last that it was time she gave up the battle. She should give in. It would be terrible for all of us, but better not suffering any more.

The car awaited me. The baggage was soon found & packed, & once more we were on our way to England. It seems the sun has shone all the time we were away. The leafy lanes were long since forgotten, and a hideous four-way traffic took its place! Its momentum was something.

The return was thrilling, and there were so many good messages. So many letters of good love and photograph sittings of excellence! It was very pleasant to return home, to the new gardener, his wife and the daughter.

The Aga has gone on the blink! I don't know what is going to happen when the man in charge comes and sees what happens. But it makes life very empty without supplies! I don't quite know who to call when I am through the painting jag! Having been up to the nose with activity, I am through the list, especially as [Eileen] is not through with her cold. I wish I had an ideal place to go to!

---

[1] Mervyn Stockwood (1913–1995), Bishop of Southwark.
[2] Harold Pinter (b.1930), wrote *Betrayal* (1978).

I had a full day doing nothing. The newspapers in the morning, with the addition of the French magazine. An early visit with the eye artist, a trek around garden, not in the big sun, and then a run in the car to Anne and Michael [Tree].

Tuesday, 18 September 1979

It is very cold. It is possible the sun is at an end, at least for this August. I hate the time of the year. Nothing to look forward to, except at best time when it becomes hot. I was not at all entertained by the people I saw. They seemed horribly dated.

A Bad Day

Was quite ready for car journey to London, but the driver was an hour and forty minutes late. As I got into the car, the alarm went off. Fortune favoured us, and with the minimum of time we were off. The shortage of petrol was our next trouble! We arrived at the Dorchester at the hour we should be leaving for the first stop. We discovered this was not on. With the minimum of time wasted, we went to see the - - - - - show and bought at several pounds higher the best books on the file. The next effort was a cocktail party given by George Weidenfeld. A strange list awaited me. I was unable to use my time talking to the friends I liked. There were too many 'friends'. At eight o'clock we left. Back at the Dorchester we talked hard and fast but I was unable to join in the feast as it was long past my bedtime and I was dying to go to sleep. Unfortunately, this did not happen at once.

Our next appointment was 'chucked' as the former Chairman had given the false instruction but the trip was cancelled as there had been a breakdown in earlier communication. I waited ¾ of an hour.

28 Dec (?) [1979]

The date is wrong – more likely October or November. This is an account of the Pembroke Ball at Wilton, which marked the birth of an heir, and, though this was not generally known at the time, the excuse for the Earl and Countess to go their separate ways. There is a hint in the slightly 'Jennifer's Diary' account that follows, that Cecil was aware of this – and it marred his enjoyment of the evening. He was devoted to the young Pembrokes. Unlike his visit to a ball at

*Wilton in 1926, during which he was thrown into the Nadder, Cecil was treated
with great respect as this ball. He sat on the long sofa in the Double Cube Room,
under the great tapestry, with the Dowager Marchioness of Salisbury on one side
of him, and Lady Diana Cooper on the other.*

I didn't enjoy myself as much as I expected to. Although there was a long
interval to fill before going off to a high class dinner with the - - - - - - , I
found myself wondering how I would last out the long banquet before-
hand, and left the party well in advance of people. There was not a group
studying the guests as they drove into the double gates but the illuminations of the trees in the park, and the illuminations of the buildings were
indeed gorgeous! There unfortunately the magic stopped. I was terribly
put out by the photographers who were placed by the entrance. And
Claire and Henry Pembroke were taken up with kisses. It was the wrong
note. The 4 great sections of lilies was wonderful.

I too was ashamed at the crowds already placed in position for the far
days off when I was ducked in the pond were too far off for me to
remember except as a lovely blur!

I found lots of people to say hello to, and was not put out by anything
except the spontaneous rejoicing. This was not present. I was alone in my
agony, but I had to pretend that all was full of spirit and guile! I talked to
Mary [Pembroke], David Herbert, the Duchess of - - - - - arrived. I
watched the Duke of York [the Prince of Wales] giving a 10-year-old
girl[1] the whirl. I didn't notice the wife of Patrick Procktor except that she
wore a new dress. Others I remember seeing among the 2 thousands
there were Michael Duff.

It was interesting to see that the lighting was too vivid and that few of
the dresses stood up.

I spent until 2 o'clock there and did not sleep when I was worn out.

3 November [1979]

The *Daily Telegraph* has added to my grief. They have put in a piece
about my death and resurrection.[2] For 2 days now we have been telling
the powers that be what they should do in the way of consequences. Even
£3,000 in income has come from [them] to an apology. Yesterday the

---

[1] Lady Emma Herbert (b.1969).
[2] The *Daily Telegraph* described Cecil as 'the late Sir Cecil Beaton' on the day of the
Wilton Ball. Following this, a journalist was dispatched to interview him at length for
the paper.

matter was 'cleared up' by a reporter coming down with a happy ending to a very sore subject. I hope the 'muddle' will now settle, and no further bother will be heaped on my terribly lacking in space head.

London

It had been such a delightful ordeal since I arrived. Then we had to get to our feet for the congenial meeting with the Queen Mother. She has the most wonderful knack with everybody of saying the easy thing. She was the perfect foil, the two of us matching each other perfectly.

I am now writing many weeks after the event, cannot remember how thrilling she was, but I was on tenterhooks of excitement most of the time. I had time to pay her compliments about her daughter, the Queen, about her own clothes, including the hat which she wore with a danger-ous fur about to spike the nape.

We had two hours of private happiness before HM had to leave for home and she left behind her a group of well-wishers. I adored her. I loved her clothes, her warmth.

Monday, the last day of December [31 December 1979]

A most terrible tragedy has overwhelmed my dear friend, Michael Duff.[1] I saw him at Mary [Pembroke]'s birthday party and was overwhelmed at the sight of him. The marvellously prepared vision that he stays prepared for himself – was now but a poor shell of his former beauty. The poor thing has become a shadow of himself. There is very little to remind one of what he was. He cannot last long! I was abject! I remember what he used to be – and now a feeble voice meant nothing more to be. The inroads into the flesh do not tell one the full story. One just sees a sort of shadow. With discretion one tried to tell him that his nose was bleeding! But it did not count. A few days more of this misery and he will surely be of the past? Poor Michael will be reduced to nothing!

I was *very* sad and considered myself fairly lucky! I have only half an atom left, but I continue on that. I have enough to live on – until I am taken off! But I suddenly feel it is a long journey away. On what am I to build my life? The answer is very vague!

---

[1] Sir Michael Duff outlived Cecil by but a few weeks, dying on 3 March 1980, at the age of 72.

1980

The usual nonsense about whether or not you had said 'Good Morning' and 'Many Happy Returns'. This unhappy mess has come too late for me. I no longer feel charitable or bad-tempered at the result. I was fast void. Luckily there were others who showed their colours. Nancy and Hugh [Smiley] found for me a very passable entry into another world.

I came home late at night with a feeling of quiet contentment that if I had not been absolved I was at any rate solved for the next day!

The garden catalogues arrive and I buy back numbers enlisted as if I were going to watch a new opening! This of course is not the case, but very likely a thin veil of my original dream is opened for a short spell. I forget in the absence of other things that my original red hot poker or Michaelmas daisy had flowered a quarter of the size expected.

Cecil writes of a production of Peter Shaffer's Amadeus.

Mozart

The triumphant applause of certain sections of the community and the irate ravings of others have kept at high pitch the very instigator of a success. In spite of feeling that interpretation of Mozart would call a very different tune to Paul Scofield's performance, I felt tremendous let down to find that at a former performance, both were out of time.

It is difficult at one performance to gauge such a tremendously varied interpretation and I would have to see the play at least three times to make final distinctions. Happily the play will run through many performances, and I may have a chance to see the play again before I can notice its particular excellences. Meanwhile Paul Scofield is happy learning new tricks at every stance! He is always at his best in a sudden reaction to a given scene, and Scofield for all I know has copied himself to the life for every turn of life and liver. He has the sort of face that makes it hard to come to terms with.

This entry, about the death of Cecil's cat, was written on 11 January 1980. Cecil and Eileen agreed that Timothy was no longer enjoying life. It was decided that next time the vet was in the area, he would come out and put Timothy to sleep. Cecil went up for his afternoon siesta and Eileen called the vet. As it happened, he was coming in that direction that very afternoon.

It transpired that on the last evening of his life, 17 January 1980, Cecil had been depressed. Billy Henderson came to read to him. He was worried about tests that he was to have, fearing that, having made a good recovery from his stroke, there might be some new illness, possibly cancer, to face.

It is not too fanciful to suggest that Timothy showed Cecil the way to escape. When he went up to bed, he had problems sleeping and asked Grant to summon the doctor. He was flustered. Dr Brown came round and gave him something to help him sleep. His last words were 'Thank you, doctor' and he drifted into a deep sleep from which he did not wake up.

It was exactly a week after the death of Timothy. Here is the last entry as written:

Timothy

I was in the study and - - - - - in the hall, when Eileen met me with the news of Timothy's death. The doctor from Salisbury had come out immediately from his deathbed scene, had listened to a short sharp visit to the puff and with the connivance of [Eileen] had taken the final step. Timmy had only a moment of indecision. Then the knife had found its position and the delay was not postponed. The life of Timothy was quickly at an end. Timothy who had been 17 years my friend was no longer.

Then Eileen and I had a troubled time sitting in the firelight, thinking about Timmy's years. Suddenly tears could not be separated. The man had gone away leaving me with the loss. Timmy had been the great friend of Smallpeice and me. He had his own ways, which would not be altered. He liked to sit on this or that chair. He liked the sunny side of the street. Now all was over and Timmy was alone, parted from us, while we were very much alone, parted from him. I took a long time coming to grips with ordinary life. I felt very lonely as I spent my time thinking back through the last 17 years. I was still alive, but Timmy had gone through to oblivion. He was perhaps lucky? Who knows?

Index

This index identifies figures in the text and occasionally those who appear in footnotes, but are not otherwise mentioned in the text. Since most people are identified in footnotes on their first appearance, the distinction '& n' is by and large omitted, unless the footnote happens to appear on a later page. Normally I insert dates in the index but as these appear wherever possible in the footnotes in the text, they have not been repeated in this index.

Nor have I indexed names mentioned in footnotes that are only there to identify characters in the text. These have been omitted since they are secondary characters, and anyone looking them up would therefore be disappointed. H.V.

* * * * *